JOSEPH SMITH
and the
DOCTRINAL
RESTORATION

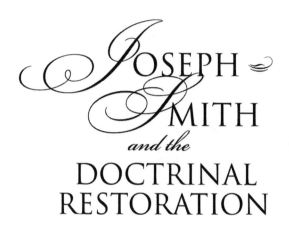

JOSEPH SMITH

and the

DOCTRINAL
RESTORATION

THE 34TH ANNUAL
SIDNEY B. SPERRY SYMPOSIUM

BYU

DESERET
BOOK

SALT LAKE CITY, UTAH

Copublished by the Religious Studies Center, Brigham Young University, Provo, Utah, and Deseret Book Company, Salt Lake City, Utah.

Library of Congress Cataloging-in-Publication Data
Sperry Symposium (34th : 2005 : Brigham Young University)
  Joseph Smith and the Restoration : the 34th Annual Sidney B. Sperry Symposium.
    p. cm.
  Includes bibliographical references and index.
  ISBN 1-59038-489-X (hardbound : alk. paper)
  1. Smith, Joseph, 1805–1844—Congresses.   2. Restoration of the gospel (Mormon doctrine)—Congresses.   3. Church of Jesus Christ of Latter-day Saints—History—19th century—Congresses.   I. Title.
  BX8695.S6S66 2005
  289.3'092—dc22   2005015828

Printed in Canada   29359
Friesens, Manitoba, Canada

10   9   8   7   6   5   4   3   2   1

CONTENTS

Contents

ACKNOWLEDGMENTS

We owe a debt of thanks to many people, without whose help this symposium and this book would not have come to fruition. Chief among them is the 2005 Sperry Symposium Committee, consisting of Susan Easton Black, Steven C. Harper, Andrew H. Hedges, Cynthia Doxey, Lloyd Newell, Mary Jane Woodger, and Patty Smith. Their willingness to serve as symposium planners and their unselfish devotion of time to review articles helped produce this book and make the symposium a fit tribute to the Restoration that was revealed through the Prophet Joseph Smith.

Our thanks and gratitude are also extended to each of the presenters for their inspiring messages and testimonies.

A great deal of gratitude is also owed to Devan Jensen and Richard Neitzel Holzapfel at the Religious Studies Center at Brigham Young University for their careful and conscientious editing and for those at Deseret Book who reviewed all our work, created the cover, and saw everything through to final publication.

Thanks also to Dr. Sidney B. Sperry, whose teachings, research, and writings continue to inspire rising generations to follow the Lord's counsel: "Teach one another words of wisdom; yea, seek ye out of the best books words of wisdom; seek learning, even by study and also by faith" (D&C 88:118).

PROLOGUE

This year the 34th annual Sidney B. Sperry Symposium, held at Brigham Young University, marks several significant anniversaries. One hundred eighty-five years ago, in the spring of 1830, the Prophet Joseph Smith experienced the First Vision when our Heavenly Father and His Son, Jesus Christ, appeared to him in Palmyra, New York, ushering in the dispensation of the fulness of all times (see Acts 3:19–21). The year 2005 also marks:

• The 200th anniversary of the birth of the Prophet Joseph Smith, born December 23, 1805.

• The 175th anniversary of the printing of the Book of Mormon, first published March 26, 1830.

• The 175th anniversary of the founding of The Church of Jesus Christ of Latter-day Saints, organized on April 6, 1830.

• The 175th anniversary of the first missionaries called in these latter days, in April 1830.

• The 170th anniversary of the calling of the Quorum of the Twelve Apostles, ordained in February 1835.

• As early as March 1829, the Lord declared that the restoration of His word would come to our generation through the Prophet Joseph Smith (see D&C 5:10). At the time, Joseph Smith was only twenty-three years old. He would live only fifteen more years. But in those fifteen very short and compressed years, Joseph Smith ushered in the fulness of times that comprised a "welding together" of all dispensations wherein everything "from the days of Adam [to] the

1

present time" would be revealed in this, the final gospel dispensation (see D&C 128:18).

It is interesting that the Lord said the Restoration would come *through,* not *by* or *from,* the Prophet Joseph Smith. The Restoration is so grand in vision, so all-encompassing in thought and doctrine, and so beyond mortal power and authority that it could not possibly have come from the Prophet Joseph, or from any other individual, for that matter. Even if Joseph Smith had been the most gifted linguist, the most learned biblical scholar, the most studied anthropologist, the most spiritual intellect on the face of the earth (which, by the way, I believe he was), he still would not have been able to restore priesthood authority without help from the authorized servants of the Lord who held it anciently.

Through the centuries, many have recognized that elements once present in the original church were missing. For hundreds of years, reformers sought to bring back what was once present—including the offices and authority of the priesthood, the organization of the Church of Jesus Christ, and the gifts of the Spirit that were exercised anciently as described in the Bible. No individual, committee, council, or creed was able to recover what was lost—until the Father and the Son appeared to Joseph Smith to inaugurate the "restitution of all things, which God hath spoken by the mouth of all his holy prophets since the world began" (Acts 3:21). From heavenly beings, the gospel was restored to the Prophet Joseph Smith, and the promise was given by the Lord that it would never be taken from the earth again or given to another people (see D&C 27:13). The ministering of angels continued, and Joseph Smith and Oliver Cowdery received the Aaronic Priesthood by the laying on of hands from John the Baptist (see D&C 13) and the Melchizedek Priesthood in the same manner from Peter, James, and John (see D&C 128:20).

Later, while translating the Book of Mormon, Joseph Smith received a commandment from the Lord to "organize His Church once more here upon the earth." Joseph was not only told the "precise day upon which, according to His will and commandment, we should proceed"[1] (April 6, 1830), but he was also informed by revelation how to conduct the organizing meeting.[2]

What have we received as a result of the Prophet Joseph Smith's work and ministry? The world has received a knowledge of God the

Eternal Father, His marvelous plan for our salvation and happiness, and an understanding of what His Son, Jesus Christ, did for us through His atoning sacrifice, which is the centerpiece of God's plan for our redemption. To the Prophet Joseph Smith were revealed the eternal principles and ordinances of the gospel of Jesus Christ that lead to eternal life in God's presence and more pages of holy scripture than have been given to any other prophet.

We accept and revere him as a prophet of God, and we declare to the world that he was called as such, but we do not worship him. In fact, many members of the Church are not even aware of Joseph Smith's final resting place.[3] As President Gordon B. Hinckley observed, "We do not worship the Prophet. We worship God our Eternal Father, and the risen Lord Jesus Christ. But we acknowledge him . . . we reverence him as an instrument in the hands of the Almighty in restoring to the earth the ancient truths of the divine gospel, together with the priesthood through which the authority of God is exercised in the affairs of His church and for the blessing of His people."[4]

A MARVELOUS WORK AND A WONDER

This year's Sperry Symposium is devoted to exploring the impact that the doctrines and scriptures restored through the Prophet Joseph Smith have had on the world in the past 175 years. For example, "today there are more than twelve million members of the Church. More than 51,000 full-time missionaries along with members of the Church are sharing the gospel throughout the nations of the earth. More than 120 million copies of the Book of Mormon have been published and have been fully translated into 74 languages. The last general conference of the Church was broadcast throughout the world in 70 different languages. Temples are beginning to dot the earth. Millions of lives are being blessed around the world by the humanitarian and welfare efforts of the Church. More than 16,000 individuals [and more] have been helped by the Perpetual Education Fund. The seminary and institute programs of the Church are blessing the lives of more than 800,000 teenagers and young adults in 144 countries. Countless individual lives are being blessed in ways that cannot be measured."[5]

Those of us living today have inherited a great legacy. We are the beneficiaries of what the scriptures describe as "a marvelous work and a wonder" (see 2 Nephi 25:17; 27:26). The worldwide Church, organized and established 175 years ago, is indeed the very kingdom of God on the earth. It is the restored Church of Jesus Christ. As envisioned by Daniel, it is the stone cut out of the mountain without hands, rolling forth across the earth in majesty and power (see Daniel 2:34–35, 44). As Isaiah foresaw, this Church has been raised up in the tops of the mountains like an "ensign," or banner, and now waves to all the world, inviting people from every nation to come and partake of the blessings of the Restoration and the gathering of Israel (see Isaiah 5:26; 11:10, 12; 18:1–3). As prophesied, the Church will continue to rise out of obscurity and eventually become an object of political and religious interest to every person in the world (see D&C 1:30; Revelation 14:6).[6] It will one day inundate "the earth as with a flood" to bear testimony of Jesus Christ and His resurrection from the dead (see Moses 7:62). In our modern world, which seems to be rapidly slouching into Sodom and Gomorrah–like conditions, the restored gospel of Jesus Christ is becoming more and more a "defense, and . . . a refuge from the storm" for millions across the earth (see D&C 115:6). The gospel of Jesus Christ has been restored that its light may be "a standard for the nations" to look to (D&C 115:5).

"Mormonism," Elder Orson F. Whitney observed, "is not a mere sect among sects, one more broken off fragment of a degenerate and crumbling Christianity. It is the pure, primitive Christianity restored—the original faith, the root of all religion; and it was not accident, but [divine] design, that [has given] it the strength of its position."[7]

OUR DAY IN CHURCH HISTORY

In describing the early, foundational events of the Restoration, Joseph Smith testified:

> The building up of Zion is a cause that has interested the people of God in every age; it is a theme upon which prophets, priests and kings have dwelt with peculiar delight; they have looked forward with joyful anticipation to the day in which we live; and fired with heavenly and joyful anticipations they have sung and written and prophesied of this

our day; but they died without the sight; *we are the favored people that God has made choice of to bring about the Latter-day glory; it is left for us to see, participate in and help to roll forward the Latter-day glory,* "the dispensation of the fulness of times, when God will gather together all things that are in heaven, and all things that are upon the earth, 'even in one.'"[8]

Saints living today have not only inherited a great spiritual legacy but also the responsibility to carry this work forward. As President Hinckley further reminded us, these are our days in the history of the Church and kingdom of God on the earth, and we have work to do: "The Lord expects so much of [Latter-day Saints] now because we are not persecuted, we are not driven, we are not on the march, we are not being burned and destroyed and troubled on all sides. We have peace, and we have the good opinion of many, many people in many, many places. How thankful we ought to be and how ambitious we ought to be to move forward this, the work of the Lord."[9]

It is our privilege to stand for the one cause that will emerge victorious! President Hinckley testified: "This Church is true. It will weather every storm that beats against it. It will outlast every critic who rises to mock it. It was established by God our Eternal Father for the blessing of His sons and daughters of all generations. It carries the name of Him who stands as its head, even the Lord Jesus Christ, the Savior of the world. It is governed and moves by the power of the priesthood. It sends forth to the world another witness of the divinity of the Lord."[10]

Thus, not only will the Church continue to stand, but we have an obligation to stand with it. As Oliver Cowdery was told, "Therefore be diligent; stand by my servant Joseph, faithfully" (D&C 6:18). The Prophet Joseph Smith laid the foundations for this work, and it is now up to us to "stand faithfully" until the capstone of Zion has been set in place.

A LIGHT THAT SHINES IN THE DARKNESS

Seventeenth-century artists employed a technique called *chiaroscuro* in which the artist created an extreme contrast between light and darkness to achieve dramatic effect and create depth. Before beginning a painting, Rembrandt would first paint his canvas black, causing the lighter colors that came later to shimmer and stand out more. Similarly, the light of the restored gospel is all the more brilliant when painted across the bleak landscape of the world. Thus, the Restoration is both a *declaration* of light and a *refutation* of darkness. In a revelation given in 1831, the Lord declared that His everlasting covenant has been sent into the world to be a *standard*, a *light* for people to seek after, and a *messenger* to prepare the way for His Second Coming (see D&C 45:9).

Our congregations sing a hymn in honor of the Restoration that contains the verse, "Praise to the man who communed with Jehovah! Jesus anointed that Prophet and Seer."[11] The focus of this symposium is to praise the Father and the Son for communing with living prophets—such great men as the Prophet Joseph Smith. When Joseph Smith walked out of the grove near his home in Palmyra, New York (as the cover of this book illustrates), a new day had dawned in the history of the world. The Restoration is real, and now, 175 years later, it is moving forward at a quickened pace to fulfill its ultimate and prophesied destiny. It is our privilege to be living in a day when the Lord is making "bare his holy arm in the eyes of all the nations" and at a time when "all the ends of the earth shall [one day] see the salvation of God" (3 Nephi 16:20).

W. JEFFREY MARSH
CHAIR, 2005 SIDNEY B. SPERRY SYMPOSIUM COMMITTEE

NOTES

1. Joseph Smith, *History of the Church of Jesus Christ of Latter-day Saints,* ed. B. H. Roberts, 2nd ed. rev. (Salt Lake City: Deseret Book, 1957), 1:64.
2. See Smith, *History of the Church,* 1:60–61.
3. Joseph Smith is buried in Nauvoo, Illinois.
4. Gordon B. Hinckley, *Be Thou an Example* (Salt Lake City: Deseret Book, 1981), 119.
5. *Church News,* January 1, 2005, 7.
6. President Ezra Taft Benson said: "We may expect to see the righteousness of the Saints and the progress of the kingdom of God continue unabated, but it will not be without opposition. The Council of the Twelve proclaimed in 1845: 'As this work progresses in its onward course, and becomes more and more an object of political and religious interest, . . . no king, ruler, or subject, no

community or individual, will stand neutral. All will . . . be influenced by one spirit or the other; and will take sides either for or against the kingdom of God'" (in Conference Report, April 1978, 46; or *Ensign*, May 1978, 32).

7. Orson F. Whitney, *The Strength of the Mormon Position,* cited in Abinadi Pratt, ed., *Pamphlets: Latter-day Tracts* (Salt Lake City: Deseret News, 1880), 23–24.

8. Smith, *History of the Church,* 4:609–10; emphasis added.

9. President Gordon B. Hinckley, member meeting, Richmond, Virginia, November 14, 1989; as cited in *Church News,* April 2, 2005, 5.

10. Gordon B. Hinckley, "Keep the Faith," *Ensign,* September 1985, 6.

11. "Praise to the Man," *Hymns* (Salt Lake City: The Church of Jesus Christ of Latter-day Saints, 1985), no. 27.

CHAPTER ONE

The Impact of the Doctrinal Restoration: How the World Was Different After Joseph Smith

ANDREW C. SKINNER

"Joseph Smith, the Prophet and Seer of the Lord, has done more, save Jesus only, for the salvation of men in this world, than any other man that ever lived in it" (D&C 135:3). What a statement! Though stunning to some, and even shocking to others, it is no exaggeration. The Prophet Joseph Smith single-handedly changed the theological landscape of the world. It was he who, after a long period of apostasy, reintroduced the world to a true knowledge of God the Father. It was he who made known to the world the full and far-reaching saving potential of Christ's atoning power. It was he who taught the doctrine and put back into operation the powers that enable all who so desire to reenter the Father's presence.

The Impact of Joseph's Personal Tutors

Latter-day Saints are not the first group of people to comprehend the greatness of Joseph Smith. From the beginning of time, God and His many prophets have known of and declared the coming of Joseph Smith to inaugurate and establish this, the dispensation of the fulness of times. President Brigham Young's well-known statement on this topic has become a classic but is well worth repeating because it is so mind-expanding! He said:

Andrew C. Skinner is dean of Religious Education at Brigham Young University.

It was decreed in the counsels of eternity, long before the foundations of the earth were laid, that he, Joseph Smith, should be the man, in the last dispensation of this world, to bring forth the word of God to the people, and receive the fulness of the keys and power of the Priesthood of the Son of God. The Lord had his eyes upon Joseph, and upon his father, and upon his father's father, and upon their progenitors clear back to Abraham, and from Abraham to the flood, from the flood to Enoch, and from Enoch to Adam. He has watched that family and that blood as it has circulated from its fountain to the birth of that man. He was fore-ordained in eternity to preside over this last dispensation.[1]

Therefore, it is not surprising that Joseph Smith was personally tutored in mortality by God as well as the many prophets who foreknew of him and his mortal sojourn. Many of the ancient prophets and patriarchs, and all of the heads of gospel dispensations, appeared to Joseph and either instructed him one-on-one or laid their hands upon his head and bestowed keys, powers, and knowledge that they had gained from Deity themselves.

Who else among all the world's leaders has stood in the presence of God the Eternal Father, His Son Jesus Christ, Adam, Noah, Raphael, Moses, Elias, Elijah, John the Baptist, Peter, James, John, Moroni, and many, many more, and received the power to bring salvation to *all* of Heavenly Father's children? We can document at least fifty-nine nonmortal or divine beings who appeared to, or were seen by, Joseph Smith in vision, each one presenting to the Prophet a divine tutorial or personalized lesson of eternal consequence for all of God's children.[2]

President John Taylor, beloved friend and trusted associate of the Prophet Joseph Smith, summed up the matter regarding his friend in these words:

Joseph Smith in the first place was set apart by the Almighty according to the councils of the gods in the eternal worlds, to introduce the principles of life among the people, of which the Gospel is the grand power and influence, and through which salvation can extend to all peoples, all nations, all kindreds, all tongues and all worlds. It is the principle that brings life and immortality to light, and places us in communication with God. God selected him for that purpose, and he fulfilled his mission and lived honorably and died honorably. I know of what I speak, for I was very well acquainted with him and was with him a great deal during his life, and was with him when he died. The principles which he had, placed him in communication with the Lord, and not only with the Lord, but with the ancient apostles and prophets; such men, for instance, as Abraham, Isaac, Jacob, Noah, Adam, Seth, Enoch, and Jesus, and the Father, and the apostles that lived on this continent, as well as those who lived on the Asiatic continent. He seemed to be as familiar with these people as we are with one another. Why? Because he had to introduce a dispensation which was called the dispensation of the fulness of times, and it was known as such by the ancient servants of God.[3]

The Prophet's divine tutorials not only introduced the Restoration in stages but also affected the way we think about God's saving plan in general, and our own lives and relationship to Deity in particular. Both Joseph Smith's life and the doctrine he restored show us just how carefully and meticulously the Lord plans events. Joseph Smith did not end up where he was by accident, just as you and I have not ended up where we are by happenstance. As Paul taught, "[God] hath made of one blood all nations of men for to dwell on all the face of the earth, and hath determined the times before appointed, and the bounds of their habitation" (Acts 17:26). Joseph Smith's experience also showed to the world the reality of heavenly beings and the closeness of an unseen realm of existence.

THE IMPACT OF THE PRINCIPLE OF REVELATION

Joseph Smith is one who seems to have lived every day of his life guided by the lodestar of revelation. This is impressive enough, but one of the reasons we have come to appreciate Joseph and his ministry so much is the assurance we have received from him that the same principle of revelation by which he lived his life and restored so much truth to the earth is available to each of us. As much as anything, the Prophet restored to the world a knowledge of, and an appreciation for, the doctrine of personal revelation—a kind of revelation that is not limited to the educated or the wealthy, not restricted to the powerful or the prelates, not intended only for those in some inner circle. But, rather, Joseph restored a knowledge of revelation that is available to all who simply call upon God in their quest for truth and in the sincerity of their souls. Is this not the lesson of Joseph's application of James 1:5?

The Prophet Joseph Smith, and all prophets since his inaugural ministry, have constantly preached that revelation is an "equal-opportunity" doctrine. Said Joseph, "The best way to obtain truth and wisdom is not to ask it from books, but to go to God in prayer, and obtain divine teaching."[4] Similarly, "Reading the experience of others, or the revelation given to them, can never give us a comprehensive view of our condition and true relation to God. . . . Could you gaze into heaven five minutes, you would know more than you would by reading all that ever was written on the subject."[5] Joseph consistently taught that "it is the privilege of the Children of God to come to God & get Revelation. . . . When *any* person receives a vision of heaven, he sees things that he never thought of before."[6] In regard to Church members, he indicated that it was the privilege of any officeholder in the Church to obtain revelations so far as it relates to his or her particular calling and duty in the Church.[7]

This is truly liberating doctrine. Both men and women are called into fellowship with God, to share equally in the glorious flood of light, knowledge, and power restored through the Prophet Joseph Smith. As Joseph found out when translating the Book of Mormon, God "imparteth his word by angels unto men, yea, not only men but women also. Now this is not all; little children do have words given unto them many times, which confound the wise and the learned" (Alma 32:23). Equal opportunities for all people to receive revelation and exaltation were inherent in the system Joseph restored.

The Impact of the First Vision

Perhaps the most important revelation of this last and greatest dispensation was Joseph Smith's First Vision of the Father and the Son. President Ezra Taft Benson certainly thought so. He declared, "The appearance of God the Father and His Son Jesus Christ to the boy prophet is the greatest event that has occurred in this world since the resurrection of the Master."[8] There are many lessons to learn from, as well as about, the First Vision.

Writing about the First Vision years after it had taken place, Joseph Smith himself said that he had thought how much he felt "like Paul [the Apostle], when he made his defense before King Agrippa, and related the account of the vision he had when he saw a light, and heard a voice" (Joseph Smith—History 1:24). In truth, the ministries of Paul and Joseph demonstrate significant parallels, and these parallels, beginning with a first vision for both, serve to help honest people see that the same reasons for accepting Paul as a bona fide servant of Jesus Christ should also lead them to accept and appreciate Joseph Smith as a genuine, duly authorized and commissioned servant of the same Lord that Paul followed.[9] When Paul came off the road to Damascus, where he was intending to persecute the Christians, at least seven things were confirmed:

- Jesus Christ is Lord.
- He is alive in heaven.
- He is a Being possessing great glory.
- Persecuting His followers is the equivalent of persecuting Him personally.
- Direct revelation is a continuing reality even after the Lord's mortal ministry ended.
- Jesus Christ has the power to change men's hearts.
- Jesus Christ continues to call men to be witnesses of Him after His death and Resurrection.

When Joseph Smith walked out of the Sacred Grove on that early spring morning in 1820, at least fourteen things were clarified or reestablished that had been lost or unknown during the previous seventeen hundred years:

- God the Father and Jesus Christ are alive and reside in heaven.
- Their relationship is a familial one—Father to Son.
- They are separate and distinct personages, not one spiritual essence.
- They possess a glory beyond description.
- They look, act, and speak like human beings.
- Humans are created in the image of the Father and the Son.
- The Father and the Son hear and answer prayers.
- The Father and the Son know individuals by name.
- There is an opponent to righteousness; he is real.
- That adversary to righteousness tries to thwart prayer.

- Revelation was a continuing reality seventeen hundred years after the so-called era of primitive Christianity.
- The Father testifies of His Son, and the Son of God deals directly with humankind.
- There had been an apostasy from Christ's Church.
- None of the churches on the earth in Joseph's day possessed the fulness of Christ's gospel.

The first visions of both Paul and Joseph Smith did have, and will continue to have, eternal consequences. Those visions inaugurated for both men a long period of direct revelation that continued until their martyrdoms. The instruction that accompanied both visions told their recipients to change their respective courses and wait for further instruction.[10] Out of these profound revelatory experiences came divine direction that blessed lives and changed the way countless humans looked at God's dealings with mortals. Both Paul and Joseph added to a corpus of prior revelations given by God to the human family in order to raise a new generation to a higher level. The essence of all these revelations was centered in Jesus Christ and His Atonement. The Apostle John declared that the *testimony of Jesus* was the spirit of prophecy (see Revelation 19:10). That is to say, the essence, or life-force, of prophecy is a knowledge of what Jesus has done and will yet do for the world. Thus, the essential job of every prophet is to testify personally of Jesus Christ. "And in the case of the great prophets Paul and Joseph Smith, they did so on the basis of their eyewitness contact with Christ."[11]

PAUL AND JOSEPH SMITH

The Prophet made many references to Paul, both explicit and implicit, throughout his life.[12] He constantly invoked the example and language of Paul to illustrate the way the Restoration unfolded and to describe the continuous, unchanging nature of opposition to divine truth and the work of the Father and the Son. Thus, one of the undervalued, perhaps unappreciated, aspects of the Restoration is the increased understanding of previous dispensations it provides—especially of Paul's day, the doctrine the ancient Apostle taught, what he thought and felt, and the social and cultural context of the gospel restoration of the first century.

Significantly, Paul's time was much like Joseph's. We can learn much about each period by studying the other. Both Joseph Smith and Paul endured monumental challenges to their integrity and teachings as a result of their first visions. For example, in describing his own encounters with opposition and persecution over his First Vision, Joseph Smith quoted the experience of the ancient Apostle:

> There were but few who believed him; some said he was dishonest, others said he was mad; and he was ridiculed and reviled. But all this did not destroy the reality of his vision. He had seen a vision, he knew he had, and all the persecution under heaven could not make it otherwise; and though they should persecute him unto death, yet he knew. . . . So it was with me. . . . And though I was hated and persecuted for saying that I had seen a vision, yet it was true; and while they were persecuting me, reviling me, and speaking all manner of evil against me falsely for saying so, I was led to say in my heart: Why persecute me for telling the truth? (Joseph Smith—History 1:24–25)

Paul gave us some appreciation for how the message of his vision was received among his non-Christian contemporaries. "For the Jews require a sign, and the Greeks seek after wisdom: but we preach Christ crucified, unto the Jews a stumblingblock, and unto the Greeks foolishness" (1 Corinthians 1:22–23). In other words, it was not easy to preach the message of Christ in an environment of Jewish superiority and Greek intellectualism. But, continued Paul, "the foolishness of God is wiser than men; and the weakness of God is stronger than men. . . . God hath chosen the foolish things of the world to confound the wise; and God hath chosen the weak things of the world to confound the things which are mighty" (1 Corinthians 1:25, 27).

Echoing the words of Paul, Joseph Smith presented a revelation during a special conference of elders at Hiram, Ohio, in November 1831, in which the Lord told His servants not to mind the wisdom of the world nor pay attention to worldly estimations of weakness and foolishness. For "the weak things of the world shall come forth and break down the mighty and strong ones, that man should not counsel his fellow man, neither trust in the arm of flesh . . . that the fulness of my gospel might be proclaimed by the weak and the simple unto the ends of the world. . . . Behold, I am God and have spoken it;

these commandments are of me, and were given unto my servants in their weakness, after the manner of their language, that they might come to understanding" (D&C 1:19, 23–24). One notes that the words of Joseph Smith and those of Paul are truly interchangeable.

Many so-called "hearers of the word" in the first century regarded the vision of Paul as foolishness. And many investigators in the dispensation of the fulness of times have regarded Joseph Smith's First Vision as a "delusion."[13] It has been observed that most of the objections raised against Joseph Smith's First Vision also call into question Paul's experience with equal force.[14] For example, one of the points of attack leveled against Joseph Smith's First Vision is that the Prophet did not describe his experience until a dozen years after it happened, and then he issued multiple versions of it thereafter. However, critics should have realized this is perfectly consistent with the timing of Paul's report of his first vision and his subsequent republicizing of it. The first known mention of Paul's dramatic experience is found in 1 Corinthians 9:1, written about two dozen years after it happened: "Am I not an apostle? am I not free? have I not seen Jesus Christ our Lord? are not ye my work in the Lord?"

In fact, arguments regarding the historical validity of an event that are based on the closeness of that event to the time it first appears in written form present a problem for the whole New Testament as well. According to tradition, the Gospel of John was composed between AD 90 and 100. And the earliest extant fragment of John's Gospel is dated even later—to around AD 110–30 on paleographical grounds.[15] That means at least seventy years went by from the time the Savior's mortal ministry took place until the time John wrote his Gospel account. Yet no committed Christian who believes the New Testament to be the word of God would dismiss the Gospel of John as untrustworthy.

Other attacks leveled against Paul in his day and Joseph Smith in his (and beyond) attempted to appeal to the principle of empirical evidence as well as the irrationality of believing that God is literally, physically, a resurrected Being. More to the point, in Joseph's day, how could anyone seriously believe that such a God would appear to a teenage boy and call into question all other denominations? However, both Paul and Joseph Smith taught that the natural man—the man or woman devoid of the Spirit of God—does not and cannot receive knowledge conveyed by the Spirit of God. Here are Paul's words: "But the natural man receiveth not the things of the Spirit of God: for they are foolishness unto him: neither can he know them, because they are spiritually discerned" (1 Corinthians 2:14). Compare that statement with one translated by Joseph Smith from the gold plates: "For the natural man is an enemy to God, and has been from the fall of Adam, and will be, forever and ever, unless he yields to the enticings of the Holy Spirit, and putteth off the natural man and becometh a saint through the atonement of Christ the Lord, and becometh as a child, submissive, meek, humble, patient, full of love, willing to submit to all things which the Lord seeth fit to inflict upon him, even as a child doth submit to his father" (Mosiah 3:19).

No insignificant parallel here! Neither Joseph Smith nor Paul attempted to engage their critics in debate over the philosophical possibility of resurrection or visions involving divine beings. Rather, they both humbly offered the strongest evidence possible, evidence against which there is no philosophical or logical counter: they *saw* the resurrected Lord for themselves! Said Paul: "And last of all he was *seen* of me also, as of one born out of due time" (1 Corinthians 15:8; emphasis added). Said Joseph: "And now, after the many testimonies which have been given of him, this is the testimony, last of all, which we give of him: That he lives! For we *saw* him" (D&C 76:22–23; emphasis added). Without the help of the doctrinal restoration in modern times, we would not be able to appreciate the significance of Paul's position or teaching and, thus, the consistency in the gospel of Jesus Christ over time.

The Impact of Joseph's Legacy of Sacrifice

From the moment of his First Vision onward, Joseph could never say his life was his own. The Sacred Grove inaugurated a lifetime of service to the Lord. Joseph Smith taught us by example as well as precept what it meant to live a consecrated life. (The word *consecrated* literally means "to make or declare sacred, to devote irrevocably to the worship of God."[16]) This is another lasting legacy of the Restoration. The Prophet gave to the world a template of unyielding loyalty in the face of continual hardship and persecution. The world is a different place because many individuals have hearkened to Joseph's words and modeled his behavior.

In describing his experiences, Joseph again harked back to Paul's words as found in Second Corinthians wherein the ancient Apostle spoke of his "journeyings often, in perils of waters, in perils of robbers, in perils by [his] own countrymen, in perils by the heathen, in perils in the city, in perils in the wilderness, in perils in the sea, in perils among false brethren; in weariness and painfulness, in watchings often, in hunger and thirst, in fastings often, in cold and nakedness" (2 Corinthians 11:26–27). Joseph said of his own difficulties: "I, like Paul, have been in perils, and oftener than anyone in this generation. As Paul boasted, I have suffered more than Paul did. I should be like a fish out of water if I were out of persecution. . . . The Lord has constituted me so curiously that I glory in persecution."[17] Writing to the Church in Nauvoo during a challenging period of legal harassment that kept him out of that city, Joseph again made explicit reference to Paul's example and mentoring influence. His comment has become part of the Church's official canon of scripture, Doctrine and Covenants 127:2:

> And as for the perils which I am called to pass through, they seem but a small thing to me, as the envy and wrath of man have been my common lot all the days of my life; and for what cause it seems mysterious, unless I was ordained from before the foundation of the world for some good end, or bad, as you may choose to call it. Judge ye for yourselves. God knoweth all these things, whether it be good or bad. But nevertheless, deep water is what I am wont to swim in. It all has become a second nature to me; and I feel, like Paul, to glory in tribulation; for to this day has the God of my fathers delivered me out of them all, and will deliver me from henceforth; for behold, and lo, I shall triumph over all my enemies, for the Lord God hath spoken it.

President Brigham Young was a second witness to Joseph's unrelenting hardships. Of his friend and mentor, President Young said that Joseph was

> poor, harassed, distressed, afflicted, and tormented with lawsuits, persecution upon persecution, and it cost thousands

and hundreds of thousands of dollars to keep him alive, which a few had to sustain. . . .

Joseph, our Prophet, was hunted and driven, arrested and persecuted, and although no law was ever made in these United States that would bear against him, for he never broke a law, yet to my certain knowledge he was defendant in forty-six lawsuits, and every time Mr. Priest was at the head of and led the band or mob who hunted and persecuted him. And when Joseph and Hyrum were slain in Carthage jail, the mob, painted like Indians, was led by a preacher.[18]

In spite of their sufferings, both Paul and Joseph Smith possessed a contagious optimism born of faith and hope in Jesus Christ. All members of the Church of Jesus Christ in these latter days are the beneficiaries and the inheritors of this optimistic mind-set. In addition to the trials and persecutions previously mentioned, Paul seems to have suffered throughout his life with an affliction that he called a thorn in the flesh. "And lest I should be exalted above measure through the abundance of the revelations, there was given to me a thorn in the flesh, the messenger of Satan to buffet me, lest I should be exalted above measure. For this thing I besought the Lord thrice, that it might depart from me" (2 Corinthians 12:7–8).

An important lesson from this comment is that all mortals, even the most dedicated, righteous servants of the Lord, will have afflictions to endure throughout mortality. But the Lord's power and grace are sufficient to make weak things strong. Thus, the Lord's response to Paul's petition regarding his thorn in the flesh and Paul's subsequent response to the Lord are comforting and fortifying: "And he [the Lord] said unto me, My grace is sufficient for thee: for my strength is made perfect in weakness. Most gladly therefore will I rather glory in my infirmities, that the power of Christ may rest upon me" (2 Corinthians 12:9).

It is important to emphasize that Joseph Smith came across this same concept, in almost the same language used by Paul, when he was translating Ether 12:27 of the Book of Mormon:

"And if men come unto me I will show unto them their weakness. I give unto men weakness that they may be humble; and my grace is sufficient for all men that humble themselves before me; for if they humble themselves before me, and have faith in me, then will I make weak things become strong unto them."

In addition to Paul and Joseph Smith, other of the Lord's prophets have recognized that weaknesses and problems are inherent in mortality. Most of these challenges come as a result of the Fall of Adam and therefore impose limitations on all of us. We cannot escape them. But we can overcome them through the grace, or enabling power, granted unto mortals through the Atonement. "It is not just in the next life that the 'weak things' are made strong through Christ. The Savior's grace is sufficient even in mortality to buoy up the spirit, to strengthen and spiritually enlarge one above natural abilities."[19] The prophet Ammon in the Book of Mormon described how much God can help us, saying, "Yea, I know that I am nothing; as to my strength I am weak; therefore I will not boast of myself, but I will boast of my God, for in his strength I can do all things" (Alma 26:12).

Precisely because of the doctrinal restoration accomplished through Joseph Smith, we are able to recognize that even those who are not of our faith have been inspired to see that God gives to all men weakness that all may humbly learn to rely upon Him, *and* that once we have entered into a covenant partnership with Him, He has unlimited resources to make us into something we could not even fathom beforehand. C. S. Lewis observed:

> When a man turns to Christ and seems to be getting on pretty well (in the sense that some of his bad habits are now corrected), he often feels that it would now be natural if things went fairly smoothly. When troubles come along— illnesses, money troubles, new kinds of temptation—he is disappointed. These things, he feels, might have been necessary to rouse him and make him repent in his bad old days; but why now? Because God is forcing him . . . into situations where he will have to be very much braver, or more patient, or more loving, than he ever dreamed of being before. It seems to us all unnecessary: but that is because we have not yet had the slightest notion of the tremendous thing He means to make of us. . . .
>
> Imagine yourself as a living house. God comes in to rebuild that house. At first, perhaps, you can understand what He is doing. He is getting the drains right and stopping the leaks in the roof and so on: you knew that those jobs needed doing and so you are not surprised. But presently He

starts knocking the house about in a way that hurts abominably and does not make sense. What on earth is He up to? The explanation is that He is building quite a different house from the one you thought of—throwing out a new wing here, putting on an extra floor there, running up towers, making courtyards. You thought you were going to be made into a decent little cottage: but He is building a palace. He intends to come and live in it Himself. . . .

He said (in the Bible) that we were "gods" and He is going to make good His words. If we let Him—for we can prevent Him, if we choose—He will make the feeblest and filthiest of us into a god or goddess, a dazzling, radiant, immortal creature, pulsating all through with such energy and joy and wisdom and love as we cannot now imagine, a bright stainless mirror which reflects back to God perfectly (though, of course, on a smaller scale) His own boundless power and delight and goodness.[20]

Some of the most magnificent declarations uttered by the Prophet Joseph about the eternal triumphs we may expect through God's power came in the midst of some of his most terrible trials. Said Joseph as he was incarcerated in Liberty Jail: "Do not think that our hearts faint, as though some strange thing had happened unto us, for we have seen and been assured of all these things beforehand, and have an assurance of a better hope than that of our persecutors. Therefore God hath made broad our shoulders for the burden. We glory in our tribulation, because we know that God is with us, that He is our friend, and that He will save our souls."[21]

For me personally, the most profound of the Prophet's inspiring exhortations are those Liberty Jail revelations we all know so well but sometimes forget or fail to comprehend. "My son, peace be unto thy soul; thine adversity and thine afflictions shall be but a small moment; and then, if thou endure it well, God shall exalt thee on high; thou shalt triumph over all thy foes" (D&C 121:7–8).

For his total service and sacrifice, the Prophet Joseph Smith was promised a crown of exaltation and given the pattern for the way in which God will deal with each of us. To Joseph the Lord declared: "I am the Lord thy God, and will be with thee even unto the end of the world, and through all eternity; for verily I seal upon you your exaltation, and prepare a throne for you in the kingdom of my Father, with Abraham your father. Behold, I have seen your sacrifices, and will forgive all your sins; I have seen your sacrifices in obedience to that which I have told you. Go, therefore, and I make a way for your escape, as I accepted the offering of Abraham of his son Isaac" (D&C 132:49–50).

Though Joseph Smith ultimately did escape the grasp of his enemies, it might not have been the way he originally thought it would—though he finally came to know that he would suffer a martyr's death (see D&C 135:4). John Taylor said Joseph was "like most of the Lord's anointed in ancient times, [who] . . . sealed his mission and his works with his own blood" (D&C 135:3). So it was with most of the ancient Apostles, including Peter and Paul. Our knowledge of Peter's and Paul's martyrdoms comes from sources outside the canon of scripture. The early church historian Eusebius (c. 260–339), whose *History of the Church* fills in many gaps in our knowledge about the early church, recorded: "So it came about that this man [Nero], the first to be heralded as a conspicuous fighter against God, was led on to murder the apostles. It is recorded that in his reign Paul was beheaded in Rome itself, and that Peter likewise was crucified."[22]

Eusebius's perspective on Peter and Paul was further informed by another of the early church's theologians, Origen (c. 185–254). Eusebius wrote: "Peter . . . came to Rome where he was crucified, head downwards at his own request. What need be said of Paul, who from Jerusalem as far as Illyricum preached in all its fulness the gospel of Christ, and later was martyred in Rome under Nero? This is exactly what Origen tells us in Volume III of his *Commentary on Genesis.*"[23]

Our English word *martyr* is a loanword from Greek and originally meant "witness." Truly, Peter, Paul, and Joseph were such true and faithful witnesses that they gave their very lives for the cause of revealed truth. All three were killed for restoring to the world a correct understanding of the nature of God the Father and His Son, Jesus Christ. All three died at the hands of unscrupulous men, who were lovers of self more than lovers of God. The rough treatment and eventual deaths of Peter, Paul, and Joseph can be laid squarely at the feet of political rulers—not a happy parallel, but an important one as we examine the history of the interaction between governments and God's people through the ages.

THE PROFUNDITY OF JOSEPH SMITH'S INTIMATE ACQUAINTANCE WITH DEITY

When all is said and done, no one was better acquainted with God than the Prophet Joseph Smith. He stood in the presence of the resurrected Lord a number of times. And though others, like Paul for example, speak of similar experiences (Paul records seeing the Lord on three other occasions after his Damascus experience), I believe there is a difference between Joseph Smith and others. The depth of Joseph's association with and understanding of Deity seems greater, so much so that Joseph's seeric powers come through with an intensity, constancy, majesty, and directness matched by few other personalities in all of scripture.

First, in canonized scripture Joseph speaks of seeing *both* the Father and the Son a number of times: during his First Vision in 1820, in a vision in 1832 that is so spectacular it is called "The Vision" (see D&C 76:20), and in an 1836 vision in the Kirtland Temple. Regarding the latter he said: "The heavens were opened upon us, and I beheld the celestial kingdom of God, and the glory thereof, whether in the body or out I cannot tell. I saw the transcendent beauty of the gate through which the heirs of that kingdom will enter, which was like unto circling flames of fire; also the blazing throne of God, whereon was seated the Father and the Son" (D&C 137:1–3). While other prophets may have had such experiences, they do not mention them. Joseph Smith alone helps us to see that the nature and person of Jesus Christ can only be fully comprehended and appreciated by gaining a knowledge of God the Father as well. This is a truly remarkable and unique aspect of the Restoration of the latter days. What the doctrinal restoration does, purely and simply, is reintroduce the world to a knowledge of God the Father (much the same way the same kind of restoration did during the meridian dispensation) after a long period of apostasy.

In addition to his mention of Elohim in scriptural passages, Joseph Smith also discussed God the Father in many of his non-canonical sermons, writings, musings, and dialogues. This rich and deep contact with and understanding of the nature and person of Elohim is nowhere better demonstrated than in the Prophet's 1844 sermons, especially the King Follett discourse. In that magnificent sermon, delivered before some 20,000 Saints at the April conference of the Church in Nauvoo, the Prophet asked and answered the question regarding what kind of being God is.

The necessity of possessing the right answer to the question about the nature of God is simple according to Joseph Smith:

> If men do not comprehend the character of God, they do not comprehend themselves. . . . The Scriptures inform us that "This is life eternal that they might know thee, the only true God, and Jesus Christ whom thou hast sent."
>
> If any man does not know God, and inquires what kind of a being he is,—if he will search diligently his own heart— if the declaration of Jesus and the apostles be true, he will realize that he has not eternal life; for there can be eternal life on no other principle.[24]

When one reads and ponders material like the King Follet discourse, one quickly realizes that there is not another person besides Joseph Smith to whom we may go to find such depth of insight about Deity. The reason Joseph spent so much time dwelling on this information about God was to bless the Saints. "I want you all to know him, and to be familiar with him," Joseph said.[25]

What are some of the critical concepts Joseph Smith taught about God the Father that are not articulated elsewhere in such clarity?

- "The Father has a body of flesh and bones as tangible as man's" (D&C 130:22).
- The Father is "the Eternal God of all other gods" (D&C 121:32).
- "In the beginning, the head of the Gods called a council of the Gods; and they came together and concocted a plan to create the world and people it."[26]
- "God himself was once as we are now, and is an exalted man, and sits enthroned in yonder heavens!"[27]
- "[God] was once a man like us. . . . God himself, the Father of us all, dwelt on an earth, the same as Jesus Christ himself."[28]
- "[We] have got to learn how to be Gods . . . and to be kings and priests to God, the same as all Gods have done before [us], namely, by going from one small degree to another, and from a small capacity to a great one; from grace to grace, from exaltation to exaltation, until [we] attain to the resurrection of the dead,

and are able to dwell in everlasting burnings, and to sit in glory as do those who sit enthroned in everlasting power."[29]

- "When we are ready to come to [God], he is ready to come to us."[30]

All of these insights about God the Father that came through the Prophet Joseph Smith present us with new information that is unique or uniquely stated in Christian theology. This is a profound and lasting consequence of the doctrinal restoration. The great Prophet of the Restoration knew God the Father in a special, intimate way. And yet there remained with Joseph a profound respect for Deity that eschewed any hint of inappropriate familiarity.

Another profound aspect of Joseph Smith's intimate association with Deity deserves to be noted. Often the canonized thoughts and words expressed by Joseph Smith were, in actuality, the thoughts and very words of the Lord Himself. Much of the doctrine and theology imparted to us by Joseph Smith is composed of nothing less than the direct, first-person declarations of Jesus Christ. Often Joseph was simply the amplifier through whom the Lord's own words passed to others.

Even a cursory examination of the Doctrine and Covenants shows how often Joseph Smith was simply relaying the actual declarations of the Lord in unmistakable language to various recipients:

- Four sections of the Doctrine and Covenants begin with the declaration "Behold, I am God."
- At least twenty-nine sections begin with the direct expression of the Lord "Behold [or Verily], I say unto you."
- At least thirty-seven sections of the Doctrine and Covenants begin with "Thus saith the Lord" or a slight variation of that formula.
- At least ten sections open with "Hearken and listen to the voice [words] of Jesus Christ" or some slight variation of that direct call to give undivided attention to the Lord Himself.

What the Apostle Paul said of his day and ministry may be said even more intensely and literally about Joseph Smith's day: "For who hath known the mind of the Lord, that he may instruct him? But we have the mind of Christ" (1 Corinthians 2:16). We have the mind of Christ, and we have it through the Prophet Joseph Smith!

THE IMPACT OF THE KEYS OF THE KINGDOM

From Joseph's interactions with God and angels there have come to us the keys to perform the ordinances of exaltation for both the living and the dead. This is one of the most important of the Restoration's many facets.

Keys are conduits of power and information. The revelations of the Restoration speak of keys in two major senses: one is the power and authority to *direct* the priesthood and the Church; the other is the means to reveal, to discover, to bring to light things unknown or hidden. In this second sense, for example, "Joseph Smith and Oliver Cowdery were given the *keys* to translate and bring hidden scriptures to light" (see D&C 6:24–28).[31] For our discussion, we will define the keys of the kingdom of God in the first sense, as the right and power to direct and govern the Lord's affairs on this earth. Joseph Smith taught, "The fundamental principles, government, and doctrine of the Church are vested in the keys of the kingdom."[32] These keys are part of the higher or Melchizedek Priesthood. As revealed to the Prophet Joseph Smith, this higher priesthood, which encompasses the Aaronic and Levitical Priesthood,[33] holds "the keys of all the spiritual blessings of the church" and "the mysteries of the kingdom of heaven" (D&C 107:18–19); it "holds the right of presidency, and has power and authority over all the offices in the church in all ages of the world" (D&C 107:8). Like God Himself, the Melchizedek Priesthood is eternal. The Prophet Joseph Smith said, "The priesthood is an everlasting principle, and existed with God from eternity, and will to eternity."[34]

The Melchizedek Priesthood was instituted "prior to the foundation of this earth" said the Prophet Joseph, and "is the channel through which the Almighty commenced revealing His glory at the beginning of the creation of this earth, and through which He has continued to reveal Himself . . . and through which He will make known His purpose to the end of time."[35] This is critical doctrine, and without the revelations and work of Joseph Smith we would not know these things.

Consider what knowledge has come to us as a direct result of Joseph Smith's instruction. He revealed that before the time of the Old Testament patriarch Melchizedek, the higher priesthood was called "the Holy Priesthood after the Order of the Son of God." But out of respect or reverence for the name of Deity, its name was changed to the Melchizedek Priesthood in honor of the great Patriarch (see D&C 107:2–4). Joseph taught that all the prophets in ancient times held the Melchizedek Priesthood.[36] Furthermore, he said that the Melchizedek Priesthood is the power by which men and women become like our heavenly parents, heirs of our Heavenly Father's kingdom and joint heirs with Jesus Christ, possessing every power and every blessing the Father and the Son possess.[37] This is at the very core of God's work and glory (see Moses 1:39).

Joseph Smith revealed that the first person on this earth to possess the keys of the priesthood was Adam. In fact, our first father holds the keys of presidency over *all* dispensations and eras of the gospel. He is the presiding high priest, under Christ's direction, over all the earth. Noah stands next to Adam in priesthood authority,[38] and "after these two come all the heads of the different gospel dispensations, together with a host of other mighty prophets."[39] Not the least of these are Elijah, who held the keys of the sealing power in ancient Israel (see D&C 27:9; 110:13–16), and Nephi the son of Helaman, who held the keys of the sealing power among the Nephites (see Helaman 10:4–10).

The scriptures given through Joseph Smith speak of others who hold keys. Another Book of Mormon prophet, Moroni, holds "the keys of the record of the stick of Ephraim" (D&C 27:5). The prophet Moses holds the keys of the gathering of Israel and the leading of the ten tribes from the land of the north (see D&C 110:11). A prophet named Elias holds the keys of the Abrahamic covenant (see D&C 110:12).[40] An angel named Raphael holds the keys of his dispensation (see D&C 128:21). The chief Apostles, Peter, James, and John, held the keys of the kingdom of God on the earth in their day (see D&C 27:12–13; 128:20).

All of these specific keys we have mentioned constitute the keys of the kingdom of God. And all of these prophets who held keys, and many other "divers angels, from Michael or Adam down to the present time," have returned in these latter days to the Prophet Joseph Smith and declared "their dispensation, their rights, their keys, their honors, their majesty and glory, and the power of their priesthood," according to D&C 128:21. Joseph Smith and his successors have been, and now are, the possessors of all the keys and powers of the kingdom of God that are possible for mortal men to possess.

KEYS AND SEALING POWER

Among the keys of authority and power bestowed upon the Prophet Joseph Smith, none are of greater or more far-reaching significance than those given by Elijah.[41] This ancient prophet held the keys of the kingdom in his day; he held the keys of presidency and the keys of the sealing power that constitute the fulness of the Melchizedek Priesthood. President Joseph Fielding Smith said that "it is that sealing power which gave [Elijah] the right and authority to officiate. And the Lord said unto him, 'That which you bind on earth shall be bound in heaven.' That is how great his power was, and in that day Elijah stood up and officiated for the people in the sealing power."[42]

So great and important are the keys of the sealing power that sometimes we equate the keys of the kingdom with the keys of the sealing power. The "sealing power puts the stamp of approval upon every ordinance that is done in this Church and more particularly those that are performed in the temples of the Lord."[43] And as the revelation states, "All covenants, contracts, bonds, obligations, oaths, vows, performances, connections, associations, or expectations, that are *not* made and entered into and sealed by the Holy Spirit of promise, of him who is anointed . . . whom I have appointed on the earth to hold this power, . . . and there is never but one on the earth at a time on whom this power and the keys of this priesthood are conferred . . . are of no efficacy, virtue, or force in and after the resurrection from the dead; for all contracts that are not made unto this end have an end when men are dead" (D&C 132:7; emphasis added).

The sealing powers for the living and the dead constitute the fulness of the priesthood. We can receive a fulness of the priesthood only in the temples of the Lord. The Prophet Joseph Smith declared: "If a man get a fulness of the priesthood of God, he has to get it in the same way that Jesus Christ obtained it, and that was by keeping all the commandments and obeying all the ordinances of the house of the Lord."[44]

Further commenting on the Prophet's words, President Joseph Fielding Smith stated: "Let me put this in a little different way. I do not care what office you hold in this Church—you may be an apostle, you may be a patriarch, a high priest, or anything else—you cannot receive the fulness of the priesthood unless you go into the temple of the Lord and receive these ordinances of which the Prophet speaks. No [one] can get the fulness of the priesthood outside of the temple of the Lord."[45] But the fulness of the priesthood *is* available to anyone who is worthy to enter the house of the Lord.

There is no exaltation in the kingdom of God without the fulness of priesthood, including the sealing keys. Thus, the fulness of the priesthood or the sealing power might also be termed the keys of exaltation. Again, President Smith said: "Only in the temple of the Lord can the fulness of the priesthood be received. Now that temples are on the earth, there is no other place where the endowment and the sealing powers for all eternity can be given. No man [or woman] can receive the keys of exaltation in any other place."[46]

In the temples of the Lord that now dot the earth, men and women can be sealed as husbands and wives for eternity. Children can be sealed to parents in family units forever. "What a glorious privilege it is to know that the family organization will remain intact."[47] Through the doctrinal restoration, we know that what is enacted on earth by the Lord's authorized stewards is bound in heaven. What value can be put on this knowledge? There is great comfort in knowing this. There is great security. There is great stability. There is a great anchor that comes to the soul in knowing this. Has any aspect of the Restoration had greater impact on the entire human family than the return of the keys of the priesthood—the sealing power of eternity?

My father died when I was young. I idolized him. Those were dark days. But tremendous peace, security, and motivation to carry on came from my knowledge that we had been to the temple and had been sealed as a family for eternity. I believe there would be significant value in having mothers and fathers spend some time with their children talking about the ordinances of eternity and the sealing power that binds families together forever. I believe our children would be more secure in their faith, better prepared to face life's challenges, and come to regard living prophets with a new love and appreciation if they could understand the incomparable sealing

power, found in the temples of the Lord because of the ministry of
the Prophet Joseph Smith.

CONCLUSION

There are invaluable, even incomparable, benefits that have
issued forth from the restoration of all things through the Prophet
Joseph Smith. Humankind has been impacted in profound ways.
First, we see that God is consistent. He has had a plan for His children from before this world was created, and that plan has been
administered through prophets who have held priesthood power and
priesthood keys.

Second, we see that God has fulfilled and is fulfilling His prophecies and promises concerning the restoration of all things in this, the
dispensation of the fulness of times. We may have perfect confidence
and trust in Him. He has the power to fulfill all His purposes, which
are perfectly just and fair. God does *not* deal in accidents or
coincidences.

Third, divine beings, Gods and angels, are real and they have
ministered to men and women on earth since its creation. Divine
tutorials are powerful tools of instruction.

Fourth, not only is revelation a principle of power with prophets
but it is also available to every man, woman, and child who desires to
have it. The heavens are not closed!

Fifth, the restoration of all things is founded on the First Vision,
the most important event since the Resurrection of Jesus Christ.

Sixth, the doctrinal restoration in this dispensation teaches us
about all other dispensations: what they were like, how God dealt
with His children in those dispensations, and what challenges previous prophets and apostles (Paul and others) had to contend with.

Seventh, our gratitude for the Prophet Joseph Smith will continue to increase as we expand our understanding of the doctrinal
restoration—as we begin to comprehend the magnitude of his
prophetic office and calling, and the depth of his association with
God the Father and His Son Jesus Christ. The doctrinal restoration
reintroduced the world to a knowledge of God the Father.

Eighth, every aspect of the doctrinal restoration points to the fulness of the priesthood and the culminating power we call the keys of

the sealing power. This power is so great that it has an impact on both the living and the dead for eternity.

Ninth, our gratitude and respect for all of Joseph's successors will increase profoundly as we are able to understand the nature of the power and authority held by all the Presidents of the Church up to the current day.

Tenth, knowing that the keys and fulness of the priesthood are upon the earth and available to all who desire them gives us security and stability in a world that is horribly unstable. It gives us assurance of the continuation of the bonds of love and association with friends and family through the eternities.

All of this is made possible by the Father and the Son through the great Prophet of the Restoration. God be thanked for Joseph Smith and his successors.

NOTES

1. Brigham Young, *Discourses of Brigham Young,* comp. John A. Widtsoe (Salt Lake City: Deseret Book, 1971), 108.

2. See H. Donl Peterson, *Moroni: Ancient Prophet, Modern Messenger,* Salt Lake City: Deseret Book, 2000, pp. 148–150. See also chapter 21 in this volume.

3. John Taylor, in *Journal of Discourses* (London: Latter-day Saints' Book Depot, 1854–86), 21:94.

4. Joseph Smith, *History of the Church of Jesus Christ of Latter-day Saints,* ed. B. H. Roberts, 2nd ed. rev. (Salt Lake City: The Church of Jesus Christ of Latter-day Saints, 1932–51), 4:425.

5. Joseph Smith, *Teachings of the Prophet Joseph Smith,* comp. Joseph Fielding Smith (Salt Lake City: Deseret Book, 1976), 324.

6. Joseph Smith, *Words of Joseph Smith,* comp. and ed. Andrew F. Ehat and Lyndon W. Cook (Provo, UT: Religious Studies Center, Brigham Young University, 1980), 13–14; emphasis added.

7. See Smith, *History of the Church,* 2:477.

8. Ezra Taft Benson, in Conference Report, April 1971, 20.

9. See Richard Lloyd Anderson, "Parallel Prophets: Paul and Joseph Smith," in *BYU Fireside and Devotional Speeches, 1982–83* (Provo, UT: Brigham Young University Press, 1983), 177.

10. See Anderson, "Parallel Prophets," 178.

11. Anderson, "Parallel Prophets," 178.

12. For Joseph Smith's explicit references to Paul in modern scripture see D&C 18:9; 74:1–6; 127:2; 128:13, 15–16; JS—H 1:24; and Article

of Faith 13. For many of Joseph Smith's references to Paul outside
of scripture, see Smith, *Teachings:* as author of Epistle to Hebrews,
59–60; an example of industry and patience, 63; labored unceas-
ingly in the gospel, 63; summary of life and labors of, 63–64; did
not seek honors of this life, 64; to receive a crown of righteousness
at Jesus's Second Coming, 64; had the Second Comforter, 151;
received a visit from and was taught mysteries of godliness by Abel,
169–70; was acquainted with and instructed by Enoch, 170;
description of, 180; a good orator, 180; caught up to third heavens,
247, 301, 304, 311, 323; knew things unlawful to utter, 247, 305,
323; had to be baptized for remission of sins, 265; was all things to
all men to save some, 306; was persecuted, 32; quoted: on hasty
ordinations, 42; on sacrifice offered by Abel, 59; on gospel taught
to Abraham, 60; on necessity of the Resurrection of Jesus Christ,
62; on Second Coming of Jesus, 63–65, 286; on receiving crown of
righteousness, 63–64; on apostasy in Church at Ephesus, 67; on
love of husbands and wives, 88–89; on doctrine of election, 149,
189; on ministry of angels, 158; on dispensation of the fulness of
times, 159, 168; on baptism of children of Israel, 159; on purposes
and order of God, 158; on baptism for the dead, 179, 201, 222; on
spiritual gifts, 202, 207, 243–45; on gift of prophecy, 209, 244–46;
on order in the Church, 209; on offices in the Church, 244–45; on
necessity of having Spirit of God, 247; on three degrees of glory,
311, 359, 374; on rebaptism, 263, 336; on wisdom of the world,
300; on being yoked to unbelievers, 306; on priesthood and ordinances, 308; on seeking after the dead, 356; on plurality of gods,
370–71; on earthly likeness to heavenly things, 373 (Robert J.
Matthews's index of *Teachings,* 422).

13. So said Charles Francis Adams in 1844; quoted in Hyrum L. Andrus,
Joseph Smith: The Man and the Seer (Salt Lake City: Deseret Book,
1979), 1.

14. See Anderson, "Parallel Prophets," 178.

15. See F. F. Bruce, *The New Testament Documents—Are They Reliable?*
(Grand Rapids, MI: Eerdmans, 1985), 17.

16. *Merriam-Webster's Collegiate Dictionary,* 11th ed., s.v. "consecrate."

17. Smith, *History of the Church,* 6:408.

18. Young, *Discourses of Brigham Young,* 465–66.

19. Joseph Fielding McConkie, Robert L. Millet, and Brent L. Top,
Doctrinal Commentary on the Book of Mormon (Salt Lake City:
Bookcraft, 1992), 4:301.

20. C.S. Lewis, *Mere Christianity* (New York: Touchstone, 1996), 176.

21. Smith, *History of the Church,* 3:227.

22. Eusebius, *The History of the Church from Christ to Constantine,* trans.
G. A. Williamson (London: Penguin Books, 1989), 62.

23. Eusebius, *History of the Church*, 65.

24. Smith, *Teachings*, 343–44.

25. Smith, *Teachings*, 345.

26. Smith, *Teachings*, 349.

27. Smith, *Teachings*, 345.

28. Smith, *Teachings*, 346.

29. Smith, *Teachings*, 346–47.

30. Smith, *Teachings*, 350.

31. Bruce R. McConkie, *Mormon Doctrine*, 2nd ed. (Salt Lake City: Bookcraft, 1966), 410; emphasis added.

32. Smith, *Teachings*, 21.

33. See Smith, *Teachings*, 166.

34. Smith, *Teachings*, 157.

35. Smith, *Teachings*, 166–67.

36. See Smith, *Teachings*, 181.

37. See Smith, *Teachings*, 308–9, 322.

38. See D&C 78:16; see also Smith, *Teachings*, 157.

39. McConkie, *Mormon Doctrine*, 412.

40. See Joseph Fielding Smith, *Doctrines of Salvation*, comp. Bruce R. McConkie (Salt Lake City: Bookcraft, 1954), 3:126–27.

41. See Smith, *Doctrines of Salvation*, 3:126.

42. Smith, *Doctrines of Salvation*, 3:127.

43. Smith, *Doctrines of Salvation*, 3:129.

44. Smith, *Teachings*, 308.

45. Smith, *Doctrines of Salvation*, 3:131.

46. Smith, *Doctrines of Salvation*, 3:133.

47. Smith, *Doctrines of Salvation*, 3:129.

CHAPTER TWO

CONTINUING THE PROGRAM OF THE PROPHET

MILTON V. BACKMAN JR.

One of the significant contributions of Joseph Smith was to establish a program that enabled other leaders to continue the work which he restored. This program included not only teaching others essential gospel principles but training others to record, publish, and preserve his historical records. These records included doctrinal contributions and descriptions of his experiences. Following the martyrdom of Joseph Smith, the Quorum of the Twelve Apostles was the only group of leaders who continued this vital program of the Prophet.

RECORDING AND PRESERVING HISTORICAL RECORDS

The accomplishments of Joseph Smith, including his doctrinal contributions, have been preserved in a variety of documents. One of Joseph Smith's early contributions was to establish a program which preserved historical records. The period of intense record keeping under Joseph Smith's direction began when the Church was organized on April 6, 1830, and continued until his death on June 27, 1844. During these fourteen years, Joseph Smith kept a variety of records and appointed others to record, write, and publish the history of the Church. These records described his activities, teachings, visions, prophecies, and many other gifts of the Spirit. The importance of these records is evident by the fact that so many were

Milton V. Backman Jr. is professor emeritus of Church history and doctrine at Brigham Young University.

preserved amid intense persecution and subsequent migrations of Latter-day Saints. If Joseph Smith had been a fraud, as he was sometimes accused, it is difficult to understand why he was so concerned and so involved in recording and preserving the history of the Church.[1]

On the day the Church was organized, the Prophet recorded a revelation which specified, "Behold, there shall be a record kept among you" (D&C 21:1). Shortly following the recording of this revelation, Oliver Cowdery was called to be the first Church historian and he was the first Latter-day Saint to publish an early history of the Restoration. This history, which was printed in Kirtland in the *Latter-day Saints' Messenger and Advocate* in 1834 and 1835, described the visitations and teachings of Moroni, the coming forth of the Book of Mormon, and the restoration of the priesthood.[2] Selections from that publication have been inserted as a note in the current edition of our Pearl of Great Price (see Joseph Smith—History, 58–59).

HISTORIES

Based on records that have survived, Joseph Smith's personal involvement in writing history began in November 1832 when he commenced an autobiography that he wrote partly with his own pen and dictated other portions to his clerk, Frederick G. Williams. This autobiography included a brief account of his family, boyhood experiences, and education. He recalled that because of the poverty of his family, his formal education was neglected and all he learned were the rudiments of reading, writing, and arithmetic. He also wrote an account of his First Vision in this manuscript, which is the only account of that vision in his own handwriting. He included in this 1832 record many doctrinal concepts that he learned from the Lord in 1820, such as the reality of the Atonement and the Second Coming. He also described in that history events relating to the coming forth of the Book of Mormon.[3]

Although the 1832 autobiography was not published during the life of Joseph Smith, concepts included in that record were included in a missionary pamphlet published by Orson Pratt in 1840. This pamphlet, entitled "An Interesting Account of Several Remarkable Visions," was based upon information that Elder Pratt had learned from Joseph Smith and was the first publication by a Latter-day Saint of the Prophet's First Vision.[4] Moreover, selections from that pamphlet were included in Joseph Smith's Wentworth Letter, which was published in the *Times and Seasons* in March 1842. This 1842 history contained the first published account written by Joseph Smith of his First Vision and included the Articles of Faith, both later published in the Pearl of Great Price.[5]

JOURNALS

In the 1830s and early 1840s, Joseph Smith also recorded his experiences in journals. The earliest journals that have been preserved include his experiences between November 27, 1832, and April 3, 1836 (except for the period from December 1834 to September 1835). Although portions of the earliest journal were written by Joseph, most of the information recorded in 1835 and 1836 was dictated to scribes. In 1836 he recorded in his journal daily events that occurred during the greatest Pentecostal season in the history of the restored Church.[6] Selections from these journal entries were included in the history of the Church, and his account of his vision of the celestial kingdom is now section 137 in the current edition of the Doctrine and Covenants.[7] The last entry in that journal is a description of a vision in the Kirtland Temple during which Joseph Smith and Oliver Cowdery saw the Savior and received keys of the priesthood from Moses, Elias, and Elijah.[8] This account became section 110 of our Doctrine and Covenants.

Joseph Smith recognized his deficiencies and imperfections in conveying his ideas in writing, and his temporal responsibilities continued to increase after he was forced to flee from Kirtland in January 1838. Subsequently, after moving to Missouri early in 1838 and to Nauvoo in May 1839, many of his activities were recorded in journals that were almost entirely written by his scribes. These scribes traveled with him and recorded in their words Joseph's activities and teachings.[9] Shortly before his martyrdom, Joseph declared, "For the last three years I have a record of all my acts and proceedings, for I have kept several good, faithful, and efficient clerks in constant employ: they have accompanied me everywhere, and carefully kept my history, and they have written down what I have done, where I have been, and what I have said; . . . I have [a] written testimony to prove my actions."[10]

LETTERS

The journals and letters of Joseph, especially those that were written and dictated by him, provide a glance into his daily life, his love for his family, his personality, and his teachings. Today more than ninety of Joseph Smith's letters have survived, and most of these are currently located in the Church Archives. One of these documents, Joseph Smith's March 20, 1839, letter to the Church written in the Liberty Jail, was initially published in the *Times and Seasons* (May and July 1840). Excerpts from that twenty-nine-page letter were included in the 1876 edition and the current edition of the Doctrine and Covenants as sections 121, 122, and 123.[11]

REVELATIONS

Joseph Smith's doctrinal contributions are not only found in his historical writings but also in his revelations. The earliest reference to Joseph Smith compiling the revelations he had received was in July 1830, and throughout the remainder of his life he continued to arrange and copy revelations. The initial efforts to publish these documents began in November 1831 when Joseph Smith and a council of high priests selected for publication more than sixty revelations that he had received. This work, entitled the Book of Commandments, contained sixty-five revelations and was to be published in the first Mormon press established in Independence, Missouri. During its publication, however, the press was destroyed by a mob. Meanwhile, William W. Phelps, a convert and former publisher who was called to establish this press, printed some of Joseph's revelations in 1832 and 1833 in the first Mormon periodical, the *Evening and Morning Star.*[12]

In 1835, under the direction of Joseph Smith, Latter-day Saints replaced the Book of Commandments with the first edition of the Doctrine and Covenants. Joseph Smith set many precedents as he prepared the first edition of this work for publication. For example, a committee was appointed by the high council to assist Joseph Smith in compiling or determining the revelations that should be published and in editing the revelations. This committee included the First Presidency of Joseph Smith, Sidney Rigdon, Frederick G. Williams, and Oliver Cowdery. Oliver Cowdery at that time was involved in reprinting revelations that had been printed in the Book of

Commandments in a new edition of the *Evening and Morning Star,* which was being printed in Kirtland. He wrote in that periodical that he was correcting errors in the initial printing of the revelations because he had access to more reliable copies of the manuscripts.[13]

The editing of the revelations by the committee included other changes. There is no indication in the writings or revelations of Joseph Smith that he was given perfect, final language as he recorded the revelations. Rather, he was inspired in fundamental thoughts. As suggested by Orson Pratt, Joseph received ideas from God and clothed those ideas with words that came to his mind. In the preface to that work we read, "These commandments are of me, and were given unto my servants in their weakness, after the manner of their language, that they might come to understanding" (D&C 1:24). Subsequently, editorial changes were not only made to correct errors by scribes and publishers, but words were inserted by editors to throw increased light upon subjects unfolded in the revelations. For example, since there were developments in Church government in the early 1830s with new officers being appointed (such as counselors to bishops), words, phrases, and sentences were added so that instructions would apply to officers not in the Church at the time the initial revelations were given. There was also a combining of revelations. What is now section 42 contains instructions on the law of consecration and stewardship, which Joseph Smith received on February 9 and February 23, 1831.[14]

The committee also changed the name of that work to *Doctrine and Covenants,* and this first edition included seven lectures on faith delivered in Kirtland, which Joseph Smith approved. These theological discussions appeared under the heading of "Doctrine"; and the second part, consisting of 103 revelations, was included under the title "Covenants and Commandments."[15]

Joseph Smith also supervised the publication of a second edition of the Doctrine and Covenants. On June 12, 1844, two weeks before the martyrdom, a notice appeared in the *Nauvoo Neighbor* that a new edition of the Doctrine and Covenants would be available in about one month.[16] The martyrdom of Joseph and the wounding of John Taylor interrupted the final publication date, but this new edition contained seven revelations that Joseph Smith received between 1834 and 1844. These sections included information about building a temple in Nauvoo and an epistle regarding baptism for the dead that was to be performed in that sacred building (see D&C 127–28). One other section was added immediately prior to its publication. This new section was a tribute written by John Taylor describing the martyrdom of Joseph and Hyrum and identifying some of Joseph's remarkable accomplishments (see D&C 135).[17]

ADDITIONAL CHURCH RECORDS

In addition to histories, journals, letters, and revelations, Joseph supervised the recording and preserving of many other historical documents during the 1830s and early 1840s. These records included proceedings of meetings and quorum and temple records.[18] One of these valuable documents recorded in Kirtland between October 1832 and November 1837 was the Kirtland Council Minute Book. This record included proceedings of meetings and discussions of church policies and procedures. There is a description in this document kept by Joseph's scribe, Frederick G. Williams, of the historical setting of section 88 of our Doctrine and Covenants and accounts of meetings of the School of the Prophets. It also included a description of ordinances performed during the first term of that school and the vision of the Savior and angels to participants on March 18, 1833.[19]

PRESERVING THE TEACHINGS OF JOSEPH SMITH

One of the significant contributions of Joseph Smith's scribes and other members was to record Joseph Smith's sermons. Although Joseph Smith delivered more than 250 public sermons, historians have located no notes, outlines, or recorded speeches prepared by Joseph Smith. Even though no one attending these meetings recorded verbatim his sermons, a summary of about fifty sermons has survived.[20] One of the most faithful recorders of his teachings was Wilford Woodruff, who kept one of the most detailed diaries that has ever been preserved. After taking copious notes, he generally, after a brief period, transcribed them into more detailed accounts.[21]

Two other major contributors to preserving the teachings of Joseph were Willard Richards (Church historian) and William Clayton (Joseph's private secretary). Both of these men were present with the Prophet during many occasions in Nauvoo and traveled with the Prophet and recorded in journals his teachings as they unfolded in meetings and conversations with others.[22] William Clayton, for example, recorded Joseph Smith's distinct doctrinal contributions relating to the Godhead, celestial marriage, Adam and the priesthood, angels, the future state of the earth, and degrees in the celestial kingdom. Information recorded in that journal and records kept by Willard Richards are currently published as sections 129, 130, and 131 of the Doctrine and Covenants.[23] Moreover, William Clayton wrote as Joseph dictated the revelation on celestial marriage (see D&C 132).[24]

Thomas Bullock and Willard Richards also recorded some of Joseph Smith's discourses. One of the last and most famous sermons of Joseph Smith, known as the King Follett discourse, probably contained more distinct teachings than any other reported sermon. It was recorded by Wilford Woodruff, Thomas Bullock, William Clayton, Willard Richards, and others.[25]

WRITING AND PUBLISHING THE HISTORY OF THE CHURCH

While living in Far West, Missouri, in April 1838, Joseph Smith commenced writing a history of the Church. Because so many inaccurate reports had been circulated about his experiences, he decided to record events in relation to the Church as they had transpired. In this history he described his birth, family, move to New York, and early visions, and the coming forth of the Book of Mormon. This manuscript, which was completed in 1839, served as the beginning of Joseph Smith's *History of the Church,* was accepted as scripture (as truth and revelation) in 1880 in Utah, and was included in the Pearl of Great Price under the heading "Joseph Smith—History."[26]

The major contributor to the *History of the Church* was Willard Richards. In August 1841, this Apostle was called by Joseph Smith to be his private secretary and general clerk for the Church. At that time, only 157 pages had been written of that history.[27]

Howard Coray, one of the new converts who helped write the history, recalled that after meeting Joseph Smith in Nauvoo in 1840, he was called to serve as one of Joseph's clerks. Shortly thereafter, he recalled, he was "busily employed in his office, copying a huge pile of letters into a book." After he had finished that project, Joseph Smith assigned him to assist others in compiling the history of the Church. Being a new member, he knew very little about that history, but

Joseph instructed him that he was to take the records that he gave him, combine and arrange the information in chronological order, and make necessary corrections and improvements in the grammar of the works he cited.[28]

CONTINUING THE HISTORICAL PROGRAM OF THE PROPHET

The project of writing the history of the Church was not interrupted by the martyrdom of Joseph and Hyrum on June 27, 1844. While in the Carthage Jail, Joseph Smith informed his private secretary, Willard Richards, to continue the history that he and others were writing. At that time, Church historians had completed the manuscript of the history up to August 5, 1838. Following the death of the Prophet, the Apostles were the only priesthood quorum prepared to continue the historical program established by Joseph Smith. Elder Willard Richards continued to serve as custodian of Church records and compiler and writer of the history of the Church. Two other leaders who were not Apostles but who had been serving as scribes to the Prophet, William Clayton and Thomas Bullock, continued to help with historical projects that were then being supervised by the Twelve. Prior to the exodus from Nauvoo in 1846, the history of the Church was completed to March 1843 under Elder Richards's direction.[29]

Following the death of Joseph Smith, another Apostle, Elder John Taylor, continued to be in charge of the printing establishment and to serve as editor of the *Times and Seasons*. The format of the paper did not change after the martyrdom. The publication of the history of the Church continued, and the policy of publishing articles describing doctrinal contributions of Joseph Smith, gospel discussions, missionary activities, minutes of meetings, and instructions to Latter-day Saints by Church leaders was not interrupted. A few days following the martyrdom, this periodical also published an account of the assassination of Joseph and Hyrum.[30]

Meanwhile, under the direction of the Twelve, Willard Richards, with the assistance of others, gathered and transported across the plains many valuable Church records. These records included histories, journals, letters, revelations, minutes of meetings, and temple and quorum records. These documents enabled historians to continue writing the history of the Church and to compile teachings of Joseph Smith based upon notes recorded by his contemporaries.[31]

Following the death of Elder Richards in March 1854, this historical project continued under the direction of two other Apostles, Elder George A. Smith, the new Church historian, and his assistant, Elder Wilford Woodruff.[32] Since the Apostles and others who completed that history were close associates of the Prophet who had lived in Nauvoo, they were witnesses of many of Joseph Smith's activities and gospel discussions. They also based this history on what they regarded as the most reliable sources, and although they did not employ some of the modern standards of historiography, especially in using and citing sources, they testified that the history they completed was one of the most authentic ever written.[33]

The history of the Church up to the martyrdom of Joseph and Hyrum was finally finished in August 1856, twenty-six years after Joseph had received the revelation to keep a record and twelve years after his death. This multivolume work eventually numbered more than two thousand pages and was one of the most detailed accounts of the rise and early history of a church that has ever been written and compiled by participants.[34]

1876 Edition of the Doctrine and Covenants

The transportation of historical records to Utah not only aided historians in completing the history of the Church but also provided the basis for the publication of a new edition of the Doctrine and Covenants. In harmony with precedents set by the Prophet Joseph Smith, Church leaders published the 1876 edition of the Doctrine and Covenants that included twenty-six new sections. Many of these revelations were based on Joseph Smith's teachings and revelations that were recorded by contemporaries. These revelations included sections 125, 126, 129–32, and 136 in our current edition of the Doctrine and Covenants.[35] Many who did not accept the leadership of President Brigham Young and the Apostles did not understand or embrace many of the most distinct theological contributions of Joseph Smith that were included in these revelations.

Following the martyrdom of the Prophet, John Taylor testified in an inspired tribute to this leader that Joseph Smith in the short space of twenty years did more, save Jesus only, for the salvation of men than any other man in this world. While identifying his most significant contributions, he declared that Joseph translated the Book of Mormon by the gift and power of God and published it on two continents. He also emphasized that Joseph Smith brought forth the revelations and commandments that compose the Doctrine and Covenants. He further stated that this man who lived great and died great in the eyes of God and who sealed his testimony with his blood brought forth many other wise documents and instructions for the benefit of the children of men (see D&C 135:3).

The significant contributions of many leaders who continued the historical program of the Prophet Joseph Smith and followed President Brigham Young westward preserved and published many documents that enable us to gain a greater understanding and appreciation of the doctrinal contributions of Joseph Smith.

NOTES

1. Dean C. Jessee, "The Reliability of Joseph Smith's History," *Journal of Mormon History* 3 (1976): 27–35.

2. Jessee, "Reliability," 30–31; Joseph Smith, *The Papers of Joseph Smith,* comp. and ed. Dean C. Jessee (Salt Lake City: Deseret Book, 1989), 1:11–96; *Latter-day Saints' Messenger and Advocate,* October 1834, 13–16; November 1834, 41–43; February 1835, 78–80; March 1835, 95–96; April 1835, 108–9; July 1835, 155–58; October 1835, 195–202.

3. Joseph Smith, *Personal Writings of Joseph Smith,* comp. and ed. Dean C. Jessee (Salt Lake City: Deseret Book, 2002), 9–20.

4. Smith, *Papers,* 1:387–401.

5. Smith, *Papers,* 1:427–37.

6. Smith, *Personal Writings,* 21–219.

7. Smith, *Personal Writings,* 174–77.

8. Smith, *Personal Writings,* 218–19.

9. Smith, *Personal Writings,* 2–3; Smith, *Papers,* 2:211, 301, 334–35. From March to October 1838 his journals were kept by George W. Robinson and James Mulholland and his Illinois journals were primarily recorded by his scribe, Willard Richards.

10. Joseph Smith, *History of the Church of Jesus Christ of Latter-day Saints,* ed. B. H. Roberts, 2nd ed. (Salt Lake City: Deseret Book, 1957), 6:409. The original source entry was Joseph Smith, Diary, by Willard Richards; see Joseph Smith, *The Words of Joseph Smith,* comp. and ed. Andrew F. Ehat and Lyndon W. Cook (Provo, UT:

Religious Studies Center, Brigham Young University, 1980), 373–74, 406.

11. Smith, *Personal Writings,* 429–46; Lyndon W. Cook, *The Revelations of the Prophet Joseph Smith* (Provo, UT: Seventy's Mission Bookstore, 1981), 239–42.

12. Smith, *History of the Church,* 1:104, 222–34, 390; Milton V. Backman Jr., *The Heavens Resound: A History of the Latter-day Saints in Ohio, 1830–1838* (Salt Lake City: Deseret Book, 1983), 90–92.

13. Kirtland Council Minute Book, Church Archives, 74–76; *Evening and Morning Star* (Kirtland, Ohio), September 1834, 192; Robert J. Woodford, "The Historical Development of the Doctrine and Covenants" (Ph.D. diss., Brigham Young University, 1974), 1:38–40. Although in this work I have cited Woodford's dissertation, selections from that work were published in Daniel H. Ludlow, ed., *Encyclopedia of Mormonism* (New York: Macmillan, 1992), 1:425.

14. Smith, *History of the Church,* 1:173; Backman, *Heavens Resound,* 217; Woodford, 1:7–11, 46–47; Cook, *Revelations,* 59–61. Approximately two hundred manuscript copies of revelations in the Doctrine and Covenants have been preserved, but only a few can be identified as originals. In many instances, immediately after revelations were recorded they were copied and recopied, with errors occurring in the manuscripts (Woodford, "Historical Development," 1:12).

15. Woodford, "Historical Development," 1:41–42; Backman, *Heavens Resound,* 217.

16. *Nauvoo Neighbor,* June 12, 1844, 235.

17. Woodford, "Historical Development," 1:54–56; Smith, *History of the Church,* 4:164; 5:264, 273; *Times and Seasons,* January 15, 1842, 667. The new sections included in the 1844 edition are currently sections 103, 105, 112, 119, 124, 127, 128, and 135.

18. Selections from a variety of Church records were published in early LDS periodicals and in the *History of the Church* (Jessee, "Reliability," 31–35).

19. Kirtland Council Minute Book, December 27, 1832; March 18, 1833, Church Archives; see also Smith, *History of the Church* 1:322–24, 334–35.

20. Ronald K. Esplin, "Joseph, Brigham and the Twelve: A Succession of Continuity," *BYU Studies* 21 (Summer 1981): 304; see also Smith, *Words of Joseph Smith,* xii.

21. Smith, *Words of Joseph Smith,* xii.

22. Smith, *Papers,* 2:211, 301, 334–35; Smith, *Words of Joseph Smith,* index.

23. George B. Smith, ed., *An Intimate Chronicle: The Journals of William*

Clayton (Salt Lake City: Signature Books, 1995), 95–97, 128, 515–19; Smith, *Words of Joseph Smith,* 168–73, 202–3.

24. Smith, *History of the Church,* 5:500–501.
25. Smith, *Words of Joseph Smith,* 340–62; see also Donald Q. Cannon and Larry E. Dahl, *The Prophet Joseph Smith's King Follett Discourse* (Provo, UT: Religious Studies Center, Brigham Young University, 1990).
26. Smith, *Personal Writings,* 226–39; Smith, *Papers,* 1:265.
27. Jessee, "Reliability," 34–35.
28. Howard Coray, Journal, typescript, L. Tom Perry Special Collections, Harold B. Lee Library, Brigham Young University, 8–10.
29. Smith, *History of the Church* 7:242–43; Jessee, "Reliability," 34–35.
30. *Times and Seasons,* July 1, 1844, 568.
31. Jessee, "Reliability," 35–36; Smith, *Words of Joseph Smith,* xv–xviii.
32. Jessee, "Reliability," 35–36.
33. Smith, *History of the Church,* 7:242–43. Jessee, "Reliability," 24–27, considers the writing of the *History of the Church* in relationship to historical practices in the mid-nineteenth century.
34. Jesse, "Reliability," 34–36; *Deseret News,* January 20, 1858, 363.
35. Woodford, 75–81; *Deseret News,* September 27, 1876, 553. In addition to the sections in the Doctrine and Covenants included in the text, other revelations which were added were sections 2, 13, 85, 87, 108–11, 113–18, 120–23.

CHAPTER THREE

THE ARTICLES OF FAITH: ANSWERING DOCTRINAL QUESTIONS OF THE "SECOND GREAT AWAKENING"

ROSEANN BENSON

Joseph Smith lived in the postcolonial period often called the "Second Great Awakening," or the "Great Reformation of the Nineteenth Century," which began at the end of the eighteenth century and continued into the first half of the nineteenth century.[1] The disestablishment of the alliance between church and state created an era characterized by widespread interest in religious regeneration and revival. Continuing disagreement about doctrine, practice, and church government by mainstream European Protestant churches caused further splintering of Protestantism in America into a variety of new sects.[2] As a young man, Joseph described vividly the local Presbyterian, Baptist, and Methodist "war of words and tumult of opinions" for converts in the vicinity of his home (Joseph Smith—History 1:8–9). With religious freedom relatively unknown elsewhere, the lack of state monies sponsoring a particular religion caused the various sects to compete for members, resulting in a distressing and confusing situation for undecided seekers like the Smith family.[3]

In a now-famous document written in March of 1842 at the particular request of John Wentworth, editor of the *Chicago Democrat,* Joseph Smith gave a brief overview of his own religious experiences, the contents of the Book of Mormon, and a general history of the Church to that point designed for individuals unfamiliar with the

RoseAnn Benson is a part-time instructor of ancient scripture and Church history and doctrine at Brigham Young University.

46

Restoration and the principles of the gospel.[4] The document, called by Latter-day Saints the Wentworth Letter, concluded with a list of thirteen unnumbered statements clarifying central beliefs of the "faith of the Latter-day Saints," later titled the "Articles of Faith." The Articles of Faith, authored by Joseph Smith, reflect the new religious freedom of the Second Great Awakening and the questions that this freedom engendered, while at the same time setting forth and clarifying some of the doctrines of a unique tradition—neither Catholic nor Protestant but uniquely Latter-day Saint.

During the twenty-two years that had passed since Joseph's First Vision and twelve years since the official organization of the Church, scores of revelations and Latter-day Saint newspapers and pamphlets had set forth important doctrines. Many of these seminal doctrines, however, were not included in these thirteen brief statements of belief. Instead, it appears that the Prophet Joseph responded primarily to many of the conflicting philosophies and traditions of the day espoused in Catholicism, Deism, Calvinism, Arminianism, Lutheranism, Universalism, and Restorationism, as well as to millennialist expectations, in the process of clearly setting forth some central Latter-day Saint beliefs.[5] The proliferation of Protestant sects in America necessitated that each sect delineate differences from other sects by statements of belief, some requiring a profession of faith to their particular articles for membership and communion. The Articles of Faith briefly outline central beliefs, many long debated in Christianity, and provide a starting point for pronouncing Latter-day Saint doctrine.

Reverend George Moore, a Unitarian minister in Nauvoo, Illinois, commented that "Smith makes it a point not to agree with anyone in regard to his religious opinions."[6] For example, in the first ten articles of faith, Latter-day Saint beliefs contrast sharply with commonly held Christian doctrines like the nature of the Trinity, original sin, total depravity, limited atonement, predestination, free will, grace versus works, infant baptism and baptism by sprinkling, priesthood of all believers, *sola scriptura,* and postmillennialism. The Articles of Faith also answer questions regarding church organization, priesthood authority, and the presence or cessation of spiritual gifts, prophecy, seership, and revelation.

Godhead

Article 1: We believe in God, the Eternal Father, and in His Son, Jesus Christ, and in the Holy Ghost.

The first article is a general statement about the Godhead, confirming Latter-day Saint membership and fellowship with all Christianity through a profession of faith in Christ's divine Sonship. Latter-day Saints familiar with First Vision accounts and other revelations received by Joseph Smith (see D&C 20:17–29; 130:22) understand this article to define the Godhead as three separate beings; in the wording, however, Joseph did not emphasize this fact.

Nevertheless, in the context of the Wentworth document, which includes an account of the First Vision, it is very clear that the Prophet Joseph rejects the traditional Catholic and Protestant view of the Trinity expressed in the extrabiblical Nicene Creed[7] and announces the Latter-day Saint belief in Heavenly Father and Jesus Christ as separate and distinct beings. In Christian theology, this belief is called "social trinitarianism."[8]

Adam's Transgression

Article 2: We believe that men will be punished for their own sins, and not for Adam's transgression.

Article 2 rejects the traditions of original sin, total depravity, and predestination.[9] The imputation of the sin of Adam to his posterity is called original sin.[10] This idea, generally credited to Augustine, teaches that all are born sinful and guilty; therefore, humankind is completely and helplessly affected by the Fall (total depravity), and, from this state, only a few (limited atonement) that God has elected (predestined) will be saved.

The Prophet Joseph taught instead that our first parents acted in harmony with God's divine plan[11] and that "Adam did not commit sin in eating the fruits for God had decreed that he should eat and fall, but [also] in compliance with the decree he should die" (see Moses 3:17).[12] Further, he explained "that it [Adam and Eve's transgression] is [all] washed away by the blood of Christ, and that it no longer exists."[13] Thus, "we are all born pure and undefiled."[14] The Prophet learned from his inspired translation of the Bible that Christ "atoned for original guilt"; therefore, children cannot be answerable for the sins of their parents because "they are whole from the foundation of the world" (Moses 6:54). Nevertheless, the fallen nature of man and his world is acknowledged in this passage: "children are conceived in sin" (Moses 6:55), meaning that fallen and mortal human beings beget mortal children in a fallen world.

While clarifying the divinely ordained role of Adam and Eve and discarding the ideas of original sin and the total depravity of man, Joseph Smith was convinced of the "fallenness" of man and his need for redemption (see Moses 5:13). He admitted, "I have learned in my travels that man is treacherous and selfish, but few excepted."[15] Further, he lamented, "All are subjected to vanity while they travel through the crooked paths and difficulties which surround them. Where is the man that is free from vanity? None ever were perfect but Jesus."[16] The natural inclinations of humankind rule him, for "in this world, mankind are naturally selfish, ambitious and striving to excel one above another" (see D&C 121:35–39).[17] Instead of original sin, the Prophet Joseph taught that while humans inherit a fallen nature, each individual is responsible for his or her own choices.[18] Thus, Joseph placed the Latter-day Saints firmly in the camp of "free will."[19]

GRACE AND WORKS

Article 3: We believe that through the Atonement of Christ, all mankind may be saved, by obedience to the laws and ordinances of the Gospel.

Joseph took issue with Martin Luther and many Protestants in explaining salvation by grace. The crucial issues regarding grace, debated for centuries, are its relationship to free will and works and the severity of man's estrangement from God, with sects disagreeing on how to overcome this estrangement. Joseph's statement of "obedience to the laws and ordinances of the gospel" perhaps might be called a kind of "works-righteousness." The previous phrase, "through the Atonement of Christ, all mankind may be saved," however, links his doctrine clearly to the grace of Christ, the unmerited help available to all humans. This article emphasizes that "all mankind may be saved"—a belief similar to that championed by Joseph's Universalist-thinking[20] grandfather, Asael Smith, and a rejection of Calvin's notions of the predestination of the elect and a limited atonement.[21] By uniting the two phrases, (1) "through the

Atonement of Christ, all mankind may be saved" and (2) "by obedience to the laws and ordinances of the Gospel," the grace of Christ and His work of salvation is preeminent. Humankind, however, must make and keep covenants with Christ in order to be saved.[22] The prophet Lehi explained the principle of agency placed before humans, who were created to act rather than be acted upon, thereby possessing the power to choose liberty and eternal life or captivity and death as they are enticed by the opposing forces of God and Satan (see 2 Nephi 2:14, 16, 27).[23] The power, then, to act or initiate change in fallen man is a gift from God to all His children.

SALVATION

Article 4: We believe that the first principles and ordinances of the Gospel are: first, Faith in the Lord Jesus Christ; second, Repentance; third, Baptism by immersion for the remission of sins; fourth, Laying on of hands for the gift of the Holy Ghost.

In article 4, Joseph linked the laws and ordinances necessary for salvation found in the previous article to the first principles and ordinances of the gospel. These simple steps are in marked contrast to Calvinistic notions of many "stages of regeneration" and the idea that an individual must be regenerated (elected or predestined) by God before he or she could have faith in Jesus Christ. Thus, Christ chose or predestined those who would believe in Him.[24] Personally illustrating the confusing teachings regarding salvation, Elder Parley P. Pratt lamented in his autobiography the anxiety he felt about his sins and the method by which they could be remitted. For example, he complained to his father, saying, "He [the local Baptist minister, W. A. Scranton] tells us we must experience a mysterious, indefinite and indefinable something called religion before we can repent and be baptized acceptably. But, if we inquire how, or by what means we are to come at this experience, he cannot tell us definitely; but will tell us that it is the work of God in the soul; which he will accomplish in his own due time, for his own elect; and that we can do nothing acceptably til this is done. . . . They will require of me to relate *an experience,* and to tell of some time and place where I had already experienced that which I am only seeking for, and have not found."[25]

While the steps set forth for spiritual rebirth in this article were clearly defined and simple by comparison, they were for those old enough to be accountable for their sins (see D&C 68:25, 27). Adding to this confusion about salvation, some religionists taught infant baptism; others taught a "baptism of believers," those mature enough to have faith and be capable of repentance. Debates were even held on the question of baptism and, in particular, infant baptism, drawing large crowds with the arguments later published.[26] Joseph Smith in both articles 2 and 4 implied a rejection of infant baptism. In the former article the rejection of infant baptism was because children are born innocent and without the taint of original sin, and it is evident in the latter article that faith and repentance require more intellectual development than that of which an infant is capable.[27]

Further, Joseph's inclusion of the laying on of hands for giving the gift of the Holy Ghost was unique at that time for Christian churches. While the first three statements in this article of faith agree with some coreligionists on conversion and the mode of baptism, the fourth point, receipt of the gift of the Holy Ghost by the laying on of hands, provides a clear contrast. The Prophet Joseph declared that the gift of the Holy Ghost does not automatically follow baptism or hopeful prayers but is instead a priesthood ordinance conferred as it was in the New Testament (see Acts 8:16–18). Additionally, he taught that the gift of the Holy Ghost should be enjoyed in the latter days "as much as it was in the Apostles' days" and that it is linked to the organization of the priesthood.[28] Part of the Protestant revolt against Catholicism was a rejection of the notion of priesthood authority held by a few and the acceptance of a "priesthood of all believers."[29] Thus, the practice of *conferring* the gift of the Holy Ghost by the "laying on of hands" to all baptized believers contrasted with that of all other sects of that day.[30] Appropriately, Joseph clarified priesthood authority in the next article of faith.

AUTHORITY

Article 5: We believe that a man must be called of God, by prophecy, and by the laying on of hands by those who are in authority, to preach the Gospel and administer in the ordinances thereof.

Article 5 declares that the three antecedents necessary to authorize preaching the gospel and performing ordinances are: (1) an individual must be called prophetically, meaning by inspiration of the

Holy Spirit; (2) this calling must be certified by a particular priest-hood ordinance, the laying on of hands; and (3) the individual announcing the calling to the one called must have authority from God. The requirement of priesthood authority separated Latter-day Saints from all Protestant churches that, in rebelling against the power of the Catholic Church, had eroded respect for its authority. The democratization of American Christianity, the expansion of popular sovereignty and egalitarian convictions, promoted self-anointed preachers and a "priesthood of all believers . . . religion of, by, and for the people." By default, then, the only authority left for Protestants to claim was the Bible.[31]

Significantly, Joseph Smith implied in this article that he received authority by the "laying on of hands." In fact, he recorded the visits of John the Baptist restoring the Aaronic Priesthood, and Peter, James, and John restoring the Melchizedek Priesthood to him and Oliver Cowdery (see Joseph Smith—History 1:68–72; D&C 13; 27:12–13; 128:20).

CHURCH ORGANIZATION

Article 6: We believe in the same organization that existed in the Primitive Church, namely, apostles, prophets, pastors, teachers, evangelists, and so forth.

Article 6 is an open-ended statement on organization that links the Church of Jesus Christ to the former-day Saints, those who lived during the first-century organization of Christ's Church. Implied in the restoration of the primitive organization is the Church's purpose as the location for the holders of priesthood authority to perform essential saving ordinances.

In this article of faith, the Prophet Joseph identified specific parts of the Apostolic Church that had been restored—namely, some of the offices by which the kingdom of God on earth is to be organized and in which those with properly conferred authority could act—adding "and so forth," indicating that circumstances might render the need for an expansion of Church officers. This is in marked contrast, for example, to Alexander Campbell's Disciples of Christ, the other main nineteenth-century restorationist tradition, which so carefully guarded congregational autonomy that no central church officers or organization existed.[32]

In the Wentworth Letter, Joseph gave a brief overview of the Book of Mormon in which he linked the Church of the western continent to that of the eastern continent. He stated that the Savior "planted the Gospel here in all its fulness, and richness, and power, and blessing; that [the ancient American church] had Apostles, Prophets, Pastors, Teachers, and Evangelists; the same order, the same priesthood, the same ordinances, gifts, powers, and blessings."[33] By listing the same offices the Apostle Paul had identified in Ephesians 4:11 in this article of faith, and referring to the Book of Mormon Church organization in the Wentworth Letter, the Prophet Joseph tied the latter-day Restoration to the ancient foundation of apostles and prophets, showing Christ at the head in both Palestine and the American continent (see Ephesians 2:20).[34]

GIFTS OF THE SPIRIT

Article 7: We believe in the gift of tongues, prophecy, revelation, visions, healing, interpretation of tongues, and so forth.

In article 7, another open-ended article, the Prophet Joseph returned to the subject of the Holy Ghost, elaborating more on this third member of the Godhead. He listed several gifts of the Spirit that were part of the Apostolic Church: tongues, prophecy, revelation, visions, healing, and interpretation of tongues. The phrase "and so forth" at the end of the article indicates that the full complement of spiritual gifts discussed by Paul in 1 Corinthians 12–14 are also an integral part of the latter-day Church. This article affirms the Savior's teaching that true believers would enjoy the "signs" of the true Church—the gifts of the Spirit (see Mark 16:15–18).

During religious camp meetings of the nineteenth century, such as the revival at Cane Ridge, Kentucky (1801), some participants manifested "signs," such as uncontrollable weeping or crying, twitching, running in circles, and doglike barking.[35] Other Protestant sects were more circumspect in regard to spiritual manifestations. Some required the rehearsal of a conversion experience prior to baptism or church membership; however, others rejected this notion, arguing that faith was rational, or that "the age of those gifts has passed away" because gifts of the Spirit "were confined to the apostolic age, and to only a portion of the saints that lived in that age."[36] Confusion about gifts of the Spirit caused eighteen-year-old Parley P.

Pratt to ask his Baptist preacher "what Jesus meant when he said, 'these signs shall follow them that believe.' He replied, that it meant these signs should follow the Apostles only."[37] In sharp contrast to both those who believed in the nonbiblical signs manifest in camp meetings and those who believed that signs had ceased after the apostolic era, Joseph Smith taught: "We believe in the gift of the Holy Ghost being enjoyed now, as much as it was in the Apostles' days . . . we also believe in prophecy, in tongues, in visions, and in revelations, in gifts, and in healings. . . . We believe in it [this gift of the Holy Ghost] in all its fulness, and power, and greatness, and glory . . . rationally, consistently, and scripturally, and not according to the wild vagaries, foolish notions and traditions of men."[38]

In Doctrine and Covenants section 46, the Prophet Joseph restated Paul's point that gifts of the Spirit are given to bless the Church (see D&C 46:10). He went even further, declaring that while every man is given gifts by the Spirit of God, the Lord gives to the leaders of the Church of Jesus Christ *all* the gifts to bless and benefit the whole Church (see D&C 46:29; emphasis added).[39]

SCRIPTURE

Article 8: We believe the Bible to be the word of God as far as it is translated correctly; we also believe the Book of Mormon to be the word of God.

Sola scriptura, the idea of relying on "the Bible alone" as the anchor of religious authority, and "biblical inerrancy," the notion that the King James Version was "without error or mistake," were strongly held beliefs in the early republic.[40] The balance, however, between biblical and traditional authority in the form of creeds and confessions was subject to debate.[41] In contrast to these ideas, Joseph, having already mostly completed his translation of the Old and New Testaments, added an interesting caveat to Latter-day Saint belief in the Bible: "as far as it is translated correctly." This statement probably alluded more to transmission than translation. His high regard for the Bible is evident in this comment: "He that can mark the power of Omnipotence, inscribed upon the heavens, can also see God's own handwriting in the sacred volume [Bible]: and he who reads it oftenest will like it best, and he who is acquainted with it, will know the hand wherever he can see it; and when once discovered, it will not only receive an acknowledgment, but an obedience to all its heavenly precepts."[42]

The eighth article of faith encapsulates Joseph's declaration that the canon is not closed and that the prophetic office with the gifts of seership and revelation is functioning. It also states that both the Bible *and* the Book of Mormon are "the word of God."

CONTINUOUS REVELATION

Article 9: We believe all that God has revealed, all that He does now reveal, and we believe that He will yet reveal many great and important things pertaining to the Kingdom of God.

While the preachers of his day rejected the First Vision,[43] saying that "it was all of the devil, that there were no such things as visions or revelations in these days; that all such things had ceased with the apostles," Joseph announced that the heavens were again open because the kingdom of God was being established on the earth (Joseph Smith—History 1:21). The idea of personal dialogue with heaven, offensive to many of his era, pervades all that Joseph Smith did, beginning with the First Vision and including the Book of Mormon, the Doctrine and Covenants, the inspired translation of the Bible, and the book of Abraham.[44] In the Wentworth Letter, Joseph shared both an account of his First Vision experience and also his visitation from Moroni with a description of the Book of Mormon plates and the Urim and Thummim, the medium by which he "translated the record by the gift and power of God"[45]—concrete claims to new revelations and revelatory instruments.

Taken alone, this article of faith intimates only that the canon of scripture is open; however, the context of the Wentworth Letter, through specific references to heavenly visitations and an ancient instrument used by Old Testament seers, provides clear evidence of prophecy, seership, and revelation. This article is open-ended and expanding because of what it promises—continuing revelation. Through this principle, Joseph declared, additional light and knowledge continues to be revealed to prophets, seers, and revelators, even today.

ZION AND MILLENNIALISM

Article 10: We believe in the literal gathering of Israel and in the restoration of the Ten Tribes; that Zion (the New Jerusalem) will be built upon the American continent; that Christ will reign personally upon the earth; and, that the earth will be renewed and receive its paradisiacal glory.

The beliefs expressed in article 10 address the religious and secular ideas of many Americans regarding the divine role of the United States. Many Americans felt that the United States was God's own country, was a "redeemer nation,"[46] and perhaps was even the stage for the Second Coming and the site of the New Jerusalem. Nathan Hatch proposes that the first generation of Americans may have anticipated the Second Coming of Christ more intensely than any generation since.[47] For example, Jonathan Edwards (1703–58) claimed, "There was a growing conviction among Americans that it was their own country that was especially chosen by God for great things."[48] From this point of view, the struggle for liberty and the rights of mankind in the American Revolution was religiously significant in that it "prepared the way" for the Second Coming of Jesus Christ.[49] "Conferences, sermons, books, plans and reforms of every sort" in the late 1820s and early 1830s indicated the high interest in the Millennium, and many, including some Latter-day Saints, thought its dawning was imminent.[50] William Miller, forerunner to the Seventh-day Adventists and leader of thousands, even calculated that the Second Coming would take place in 1843 (and then 1844).[51] Joseph's statement, then, about the events leading up to the Millennium is very much a response to a hot topic of conversation in his day.[52]

Regarding the events of this last dispensation and the events leading up to the Millennium, Joseph Smith prophesied there would be a literal gathering of Israel, a restoration of the ten tribes, and the building of Zion. The New Jerusalem would be built in America. While Latter-day Saints are premillennialists in that they believe that Christ will return to the earth at the beginning of the Millennium to usher in a peaceful reign for one thousand years, our belief has the flavor of postmillennialism because many things must be done by humankind with help from God before that great day can come.[53] Additionally, Joseph taught that paradise, similar to the Edenic state lost at the Fall of Adam, would be established on earth at this time.

CONCLUSION

It is apparent that Joseph Smith addressed many of the fundamental questions of Christianity—ideas that had divided Catholics and, later, Protestants since the "falling away" and the death of the original Apostles (see 2 Thessalonians 2:3). These same divisions had continued to his day and even now still exist. The multiplication of sects in the new republic was based on differences of opinion and the freedom to both disagree and to start new churches. The Bible was available for each individual to read, the Enlightenment encouraged people to apply rational thinking to the study of scripture, and relatively unfettered religious freedom brought debate over ideas that had previously been accepted or enforced for centuries. Joseph was born at the precise time when freedom, skepticism, and doctrinal debate were part of American religious life. This time period was the perfect confluence of circumstances for the Restoration of the gospel. In the new era of religious liberty, which spawned innumerable new sects, Joseph Smith not only responded brilliantly to the great Christian questions but also put in place many of the foundational doctrines of the "restoration of all things" to which Latter-day Saints are anchored yet today.

NOTES

1. The term *Great Awakening* identifies the revivalism of the late 1730s and early 1740s, the era of Jonathan Edwards, George Whitefield, and Gilbert Tennent, among others. It involved a more evangelical Calvinism than the Puritan, Congregational, Baptist, and Presbyterian traditions. The Second Great Awakening had several different fronts, each with distinctive characteristics. John Wesley sent Francis Asbury and others to oversee the American Methodism of the Church of England. Particularly after the War for Independence, the Methodists under Asbury's leadership took up itinerant preaching, binding their "settled" eastern centers to the western frontier.

   In 1801 at the Cane Ridge, Kentucky, "camp meeting," thousands, both the churched and the unchurched, listened to preachers, black and white, from different religions (Presbyterian, Baptist, and Methodist). Spontaneous responses to this revival included "the jerks, dancing, laughing, running, and 'the barking exercise.'" The continuation of camp revival meetings, Methodist circuit riders, and Baptist farmer-preachers brought the good news throughout the United States.

   In 1821, a more dignified revivalism began under Charles Finney in New York and continued in the major cities of the Northeast before moving to Ohio. Noll classifies Finney as the premier white American evangelist after Jonathan Edwards (Mark A.

Noll, *America's God: From Jonathan Edwards to Abraham Lincoln* [Oxford: Oxford University Press, 2002], 166–80, 564; Peter W. Williams, *America's Religions: From Their Origins to the Twenty-First Century* [Urbana: University of Illinois Press, 2002], 138–39).

2. The mix of so many religions, including traditional and upstart Protestant churches, the efforts of Methodists and Baptists to evangelize the American populace, and the proliferation of non-Calvinist and innovative churches such as Free Will Baptists, Shakers, Christians (Disciples of Christ), and Unitarian/ Universalists, fed the fires of debate and conflict over beliefs (Peter W. Williams, *America's Religions: From Their Origins to the Twenty-first Century* [Urbana and Chicago: University of Illinois Press, 2002], 147–48; Noll, *America's God*, 567).

3. For example, Joseph Smith Sr., a God-fearing man, stayed outside of religious institutions because he couldn't agree with their doctrines (Richard Bushman, *Joseph Smith and the Beginnings of Mormonism* [Champaign: University of Illinois Press, 1984], 36, 39). Joseph Smith's mother, Lucy Mack Smith, called herself a "seeker" (Lucy Mack Smith, *History of Joseph Smith by His Mother* [Salt Lake City: Bookcraft, 1901], 31, 34–36; see also Parley P. Pratt, *The Autobiography of Parley P. Pratt*, ed. Scot Facer Proctor and Maurine Jensen Proctor, rev. ed. [Salt Lake City: Deseret Book, 2000], 13n9; and Nathan Hatch, *The Democratization of American Christianity* [New Haven, NJ: Yale University Press, 1989], 6–8).

4. John Wentworth wrote a letter requesting that Joseph Smith write a document for Mr. George Bastow [Barstow], a friend of his, who was writing a history of New Hampshire. Although the book was published, Joseph Smith's manuscript was not in it. Joseph's "chapter" for the book was published in the *Times and Seasons*, March 1, 1842, 706, and in Joseph Smith, *History of the Church of Jesus Christ of Latter-day Saints*, ed. B. H. Roberts, 2nd ed. rev. (Salt Lake City: Deseret Book, 1957), 4:535–41. See also John A. Widtsoe, *The Articles of Faith in Everyday Life* (Salt Lake City: Presiding Bishopric of The Church of Jesus Christ of Latter-Day Saints, 1951), 15; Edward J. Brandt, "The Origin and Importance of the Articles of Faith," in *Studies in the Scripture, Volume 2: The Pearl of Great Price,* ed. Robert L. Millet and Kent P. Jackson (Salt Lake City: Randall Book, 1985), 18.

5. *Deists* (natural religion) believe in the existence of a God based on a commonsense approach to nature and reason rather than revelation. *Calvinism* (John Calvin) has five predominant characteristics: total depravity, unconditional election, limited atonement, irresistible grace, and perseverance of the saints. *Arminianism* (Jacobus Arminius) contains beliefs accepted by John Wesley's Methodists, who claim that God gave prevenient grace (grace before full

salvation) to all His children so that original sin could be overcome and all could choose God. Additionally, this belief included Christian perfection, meaning the ability for believers to be liberated from all sin in this life. *Lutheranism* (Martin Luther) is credited as the leader in the Protestant revolt against the authority of the pope. Lutherans rejected penance or "works righteousness" and instead embraced "salvation by grace alone." *Universalism* was a response of ordinary people to the Calvinist teachings of the Great Awakening (1740). Its central belief was that all God's children would ultimately be saved, a clear refutation of election (predestination) and limited atonement. *Restorationism* was a movement to restore the "true apostolic church," a concern of the Puritans of the seventeenth century on down to both the Latter-day Saints and Christian Churches (Disciples of Christ) in the nineteenth century.

6. Quoted in Donald Q. Cannon, "Reverend George Moore Comments on Nauvoo, the Mormons, and Joseph Smith," *Western Illinois Regional Studies* 5, no. 1 (Spring 1982):11.

7. The Nicene Creed was formulated in the fourth century in response to theological disputes over the nature of Christ and the Godhead. It affirms the idea that the divinity of Christ is of the same substance as the divinity of God, thus guarding the unity of the Trinity. This creed is accepted by Roman Catholics and most Protestants. It also begins with the phrase "we" or "I believe." This doctrine, primarily the work of Augustine, was declared in response to the radical views of Marcion and Arius regarding Christ. "It is important to note that no important Christian theologian has argued that there are three self-conscious beings in the godhead. On the contrary, Augustine's favorite analogy for the triune god was one self-consciousness with its three distinctions of intellect, will, and the bond between them" (Van A. Harvey, *A Handbook of Theological Terms* [New York City: Macmillan, 1964], s.v. "trinity").

8. David Paulsen, "Are Mormons Trinitarians?" *Modern Reformation*, November/December 2003, 40.

9. *Original Sin* in the classical Christian tradition "refers to the universal and hereditary sinfulness of man since the fall of Adam." In Augustine's view, man inherits not only the tendency to sin but also the guilt of the Fall (Harvey, *Handbook of Theological Terms*, s.v. "sin, original"). *Total depravity* is a term characterizing the power of sin on man and "means that there is nothing in man that has not been infected by the power of sin" (Harvey, *Handbook of Theological Terms*, s.v. "depravity, total"). "*Predestination* is the decree of God, whereby he hath for his own glory foreordained whatever comes to pass" (Charles Buck, *A Theological Dictionary* [Philadelphia: J. J. Woodward, 1844], s.v. "predestination"). Other doctrines associated with the Fall are *immaculate conception* and *infant damnation*.

10. Imputation is an important term in Protestant theology. Its legal meaning is "to reckon as" in terms of ascribing one man's guilt or innocence to another. In particular, Adam's sin and guilt was imputed to future generations, and Christ's righteousness was imputed to the faithful (Harvey, *Handbook of Theological Terms*, s.v. "imputation"; Buck, *Theological Dictionary*, s.v. "sin").

11. Joseph Smith, *Words of Joseph Smith: The Contemporary Accounts of the Nauvoo Discourses of the Prophet Joseph,* comp. and ed. Andrew F. Ehat and Lyndon Cook (Provo, UT: Religious Studies Center, Brigham Young University, 1980), 33, 39, 61. Spelling and capitalization have been modernized.

12. Smith, *Words of Joseph Smith,* 63.

13. Smith, *Words of Joseph Smith,* 33.

14. Smith, *Words of Joseph Smith,* 33, 79.

15. Smith, *History of the Church,* 1:443.

16. Smith, *History of the Church,* 4:358. Also cited in *The Teachings of Joseph Smith,* ed. Larry E. Dahl and Donald Q. Cannon (Salt Lake City: Bookcraft, 1997), 187.

17. Smith, *History of the Church,* 5:388. Also cited in *Teachings of Joseph Smith,* 297.

18. Mathew Davis, writing to his wife, reported that Joseph Smith taught the following regarding humans as moral, responsible, and free agents: "Although it was foreordained he [mankind] should fall, and be redeemed, yet after the redemption it was not foreordained that he [mankind] should again sin. In the Bible a rule of conduct is laid down for him. . . . If he violates that law, he is to be punished for the deeds done in the body" (Smith, *History of the Church,* 4:78–79).

19. T. Edgar Lyon, "Origin and Purpose of the Articles of Faith," *Instructor,* September 1952, 264. Charles Buck, an advocate of "free agency" as opposed to "free will," defined the latter term as an Arminian notion that "claims a part, yea the very turning point of salvation. . . . We need only certain helps or assistances, granted to men in common, to enable us to choose the path of life." On the other hand "free agency" requires "an almighty and invincible Power to renew them" because "our hearts [are] by nature wholly depraved" (Buck, *Theological Dictionary,* s.v. "free agency").

20. Universalism or universal redemption is suggested in the Greek word *apocatasis,* meaning that *all* will be saved (Harvey, *A Handbook of Theological Terms,* s.v. "apocatasis").

21. Bushman, *Joseph Smith and the Beginnings of Mormonism,* 27, 36.

22. To appreciate the radical nature of this pronouncement, one must

realize that "only fringe theologians held that humans assisted in their own salvation" (Noll, *America's God*, 28).

23. Joseph Smith believed "that a man is a moral, responsible, free agent" (Smith, *History of the Church*, 4:78–79). Further, Joseph Smith observed that "the devil could not compel mankind to do evil. . . . Those who resisted the Spirit of God, would be liable to be led into temptation. . . . God would not exert any compulsory means, and the devil could not" (Smith, *History of the Church*, 4:358).

24. Hatch, *The Democratization of American Christianity*, 170; see also E. Brooks Holifield, *Theology in America: Christian Thought from the Age of the Puritans to the Civil War* (New Haven, NJ: Yale, 2003), 42.

25. Pratt, *Autobiography*, 10–11.

26. Robert Richardson, *Memoirs of Alexander Campbell* (Germantown, TN: Religious Book Service, 1897), 2:17–29.

27. There were two prominent philosophies defending infant baptism by sprinkling: (1) because of original sin infants must be cleansed in case of premature death; and (2) baptism is equated with the Old Testament covenant of circumcision; thus, it is practiced when an infant is eight days old. Moroni 8:5–26 calls infant baptism a "gross error" and "solemn mockery before God." Repentance and baptism are for those who are accountable. In Doctrine and Covenants 68:25, 27, the age of accountability is declared to be eight years.

28. Smith, *History of the Church*, 5:26–27; see also "Editorial," *Times and Seasons*, June 15, 1842, 823.

29. This phrase is basic to the Protestant Reformation. It is a rejection of the necessity of priesthood authority for administering ordinances (sacraments) and of priesthood holders as a special class. Instead, public ministry was a vocation. Some sects completely abolished any distinction between clergy and lay members (Harvey, *Handbook of Theological Terms*, s.v. "priesthood of all believers").

30. In general Protestant belief, the "Holy Spirit . . . is given to man with faith in Christ and is, therefore, not a natural possession but a gift empowering the faithful to live free from the compulsion to sin" (Harvey, *Handbook of Theological Terms*, s.v. "Spirit—Holy Spirit").

31. Hatch, *The Democratization of American Christianity*, 6, 12, 22–24, 34, 43, 69, 128.

32. David Edwin Harrell Jr., "Christian Primitivism and Modernization in the Stone-Campbell Movement," in *The Primitive Church in the Modern World*, ed. Richard T. Hughes (Urbana, IL: University of Illinois, 1995), 111.

33. Smith, *History of the Church*, 4:538.

34. None of the Protestant sects claimed the restoration of the

priesthood, although a few individuals claimed to be prophets. Robert Matthias, who claimed to be a literal descendant of the Apostle Matthias, visited Joseph Smith in Kirtland. Joseph listened to his teachings and pronounced him a false prophet (Smith, *History of the Church*, 2:304–7). See also Richard H. Brodhead, "Prophets in America, ca. 1830: Emerson, Nat Turner, Joseph Smith," *Journal of Mormon History* 29, no. 1 (Spring 2003): 42–65; Paul E. Johnson and Sean Wilentz, *Kingdom of Matthias* (New York City: Oxford University Press, 1994).

35. "At the time, outsiders called these actions 'exercises.' Today scholars call them trances, or involuntary motor behavior, a situation in which the brain loses control of the muscles under extreme stress" (Jon Butler, Grant Wacker, and Randall Balmer, *Religion in American Life: A Short History* [Oxford: Oxford University Press, 2003], 184).

36. Campbell, "Address to the Readers of the Christian Baptist, No. IV," *Christian Baptist*, March 1, 1824; Campbell, "Essays on the Work of the Holy Spirit in the Salvation of Men, No. VII," *Christian Baptist*, February 7, 1825.

37. Pratt, *Autobiography*, 12.

38. Smith, *History of the Church*, 5:26–27; "Editorial," *Times and Seasons*, June 15, 1842.

39. Smith, *History of the Church*, 1:163–65.

40. Other individuals in nineteenth-century America produced new translations of the scriptures; for example, Alexander Campbell and Noah Webster, but neither translation achieved widespread fame or use.

41. Noll, *America's God*, 373; Holifield, *Theology in America*, 29, 260, 275, 344–45, 379.

42. Smith, *History of the Church*, 2:14.

43. Alexander Campbell's response to Joseph Smith's claims is found in "Delusion: An Analysis of the Book of Mormon; with an Examination of Its Internal and External Evidences, and a Refutation of Its Pretences to Divine Authority," *Millennial Harbinger*, February 1831. Bushman makes the point that the First Vision is called that because it is the first of many visions Joseph Smith received (*Joseph Smith and the Beginnings of Mormonism*, 56).

44. Terryl L. Givens, *By the Hand of Mormon: The American Scripture That Launched a New World Religion* (New York City: Oxford University Press, 2002), 217. This view of revelation was at the forefront of the conflict in Missouri. In "The Manifesto of the Mob," Missourians deplored the Mormons' pretensions "to hold personal communication and converse face to face with the Most High God; to receive communications and revelations direct from heaven" (Smith, *History of the Church*, 1:374–75).

45. Smith, *History of the Church,* 4:537.

46. Williams, *America's Religions,* 206, 226; Holifield, *Theology in America,* 77.

47. Hatch, *The Democratization of American Christianity,* 184. Alexander Campbell, another nineteenth-century restorationist, anticipated that a return to Christian unity and the ancient order found in the New Testament Church would usher in the millennial era. A major focus of his monthly journal, the *Millennial Harbinger,* was to promote the restoration conditions necessary for its beginning. Through the work of humankind, an earthly millennial era would precede the return of Christ, which would then bring about the resurrection of the dead, final judgment, and creation of a new heaven and earth.

    Earlier American theologians also wrote about the Millennium. For example, John Cotton in the seventeenth century believed that the world stood on the verge of a millennial age; however, it was to be a spiritual coming of Christ, not His final return, using magistrates and ministers to build the earthly New Jerusalem. Cotton Mather, in the early eighteenth century, also believed in an earthly millennium, inaugurated by Christ, that would bring about the resurrection of the Saints destined to rule with Him and destroy the earth by fire before transforming it. Then the New Jerusalem would descend as a material but ethereal city, hovering in the air above the restored earthly Jerusalem. The end of the Millennium would climax with Armageddon and the second resurrection, which would include the righteous and the wicked.

    In the mid-eighteenth century, Jonathan Edwards described the millennial era in terms of excellence, proportion, and beauty. It would be an era characterized by one church, an orderly society, and agreement on the important doctrines, all of which would precede the return of Christ (Holifield, *Theology in America,* 49, 77–78, 123–24, 300). Some contemporary biblical commentators mentioned a literal gathering of Israel in their expositions on Isaiah (Matthew Henry, *An Exposition on the Old and New Testaments with Practical Remarks and Observations* [New York: Robert Carther & Brothers, 1853], 4:70, under Isaiah 11:4).

48. Williams, *America's Religions,* 206.

49. Jon Butler, Grant Wacker, and Randall Balmer, *Religion in American Life: A Short History* (Oxford: Oxford University Press, 2003), 149.

50. Bushman, *Joseph Smith and the Beginnings of Mormonism,* 170; Hatch, *Democratization of American Christianity,* 185.

51. Williams, *American Religions,* 229–30.

52. In fact, several young men came to visit Joseph Smith on February 12, 1843, evidently asking about William Miller's prediction that

the Second Coming would occur April 3, 1843. Joseph preached them "quite a sermon" and told them "many more things would take place before Christ would come" (Smith, *History of the Church*, 5:271–72).

53. Bushman, *Joseph Smith and the Beginnings of Mormonism*, 170.

CHAPTER FOUR

JOSEPH SMITH'S EXPANSION OF OUR UNDERSTANDING OF THE PREMORTAL LIFE AND OUR RELATIONSHIP TO GOD

RANDY L. BOTT

The stage is set, the time has arrived, and the tension can be felt in the air. Every detail has been attended to, considered, and reconsidered. Calculations numbering thousands of pages have been verified and reverified. Every possible scenario has been posed and thought through, and every possible problem has been solved. We watch the final countdown. Ignition, then liftoff! The next lunar expedition has begun.

We have heard that scenario played and replayed many times. We marvel at the attention to detail that this massive team of scientists has given. No pain is too great to avoid a catastrophe. Yet some would have us believe that this earth, traveling through space at incomprehensible speeds, held in a demandingly precise orbit around the sun, with every condition essential to keep continued life on earth unerringly in place, happened by chance. Perhaps that is one reason why the Lord called the Prophet Joseph Smith to push back the curtains of conjecture and disbelief and allowed us an illuminating look into the master plan of the entire universe. Joseph said: "In the first place, I wish to go back to the beginning—to the morn of creation. There is the starting point for us to look to, in order to understand and be fully acquainted with the mind, purposes and decrees of the Great Elohim, who sits in yonder heavens as he did at the creation of this world. It is necessary for us to have an

---

Randy L. Bott is a full teaching professor at Brigham Young University.

understanding of God himself in the beginning. If we start right, it is easy to go right all the time; but if we start wrong, we may go wrong, and it will be a hard matter to get right."[1]

Amidst the confusion resulting from conflicting theories that attempt to explain what we see around us everyday, it is no wonder that sincere, honest people question whether there is purpose in life. Did we begin in some prehistoric ocean billions of years ago and through randomness miraculously evolve into this diverse and complex world? With our origins enshrouded in mysticism and the ever-changing theories of men, no wonder Joseph was compelled to say: "Thy mind, O man! if thou wilt lead a soul unto salvation, must stretch as high as the utmost heavens, and search into and contemplate the darkest abyss, and the broad expanse of eternity—thou must commune with God."[2]

What insights did the Prophet add to our understanding of who we are, why we are here, what part, if any, our current condition plays in the eternal scheme of things? The Prophet explained:

> All men know that they must die. And it is important that we should understand the reasons and causes of our exposure to the vicissitudes of life and of death, and the designs and purposes of God in our coming into the world, our sufferings here, and our departure hence. What is the object of our coming into existence, then dying and falling away, to be here no more? It is but reasonable to suppose that God would reveal something in reference to the matter, and it is a subject we ought to study more than any other. We ought to study it day and night, for the world is ignorant in reference to their true condition and relation. If we have any claim on our Heavenly Father for anything, it is for knowledge on this important subject.[3]

In order to survey the breadth and depth of Joseph's discourses on what God revealed to him, I will lightly touch upon the following topics.

GOD'S MASTER PLAN

Life was far from a cosmic accident; the great Jehovah (the premortal Jesus Christ) knew and made provisions for every possible contingency for the mortal duration of this earth. Joseph taught:

The great Jehovah contemplated the whole of the events connected with the earth, pertaining to the plan of salvation, before it rolled into existence, or ever "the morning stars sang together" for joy; the past, the present, and the future were and are, with Him, one eternal "now;" He knew of the fall of Adam, the iniquities of the antediluvians, of the depth of iniquity that would be connected with the human family. . . . He knew the plan of salvation and pointed it out; He was acquainted with the situation of all nations and with their destiny; He ordered all things according to the council of His own will; He knows the situation of both the living and the dead, and has made ample provision for their redemption, according to their several circumstances, and the laws of the kingdom of God, whether in this world, or in the world to come.[4]

Before beginning our investigation of this earth and our premortal experience, it is instructive to put ourselves in the grand eternal picture. This earth was not the first (nor will it be the last) of God's creative ventures (see Moses 1:4). As the Prophet was fulfilling his divinely given assignment to retranslate the Bible, he learned of a vision given to the ancient prophet Moses. Moses saw countless worlds with their inhabitants. His interest was piqued, and he asked to understand about these innumerable worlds. The Savior answered:

Only an account of this earth, and the inhabitants thereof, give I unto you. For behold, there are many worlds that have passed away by the word of my power. And there are many that now stand, and innumerable are they unto man; but all things are numbered unto me, for they are mine and I know them.

And it came to pass that Moses spake unto the Lord, saying: Be merciful unto thy servant, O God, and tell me concerning this earth, and the inhabitants thereof, and also the heavens, and then thy servant will be content.

And the Lord God spake unto Moses, saying: The heavens, they are many, and they cannot be numbered unto man; but they are numbered unto me, for they are mine.

And as one earth shall pass away, and the heavens thereof even so shall another come; and there is no end to my works, neither to my words.

> For behold, this is my work and my glory—to bring to
> pass the immortality and eternal life of man. (Moses 1:35–39)

Joseph learned that the act of creating, peopling, and redeeming everything on these numberless earths is the very purpose, work, and glory of God (see 1 Nephi 17:36; Moses 6:44). If accepted by the world, this one divinely revealed concept might forever change the purpose of the research and many of the methods of scientists. However, even given that expanded insight, Joseph continued to probe further. He taught that Gods have existed "one above another" forever! Couching his reasoning in the teachings of other prophets, such as the ancient patriarch Abraham, John the Revelator, and the Apostle Paul, he said:

> I learned a testimony concerning Abraham, and he reasoned concerning the God of heaven. "In order to do that," said he, "suppose we have two facts: that supposes another fact may exist—two men on earth, one wiser than the other, would logically show that another who is wiser than the wisest may exist. Intelligences exist one above another, so that there is no end to them."
>
> If Abraham reasoned thus—If Jesus Christ was the Son of God, and John discovered that God the Father of Jesus Christ had a Father, you may suppose that He had a Father also. Where was there ever a son without a father? And where was there ever a father without first being a son? Whenever did a tree or anything spring into existence without a progenitor? And everything comes in this way. Paul says that which is earthly is in the likeness of that which is heavenly, Hence if Jesus had a Father, can we not believe that *He* had a Father also? I despise the idea of being scared to death at such a doctrine, for the Bible is full of it.[5]

It would be a monumental mistake to believe that our premortal existence was the beginning of God's work and glory. Without an idea of the bigger picture, even Latter-day Saints run the risk of failing to comprehend God, and comprehending God is by definition eternal life (see John 17:3). The Prophet Joseph Smith further taught that regardless of how many gods there are, we will never—throughout all eternity—ever worship any other beings save God our Eternal Father and His Beloved Son, Jesus Christ.[6]

OUR PREMORTAL BEGINNING

Although it is clearly taught in the Bible that we are the literal offspring of God (see Matthew 6:9; Acts 17:28, 29; Hebrews 12:9), the world has, in an attempt to explain man's presence on earth without recognizing God's role in his creation, fictionalized that most important concept. However, the creation of man was a divine act and was revealed as such to man from the beginning. "Now this prophecy Adam spake, as he was moved upon by the Holy Ghost, and a genealogy was kept of the children of God. And this was the book of the generations of Adam, saying: In the day that God created man, in the likeness of God made he him; in the image of his own body, male and female, created he them, and blessed them, and called their name Adam, in the day when they were created and became living souls in the land upon the footstool of God" (Moses 6:8–9).

Not only did God create man in His own image (see Genesis 1:26–27), but He revealed that men and women in their exalted state can also be referred to as gods.[7] Most people would acknowledge that offspring have the capability of growing up to be like their parents; so it is in the eternal worlds. If we begin by accepting the revealed truth that we are literal spirit offspring of God, then it should not be difficult to accept the concept that eventually we could grow up to become like God—that we have inherited a divine potential. In fact that is exactly what Joseph Smith taught:

> The first principles of man are self-existent with God. God himself, finding he was in the midst of spirits and glory, because he was more intelligent, saw proper to institute laws whereby the rest could have a privilege to advance like himself. The relationship we have with God places us in a situation to advance in knowledge. He has power to institute laws to instruct the weaker intelligences, that they may be exalted with himself, so that they might have one glory upon another, and all that knowledge, power, glory, and intelligence, which is requisite in order to save them in the world of spirits.[8]

Given this understanding of the purpose of divinely mandated law (to help us progress toward our eternal destiny of becoming like God), one no longer is tempted to view commandments as restrictive or burdensome but sees them as manifestations of divine love that help us attain our desired goal of eternal exaltation.

Continuing his teaching of what God had revealed to him, Joseph Smith expanded our understanding of truths revealed to the ancient patriarch Abraham:

> Now the Lord had shown unto me, Abraham, the intelligences that were organized before the world was; and among all these there were many of the noble and great ones;
>
> And God saw these souls that they were good, and he stood in the midst of them, and he said: These I will make my rulers; for he stood among those that were spirits, and he saw that they were good; and he said unto me: Abraham, thou art one of them; thou wast chosen before thou wast born.
>
> And there stood one among them that was like unto God, and he said unto those who were with him: We will go down, for there is space there, and we will take of these materials, and we will make an earth whereon these may dwell;
>
> And we will prove them herewith, to see if they will do all things whatsoever the Lord their God shall command them;
>
> And they who keep their first estate shall be added upon; and they who keep not their first estate shall not have glory in the same kingdom with those who keep their first estate; and they who keep their second estate shall have glory added upon their heads for ever and ever. (Abraham 3:22–26)

THE ROLE OF AGENCY IN OUR PREMORTAL PROGRESS

From those verses we learn that many of the spirit children of God, through obedience to premortal laws (called "the gospel of God" in Romans 1:1), had distinguished themselves as "noble and great ones," implying that there must have been others who were not so noble and not so great because of their lack of diligence in obeying God's laws. In explaining the cause of the great schism in heaven, the Lord revealed to Joseph: "It came to pass that Adam, being tempted of the devil—for, behold, the devil was before Adam, for he rebelled against me, saying, Give me thine honor, which is my power; and also a third part of the hosts of heaven turned he away from me because of their agency" (D&C 29:36).

Agency was a gift given to the premortal sons and daughters of God. God would never force His children to follow rules that would automatically result in exaltation and eternal happiness. Growth toward exaltation comes because of voluntary obedience, not forced submission. As Joseph retranslated the Bible, he had revealed to him more of the details concerning the War in Heaven.

> And I, the Lord God, spake unto Moses, saying: That Satan, whom thou hast commanded in the name of mine Only Begotten, is the same which was from the beginning, and he came before me, saying—Behold, here am I, send me, I will be thy son, and I will redeem all mankind, that one soul shall not be lost, and surely I will do it; wherefore give me thine honor.
>
> But, behold, my Beloved Son, which was my Beloved and Chosen from the beginning, said unto me—Father, thy will be done, and the glory be thine forever.
>
> Wherefore, because that Satan rebelled against me, and sought to destroy the agency of man, which I, the Lord God, had given him, and also, that I should give unto him mine own power; by the power of mine Only Begotten, I caused that he should be cast down;
>
> And he became Satan, yea, even the devil, the father of all lies, to deceive and to blind men, and to lead them captive at his will, even as many as would not hearken unto my voice. (Moses 4:1–4)

From these verses we learn that the right to exercise our agency to our own exaltation or destruction was so prized by our Heavenly Father that He would not abridge it even if it meant that some of His children would be eternally excluded from His presence. Lucifer led a rebellion against God, failed, and was cast out with all who followed him. "Neither was their place found any more in heaven" (Revelation 12:8). Today those who choose to follow the adversary become "carnal, sensual, and devilish," while those who believe in the Son of God and repent of their sins will be saved (see Moses 5:13–15). Joseph later taught: "Satan was generally blamed for the evils which we did, but if he was the cause of all our wickedness, men could not be condemned. The devil could not compel mankind to do evil; all was voluntary. Those who resisted the Spirit of God, would be liable to be led into temptation, and then the association of heaven would be withdrawn from those who refused to be made partakers of such great glory. God would not exert any compulsory means, and the devil could not; and such ideas as were entertained [on these subjects] by many were absurd."[9]

Later in his life, Joseph again returned to this theme. He knew that without a correct understanding of the events that transpired in the pre-earth life, mortal man was likely to misunderstand many of the seemingly senseless happenings in mortality. He taught: "The contention in heaven was—Jesus said there would be certain souls that would not be saved; and the devil said he could save them all, and laid his plans before the grand council, who gave their vote in favor of Jesus Christ. So the devil rose up in rebellion against God, and was cast down, with all who put up their heads for him."[10]

FOREORDAINED ROLES, A REWARD FOR PREMORTAL DILIGENCE

From the Prophet Joseph Smith's translation of the book of Abraham, we learn many other vital truths. Joseph taught that many of the noble and great spirits would be foreordained to certain works here on the earth as a result of their premortal diligence (see also Alma 13). The Lord said to Abraham, "These I will make my rulers." Rather modestly, Joseph explained his foreordained role and that of many others: "Every man who has a calling to minister to the inhabitants of the world was ordained to that very purpose in the Grand Council of heaven before this world was. I suppose I was ordained to this very office in that Grand Council."[11]

As Joseph Smith continued to translate the papyrus of Abraham, he further learned that mortal life was intended to be a probationary experience: "And there stood one among them that was like unto God, and he said unto those who were with him: We will go down, for there is space there, and we will take of these materials, and we will make an earth whereon these may dwell; and we will prove them herewith, to see if they will do all things whatsoever the Lord their God shall command them" (Abraham 3:24–25).

All who know, honor, and revere the Savior recognize that He was the one who was "like unto God," foreordained to supervise the creation of the earth. However, the antecedent to "them" in verse 22 is the "noble and great ones." Could Joseph possibly be translating aright? Even that "many of the noble and great ones" were to help create the earth? It was the very plan of the Eternal Father to provide experiences and lessons necessary for His children to become like Him. Joseph Smith taught that the Father, "God," is also known as "the Creator."[12] It seems possible, therefore, that those who would eventually gain their exaltation might have played some part in the Creation of this earth to gain experience for their future creative ventures.[13] As President Joseph Fielding Smith noted: "Adam . . . helped to create this earth. He was chosen in pre-existence to be the first man upon the earth and the father of the human race, and he will preside over his posterity forever."[14]

If we knew enough and had been given sufficient power to help create the earth on which we live, we should embrace the fact that we have sufficient power to create and control our intellectual, social, spiritual, mental, and, to a degree, physical world here in mortality. Now we can transition from being an advanced organism subject to environmental control to being sons and daughters of God endowed with agency and reason in order to create and fashion our own mortal experience to some degree.

A PLACE TO BEGIN UNDERSTANDING MORTALITY

Surely the reader can see that only summary points of interest have been touched upon in this paper and that a larger, more inclusive investigation begs to be written. Perhaps that is why Joseph said: "The great plan of salvation is a theme which ought to occupy our strict attention, and be regarded as one of heaven's best gifts to mankind. No consideration whatever ought to deter us from showing ourselves approved in the sight of God, according to His divine requirement."[15]

Far from being a cosmic mistake or even a divine experiment, our mortal existence is part of an eternal story that never had a beginning and will never have an end. Nothing could be further from the truth than to believe that we are here by mistake or without a purpose. In fact, God revealed to Joseph, "I give unto you these sayings that you may understand and know how to worship, and know what you worship, that you may come unto the Father in my name, and in due time receive of his fulness" (D&C 93:19). Joseph further taught, "If men do not comprehend the character of God, they do not comprehend themselves."[16]

With the correct understanding of who God is, what our relationship is to Him, and what His Divine purpose is for us, it is much easier to view the commandments and the trials of life as stepping stones toward our future exaltation. Then the satanic opposition we constantly experience, the death of loved ones, and everything that seems so senseless and meaningless are viewed as part of God's work and glory (see Moses 1:39) and begin to make perfect sense.

When we understand from our study of the pre-earth life that every person on earth is a brother or sister with the same divine Father, then the incentive to live together in love and harmony here in mortality increases. When we see, with our expanded vision of the pre-earth life, God's perfect love for us and His infinite ability to foreknow and preplan our mortal experience, then we can accept without murmuring those things that happen to us in mortality over which we have no control. "He doeth not anything save it be for the benefit of the world; for he loveth the world, even that he layeth down his own life that he may draw all men unto him. Wherefore, he commandeth none that they shall not partake of his salvation" (2 Nephi 26:24). When we know this, then our love for and adoration of God and His Beloved Son increase exponentially.

When we finally acknowledge that this life isn't the beginning of our test of godhood, that we were tutored and successfully passed many great tests for exaltation before ever coming here (as is evidenced by the exaltation of little children who die before being able to take the tests of mortality),[17] then we can take courage that, with effort and faith, we can pass these remaining tests and eventually qualify for our desired prize of exaltation with God in the celestial kingdom.

When we see our true familial relationship to God with vision so greatly enlarged and amazingly clarified by the revelations through God's chosen prophet, Joseph Smith, then we can express eternal gratitude that we are able to bask in the understanding revealed through him. We feel like Brigham Young, who said, "I feel like shouting Hallelujah, all the time, when I think that I ever knew Joseph Smith, the Prophet."[18]

NOTES

1. Joseph Smith, *Teachings of the Prophet Joseph Smith,* comp. Joseph Fielding Smith (Salt Lake City: Deseret Book, 1976), 343.

2. Smith, *Teachings,* 137.

3. Smith, *Teachings,* 324.

4. Smith, *Teachings,* 220.

5. Smith, *Teachings,* 373; emphasis in original.

6. Smith, *Teachings,* 370.

7. For further scriptural verification, see D&C 131:1–4; 132:19–20; see also Erastus Snow, in *Journal of Discourses* (London: Latter-day Saints' Book Depot, 1854–86), 19:270–71; Joseph F. Smith, *Gospel Doctrine: Selections from the Writings and Sermons of Joseph F. Smith,* 5th ed. (Salt Lake City: Deseret Book, 1939), 276.

8. Smith, *Teachings,* 354.

9. Smith, *Teachings,* 187.

10. Smith, *Teachings,* 357.

11. Smith, *Teachings,* 365.

12. *Lectures on Faith* (Salt Lake City: Deseret Book, 1985), 3:19; see also Smith, *Teachings,* 190.

13. Joseph Fielding Smith, *Doctrines of Salvation,* comp. Bruce R. McConkie (Salt Lake City: Bookcraft, 1955), 1:74–75.

14. Smith, *Doctrines of Salvation,* 1:94.

15. Smith, *Teachings,* 68.

16. Smith, *Teachings,* 343.

17. Bruce R. McConkie, "The Salvation of Little Children," *Ensign,* April 1977, 3.

18. Brigham Young, *Discourses of Brigham Young,* comp. John A. Widtsoe (Salt Lake City: Deseret Book, 1954), 458.

CHAPTER FIVE

Joseph Smith's Contributions to Understanding the Doctrine of Eternal Marriage

DOUGLAS E. BRINLEY

President Boyd K. Packer taught Church members in three separate general conference addresses that "true doctrine, understood, changes attitudes and behavior." He explained that "the study of the doctrines of the gospel will improve behavior quicker than a study of behavior will improve behavior."[1] On another occasion, he provided this illustration of how doctrine influences both attitudes and behavior:

> Once we accept the truth of the doctrine that *we are the children of God,* that realization *changes us.* Thereafter we cannot *willingly* injure another or transgress against him. *That simple, profound doctrine has a very practical value.* It brings a feeling of self-worth, of dignity, of self-respect. Then self-pity and depression fade away. We then can yield to self-discipline and to the discipline of a loving Father and accept even the very hard lessons in life. The gospel is good medicine.[2]

This chapter will discuss five principles or concepts relative to the doctrine of eternal marriage restored by Joseph Smith that have power to positively influence a spouse or parent to make a more determined effort to succeed in marriage and family relationships. The Prophet taught that marriage is to be an eternal compact. Among

---

Douglas F. Brinley is a professor of Church history and doctrine at Brigham Young University.

those professing Christianity in our day, however, this doctrine is typically rejected because of a misunderstanding of the Savior's interchange with the Sadducees in Matthew 22.[3] This doctrine of eternal marriage is unique to Latter-day Saint theology and is found in both scripture attributable to Joseph Smith and in his sermons and writings.

DOCTRINE 1. WE LIVED IN A PREMORTAL STATE AS SINGLE ADULT BROTHERS AND SISTERS, SONS AND DAUGHTERS OF HEAVENLY PARENTS. MORTALITY IS OUR FIRST OPPORTUNITY TO MARRY AND EXPERIENCE PARENTHOOD.

Joseph Smith taught the doctrine that we were spirits before we were born (see Abraham 3:22–28; D&C 77:2; Ether 3:16–17; D&C 93:23, 29; Moses 3:5–7). To my knowledge, the Prophet did not discourse publicly that we were the *literal offspring* of heavenly parents, but the concept is inherent in his teachings about spirits, and he certainly taught it privately. For example, Eliza R. Snow's singular poem that now constitutes the lyrics to the Church hymn "O My Father" was inspired by the Prophet's comments to her. Her poem reads: "In the heav'ns are parents single? No, the thought makes reason stare! Truth is reason; truth eternal tells me I've a mother there."[4]

An account by Susa Young Gates provides insight to the origin of this idea:

> An interesting sidelight is given to this time [during which the hymn "O My Father" was written] through a possible glimpse of the thought-kernel which grew into such fragrant bloom in the full-voiced poem of Sister [Eliza R.] Snow. It was told by Aunt Zina D. Young to the writer as to many others during her life. Father Huntington lost his wife under the most trying circumstances. Her children were left desolate. One day, when her daughter Zina was speaking with the Prophet Joseph Smith concerning the loss of her mother and her intense grief, she asked the question:
>
> "Will I know my mother as my mother when I get over on the Other Side?"
>
> "Certainly you will," was the instant reply of the Prophet. "More than that, you will meet and become acquainted with your eternal Mother, the wife of your Father in Heaven."

"And have I then a Mother in Heaven?" exclaimed the astonished girl.

"You assuredly have. How could a Father claim His title unless there were also a Mother to share that parenthood?"[5]

It was about this time that Sister Snow learned the same glorious truth from the same inspired lips, and at once she was moved to express her own great joy and gratitude in the moving words of the hymn "O My Father," which includes the powerful couplet:

> Truth is reason; truth eternal
> Tells me I've a mother there.

Statements by subsequent future First Presidencies help clarify the point that spirits are the literal offspring of resurrected, exalted parents: "So far as the stages of eternal progression and attainment have been made known through divine revelation, we are to understand that *only resurrected glorified beings can become parents of spirit offspring.* Only such exalted souls have reached maturity in the appointed course of eternal life; and these spirits born to them in the eternal worlds will pass in due sequence through the several stages or estates by which the glorified parents have attained exaltation."[6]

In 1995 the First Presidency and members of the Quorum of Twelve stated: "Each [male and female] is a beloved *spirit son or daughter of heavenly parents,* and, as such, each has a divine nature and destiny. Gender is an essential characteristic of individual premortal, mortal, and eternal identity and purpose."[7]

As the offspring of heavenly parents and as male and female, every couple has a model to inspire them to succeed in marriage and family relations. Elder Dallin H. Oaks said: "Our theology begins with heavenly parents. Our highest aspiration is to be like them."[8] The significance of understanding our relationship to our Eternal Father gives meaning and purpose to marriage and provides an incentive for a couple to strive together to attain eternal life. They will make better decisions when their eternal goal is clear. On another occasion, Elder Oaks explained the value of knowing this basic principle: "There are few things more important in this life than knowing your place in mortality and your potential in eternity."[9]

The principle of how spirit children are the offspring of resurrected beings was best explained by Elder Melvin J. Ballard:

What do we mean by endless or eternal increase? We mean that through the righteousness and faithfulness of men and women who keep the commandments of God they will come forth with celestial bodies, . . . and unto them, through their preparation, there will come children, who will be spirit children. I don't think that is very difficult to comprehend and understand. *The nature of the offspring is determined by the nature of the substance that flows in the veins of the being. When blood flows in the veins of the being, the offspring will be what blood produces, which is tangible flesh and bone; but when that which flows in the veins is spirit matter [as in resurrected beings], a substance which is more refined and pure and glorious than blood, the offspring of such beings will be spirit children.*[10]

The Prophet Joseph Smith commented that resurrected beings will "be raised by the power of God, having spirit in their bodies, and not blood."[11] He taught that resurrected beings have tangible bodies: "The Father has a body of flesh and bones as tangible as man's; the Son also" (D&C 130:22). Resurrected parents produce immortal spirit children that receive a mortal body created by earthly parents. Elder Bruce R. McConkie explained, "A child is an adult spirit in a newly born body, a body capable of growing and maturing according to the providences of Him whose spirit children we all are."[12] Thus we understand that we have been children twice in our existence, once in the premortal sphere and now again in mortality.

Perhaps one of the most profound revelations of the Prophet pertains to Heavenly Father having passed through stages of progression similar to our own. In a well-known address in Nauvoo, he said: "*God himself was once as we are now, and is an exalted man, and sits enthroned in yonder heavens! That is the great secret. . . . It is the first principle of the Gospel to know for a certainty the Character of God, and to know that we may converse with him as one man converses with another, and that he was once a man like us; yea, that God himself, the Father of us all, dwelt on an earth, the same as Jesus Christ himself did.*"[13]

Application. From the above statements, a married couple can draw several conclusions: We are the literal offspring of heavenly parents. Our Heavenly Father is a husband and a parent. He passed through a mortal experience. We waited a long time as God's spirit children before this life to come to earth and obtain a body of earthly element as a counterpart to our spirit body.

When a married couple understands these concepts, they will do their best to treat each other in a manner so that each will want to be eternal partners. They will seek both individually and as a couple, through prayer, counsel from a perfect Husband and Father concerning marital or parenting difficulties. They will want to remain on the path that leads to eternal lives (see D&C 132:24). They will understand the sanctity of procreation as a special privilege granted for the first time to them, and sexual sins would be a tragic choice.

With this doctrinal understanding, what married couple would be critical or sarcastic with each other? To fight and quarrel with each other would be hurtful to the marriage, besides offending the Spirit of God. To be angry or caustic in their treatment of each other would indicate a lack of appreciation for the wonderful privilege they have been granted to finally be capable of marriage and parenthood. They would be humbled by the knowledge that in their first opportunity to marry, they must learn from each other how to function as a spouse and parent. It is in marriage that they learn the roles of husband, father, wife, mother, lover, therapist, and so forth. They will be more inclined to be supportive of each other, knowing that their ultimate goal of exaltation is unattainable alone. They would be more willing to apologize, to take responsibility, to make personal adjustments, to do whatever is needed to keep their relationship strong and viable. Divorce would thwart their goals both here and beyond this life.

Doctrine 2. Heavenly Father has a plan for His children to gain exaltation and become like Him.

Our Heavenly Father's experience with marriage and parenthood was no doubt instrumental in His formulating the plan of salvation under which we now apprentice (see Moses 1:39). The Prophet Joseph Smith said of our premortal existence: "At the first organization in heaven we were all present and saw the Savior chosen and appointed, and the plan of salvation made and we sanctioned it."[14] "We," in this case, refers to us as God's spirit children in our premortal habitation. On another occasion, the Prophet said: "God himself, finding he was in the midst of spirits and glory, . . . saw proper to institute laws whereby the rest could have a privilege to advance like himself."[15]

The Father's plan outlines the curriculum that mortals pass through to attain exaltation. An important part of the plan, not unlike that of mortal parents, calls for children to "leave home," to move away from parental controls and influences in order to find out for themselves if what their parents taught is true. The earth was framed so that we could leave home and participate in a laboratory that includes agency in choosing between good and evil. It was intended that Adam and Eve fall as a part of the plan. After both spouses had partaken, Elohim said to Jehovah, "Behold, *the man is become as one of us to know good and evil*" (Moses 4:28; emphasis added). We cannot become like God, and consequently cannot gain exaltation, without knowing good from evil.

Our birth into mortality indicates that we sustained the Father's plan in our premortal habitation. Satan rejected the divine plan, thereby preventing him and his followers from ever marrying or creating offspring, for spirits are incapable of procreation. Joseph Smith explained: "The Devil has no body, and herein is his punishment. He is pleased when he can obtain the tabernacle of man and when cast out by the Savior he asked to go into the herd of swine showing that he would prefer a swine's body to having none."[16]

Heavenly Father entrusts married couples with procreative powers to rear His spirit children who inhabit the bodies we create for them. Understanding whose children they are rearing, every couple would give their best efforts in parenting their children. No one would dare abuse or mistreat God's own children. If we fail to care for those whom the Lord assigns to us, we fail in one of the most important areas of our mortal stewardships. In fact, the penalty for violating this sacred trust, either as a spouse or a parent, is to live in a degree of glory where marriage and family relations are no longer open to us (see D&C 131:1–4; 132:17). Therefore, every Latter-day Saint couple has an incentive to be effective sweethearts and parents, because they know that if they do well in these responsibilities in this life, family associations will continue throughout eternity.

"We came to this earth that we might have a body and present it pure before God in the Celestial Kingdom," said the latter-day seer. "The great principle of happiness consists in having a body."[17]

When we were born into mortality we became a child for the second time in our existence. After we were born as spirit children in the premortal life, our spirit bodies grew to adulthood (Ether 3:17). In mortality, our earthly bodies grow to their adult stature. This union of spirit and earthly bodies provides us with the opportunity to marry and experience parenthood—a primary objective our Father had in creating the earth (see D&C 49:16–17). Joseph Smith revealed that "the head of the Gods called a council of the Gods; and they came together and concocted a plan to create the world and people it."[18] It is in this probationary state that we find a companion, marry, and consummate a marriage.

To introduce us to His plan, God called a council in which He outlined His plan. There, in that premortal existence, we learned the terms and conditions of His plan whereby we would step into mortality for a brief time to marry. At the end of our probation, we would return back to the Father's presence as married adult couples, having proven ourselves capable of living in a society with other glorified, exalted couples. For some of God's children, of course, the blessings of marriage and children are delayed till the next life, but the blessings *will* come.

Application. An understanding of the Father's plan of salvation helps a couple understand the following concepts: Heavenly Father wants us to become as He is, and His plan outlines the path we must follow to obtain eternal life. We left our premortal home to receive this endowment of flesh and bones. Understanding these concepts should cause every couple to bring their behavior into harmony with the elements of the Father's plan and to understand the importance of marriage and parenting as a sacred stewardship. In short, to be the mortal parents of Heavenly Father's spirit children should cause each parent to treat each other and each child kindly and charitably.

DOCTRINE 3. WITHOUT THE RESURRECTION, AN ETERNAL MARRIAGE WOULD BE IMPOSSIBLE.

The plan of the Father requires a Savior to redeem us from physical and spiritual death, which are the penalties for sin. Marriage and parenthood test our very souls. What spouse or parent feels completely adequate in marriage and parenting challenges? In addition, our memory of the premortal life was taken from us at birth, allowing Satan to tempt us to make decisions inconsistent with the plan of happiness. Disobeying the laws of God and not repenting result in long-range limitations that include a loss of procreative power (see D&C 131:3–4).

It was in the premortal setting that Jesus volunteered to be the Redeemer for all who repent. The penalties for sin could not be paid by a mere mortal; it required one who would be both the Son of God and of a mortal mother, one who would work out the infinite Atonement on our behalf.

Without the Savior's gift of Resurrection, death would keep us in a spirit existence similar to our premortal state, but we would be devils or angels to a devil, as Jacob explained (see 2 Nephi 9:6–8). Like Satan, we would remain spirits forever, incapable of further marriage and parenthood. President Boyd K. Packer explained Satan's damnation: "The adversary is jealous toward all who have the power to beget life. He cannot beget life; *he is impotent.* He and those who followed him were cast out and forfeited the right to a mortal body."[19] In the Resurrection we are incapable of death (see Alma 11:45). Marriage and family life will continue for those who are worthy, who married in the right place, by the right authority, and are faithful to their baptism and temple covenants (see D&C 132:19–25).

The Savior restores our souls. Joseph Smith explained: "The spirit and the body are the soul of man. And the resurrection from the dead is the redemption of the soul" (D&C 88:15–16). A mortal soul, therefore, is the combination of a mortal body created by mortal parents combined with a spirit body from immortal parents. Procreation and birth unite these two bodies for an individual's mortal probation. At death, these bodies separate, one going back to "dust," while the spirit, unable to die, moves to the spirit world. Now the good news: Jesus Christ makes it possible for our bodies to be reunited in a resurrected state with the power to create spirit children as our heavenly parents once created us.

This earth will someday become a celestial world, the habitation of those who attain exaltation, where "bodies who are of the celestial kingdom may possess it forever and ever; for, for this intent was it made and created, and for this intent are they sanctified" (D&C 88:20).

Application. Latter-day Saint married couples appreciate the

Redeemer because without His death, Atonement, and Resurrection, they could not remain married in eternity. The Resurrection restores both their earthly and spirit bodies, thus allowing them to continue the powers of life and procreation in the celestial kingdom. A couple with this doctrinal understanding would not want to frustrate the Savior's efforts in their behalf to be married beyond this life. They would feel a desire to live the principles of the gospel in a way that both would be thrilled to be married companions. Surely the hearts of both husband and wife would be softened by the realization that without the Savior's gift of Resurrection, their only opportunity to marry and be parents would be in this brief span of mortality. Because of Him, family associations organized in mortality may last forever.

Doctrine 4. Marriage is essential to exaltation (see D&C 49:15–17; 131:1–4).

The Prophet Joseph taught this principle: "Except a man and his wife enter into an everlasting covenant and be married for eternity, while in this probation, by the power and authority of the Holy Priesthood, they will cease to increase when they die; that is, they will not have any children after the resurrection. But those who are married by the power and authority of the priesthood in this life . . . continue to increase and have children in the celestial glory."[20]

If marriage were limited to this life only, how devastating death would be to family members! What soul would want to worship a God who designed such a useless and frustrating plan that has us come to earth, marry, and create children, only to have these profound feelings of love for each family member end at death? Were that the plan of God, Christianity would be a miserable philosophy. To put it frankly, if the Atonement of Jesus Christ did not have the power to resurrect men and women with immortal bodies, it would be of little use. There would be little purpose in life, marriage, or parenthood. Thankfully, God does not command marriage to be a temporary, once-in-eternity phenomenon. Without the assurance the restored gospel provides of the knowledge that marriage and family life continue beyond this probationary period, mortals would live in constant fear that a family member's death would cut short any association with that person—forever.

Application. When a couple understands that eternal marriage is exaltation, they will make their marriage a high priority to merit eternal life. They will do their best to live together in love and serve each other. Would not every husband and wife who understands these principles want to conform to the principles that lead to an eternal relationship? With an eternal perspective, couples will be more forgiving, more charitable, and more willing to sacrifice their own wants in an effort to contribute more to their own marriage.

Doctrine 5. One of Satan's primary goals is to destroy Latter-day Saint marriages and families.

A doctrine clearly misunderstood by Christian theologians is the identity and motivation of why Satan, or Lucifer, wants to destroy marriages. The Bible is unclear in its teachings about him and his origin. For example, he is said to be a snake in Genesis (see Genesis 1:1–4, 13–14), a son of the morning in Isaiah (see Isaiah 14:12), and a fallen star in Revelation (see Revelation 8:10). Without Joseph Smith's contribution to our understanding of Lucifer's identity, Latter-day Saints would not understand Satan's motivations. Through revelation, the Prophet contributed this understanding of Lucifer's rebellion:

> That Satan . . . is the same which was from the beginning, and he came before me, saying—Behold, here am I, send me. I will be thy son, and I will redeem all mankind, that one soul shall not be lost, and surely I will do it; wherefore give me thine honor.
>
> But, behold my Beloved Son, which was my Beloved and Chosen from the beginning, said unto me—Father, thy will be done, and the glory be thine forever.
>
> Wherefore, because that Satan rebelled against me, and sought to destroy the agency of man, which I, the Lord God, had given him, and also, that I should give unto him mine own power; by the power of mine Only Begotten, I caused that he should be cast down;
>
> And he became Satan, yea, even the devil, the father of all lies, to deceive and to blind men, and to lead them captive at his will, even as many as would not hearken unto my voice. (Moses 4:1–4)

> And it came to pass that Adam, being tempted of the devil—for, behold, the devil was before Adam, for he rebelled against me, saying, Give me thine honor, which is my power; and also a third part of the hosts of heaven turned he away from me because of their agency;
>
> And they were thrust down, and thus came the devil and his angels. (D&C 29:36–37)

Without an opportunity to ever marry or become a parent himself, no wonder Satan has such disdain for marriage and parenthood. Through his rebellion he forfeited the right to obtain a body of flesh and bone, thus preventing himself and his followers from ever being married or experiencing parenthood. Joseph Smith explained that Lucifer "sought for things which were unlawful. Hence he was sent down, and it is said he drew many away with him; and the greatness of his punishment is that he shall not have a tabernacle."[21]

Orson Pratt explained Lucifer's damnation in these simple terms:

> Could wicked and malicious beings, who have irradicated every feeling of love from their bosoms, be permitted to propagate their species, the offspring would partake of all the evil, wicked, and malicious nature of their parents. . . . *It is for this reason that God will not permit the fallen angels to multiply:* it is for this reason that God has ordained marriages for the righteous only: it is for this reason that God will put a final stop to the multiplication of the wicked after this life: it is for this reason that *none but those who have kept the celestial law will be permitted to multiply after the resurrection.*[22]

Application. Satan is determined to destroy marriage because he knows that marriage is at the heart of the Father's plan. When a temple marriage dissolves, Satan must laugh. On the other hand, when a couple understands that by honoring temple covenants Satan has little power over them, they are more determined to avoid his snares. In the book of Moses, there is an account of Satan's efforts to thwart Moses' mission to Egypt (see Moses 1:11–22, 26). A couple who understands Lucifer's intentions will resist any efforts to destroy their marriage. They will be more attentive to contention and efforts to destroy their unity (see 3 Nephi 11:28–29; Mosiah 4:12–23).

When a faithful couple is sealed in the temple by the Melchizedek Priesthood key restored by Elijah, death has no effect on their marital status. At death they rejoin each other as a married couple in the spirit world, where they await the Resurrection and eventual exaltation. For those who do not attain eternal life, however, the Prophet taught that they will remain "separately and singly" forever (D&C 132:17). Those who qualify for a lesser degree of glory—terrestrial, telestial, or the lower two-thirds of the celestial kingdom—will be alone forever (see D&C 131:1–4).

SUMMARY

True doctrine assists married couples to understand the purposes of marriage and parenthood in order to deal with the tests of mortality more effectively because they understand the doctrines that comprise the plan of salvation. They gain power to live together in love and happiness because they understand their potential. Doctrine outlines their opportunities to live together forever as sweethearts when they learn to love each other as mortal companions.

Latter-day Saints look to Joseph Smith with a great appreciation for restoring lost doctrines (and ordinances) essential for eternal marriage. Latter-day Saints stand alone in the Christian arena in understanding and teaching the doctrine that marriage and family relations can be eternal. As President Packer explained, such a knowledge will make Latter-day Saints more effective marriage partners and parents because they understand their potential as an eternal companionship. With an eternal perspective, they understand the significance of marriage and parenthood. Obviously without these essential doctrines they would not understand, nor could they appreciate, the plan of salvation and the Savior's gift of eternal marriage to worthy spouses. This doctrine of eternal marriage alone should cause Latter-day Saint couples to shout hallelujah whenever they hear the name of Joseph Smith!

NOTES

1. Boyd K. Packer, "Do Not Fear," *Ensign,* May 2004, 79; see also his articles "Little Children," *Ensign,* November 1986, 17, and "Washed Clean," *Ensign,* May 1997, 9.
2. Boyd K. Packer, "Hope for Troubled Hearts," in *Let Not Your Hearts Be Troubled,* 1–2; emphasis added.
3. For a discussion of the Savior-Sadducee exchange, see Bruce R.

McConkie, *Doctrinal New Testament Commentary* (Salt Lake City: Bookcraft, 1965), 1:546–49.

4. "O My Father," *Hymns* (Salt Lake City: The Church of Jesus Christ of Latter-day Saints, 1985), no. 292.

5. Susa Young Gates, *History of the Young Ladies' Mutual Improvement Association* (Salt Lake City: Deseret News, 1911), 16.

6. First Presidency and Quorum of the Twelve Apostles, *Messages of the First Presidency*, comp. James R. Clark (Salt Lake City: Bookcraft, 1971), 5:34; emphasis added.

7. "The Family: A Proclamation to the World," *Ensign*, November 1995, 102; emphasis added; herein designated as "proclamation."

8. Dallin H. Oaks, "Apostasy and Restoration," *Ensign*, May 1995, 87.

9. Dallin H. Oaks, "The Gospel in Our Lives," *Ensign*, May 2002, 35.

10. Melvin J. Ballard, "The Three Degrees of Glory," discourse at the Ogden Tabernacle, September 22, 1922 (Salt Lake City: Deseret Book, n.d.), 10; emphasis added.

11. Joseph Smith, *History of the Church of Jesus Christ of Latter-day Saints*, ed. B. H. Roberts, 2nd ed. rev. (Salt Lake City: Deseret Book, 1960), 4:555.

12. Bruce R. McConkie, "The Salvation of Little Children," *Ensign*, April 1977, 3.

13. Joseph Smith, *Teachings of the Prophet Joseph Smith*, comp. Joseph Fielding Smith (Salt Lake City: Deseret Book, 1972), 345–46.

14. Joseph Smith, *The Words of Joseph Smith*, ed. Andrew F. Ehat and Lyndon W. Cook (Provo, UT: Religious Studies Center, Brigham Young University, 1980), 60.

15. Smith, *Teachings*, 354.

16. Smith, *Words of Joseph Smith*, 60.

17. Smith, *Words of Joseph Smith*, 60.

18. Smith, *Teachings*, 349.

19. Boyd K. Packer, "Our Moral Environment," *Ensign*, May 1992, 66; emphasis added.

20. Smith, *History of the Church*, 5:391; emphasis added.

21. Smith, *Teachings*, 297.

22. Orson Pratt, "Power and Eternity of the Priesthood," *The Seer*, 1853, 156–57.

CHAPTER SIX

JOSEPH SMITH AND ABRAHAM LINCOLN

RICHARD LYMAN BUSHMAN

In a letter to his friend John Stuart, dated March 1, 1840, Abraham Lincoln wrote that Joseph Smith had recently passed through Springfield, Illinois. In a tantalizingly brief report, Lincoln told Stuart that "Speed [another close friend] says he wrote you what Jo. Smith said about you as he passed here. We will procure the names of some of his people here and send them to you before long."[1] The nature of Joseph's comment on Stuart can only be surmised. Joseph had spent the winter in Washington D.C., vainly seeking compensation for the Saints' losses in Missouri in 1839. He was returning to Nauvoo in the early spring when he passed through Springfield. John Stuart was Lincoln's law partner and a member of Illinois's congressional delegation. The Illinois delegation had gone out of their way to assist Joseph and his legal counselor Elias Higbee in making their case in Washington. Likely Joseph was grateful to Stuart and said so in Springfield.[2]

The letter is a reminder that Smith and Lincoln resided in the same state for five years before Joseph's death in 1844. In 1840 Lincoln was completing his third term in the state legislature, where he was the Whig floor leader. Joseph was recovering from the Mormons' expulsion from Missouri and organizing a new gathering place in Illinois. The Prophet was a little over three years older than

---

Richard Lyman Bushman is Gouverneur Morris Professor of History emeritus at Columbia University.

Lincoln, who had been born February 12, 1809. Though they probably never met face to face, the two men illustrate the possibilities for obscure men to reach great heights in the swarming confusion and institutional fluidity of antebellum America. Both were plungers and seekers, and both struggled to understand how God worked His will in human affairs.[3] A comparison of their lives is one way to measure the accomplishments of each of these extraordinary men. Joseph, usually viewed within the Mormon context, may appear in a new light when brought onto a larger stage.

BEGINNINGS

Abraham Lincoln was the middle South and Joseph Smith was the Yankee version of back-country men who transcended their origins and went on to eminence and notoriety on the national scene. They took entirely different paths, Lincoln in law and politics and Joseph in religion and church leadership. Their religious beliefs stood at the opposite ends of the spectrum too. Lincoln did not believe in the redemption of Jesus Christ, was not known to pray, and attended church haphazardly. His God was an ominous presence who controlled events down to the finest detail but was beyond human influence. Joseph's God spoke to him, forgave him, and led His people like a kind, demanding father with ambitions for His children. Lincoln's deity was remote and impersonal, Joseph's intimate and involved.

The family histories of the two men followed roughly similar patterns. The first Lincolns immigrated from England to Massachusetts in 1637, just one year before Robert Smith, Joseph's first American ancestor, landed in Boston. Over the generations, the Lincolns migrated southward, first to New Jersey, then to Pennsylvania and Virginia. Probably because the Smiths stayed put in Topsfield, Massachusetts, while the Lincolns kept moving, none of the Lincolns achieved the eminence of Joseph's great-grandfather Samuel Smith, who was town meeting moderator and representative to the General Court. Lincoln's ancestors were plain farmers and planters, respectable but of no particular distinction.[4]

Despite the spatial separation and differences in stability and mobility, family patterns converged again with Lincoln's and Joseph's grandfathers. Their lives tracked so closely that one is inclined to think they followed a common pattern for this generation of

Americans. Lincoln's grandfather, also an Abraham Lincoln, moved west from Virginia to Jefferson County, Kentucky, in 1782, nine years before Joseph's grandfather Asael left coastal Massachusetts for Tunbridge, Vermont. The West was the way to go in the late eighteenth century. Abraham's son Thomas, the future president's father, then moved from farm to farm in Kentucky, Indiana, and Illinois, just as Joseph Sr. moved seven times in fourteen years in Vermont and New Hampshire before settling in Manchester, New York. The narrow margin between success and failure in early American farming, combined with the plentitude of land, made frequent migration both a possibility and a necessity for families on the lower edge of the rural economy.

Both the Lincolns and the Smiths went through a decline in fortunes over their lifetimes. Thomas Lincoln at one time owned three farms. When he purchased more land, he paid in cash. But his circumstances steadily worsened as he moved from Kentucky to Indiana and then to Illinois. His Kentucky properties turned out to have precarious titles, and he sold them at a loss before moving to Indiana. There he farmed remote frontier lots with little access to markets and grew poorer and poorer. Similarly, Joseph Smith Sr., as a young man, owned a substantial farm and a store in Vermont and then lost both through a failed business venture. Both the Smiths and the Lincolns purchased land on credit late in life. The Lincolns did a little better at the end. They completed payment on half of their Indiana land and sold it for $125 before they made their final move to Illinois in 1830. The Smiths lost their Manchester property when they could not meet the mortgage payment and thereafter were dependent on their children and friends. Both families were caught in the downward economic trend that ensnared many rural families—contrary to the American myth of ever-increasing prosperity.

The two families' ways of living were much the same. When the Lincolns moved to Indiana in 1816 (the same year the Smiths moved to Palmyra), eight people crowded into their rough-hewn cabin; a few years later, after contracting for a farm, the Smiths stuffed ten family members into their Manchester log house. Both Lincoln and Joseph cleared land and helped their fathers plant crops. Lincoln followed a horse along the furrows as he plowed; the Smiths probably owned animals but not necessarily draft animals. They may have used hoes like the first settlers or borrowed oxen from the neighbors.[5]

CULTURE

Neither boy spent much time in school. Lincoln's stepmother, Sarah Bush Johnston, who replaced Lincoln's deceased mother, Nancy Hanks, when he was ten, sent the two Lincoln children and her own three to school, but Lincoln had less than a year of sporadic instruction as a boy, probably about the same as Joseph. Of the two, Lincoln was the more avid learner. He could spell down anyone in the school and did all the writing and ciphering for the family while still a teenager. Later stories were told of his taking a book to the fields for reading while the horse rested at the end of a furrow. He did not have access to many books but read a few avidly—Weems's *Life of Washington,* Defoe's *Robinson Crusoe,* Bunyan's *Pilgrim's Progress,* Aesop's *Fables,* and the Bible. Joseph could have obtained books from the Manchester lending library or the Palmyra bookstores, but he had little interest. One early acquaintance said he read a few adventure stories, but he was not bookish. The family studied the Bible, and, like Lincoln, Joseph must have spent time with the scriptures. But according to Joseph's mother, her son did not share Lincoln's appetite for reading.[6]

Lincoln began to experiment with language early. While a teenager he composed a piece of doggerel for his copybook:

> *Abraham Lincoln*
> *his hand and pen*
> *he will be good*
> *but god knows When.*[7]

When he was about nineteen, he wrote a humorous account of his sister Sarah's wedding night in biblical language, titling it "The Chronicles of Reuben." This and other satirical sallies showed Lincoln's affinity for coarse, frontier humor and his interest in words. While living with his father, he spent time at the village store trading quips and developing a reputation as a teller of tales. The scraps of writing revealed his wish to hold on to those words and make them work better. In this way, he was far ahead of Joseph, who is not known to have written a word until he was in his twenties. Joseph's

wife said when she married him at age twenty-one he could not compose a decent letter. To the end of his life he made spelling errors.

Joseph's mind turned more to religious questions and the supernatural. Before he was thirteen, he was questioning the state of his
soul and asking how he could find forgiveness. The babble of preaching in the burned-over district confused him and prevented him
from enjoying a stable religion. He did not turn to books for his
answers but to spiritual inquiries and prayer. Lincoln probably went
to church with Thomas Lincoln, who joined the Pigeon Creek Baptist
Church when Lincoln was fourteen, the very age when Joseph's questioning was reaching a crisis, but in Lincoln's case, exposure to his
father's religion did not result in conversion or even faith. He did not
ask God for help or come to any resolution in his soul. Sarah Bush
Lincoln said that Abraham "had no particular religion—didn't think
of that question at that time, if he ever did—He never talked about
it."[8] He would not even sing religious songs. He relied on his own
reasoning and even tried to close down religious emotions. Joseph
was awash in religious anxieties that he quieted through prayer.

Lincoln lived in an environment as electric with superstition and
the supernatural as Joseph's, but he never took to folk magic. Joseph
found a seerstone when he was sixteen or seventeen, which he used
to find lost objects and help his father on treasure quests.[9] Lincoln's
rationality raised a wall against the supernatural searches of his
neighbors. He never took an interest in the magical or yearned to get
in touch with unseen powers. His adolescent mind went to books,
while Joseph's was caught up in visions and seerstones. Lincoln's reason kept the supernatural at bay. His mind was not furnished with
the treasure lore that awakened Joseph to the play of supernatural
forces and the possibility of unseen worlds.

And yet religion did seep into Lincoln's mind. He wrote the
words of an Isaac Watts hymn into his copybook, and as a boy he
would parody Sunday sermons by repeating them "word for word"
on a stump when back home after service, "mimacing the Style &
tone of the old Baptist Preachers."[10] Protestant language and thus
Protestant thought shaped his fundamental categories of understanding. Through regular attendance at his father's and mother's
Baptist church, Lincoln may have had more knowledge of religion
than Joseph, whose parents did not regularly attend church. When

his mother, Lucy, joined the Presbyterians, Joseph Jr. stayed home with his father. Joseph possessed religious sensibilities that Lincoln lacked but had less exposure to doctrine and Christian culture.

Personal Growth

Until he was twenty-two, Lincoln gave few signs of unusual ambition or particular genius. At age seventeen, he got a job helping an Ohio ferryman sixteen miles from his father's Spencer County, Indiana, farm. Two years later Lincoln constructed a flatboat with a friend and floated a load of farm produce down the Ohio and Mississippi Rivers to New Orleans, where he experienced the excitement of the nation's most cosmopolitan city. But he returned only to sink once more into the dull routine of farm work and odd jobs. One biographer, Benjamin Thomas, says of this period that Lincoln "seemed to be drifting into the same unimaginative life of a pioneer farmer or hired hand that had become the lot of his father and those about him." Later Lincoln called himself "a piece of floating driftwood."[11]

Lincoln's one daring step was to break free from his father's household. When, after a hard winter, Thomas Lincoln moved once more, this time to Coles County, Illinois, Abraham was not in the party. Instead, he made plans for another flatboat excursion to New Orleans with two friends. He got as far as St. Louis and then returned to New Salem, a village on the Sangamon River that they had visited on their way downstream. Lincoln had been offered a job as a storekeeper there, and, on reflection, he considered this a better opportunity than the New Orleans voyage.

In New Salem in 1831, Lincoln's ambition kicked in. For the next three years he turned himself into a politician headed for Whig party leadership and eventually the presidency. He began studying grammar and mathematics to improve his writing and thinking. His skill in frontier rhetoric and competence in storekeeping won the admiration of locals, who elected him captain of the militia. He was chosen postmaster, took up surveying, and began reading law. Gaining confidence and finding politics fascinating, he ran for the state legislature unsuccessfully in 1832, but then in 1834 he was elected. In three short years, from age twenty-two to twenty-five, he suddenly bloomed. A man who knew him well said Lincoln had "a strong conviction that he was born for better things than then seemed likely or even possible."[12] That vision of himself took over in New Salem.

Joseph's adolescence had a different character than Lincoln's, but the years from age twenty-two to twenty-five were also his time of blossoming. Until 1827 when he turned twenty-two, Joseph had been a seeker who had actually done little. God and Christ had appeared to him, he had been visited by an angel, the grand mission to translate had been declared to him, and he was ready, but all was anticipation rather than accomplishment. He may even have been uncertain and confused about when he was to begin and how he was to go about his work. How was he, a barely literate boy, to translate? It must have seemed like a mysterious and forbidding task.

Then, as he turned twenty-two, the work began. He obtained the plates and the interpreters, and with Emma scribing at first and then Martin Harris, he started to dictate. After the loss of the first manuscript, he wrote the rebuke he received from the Lord, the first of the written revelations to comprise the Book of Commandments. For a year and a half, from the winter of 1828 to the summer of 1829, words poured from him in a flood. The bulk of the Book of Mormon was translated in three months: more than five hundred pages of sermons, prophecies, visions, wars, miracles, journeys, and admonitions. The young man who was not known to have read a book or preached a sermon produced a book full of sermons and theological declarations. In March 1830, three months after his twenty-fourth birthday, the Book of Mormon was published. A few weeks later, he organized a church with himself as the first elder. That summer he received the revelation of Moses that commenced the revision of the Bible. In the fall he dispatched missionaries to locate the site of the New Jerusalem where the City of Zion was to be built in preparation for the Lord's Second Coming. When he arrived in Kirtland, Ohio, a month after his twenty-fifth birthday, he could present himself as Joseph the Prophet with a string of accomplishments to support the claim.

The same three years in the life cycle, from twenty-two to twenty-five, launched the careers that would bring Lincoln and Joseph to their eminent positions in the political and religious histories of the nation. Lives that had been obscure, private, and in Lincoln's case unpromising, suddenly entered the public scene. James

Gordon Bennett, the bustling New York reporter who visited Palmyra in 1831, would write a report on Joseph that began, "You have heard of MORMONISM—who has not?"[13] This was the time of emergence for both men. But there the similarities cease; from then on, the shape and character of their careers differed drastically.

Lincoln began his ascent at the bottom, as the American myth of personal progress required. He developed skills as a storekeeper, public speaker, surveyor, and lawyer, and then ran for office. He failed the first time but did not give up. On the next try he was elected. He ascended gradually as would be expected for one climbing a tall peak. Not so with Joseph. He burst onto the public scene with a masterpiece, the Book of Mormon, one of the world's most influential books. He made no preparations, did not attend school, did not experiment with smaller writings, and did not read in preparation. Under inspiration, he precipitously dictated a 584-page book. Then, without pause, he went on to the book of Moses and the heaven-daring task of revising the Holy Bible. Rather than ascending gradually, taking a few small steps at first, Joseph made a series of grand gestures, including the organization of a new church, which he said was the one true church among all others. The curve of his achievements, instead of rising gradually, ascended almost vertically in the first three years, making him prophet and seer from the beginning rather than as an accumulation over time. Instead of working his way up, Joseph catapulted into prominence.

The spirit and motive of the two emergences had a different cast, too. Lincoln was driven by ambition coupled with a thrilling sense of his own powers. In New Salem, he began to glimpse his own destiny and yearned to fulfill it. He took steps to acquire the skills, put himself forward for public office, and sought out promising friendships. He was ambitious in the best sense of the word, aggressively carving the path he wished to follow.

Joseph may have been ambitious, but that is not the impression left in his writings. He sought forgiveness and understanding, but he did not seek office or elevation. These came to him; in a sense, they were thrust upon him. Instead of being the product of diligence, talent, and calculation, Joseph's work was given to him. He sought help from God but always received more responsibilities than he bargained for. Asking at age seventeen if his sins were forgiven, he was told he was to translate the Book of Mormon. He learned to look in a seerstone for lost objects and then was given a Urim and Thummim to translate reformed Egyptian. He asked which church was right and was told to organize a new one. The work kept inflating beyond his expectations. Everything he took up exceeded his initial projection. Rather than being driven by personal ambition, he worked under divine command.

CONFLICT

While taking divergent paths, Joseph and Lincoln passed through the same dark plain early in life. They both struggled with skepticism about the scriptures and the Christian religion. Lincoln's encounter is more fully documented and had a more lasting effect, but there is good evidence Joseph also had a bout with what was then called "infidelity." The term referred to a conglomerate of beliefs put forward by Thomas Paine in *The Age of Reason,* Ethan Allen in *Reason the Only Oracle of Man,* David Hume in *On Miracles,* C. F. Volney in *Ruins of Civilizations,* and other works in a similar vein. The upshot of this complex body of writings was to throw the authenticity of the scriptures into question and to undermine belief in Jesus as the Son of God and Savior of mankind. Some writers verged on atheism; others ended up with differing varieties of Deism that found God in nature rather than the Bible.

Both Lincoln and Joseph explored these ideas in informal discussion societies modeled roughly after Benjamin Franklin's Junto Society a century earlier. All around the country, ambitious young men gathered to read and talk with the aim of "improving" themselves. In these informal gatherings, they could try out ideas too scandalous for discussion in church or family. These small circles had been forming at various levels of society throughout the eighteenth century, and by the 1820s they had sprung up in tiny villages like Palmyra and New Salem among people with as little education as Joseph Smith and Abraham Lincoln. In Joseph's case, local printers, men in touch with wider currents of thought, formed a "juvenile debating club," which gathered in the red schoolhouse on Durfee Street to "solve some portentous questions of moral or political ethics."[14] In Lincoln's New Salem, intellectually oriented young professionals-in-the-making got together to read their writings to each other.

Among his friends, Lincoln was able to express doubts that had probably been forming since attending church with Thomas Lincoln's Pigeon Creek Baptists. How much he read of infidel writings is not known, but he came to question the inspiration of the Bible and to reject the efficacy of Christ's redemption, just as if he had absorbed Thomas Paine. At the end of his wrestle with skepticism, however, Lincoln did not come out in the glowing sunshine of Paine's Deism. Paine doubted the Bible but had infinite faith in nature, which he thought bore constant witness to the benevolence and might of the Creator. The evidence of God's handiwork was everywhere, Paine thought, and it was the privilege and joy of mankind to contemplate nature's wonders. Lincoln found only determinism in nature—the iron law of necessary causes. The God that remained for him after the Bible, as one commentator has put it, was the Calvinist God of predestination and indifference to human wishes, without a redeeming Christ or a comforting Holy Spirit.[15] Lincoln fused the scientific doctrine of necessity—that everything, even human thought, was caused and therefore predetermined— with the Calvinist principle of predestination. Lincoln's God was less the Creator of glorious nature than a distant Providence that ruled and determined all human affairs without visible concern for anyone's happiness or will.

Joseph passed through the rigors of skepticism without being scarred or frightened. He may have first encountered infidelity at the Palmyra debating society. Oliver Cowdery spoke of a time when Joseph questioned the existence of God.[16] The sure evidence that he had encountered skepticism was the passage in his 1832 history about nature testifying to God's existence. The sun, the moon, the stars, the earth, and man "walking forth upon the face of the earth in magesty . . . all these bear testimony and bespeak an ominpotant and omnipreasant power."[17] The sentiments are pure Deism and would have been recognized by anyone who had stood up to infidelity as Lincoln and Joseph did. Later the men in Zion's Camp were surprised at how well Joseph grasped the case for skepticism. One Sunday when the marchers were trying to disguise their Mormon identity before a crowd of curious onlookers, Joseph spoke for an hour pretending to be a "liberal free-thinker." According to George A. Smith, "Those present remarked that he was one of the greatest reasoners they ever heard."[18]

Joseph quickly passed beyond Deism, overcome by his "marvilous experience," as he called it in the 1832 history.[19] The presence of heavenly angels left no room for further doubt. But the skeptical arguments remained in the background of his mind. The "constitution" of the church, written soon after the organization, named the overcoming doubts about the Bible as one purpose of Joseph's revelations. The Book of Mormon, the revelation said, proved to the world "that the holy scriptures are true, and that God does inspire men and call them to his holy work" (D&C 20:11).

AMERICA AND GOD

Lincoln thus entered adult life with belief in a God as a controlling will, standing over all existence, determining every outcome but showing no empathy or compassion. Joseph, on the other hand, had experienced the presence of a speaking God. Joseph's God mingled His will with human exertion, had plans for the human race, and responded to questions and desires. He punished and rewarded, blessed and withheld, rebuked and revealed. Joseph's God was as immanent as any God in nineteenth-century religion.

Lincoln's idea for America was, not surprisingly, empty of religious purpose. He did not believe that the nation could please the withdrawn Calvinist Being who ruled everything. God did not instruct the nation in how to conduct itself. Although He controlled everything that transpired, He did not necessarily manifest Himself in any government, house of worship, religious creed, body of doctrine, or righteous work. He was above all human striving and belief. A righteous God, He brought the nation to righteousness in His own way and in His own time.

Lincoln's chief hope for the nation was to establish a justice that would allow human beings to thrive in purely worldly terms. He embraced Whig hopes for a prosperous, industrious people who would labor and be rewarded for their work. He wanted to fashion an economy where workers would not be drawn into the downward spiral of poverty that had trapped Thomas Lincoln. He believed that the development of the market economy would enable an individual to rise from hired laborer to independent worker to employer—in a factory, store, or farm. The happiness of extracting oneself from the mire of poverty was the best that Lincoln hoped for Americans. He hated slavery for denying captive workers the benefits of their own labor. "Unrequited toil" was the sin of slavery.[20] He feared that certain forms of factory work would enslave white laborers in the same injustice. He had a Hamiltonian vision of a people fulfilling themselves through creative and rewarded labor. A properly functioning, justly organized market economy was for Lincoln the essence of the good society.

Joseph's revelations passed judgment on the market economy and found it wanting. One revelation said quite radically that men were to be equal in earthly property that they might be equal in heavenly goods (see D&C 78:5–6). The world lay in sin because of gross economic inequality (see D&C 49:20). One revelation proposed a system of consecrating property and redistributing it to assure work and the elimination of poverty (see D&C 42:30–39). But these egalitarian principles were not ones Joseph would die for. He attempted a thorough consecration of property in Jackson County, Missouri, from 1831 through 1833; partially in Far West, Missouri, in 1838; and not at all in Nauvoo, Illinois, after its settlement in 1839. Equality of property was an ideal rather than a functioning necessity. If the poor could be cared for through capitalist enterprise, no objections would be raised. In Nauvoo, he encouraged the men of property to set up mills to employ the poor and said nothing about redistributing the profits. His main concern was to provide employment and a comfortable life for all his people.

Joseph's greater concern was for the Saints' spiritual education. He once wrote that nothing could prevent divine knowledge from pouring from heaven on the heads of the Latter-day Saints (see D&C 121:33). In his plat for the original City of Zion, he placed twenty-four temples at the center, saying nothing about shops, factories, or theaters. The dominant structure in Nauvoo was its huge temple, far out of proportion to the means of the people and any other architecture. Joseph put spiritual instruction above all other values in his city, believing that virtue would flow from this knowledge. By the end of his life, he hoped to cover the country with such cities and temples. His vision of America was a nation of Zion cities, prosperous, to be sure, but also righteous and divinely instructed. He wanted his people to grow in divine intelligence by contemplating the words of God in scripture and reading from all good books on every possible topic. This young man who may never have read a book before age twenty, and who had minimal schooling, made education and divine instruction the premier value of his Zion cities.

THEODICY

Of the two men, Joseph seems to be the happy warrior filled with bright hopes and spiritual desires, and Lincoln the glum materialist who had no other dream than to let Americans get rich. At first glance, it appears that Lincoln thought it was hopeless to strive for God because God was out of reach. But this abbreviated caricature does not do him justice, nor is it right to think of Joseph as invariably optimistic and cheerful. Lincoln's spiritual depths were plumbed in the tragedy of the Civil War, and after the Missouri expulsion, a despairing and angry Joseph wondered if God had failed him.

In Lincoln's thinking, the Civil War was proof of God's implacability. Why was the war prolonged while hundreds of thousands died? Justice was clearly on the side of the North; surely a fight against slavery was a battle for the good. He did believe it was God's will that government of the people, by the people, and for the people should be established on the earth and that slavery should end. Why, then, did the North not overcome the South without all the bloodshed? Lincoln could only conclude that the ways of the Almighty were incomprehensible to man. God clearly willed the war to go on, however bloody, though Lincoln could not fathom why, stating, "The Almighty has His own purposes."[21] Lincoln bowed before this divine opacity in humble incomprehension. He did not call down the wrath of God on the sinning slave owners, self-righteously proclaiming that God was a Yankee. He did not see the Redeemer in the fires of a hundred circling Northern camps. Lincoln's God did not take sides; He was everywhere, North and South.

Out of Lincoln's bafflement came not wrath or vindictiveness but compassion. Because it was God that determined all, no one could judge his enemy or himself. All were helpless before the Divine might. "With malice toward none; with charity for all," he wrote in his second inaugural address in 1865, let us "bind up the nation's wounds."[22] The distance of God reduced Lincoln to utter humility, stripping away all judgment and wish for retribution. In the end, his belief in a distant God ennobled the president. It made him capable, Job-like, of bearing the sorrows of the nation and of solving conundrums of human suffering.

Lincoln's faith in the controlling power of Divine Providence made him look for the hand of God everywhere—in the events of history and even in his own actions. In the course of the war, he came to believe that he was himself an instrument of God. He told a group of visiting clergymen that it was his "earnest desire to know the will of Providence" on freeing the slaves. *"If I can learn what it is I will do it!"*[23] In the extremities of the nation's trial, he longed for personal revelation that would enable him to see clearly, and he believed it came. One associate remembers Lincoln saying:

> That the Almighty does make use of human agencies, and directly intervenes in human affairs, is . . . one of the plainest statements of the Bible. I have had so many evidences of his direction, so many instances when I have been controlled by some other power than my own will, that I cannot doubt that this power comes from above. I frequently see my way clear to a decision which I am conscious that I have no sufficient facts upon which to found it. But I cannot recall one instance in which I have followed my own judgment, founded upon such a decision, where the results were unsatisfactory. . . . I am satisfied that when the Almighty wants me to do or not to do a particular thing, he finds a way of letting me know it.[24]

Toward the end he relied more and more on the inner light, an occasional "presentiment" of revelation, and possibly his own dreams.[25] In a biblical culture, the logic of revelation overcame his sense of God's indifference to human wishes. As one scholar has said, under the duress of war Lincoln came to think of himself as a "latter-day Moses learning God's will on the presidential mountain and bringing it down to the people."[26] "I should be the veriest shallow and self-conceited blockhead upon the footstool [of the earth]," Lincoln said to Noah Brooks on election day in 1864, "if, in my discharge of the duties which are put upon me in this place, I should hope to get along without the wisdom which comes from God and not from men."[27] Revelation did not clarify God's purposes for Lincoln—the prolonged, bloody war still baffled him—but he believed that Providence had made the president an instrument of its will.

Joseph's God, though immanent and communicative from the start, was no less perplexing. After directing the Saints to build Zion, after requiring them to sacrifice so much, why did He not come to their defense against their persecutors? Rather than making defeats easier to bear, this made them all the more perplexing. Why should the Saints' enemies be allowed to frustrate God's own work? Having confidence that God was on their side made the triumph of their enemies more confusing. John Corrill, an early Kirtland convert and leading figure in Missouri, left the Church in 1839 and explained to Joseph exactly why: Everything he attempted had failed. Wherever the Saints had founded a city under God's direction, they had been attacked and expelled. When nothing went right, how could one say God was in it?[28]

In his public letters, Joseph offered constant reassurance to the Saints. They were not abandoned; their cause was just; God would soon come to their aid. But in his private contemplations, Joseph brought the same questions to his prayers: Why had they been driven? Why was he separated from his family? Where is thy pavilion, O God? The answer was as difficult as Lincoln's: It is all for your experience, my son, Joseph was told. Remember that I the Lord descended below all things too. Are your sufferings greater than mine? The answer to Joseph was, You must bear it. I did, and so must you. In the end you will see it all had a purpose in giving you experience (see D&C 121:1–8; 122:1–8).[29] Lincoln's ponderings led him to reflect on God's imponderable will. Joseph's revelations told him that life was an inescapable trial that brought suffering even to Christ.

Events drove both men into the heart of darkness, where the right does not prevail and God absents Himself. Both tried to affirm that God was present, though invisible and inexplicable. Neither was embittered by the miseries they saw. Lincoln advocated charity toward all. Joseph wrote after five months in a Missouri prison that the way of the priesthood, despite the evils wrought by men, was persuasion, love, and long-suffering. He knew that power corrupted nearly everyone—including the men who had beaten and driven his people—but the answer was not power against power but gentleness, meekness, and love unfeigned (see D&C 121:37–44).

ENDINGS

Joseph died in 1844 just as Lincoln, somewhat falteringly, came on the national scene. Lincoln was elected to Congress in 1846 but made no impression. He was an unsuccessful candidate for the United States Senate in 1854 and ran again unsuccessfully against Stephen Douglas in 1858. Though defeated both times, he was on hand to lead the Republican Party as it took form after 1856. He was fifty-one when elected president. Joseph had died at age thirty-eight, the age at which Lincoln first entered the House of Representatives. The Prophet's accomplishments were compressed into sixteen years, from the time he began translating the Book of Mormon in 1828 until his murder in June 1844. No one would remember Lincoln today if he had died at thirty-eight.

They both died significantly. Neither passed from this life by natural causes. Their deaths by assassins' bullets were a culmination, a punctuation mark, on their lives and accomplishments. Lincoln died for breaching the South's slave system, Joseph for claiming divine authority. Their deaths were seen as sacrifices for the causes they lived for, testaments of their works. The form of their deaths hallowed the memory of their lives.

Lincoln was remembered for emancipating the slaves and saving the Union, but that was not his only legacy to the nation. He had defined the core of American values as the individual's right to pursue wealth. The evil of slavery was its denial of the fruits of labor to the people who had labored. Lincoln's aim was to create an economy in which Thomas Lincoln could rise from poverty on his farm, or an enterprising entrepreneur could accumulate goods through a little business—as Lincoln himself had risen through a law practice and politics. That form of economic justice was the highest ideal Lincoln entertained for the United States. His dreams for America were almost solely economic. We fought the war, he said in 1861, to preserve a government whose "leading object is, to elevate the condition of men—to lift artificial weights from all shoulders—to clear the path of laudable pursuit for all—to afford all, an unfettered start, and a fair chance, in the race of life."[30] His ideals led to industrialization, corporations, consumerism, and unfettered individual ambition—not that he advocated these outcomes, but nothing in his vision stood in their way. His Republican Party sponsored the industrialization of America, and his distant God required nothing particular of the nation. Lincoln could imagine nothing more transcendent than an equal opportunity for everyone to get ahead. "For Lincoln," writes Gabor Borritt, the foremost scholar of Lincoln's economic thought, "unobstructed upward mobility was the most important ideal America strove for."[31]

Joseph's more complex view of human destiny was far more contentious. He interfered too much in human affairs, disaffected Mormons complained. He insisted on brotherhood and service and the consecration of properties to the greater good in direct contradiction to American individualism. Rather than freeing people from constraints, Joseph bound them together. Joseph's aim was Zion, an exalted society based on faith and common devotion to a great cause. He wanted his bruised father to become a priest of God and enjoy an inheritance in a promised land. The factories and rail lines of Lincoln's postbellum America would have interested Joseph only insofar as they facilitated the gathering to Zion and the creation of an equitable society. Lincoln took human nature as he found it, self-interested, ambitious, energetic, and tried to create a social order in which this natural man could enjoy his just deserts. Joseph built institutions to instruct men spiritually, to put them in touch with God, and to help them find the divine potential within themselves. The temple, not the marketplace, was the pivotal institution of his cities.

The two men were opposites and the same. They both rose from the lowest levels of American society to unexpected notoriety and influence. The circumstances of their lives plunged them both into existence's darkest mysteries. Why does injustice prevail? Where is God when the good suffer? Both retained a belief that, however dark the way, God rules over all. In the end, Lincoln even saw the need for personal revelation. But their beliefs about God and His expectations for humankind divided Joseph and Lincoln fundamentally. One believed that God left people to fend for themselves in a self-interested world. The other believed that God wanted His children to live together in love and to help each other become gods themselves. Lincoln's program resulted in factories, merchandise, markets, and a population of workers; Joseph's in temples, cities, and a Zion people.

Lincoln's regard for individual rights led him to plow around the hard, wet, heavy Mormon log rather than split, burn, or move it.[32] He did not raise his voice against the Mormons when public animosity was rising dangerously.[33] He looked on with his characteristic compassion—generous, respectful, and uncomprehending. He could find no basis in his religion to do more than leave the Mormons alone, but that was all they wanted. While Lincoln's Republicans fostered industrialization, Joseph's Mormons organized Zion cities in the desolation of the Great Basin as monuments to the vision of their founding prophet.

NOTES

1. Abraham Lincoln to John T. Stuart, March 1, 1840, in Roy P. Basler, ed., *Collected Works of Abraham Lincoln* (New Brunswick: Rutgers University Press, 1953), 1:206. I am grateful to Val H. Sederholm for this reference.

2. Joseph arrived in Nauvoo on March 4, 1840. Joseph Smith, *History of the Church of Jesus Christ of Latter-day Saints,* ed. B. H. Roberts, 2nd ed. rev. (Salt Lake City: Deseret Book, 1957), 4:89. In the fall presidential elections Lincoln ran to be a Whig elector for president and was scratched from many Mormon ballots. The removal of his name from the list of ten electors was not intended as a slight. The Mormons, who were backing William Henry Harrison over Martin Van Buren, wanted to placate the Democrats by writing in the name of Democratic elector, James H. Ralston. Lincoln's name was chosen for deletion because he happened to be at the bottom of the list. He showed no signs of bearing a grudge; in December 1840 he voted with the vast majority in favor of the Nauvoo charter (G. U. Hubbard, "Abraham Lincoln as Seen by the Mormons," *Utah Historical Quarterly* 31 [Spring 1963]: 93–94). John C. Bennett reported all this in *Times and Seasons,* January 1, 1841.

3. Information about Lincoln in this essay comes from Benjamin P. Thomas, *Abraham Lincoln: A Biography* (New York: Alfred A. Knopf, 1952); Allen C. Guelzo, *Abraham Lincoln: Redeemer President* (Grand Rapids, Michigan: William B. Eerdmans, 1999); and David Herbert Donald, *Lincoln* (New York: Simon and Schuster, 1995). Joseph Smith's life is laid out in Donna Hill, *Joseph Smith: The First Mormon* (Garden City, New York: Doubleday, 1977), and in Richard Lyman

Bushman, *Joseph Smith: Rough Stone Rolling* (New York: Alfred A. Knopf, 2005).

4. John Lincoln (1716–1788), Lincoln's great-grandfather and of the same generation as Samuel Smith, was the son of a niece of New Jersey's royal governor. John owned a large farm in the Shenandoah Valley (Donald, *Lincoln*, 21).

5. Don Enders provided information on the evidence for animals. Archeological evidence points to a possible animal shelter on the Smiths' Manchester property.

6. On Joseph's school attendance, see Mark Ashurst-McGee, "The Josiah Stowell Jr.—John S. Fullmer Correspondence," *BYU Studies* 38, no. 3 (1999): 113; Christopher M. Stafford, Statement (1885), and John Stafford, Statement (1881), in Dan Vogel, ed., *Early Mormon Documents*, 5 vols. (Salt Lake City: Signature Books, 1996–2003), 2:194, 122. Michael Quinn refers to the "myth" of Joseph's ignorance and points to the ample opportunities for extensive reading in the village bookstores and nearby libraries. Michael D. Michael, *Early Mormonism and the Magic World View*, 2nd. ed. rev. (Salt Lake City: Signature Books, 1998), 179–93. On reading cheap fiction, see Pomeroy Tucker, *Origin, Rise, and Progress of Mormonism* (New York: D. Appleton, 1867), 17. On Joseph's reading the Bible, see Lucy Mack Smith, *Biographical Sketches of Joseph Smith the Prophet and His Progenitors for Many Generations* (Liverpool, Eng.: S. W. Richards, 1853), 84.

7. *Collected Works*, 1: 1.

8. Guelzo, *Abraham Lincoln*, 38.

9. Richard Bushman, *Joseph Smith and the Beginnings of Mormonism* (Chicago: University of Illinois Press, 1984), 69.

10. Guelzo, *Abraham Lincoln*, 38.

11. Thomas, *Abraham Lincoln*, 18, 20, 24.

12. Guelzo, *Abraham Lincoln*, 120.

13. Leonard J. Arrington, "James Gordon Bennett's 1831 Report on 'The Mormonites,'" *Brigham Young University Studies* 10 (Spring 1970): 357.

14. Turner, *Gorham's Purchase*, 214, in *Early Mormon Documents*, ed. Dan Vogel (Salt Lake City: Signature Books, 1996–2003), 3:49–50.

15. Guelzo, *Abraham Lincoln*, 153.

16. *Messenger and Advocate*, February 1835, 78.

17. "History, 1832," in Joseph Smith, *The Personal Writings of Joseph Smith*, ed. Dean C. Jessee (Salt Lake City: Deseret Book, 2002), 11.

18. George A. Smith, "My Journal," *Instructor*, January 1946, 182.

19. "History, 1832," in *Personal Writings*, 9.

20. Second Inaugural Address, March 4, 1865, in *Collected Works*, 8:333.

21. Second Inaugural Address, March 4, 1865, in *Collected Works*, 8:333.

22. Second Inaugural Address, March 4, 1865, in *Collected Works*, 8:333.

23. *Collected Works*, 5:420, 424.

24. L. E. Chittenden, "Register of the Treasury," in *Recollections of President Lincoln and His Administration* (New York: Harper and Brothers, 1891), 448.

25. The evidence of Lincoln's turn to the supernatural is summed up in Richard N. Current, *The Lincoln Nobody Knows* (New York: Hill and Wang, 1958), chap. 3.

26. Melvin B. Endy Jr., "Abraham Lincoln and American Civil Religion: A Reinterpretation," *Church History* 44 (June 1975): 232.

27. Guelzo, *Abraham Lincoln*, 462.

28. Corrill, *Brief History*, 48.

29. The complicated meanings of the word "experience" are discussed by Martin Jay in *Songs of Experience: Modern American and European Variations on a Universal Theme* (Berkeley: University of California Press, 2005).

30. Message to Special Session of Congress, July 4, 1861, in *Collected Works*, 4:438.

31. G. S. Boritt, *Lincoln and the Economics of the American Dream* (Memphis, TN: Memphis State University Press, 1978), 277. For a discussion of Lincoln and the postwar rise of corporations, see Guelzo, *Abraham Lincoln*, 457–61.

32. The comment was made to T. B. Stenhouse, who was inquiring after the president's attitude toward the Mormons (quoted in Preston Nibley, *Brigham Young, the Man and His Work* [Salt Lake City: Deseret News, 1936], 369).

33. Hubbard, "Abraham Lincoln," 93; Aryeh Maidenbaum, "Sounds of Silence: An Aspect of Lincoln's Whig Years," *Illinois Historical Journal* 82 (Autumn 1989): 167–76.

CHAPTER SEVEN

JOSEPH SMITH AND THE RESTORATION OF TEMPLE SERVICE

RICHARD O. COWAN

President Gordon B. Hinckley declared that "no member of the Church has received the ultimate which this Church has to give until he or she has received his or her temple blessings in the house of the Lord."[1] President Thomas S. Monson, in like spirit, affirmed that the construction of temples "is the ultimate mark of maturity" of the Church in a given area.[2] In former dispensations, sacred temples had at least two major functions. First, they were regarded as places of contact between heaven and earth, or of communication between God and man (see, for example, Exodus 25:8, 22). Second, these sacred structures were also places for performing holy priesthood ordinances (see D&C 124:38). Both of these significant functions would need to be a part of the "restitution of all things" (Acts 3:21) when the Lord would "gather together in one all things" during "the dispensation of the fulness of times" (Ephesians 1:10). Joseph Smith would be intimately involved in this restoration of temple service, and it would constitute a major contribution of his ministry.

In 1823 the angel Moroni anticipated the restoration of temple service when he told Joseph Smith about the existence of the Book of Mormon record. The angelic visitor emphasized that the gospel needed to go forth so that a people might be prepared for Christ's millennial reign.[3] The angel then cited several biblical prophecies

Richard O. Cowan is a professor of Church history and doctrine at Brigham Young University.

related to the Second Coming, including the words of Malachi, which he paraphrased: "Behold, I will reveal unto you the Priesthood, by the hand of Elijah the prophet, before the coming of the great and dreadful day of the Lord" (D&C 2:1). The priesthood keys which Elijah restored thirteen years later (see D&C 110:13–16) were essential to the work done in temples.

The first known specific reference to a latter-day temple came one year after the restored Church was organized. When Joseph Smith and a group of elders went to Missouri during the summer of 1831, the Prophet learned that Independence in Jackson County was to be the "center place" for the future city of Zion and that the temple lot was to be situated just west of the courthouse (see D&C 57:1–3). On August 3 he placed a cornerstone marking the location of the future temple.[4] Meanwhile, the Latter-day Saints had begun settling around Kirtland in northeastern Ohio.

THE KIRTLAND TEMPLE AND THE RESTORATION OF TEMPLE WORSHIP

An 1832 revelation instructed Joseph Smith to convene the "school of the prophets" to prepare those who would go forth to preach. In many ways the meetings of this school, which was called a "solemn assembly," foreshadowed temple worship. For example, only the worthy were to attend. This spiritual preparation of those present was symbolized by sacred initiatory ordinances: "Purify your hearts, and cleanse your hands and your feet before me that I may make you clean" (D&C 88:74; see also vv. 70, 75, 127, and 134).

The Lord directed the brethren to "establish a house" to accommodate the school (D&C 88:119). Six months later, on June 1, 1833, the Lord chastised the Saints for their failure to move forward with the building of this house, in which He would "endow" them "with power from on high." The temple was not to be built "after the manner of the world," the Lord emphasized, but according to a plan He promised to reveal (D&C 95:8, 13–14). In a conference that convened just two days later, Joseph Smith and his counselors were appointed to obtain a "draft" or plan for the building.[5]

Frederick G. Williams, second counselor in the First Presidency, described how the Lord gave them a vision in fulfillment of His promise. After the Presidency saw in vision the building's exterior, it seemed to move right over them so they could equally well see its interior. Later, while speaking in the completed temple, Williams testified that the hall in which they were convened coincided in every detail with the vision given to the Prophet.[6]

The Lord had specified that the temple should include a chapel on the ground floor and a similar hall on the second floor for educational purposes (see D&C 95:15–17). An unusual feature of these rooms would be multiple pulpits at each end bearing initials identifying the respective authority of the priesthood officers seated in them. The Lord not only revealed the size and use of the temple's two main rooms, Elder Orson Pratt affirmed, but He also revealed "the order of the pulpits, and in fact everything pertaining to it was clearly pointed out by revelation. God gave a vision of these things, not only to Joseph but also to several others, and they were strictly commanded to build according to the pattern revealed from the heavens."[7] Seating in each auditorium was reversible, enabling the congregation to face either end of the room. Truman O. Angell, a supervisor of construction, later recalled that "the leading mechanic" urged Joseph to modify the seating arrangements in the temple. Joseph refused because "he had seen them in vision."[8]

In the light of these revelations concerning the Kirtland Temple, Joseph Smith drew up similar plans for the temple at Independence. On June 25, 1833, he sent his plat for the city of Zion to the Saints in Missouri.[9] The following month, however, attacks against the Saints in Jackson County escalated, ending any hopes for building a temple there at that time. The Saints in Kirtland enjoyed more success in building their temple. Actual construction began in June 1833. Joseph Smith personally led a group in search of suitable stone for the temple. A source was found two miles south of the building site, and they immediately quarried a wagonload. The Saints were so impoverished at this time, an early member recalled, that "there was not a scraper and hardly a plow that could be obtained."[10] Nevertheless, the Prophet observed, "Our unity, harmony and charity abounded to strengthen us to do the commandments of God."[11] Following the return of Zion's Camp in the fall of 1834, work on the temple went forward more rapidly. "Great exertions were made to expedite the work of the Lord's house," the Prophet noted, "and notwithstanding it was commenced almost with nothing, as to means, yet the way opened as we proceeded, and the Saints rejoiced."[12] Joseph Smith continued to lead the way: "Come, brethren," he admonished, "let us go into the stone-quarry and work for the Lord."[13]

Throughout construction, women played a key part. Under Emma Smith's direction, they "made stockings, pantaloons and jackets" for the benefit of the temple workmen.[14] Polly Angell, the construction supervisor's wife, recalled how Joseph Smith remarked, "Well sisters, you are always on hand. The sisters are always first and foremost in all good works. Mary was first at the resurrection; and the sisters now are the first to work on the inside of the temple."[15]

Great spiritual blessings followed this period of sacrifice. On January 21, 1836, the First Presidency met during the afternoon in the room above the printing office and were washed "in pure water." That evening "at early candle-light," the Presidency and others met in the west room of the temple attic, Joseph Smith's office, where they anointed one another with consecrated olive oil and pronounced blessings and prophecies.[16] Then "the heavens were opened," the Prophet recorded, and he "beheld the celestial kingdom of God, and the glory thereof." When he saw his brother Alvin in that kingdom, he "marveled" because Alvin had died before the gospel was restored and consequently had not been baptized by proper priesthood authority. But the Lord declared: "All who have died without a knowledge of this gospel, who would have received it if they had been permitted to tarry, shall be heirs of the celestial kingdom of God" (D&C 137:6–8). This revealed assurance would become the doctrinal foundation for performing vicarious ordinances in behalf of the dead.

Concerning this occasion, the Prophet testified: "Many of my brethren who received the ordinance [of washing and anointing] with me saw glorious visions also. Angels ministered unto them as well as to myself, and the power of the Highest rested upon us, the house was filled with the glory of God, and we shouted Hosanna to God and the Lamb. . . . Some of them saw the face of the Savior, and . . . we all communed with the heavenly host."[17]

Some of the most memorable spiritual experiences occurred on Sunday, March 27, 1836, the day Joseph Smith dedicated the temple. The climax of the daylong service was the dedicatory prayer, which had been given to the Prophet by revelation. After expressing gratitude for God's blessings, Joseph prayed with tears flowing freely that the Lord would accept the temple which had been built "through great tribulation . . . that the Son of Man might have a place to manifest himself to his people." Specifically, he prayed: "We ask thee, Holy Father, that thy servants may go forth from this house armed with thy power, and that thy name may be upon them, and thy glory be round about them, and thine angels have charge over them" (D&C 109:5, 22). This prayer would become a pattern for other temple dedicatory prayers.

Following the prayer, the choir sang "The Spirit of God," a hymn written by William W. Phelps in anticipation of the temple's dedication. After the sacrament was administered and passed to the congregation, Joseph Smith and others testified that they saw heavenly messengers present during the service. The dedication concluded with the entire congregation standing and rendering the sacred "Hosanna Shout": "Hosanna, hosanna, hosanna to God and the Lamb, amen, amen, and amen."

That evening more than four hundred priesthood bearers met in the temple. Joseph Smith instructed the brethren that they should be prepared to prophesy when directed by the Spirit. The Prophet recorded: "Brother George A. Smith arose and began to prophesy, when a noise was heard like the sound of a rushing mighty wind, which filled the Temple, and all the congregation simultaneously arose, being moved upon by an invisible power."[18]

One week later, on April 3, which was Easter Sunday, the resurrected Lord Jesus Christ appeared, accepted the temple, and promised to manifest Himself therein "if my people will keep my commandments, and do not pollute this holy house" (D&C 110:8). Moses, Elias, and Elijah then bestowed special priesthood keys. Interestingly, this was also Passover weekend, and for centuries Jewish people had anticipated that Elijah would return at Passover time. Through the sealing keys restored by Elijah, priesthood ordinances performed on earth can be "bound" or "sealed" in heaven; also, Latter-day Saints can perform saving priesthood ordinances in behalf of loved ones who died without the opportunity of accepting the gospel in person. In this way, the hearts of the children are turning to their fathers.

Thus, the Lord's house in Kirtland certainly was a place of

revelation between God and man—the first of the two basic functions of temples. Yet there were no specific provisions for ordinances. The Kirtland Temple was more of a multipurpose building intended for general meetings and education. Specifically, Brigham Young pointed out, it "had no basement in it, nor a font, nor preparations to give endowments for the living or the dead."[19] Hence, as Elder Boyd K. Packer wrote in summary: "The design of the temple was preliminary. It was built as a house wherein the Lord could reveal Himself to His servants, where other heavenly beings could restore priesthood keys essential to the salvation of mankind, and where the faithful Saints would be blessed with an increase of spiritual power and enlightenment."[20] In fact, Elder Harold B. Lee believed that the restoration of these keys was "sufficient justification for the building of [this] temple."[21]

Thus, in Kirtland, Joseph Smith laid the foundations for temple service that would be built upon in later years. Brigham Young explained that the ordinances as administered in the Kirtland Temple were not as complete as they would be in later times. He noted that in Kirtland the "first Elders . . . received [only] a portion of their first endowments, or we might say more clearly, some of the first, or introductory, or initiatory ordinances, preparatory to an endowment."[22]

Unfortunately, the glorious period in Kirtland did not last long. By 1837, the spirit of apostasy divided Church members. In January 1838 Joseph Smith and other faithful Saints were forced to flee for their lives. They established their homes at Far West in northern Missouri, where the Saints who were earlier expelled from Jackson County were also gathering. Here Joseph received a revelation directing them to build another temple. It was to be for "the gathering together of my saints, that they may worship me" (D&C 115:8). Thus, this building, like the Kirtland Temple, was for general purposes rather than specifically for ordinances. Cornerstones were laid on July 4, but in October, Governor Lilburn W. Boggs's order that the Mormons be exterminated or driven from the state of Missouri prevented any further work on this temple.

THE NAUVOO TEMPLE AND THE RESTORATION OF ORDINANCES

The Saints found a new home in Illinois, where they built their city of Nauvoo. The practice of vicarious baptisms for the dead was taught for the first time in the present dispensation on August 15, 1840, at the funeral of Seymour Brunson.[23] Joseph Smith noted that in the congregation there was a widow whose son had died without baptism. He read from 1 Corinthians 15:29 on baptism for the dead "and remarked that the Gospel of Jesus Christ brought glad tidings of great joy" to this widow and to all mankind. He indicated that the Saints "could now act for their friends who had departed this life, and that the plan of salvation was calculated to save all who were willing to obey the requirements of the law of God."[24] Almost immediately Church members eagerly began performing the ordinance of baptism in the Mississippi River in behalf of deceased loved ones.

"Brother Joseph has opened a new and glorious subject of late, which has caused quite a revival in the Church; that is being baptized for the dead," Vilate Kimball wrote to her husband, Heber, who was away on a mission. "Since this order has been preached here, the waters have been continually troubled. During the conference there were some times from eight to ten elders in the river at a time baptizing."[25]

Joseph Smith continued to give emphasis to this principle. Minutes of a conference held in 1842 record that he referred to "the wisdom and mercy of God in preparing an ordinance for the salvation of the dead. . . . Those Saints who neglect it in behalf of their deceased relatives, do it at the peril of their own salvation."[26]

Typically these baptisms were done for family members. Of sixty-six names in one record, sixty were grandparents or even closer relatives. Members of Joseph Smith's own family, for example, received baptism in behalf of close relatives: Hyrum was baptized for his brother Alvin. Emma received the ordinance for her father, mother, two sisters, an uncle, and an aunt. The Prophet's mother, Lucy, was baptized for a sister, her parents, and all four of her grandparents. Samuel H. Smith was baptized for an uncle, while his brother Don Carlos received this ordinance in behalf of General George Washington as "friend."[27]

Elder Wilford Woodruff later reflected the enthusiastic spirit in which these early ordinances were performed: "How did we feel when we first heard [that] the living could be baptized for the dead? We all went to work at it as fast as we had an opportunity, and were baptized for everybody we could think of, without respect to sex. I went and was baptized for all my friends, grandmothers, and aunts, as [well as for] those of the male sex; but how was it? Why, by-and-by, it was revealed, through the servants of the Lord, that females should be baptised for females, and males for males."[28] This is an illustration of how the Lord unfolded His work "line upon line, precept upon precept" (2 Nephi 28:30).

By 1844, the year of the Prophet's martyrdom, some 15,722 baptisms had been performed in behalf of the dead. With gratitude, one Saint wrote: "What a glorious thing it is that we believe and receive the fulness of the gospel as it is preached now and can be baptized for all of our dead friends. . . . Oh, mother, if we are so happy as to have a part in the first resurrection, we shall have our children just as we laid them down in their graves."[29] While these ordinances were being inaugurated, the Saints had already turned their attention to building the temple. A revelation received January 19, 1841, directed the Saints to build a house "for the Most High to dwell therein" and restore that which had been lost. The Lord also declared that the ordinance of baptism for the dead "belongeth to my house" (D&C 124:27–30). Hence, the Nauvoo Temple, like holy sanctuaries in former dispensations, was to serve the dual purpose of being a place of contact between God and man and also an edifice where sacred priesthood ordinances could be performed.

At about this same time, Joseph received several proposals for the temple's design, but none pleased him. When William Weeks, a recent convert who was an architect and builder from New England, came in with his plans, "Joseph Smith grabbed him, hugged him and said 'you are the man I want.'"[30] Later, when Weeks questioned the appropriateness of placing round windows on the side of the building, the Prophet responded: "I wish you to carry out *my* designs. I have seen in vision the splendid appearance of that building . . . and will have it built according to the pattern shown me."[31] The Nauvoo design followed the general plan of the earlier temple in Kirtland with the addition of a baptismal font in the basement and facilities for other sacred ordinances in the attic story.

Cornerstones were laid during a solemn ceremony on April 6, 1841. Joseph Smith declared: "This principal corner stone in representation of the First Presidency, is now duly laid in honor of the Great God; and may it there remain until the whole fabric is completed; and may the same be accomplished speedily; that the Saints may have a place to worship God, and the Son of Man have where to lay His head."[32]

On November 8, the Prophet dedicated a temporary font in the temple's basement. In coming weeks he and members of the Twelve frequently officiated in the temple. On December 28, 1841, for example, Joseph Smith recorded: "I baptized Sidney Rigdon in the font, for and in behalf of his parents; also baptized Reynolds Cahoon and others."[33]

While the Saints were sacrificing to build the temple, the Lord was unfolding important temple-related blessings. Endowment instructions were first given in the large "assembly room" on the second floor of Joseph Smith's red brick store. On May 4, 1842, he "spent the day in the upper part of the store . . . in council with [seven brethren], instructing them in the principles and order of the Priesthood, attending to washings, anointings, endowments and the communication of keys pertaining to the Aaronic Priesthood, and so on to the highest order of the Melchisedek Priesthood, setting forth . . . [the] principles by which any one is enabled to secure the fulness of those blessings which have been prepared for the Church of the First Born."[34]

After giving these first endowments, the Prophet turned to Brigham Young and remarked: "Brother Brigham, this is not arranged perfectly; however we have done the best we could under the circumstances in which we are placed. I wish you to take this matter in hand: organize and systematize all these ceremonies."[35]

By means of two letters written during the first week of September 1842, the Prophet gave yet further instructions concerning work for the dead. He emphasized the importance of having a recorder present, not only to keep an accurate record but also to ensure that each ordinance is done properly (see D&C 127:6; 128:3). The Prophet linked this keeping of proper records with the power to bind or loose on earth and have this action recognized in heaven (see D&C 128:8–9; compare Matthew 16:18–19). Finally, expanding on the writings of Paul, Joseph Smith declared that "they [the fathers] without us cannot be made perfect—neither can we without our dead be made perfect," and that there must be "a welding link" established through ordinances for the dead (D&C 128:15, 18).

Among the other blessings unfolded during these years was eternal marriage. In May 1843 the Prophet instructed the Saints that in order to attain the highest degree of the celestial kingdom, one must enter the new and everlasting covenant of marriage (see D&C 131:1–4). Two months later he recorded a revelation that, among other things, declared: "If a man marry him a wife in the world, and he marry her not by me nor by my word, and he covenant with her so long as he is in the world and she with him, their covenant and marriage are not of force . . . when they are out of the world" (D&C 132:15). On the other hand, the Lord promised:

> If a man marry a wife by my word which is my law, and by the new and everlasting covenant, and it is sealed unto them by the Holy Spirit of promise, by him who is anointed, unto whom I have appointed this power and the keys of this priesthood; and it shall be said unto them—Ye shall come forth in the first resurrection; and if it be after the first resurrection, in the next resurrection; and shall inherit thrones, kingdoms, principalities, and powers, dominions, all heights and depths . . . it shall be done unto them in all things whatsoever my servant hath put upon them, in time, and through all eternity; and shall be of full force when they are out of the world; and they shall pass by the angels, and the gods, which are set there, to their exaltation and glory in all things, as hath been sealed upon their heads, which glory shall be a fulness and a continuation of the seeds forever and ever. (D&C 132:19)

Reflecting on what Joseph Smith had taught him about this principle, Parley P. Pratt recorded: "During these interviews he taught me many great and glorious principles concerning God . . . and the heavenly order of eternity. It was at this time that I received from him the first idea of eternal family organizations. . . . It was from him that I learned that the wife of my bosom might be secured to me for time and all eternity. . . . I had loved before, but I knew not why. But now I loved—with a pureness—an intensity of elevated, exalted feeling, which would lift my soul from the transitory things of this grovelling sphere and expand it as the ocean."[36]

The Lord had revealed that the temple needed to be built so that "the fulness of the priesthood" might be revealed (D&C 124:28). Joseph Smith taught that this can be achieved only through temple ordinances. During the final year of his life, the Prophet communicated to others, particularly the Twelve, all the power needed to build the kingdom of God on the earth. Orson Hyde later recalled: "He conducted us through every ordinance of the holy priesthood, and when he had gone through with all the ordinances he rejoiced very much, and [said], now if they kill me you have got all the keys, and all the ordinances and you can confer them upon others, and the hosts of Satan will not be able to tear down the kingdom."[37] Nearly a half-century later, President Wilford Woodruff recalled the Prophet's instructions given in March 26, 1844, just three months before his martyrdom:

> He stood upon his feet some three hours. The room was filled as with consuming fire, his face was as clear as amber, and he was clothed upon by the power of God. . . . "I have had sealed upon my head every key, every power, every principle of life and salvation that God has ever given to any man who ever lived upon the face of the earth. . . . Now," said he addressing the Twelve, "I have sealed upon your heads every key, every power, and every principle which the Lord has sealed upon my head. . . . I tell you, the burden of this kingdom now rests upon your shoulders; you have got to bear it off in all the world, and if you don't do it you will be damned."[38]

The Lord had explained that the Melchizedek Priesthood holds "the keys of all the spiritual blessings of the Church—to have the privilege of receiving the mysteries of the kingdom of heaven, to have the heavens opened" and thereby "to enjoy the communion and presence of God the Father, and Jesus the mediator of the new covenant" (D&C 107:18–19). Earlier, he had explained that this priesthood "holdeth the key of the mysteries of the kingdom, even the key of the knowledge of God," and specifically that "in the ordinances thereof, the power of godliness is manifest" (D&C 84:19–20). It is through the ordinances of the temple endowment and of eternal sealings, put in place through the Prophet Joseph Smith, that these promises are fulfilled.

During Joseph Smith's lifetime, a total of sixty-five living individuals (thirty-six men and twenty-nine women) received the endowment. Following the Prophet's martyrdom, when the Nauvoo Temple was sufficiently completed, some five thousand additional individuals received their endowment. But the Prophet had anticipated a further expansion of this work to include even performing these ordinances in behalf of the dead. Elder Wilford Woodruff recorded Joseph's words on January 21, 1844: "How are [the Saints] to become Saviors on Mount Zion? By building their temples, erecting their baptismal fonts, and going forth and receiving all the ordinances, baptisms, confirmations, washings, anointings, ordinations and sealing powers upon their heads, in behalf of all their progenitors who are dead, and redeem them that they may come forth in the first resurrection and be exalted to thrones of glory with them; and herein is the chain that binds the hearts of the fathers to the children, and the children to the fathers, which fulfills the mission of Elijah."[39]

In fulfillment of the Prophet's vision, the restoration of temple service continued. Endowments for the dead were inaugurated early in 1877. Then in 1894, when Church leaders were instructing the Saints to be sealed to their progenitors as far back as possible, an organization now known as the Family History Department was established to provide needed help with genealogical research. During the twentieth century, computers remarkably facilitated this work. As the twenty-first century was dawning, the Lord through President Gordon B. Hinckley made temples accessible in an unprecedented way to Latter-day Saints worldwide. All these developments built on the foundation established through the Prophet Joseph Smith.

NOTES

1. Gordon B. Hinckley, in Conference Report, October 1997, 68.
2. John L. Hart, "Chilly Morning Rites Start Temple," *Church News*, October 17, 1987, 3.
3. Joseph Smith, *History of the Church of Jesus Christ of Latter-day Saints*, ed. B. H. Roberts, 2nd ed. rev. (Salt Lake City: Deseret Book, 1960), 4:537.
4. Smith, *History of the Church*, 1:199.
5. Smith, *History of the Church*, 1:352.
6. Truman O. Angell Autobiographical Sketch, ms, L. Tom Perry Special Collections, Harold B. Lee Library, Brigham Young University, 3, quoted in Marvin E. Smith, "The Builder," *Improvement Era*, October 1942, 630.

7. Orson Pratt, May 5, 1870, in *Journal of Discourses,* 13:357; see also 14:273.

8. Karl Ricks Anderson, *Joseph Smith's Kirtland* (Salt Lake City: Deseret Book, 1989), 157.

9. Smith, *History of the Church,* 1:357–62.

10. Benjamin F. Johnson, *My Life's Review* (Mesa, AZ: 21st Century Printing, 1992), 16.

11. Smith, *History of the Church,* 1:349.

12. Smith, *History of the Church,* 2:167.

13. Heber C. Kimball, in *Journal of Discourses,* 10:165.

14. Kimball, in *Journal of Discourses,* 10:165.

15. Edward Tullidge, *The Women of Mormondom* (New York: Tullidge and Crandall, 1877), 76.

16. Smith, *History of the Church,* 2:379.

17. Smith, *History of the Church,* 2:381–82.

18. Smith, *History of the Church,* 2:428.

19. Brigham Young, in *Journal of Discourses,* 18:303.

20. Boyd K. Packer, *Holy Temple* (Salt Lake City: Bookcraft, 1980), 43.

21. Harold B. Lee, "Correlation and Priesthood Genealogy," address at Priesthood Genealogical Research Seminar, 1968 (Provo, UT: Brigham Young University Press, 1969), 60, quoted in Richard O. Cowan, *Temples to Dot the Earth* (Springville, UT: Cedar Fort, 1997), 33.

22. Brigham Young, in *Journal of Discourses,* 2:31.

23. Smith, *History of the Church,* 4:179; see also D&C 124:132.

24. Joseph Smith, *The Words of Joseph Smith,* comp. and ed. by Andrew F. Ehat and Lyndon W. Cook (Provo, UT: Religious Studies Center, Brigham Young University, 1980), 49.

25. Vilate Kimball to Heber Kimball, October 11, 1840, Church Archives, The Church of Jesus Christ of Latter-day Saints.

26. Smith, *History of the Church,* 4:426.

27. "A Most Glorious Principle," in *Children of the Covenant* (Salt Lake City: Genealogical Society of Utah, 1937), 129–30.

28. Wilford Woodruff, in *Journal of Discourses,* 5:85.

29. Sally Carlisle Randall to Betty Carlisle, Nauvoo, April 21, 1844, Church Archives.

30. J. Earl Arrington, "William Weeks, Architect of the Nauvoo Temple," *BYU Studies* 19 (Spring 1979): 340.

31. Smith, *History of the Church,* 6:196–97.

32. Smith, *History of the Church,* 4:329.

33. Smith, *History of the Church,* 4:446–47, 454, 486.

34. Smith, *History of the Church,* 5:1–2.

35. L. John Nuttall diary, February 7, 1877, quoted in *BYU Studies* 19 (Winter 1979): 159 fn.

36. Parley P. Pratt, *Autobiography of Parley Parker Pratt,* ed. Parley P. Pratt Jr. (Salt Lake City: Deseret Book, 1966), 297–98.

37. Orson Hyde, *Times and Seasons,* September 15, 1844, 651.

38. Wilford Woodruff, address given February 23, 1892, in Brian H. Stuy, comp., *Collected Discourses Delivered by President Wilford Woodruff, His Two Counselors, the Twelve Apostles, and Others* (Sandy, UT: B.H.S. Publishing, 1988), 383.

39. Smith, *History of the Church,* 6:184; compare *Wilford Woodruff's Journal,* January 21, 1844, 2:341–42.

CHAPTER EIGHT

"SOMETHING BETTER" FOR THE SISTERS: JOSEPH SMITH AND THE FEMALE RELIEF SOCIETY OF NAUVOO

JILL MULVAY DERR AND CAROL CORNWALL MADSEN

[1]One of the least-tapped sources in the ongoing effort to retrieve the teachings of the Prophet Joseph Smith is the minutes of the Nauvoo Relief Society, or, more properly, "A Record of the Organization, and Proceedings of The Female Relief Society of Nauvoo."[2] The six sermons the Prophet delivered to the women of the Church between March and August 1842 comprise the heart of this important and long-cherished document.[3] In these foundational sermons, Joseph Smith instructed women regarding "the order of the priesthood," including the keys, offices, ordinances, gifts, and blessings of the priesthood. He thereby prepared them to participate in the sacred ordinances to be administered in the Nauvoo Temple at its completion. He also encouraged the sisters in their important charitable work and expounded at length upon the broader meaning of charity.

Under Joseph Smith's direction, the Relief Society was organized midway through the seven years, 1839–46, that the Church located its headquarters and many of its members on a bend of the upper Mississippi River at Nauvoo, Illinois. The Society provided a unique forum for the Prophet Joseph's teachings, and his 1842 addresses to the women reflect both the sublime principles he taught his followers and the turmoil he experienced throughout that year. As

---

Jill Mulvay Derr is managing director of the Joseph Fielding Smith Institute for Latter-day Saint History at Brigham Young University.
Carol Cornwall Madsen is a senior research fellow at the Joseph Fielding Smith Institute for Latter-day Saint History at Brigham Young University.

disbelievers' unrelenting attempts to dismantle his work and impugn his claims conspired to draw the Prophet's focus to compelling legal and political matters during 1842, he remained undeterred from completing his commission to introduce the saving ordinances of the gospel to Church members, construct a temple wherein they could be administered, enlarge the Saints' understanding of vicarious work, deliver the keys of discernment between truth and error, and preach the nature of God, heaven, and earth. He organized the women of the Church "according to the law of heaven," as Elder John Taylor of the Quorum of Twelve Apostles explained,[4] and "in the Order of the Priesthood after the pattern of the Church," as Relief Society charter member Sarah Kimball recalled.[5]

Joseph Smith greeted the year 1842 with much optimism. He was delighted with the progress on the temple, where "the fulness of the gospel" could be restored. This was the day, he recorded, "in which the God of heaven has begun to restore the ancient order of His kingdom unto His servants and His people,—a day in which all things are concurring to bring about the completion of the fulness of the Gospel." He rejoiced that the people looked to the completion of the temple "as an event of the greatest importance to the Church and the world" and that they were willing to sacrifice to bring that day to pass.[6] Indeed, women's anticipated assistance in moving forward the work on the temple led to the establishment of the Relief Society.

Sarah M. Kimball's idea for a sewing society to provide clothing for construction workers on the Nauvoo Temple was probably informed by the benevolent societies that thrived throughout the United States during the early part of the nineteenth century. The writing of a constitution for the group by Sarah's friend Eliza R. Snow reflected practice well established in various associations in the new American republic. Upon seeing the women's constitution, however, Joseph Smith declared, "Tell the sisters their offering is accepted of the Lord, and He has something better for them."[7] They thus abandoned their original plans in favor of the Prophet's inspired design of organization. On Thursday afternoon, March 17, 1842, twenty women met with him in the "Lodge Room" above his red brick store to be organized after the pattern of the Church, with a president and counselors set apart by the laying on of hands.[8] Thirty-eight-year-old

Emma Hale Smith, Joseph's wife, was elected president.[9] Within six months, the members of the newly organized Relief Society learned what Joseph meant by "something better." The new Society served effectively as a charitable institution for the welfare of Church members.[10] But for society members themselves, it became a female "school of the prophets" wherein Joseph revealed important doctrine and instructions relating to their eternal welfare.

"The Society is not only to relieve the poor but to save souls," Joseph told the sisters when he addressed them on June 9, 1842.[11] With energy and clarity he taught them principles that would lead to salvation and the eternal duration of marriage and family relationships. Much as he had earlier instructed Church leaders and elders in the School of the Prophets preparatory to their receiving the endowment in the house of the Lord at Kirtland, Joseph instructed the sisters of the Relief Society preparatory to the completion of the Nauvoo Temple, where worthy women and men would receive the full endowment and sealing ordinances.[12]

Two of his sermons made explicit his plan to instruct the women in the blessings of the priesthood relating to the temple. At the first, delivered on March 30, he expressed concern over the rapid growth of the Relief Society, whose membership had increased by fifty-five. He had hoped, he said, that the Society would "grow up by degrees." It "should commence with a few individuals," he counseled, and "thus have a select Society of the virtuous and those who will walk circumspectly." He acceded to its rapid growth, but he advised: "Go into a close examination of every candidate." Subsequently each potential member was required to present a certificate attesting to her faithfulness and good character.[13] He charged the sisters to "purge out iniquity" and affirmed the importance of unity, counseling that "all must act in concert or nothing can be done."[14]

He announced that "the Society should move according to the ancient Priesthood." This, he declared, required "a select Society separate from all the evils of the world, choice, virtuous and holy."[15] This was the beginning of the Society's understanding of his repeated references to the "ancient Priesthood."

The "ancient Priesthood" to which he alluded is the patriarchal order of the Melchizedek Priesthood and its ordinances, with the covenant of marriage and the family unit at its center. President Ezra

Taft Benson explained: "The order of the priesthood spoken of in the scriptures is sometimes referred to as the patriarchal order because it came down from father to son. But this order is otherwise described in modern revelation as an order of family government where a man and a woman enter into a covenant with God—just as did Adam and Eve—to be sealed for eternity, to have posterity, and to do the will and work of God through their mortality."[16] The ancient priesthood was governed by keys representing God's authority, which "open God's greatest blessings, including the 'privilege of receiving the mysteries of the kingdom of heaven, . . . [and] the communion and presence of God the Father, and Jesus'" (D&C 107:19).[17] A revelation to Joseph Smith identified "the mysteries of the kingdom" as "the key to the knowledge of God," as manifest in the temple ordinances of the Melchizedek Priesthood (D&C 84:19–20). Thus, when the Prophet declared that Relief Society sisters "should move according to the ancient Priesthood," he invited them to prepare for the sacred ordinances to be administered in the temple. One by one through the holy endowment, these women would come to understand "the mysteries of the kingdom." As they were sealed with their husbands in the new and everlasting covenant of marriage, they would enter the patriarchal order of the Melchizedek Priesthood.

In this same sermon, Joseph repeated what he had proclaimed three months earlier in January. Looking forward to the completion of the temple, Joseph had rejoiced that God was initiating the restoration of "the ancient order of His kingdom" and the preparation of "the earth for the return of His glory . . . and a kingdom of Priests and kings to God and the Lamb, forever, on Mount Zion."[18] The organization of the Relief Society was instrumental in this restoration, for he intended, he said, "to make of this Society a kingdom of priests as in Enoch's day—as in Paul's day."[19] Women would be included in the anticipated temple blessings, which would distinguish Latter-day Saints as "a chosen generation, a royal priesthood, an holy nation, a peculiar people" (1 Peter 2:9). Their new organization was to be the vehicle by which the Prophet could nurture a society of holy women in God's kingdom. Eliza R. Snow, the secretary of the Nauvoo society, who became Relief Society president in Utah, made frequent references in her sermons to the connection between the Relief Society organization and the promises of the temple. In 1905 Bathsheba W. Smith, fourth general president of the Relief Society, also recalled that the Prophet Joseph "wanted to make us, as the women were in Paul's day, 'A Kingdom of priestesses.' We have that ceremony in our endowments as Joseph taught."[20]

At the Society's April 28 meeting, Joseph expanded on his earlier allusions to the temple. No other sermon he delivered to the Relief Society was as instructive or as spiritually expansive. His diary entry for that day records that "at Two o'clock after-noon met the members of the 'Female relief Society' and after presiding at the admission of many new members,[21] gave a lecture on the pries[t]hood shewing how the Sisters would come in possession of the privileges & blessings & gifts of the priesthood & that the signs should follow them. such as healing the sick casting out devils &c. & that they might attain unto these blessings, by a virtuous life & conversation & diligence in keeping all the commandments."[22]

Joseph Smith took as his text the twelfth chapter of 1 Corinthians, explicating Paul's discussion of spiritual gifts and the importance of all members of the body acting unitedly (see 1 Corinthians 12:14–31). Joseph emphasized how everyone, acting in his or her place, whatever the calling, was essential to building the kingdom. The words echoed his 1832 revelation on priesthood, which admonished "every man [to] stand in his own office, and labor in his own calling" (D&C 84:109).[23] Sensing his impending death, he explained to the sisters that "inasmuch as they would not long have him to instruct them," he was going "to point out the way for them to conduct [themselves] that they might act according to the word of God."[24] He urged them to be faithful and, especially, to be charitable, not only with their material means but also with their powers of forgiveness.[25] Joseph also counseled the women to take on the responsibility of their own salvation. "After this instruction," he declared, "you will be responsible for your own sins. It is an honor to save yourself—all are responsible to save themselves."[26] While this was not a new religious concept, there were, nonetheless, women who believed their salvation depended on the good works of their husbands. As late as 1878, for instance, Eliza R. Snow, meeting with members of the Spring City, Utah, ward Relief Society, felt constrained to clarify this misconception. "Joseph organized a female relief society according to the conmmagment [commandment] of

God," the minutes reported; "his wife Emma was pres and she [Eliza] was secretary some thought that the bretheren would save us and we had nothing to do but this was not the case we had just as much to do as they had and had as great labor to do and would receive just as much blessings."[27] An assertion of female moral agency and account- ability, Joseph Smith's admonition led women to a path of spiritual maturity and independence in making choices for themselves and accepting responsibility for their own spiritual progression.

Joseph Smith then reflected on Paul's discourse on gifts of the Spirit in 1 Corinthians and on the Savior's promise regarding such gifts as found in the Gospel of Mark. "The time had not been before," Joseph said, "that these things could be in their proper order," but now, he continued, "no matter who believeth; these signs, such as healing the sick, casting out devils &c. should follow all that believe whether male or female."[28] A revelation Joseph received concerning spiritual gifts in March 1831 expanded upon the gifts listed by the Apostle Paul, emphasizing that "these gifts come from God, for the benefit of the children of God" (D&C 46:26). Like the blessings of the priesthood, spiritual gifts accompanied and indeed testified of the return of the gospel of Christ to the earth. These gifts had been abun- dantly manifest in the house of the Lord in Kirtland, and Joseph surely anticipated the presence of such gifts in the temple at Nauvoo.[29]

After sustaining the exercise of this kind of charismatic expres- sion, Joseph returned to the topic with which he began and admon- ished Relief Society sisters to "stand and act in the place appointed, and thus sanctify the Society and get it pure." He reiterated, "Every one should aspire only to magnify his own office." He exhorted the women: "You need not be tearing [down] men for their deeds, but let the weight of innocence be felt; . . . Not war, not jangle, not contra- diction, but meekness, love, purity, these are the things that should magnify us." To do like Jesus, he counseled, "you must enlarge your souls toward others" and "carry your fellow creatures to Abram's bosom."[30] Joseph's discussion of spiritual gifts, like that of the Apostle Paul, concluded with an emphasis on charity (see 1 Corinthians 13). It was a theme to which Joseph would repeatedly return.

In his April 28 sermon to the sisters, Joseph anticipated the com- pletion of the temple and alluded to its blessings for women. "The church is not now organized in its proper order, and cannot be until the Temple is completed," he declared. He was anxious to prepare the Saints for that great event. Exhorting the sisters to "concentrate their faith and prayers and confidence in those whom God has appointed to lead," Joseph explained that "the keys of the kingdom are about to be given them, that they may be able to detect every thing false— as well as to the Elders." These promised keys gave recipients the power of discernment, a gift of deep importance to Joseph.[31] He explained that he was delivering the keys "to this Society and to the Church" because "the world would not be troubled with him a great while." The sense of foreboding in his words was long remembered by Bathsheba W. Smith, who recalled that the Prophet had offered the invocation at the meeting, his voice trembling as he spoke, and that later in the meeting he had said that according to his prayer, "God had appointed him elsewhere." He even repeated the prophecy, declaring, "According to my prayer I will not be with you long to teach and instruct you."[32] This foreboding underscored his urgency to teach the culminating doctrines of priesthood.[33]

At the end of this long and historic sermon, Joseph once again promised the sisters future blessings for their faithfulness. "I now turn the key to you in the name of God," he declared, "and this Society shall rejoice and knowledge and intelligence shall flow down from this time—this is the beginning of better days to this Society." With those words Joseph metaphorically opened the door to spiritual knowledge and blessings for women.[34] He had employed nearly identical words in addressing the Kirtland elders quorum prior to the first missionary efforts in Europe: "This night the key is turned to the nations."[35] His brother Hyrum later invited Saints remaining in Kirtland to travel to Nauvoo to build the temple "wherein their dead may be redeemed, and the key of knowledge that unfolds the dispensation of the fulness of times may be turned, and the mysteries of God be unfolded."[36] The unfolding "mysteries of God" and "knowledge and intelligence" flowing down from heaven would teach the repentant and faithful how to attain eternal life, life in the presence of God. "If you live up to your privileges," Joseph promised the women that day, "the angels cannot be restrain'd from being your associates—females, if they are pure and innocent can come into the presence of God."[37]

The effect of Joseph's words upon the women was stunning. Nancy Alexander Tracy testified that when Joseph spoke "he was so full of the spirit of the Holy Ghost that his frame shook and his face shone and looked almost transparent."[38] Mercy Thompson remembered that Joseph gave "directions and counsels to the sisters calculated to inspire them to efforts which would lead to celestial glory and exaltation."[39] Two priesthood leaders added their witness to Joseph Smith's instruction preparing the sisters to receive in the temple the priesthood ordinances and blessings that would in turn prepare them to "see the face of God" (D&C 84:22–23).

In the afternoon of May 27, the women convened in the "Grove" in Nauvoo because the upper room in Joseph's store had accommodated so few of them the day before. Bishop Newel K. Whitney attended the meeting with Joseph, explaining that he had come purposely to hear the Prophet speak. But it was Bishop Whitney who delivered the sermon that day, not the Prophet, who was unwell. The bishop exuberantly confirmed Joseph's promise in turning the key of knowledge and intelligence. "I rejoice that God has given us means whereby we may get intelligence and instruction," he declared, admonishing the sisters, "Rejoice in the prospect of what lays before."[40] Just three weeks earlier, on May 4, Whitney and eight other men had met with Joseph in the upper room of the red brick store to be instructed by the Prophet in "the principles and order of the Priesthood," the initiation of the ritual of the full endowment. On that occasion the Prophet revealed for the first time the saving ordinances of the gospel, which, he promised, would be administered to all the Saints when the temple was completed. To ensure that the ordinances of salvation and the keys of authority would be delivered to the Church, and that a corps of men and women would be ordained to administer these ordinances, the Prophet Joseph, aware of the precarious state of his own safety, taught and performed these vital temple rites before the temple was completed.[41]

Bishop Whitney affirmed the importance of the Relief Society as a vehicle for the sisters to "prepare for those blessings which God is soon to bestow upon us." "It becomes us to prepare," he advised, "by striving for union one with another." In the creation of man, both male and female, he continued, God bestowed "certain blessings peculiar to a man of God, of which woman partook, so that without the female all things cannot be restor'd to earth—it takes all to restore the Priesthood."[42] This affirmation came from Whitney's new understanding of the temple-based patriarchal order of the Melchizedek Priesthood, whose blessings are bestowed only on husbands and wives together. Only in union, Whitney had recently learned, could a man or woman attain the highest degree of the celestial kingdom (see D&C 132:19–20). Bishop Whitney echoed the Prophet's admonition to the women to bridle their tongues, for "it is impossible while finding fault with one another to be united." He counseled: "Throw the vail [*sic*] of charity over failings. . . . We may have different views of things," but "by bringing our minds and wills into subjection to the law of the Lord, [we] may come to unity." In closing his remarks, he again fervently assured the women, "There are great blessings before [you], that would astonish you if you could behold them." After again pleading for unity, he reiterated his promise that there were "blessings before [us] to be confer'd as soon as our hearts are prepar'd to receive them."

Reynolds Cahoon, a member of the temple building committee, confirmed the transcendent purpose of the Relief Society as taught by the Prophet in the spring of 1842. He expressed his sentiments during an August 13, 1843, visit to the Society: "You knew [no] doubt but this society is raisd by the Lord to prepare us for the great blessings which are for us in the House of the Lord in the Temple." Cahoon anticipated, as had Whitney, the blessings a united man and woman would receive through the sealing ordinances of the temple, and he bore witness of the distinctive and integral importance of Relief Society in relation to those blessings: "There are many Benevolent Societies abroad designd to do good but not as this ours is according to the order of God connected with the priesthood according to the same good principals & knowledge will grow out of it. . . . The Order of the Priesthood is not complete without it."[43]

In September 1843, shortly after the visit of Reynolds Cahoon, Joseph Smith's promises of the previous year reached fruition when a number of Relief Society women were introduced to the temple ceremony, Emma Smith being the first. Eventually numbering about sixty-five, these men and women met regularly with the Prophet to learn and understand the significance of the temple ordinances and to be prepared to administer the ordinances to others upon completion of the temple. Bathsheba W. Smith, an original member of the Relief Society, recalled that she "received her endowment in the upper room over the Prophet Joseph Smith's store. The endowments," she said, "were given under the direction of the Prophet Joseph Smith, who afterwards gave us a lecture or instructions in regard to the endowment ceremonies." She frequently reflected on the unique opportunity of being "led and taught . . . by the Prophet himself who explained and enlarged wonderfully upon every point as they passed along the way."[44]

The Prophet's spring 1842 sermons to the Relief Society prepared women to receive the sacred priesthood ordinances that bound men and women to God and to one another, the culminating act of unity so urgently stressed by Joseph in his visits to the Relief Society. Despite a year fraught with lawsuits, writs, and accusations, and against a backdrop of continual harassment and uncertainty, Joseph pressed on to complete his prophetic mission.[45]

When Joseph met with the Relief Society again on June 9, 1842, he addressed a second theme of his counsel to the women, the meaning of charity as Paul had explained it to the Corinthians (see 1 Corinthians 13). Joseph's sermon expanded on Paul's admonition and urged the women to exercise mercy and forgiveness as central to their charitable mission. His sermon was extraordinary when one considers the harassment and persecution he had undergone in the twelve years of his ministry. In his last sermons, particularly, the sisters came to know a tender and sensitive prophet as he revealed one of the driving forces of his nature. Having faced ridicule, hostility, spurious legal encounters, and outright persecution since he was fourteen, Joseph still emphasized mercy and forgiveness. He reminded the sisters of the counsel he had written to the Saints three years earlier while he was incarcerated in Missouri's Liberty Jail. Men cannot be compelled into the kingdom of God, he told the sisters, "but must be dealt with in long suff'ring and at last we shall save them,"[46] a reiteration of his counsel that those exercising priesthood influence must work "by persuasion, by long-suffering, by gentleness and meekness, and by love unfeigned" (D&C 121:41).

It grieved him, he said, that the Society did not reflect a fuller fellowship and instructed the members to overlook "small things" with eyes of mercy. "If one member suffer all feel it," he attested, and only "by union of feeling we obtain pow'r with God." Kindness, charity, love, and mercy were the virtues he invoked as characteristics of the godly. "Nothing is so much calculated to lead people to forsake sin as to take them by the hand and watch over them with tenderness," he observed. "When persons manifest the least kindness and love to me, O what pow'r it has over my mind." "If you would have God have mercy on you," he asserted, "have mercy on one another." While there should be no license for sin, he once again counseled, "mercy should go hand in hand with reproof." His words were a sharp deterrent to zealotry and an impassioned plea for empathy.[47]

When Joseph met again with the Relief Society many weeks later, it was obvious that a summer filled with opposition, disloyalty, threats, and disaffection had taken its toll.[48] No one, however, expected it to be the last time he would speak to the members. As they gathered together in the grove on the last day of August 1842, they saw a solemn and introspective prophet. His first words at that late summer meeting were those of gratitude that despite the exertions made by his enemies, "God had enabled him to keep out of their hands." He said, "All the fuss and all the stir against me, is like the jack in the lantern, it cannot be found." He continued, "Altho' I do wrong, I do not the wrongs that I am charg'd with doing—the wrong that I do is thro' the frailty of human nature like other men. No man lives without fault." Opposition, he noted, merely increased as the work went forward. "When I do the best I can—when I am accomplishing the greatest good," he lamented, "then the most evils are got up against me."[49] Because of the disaffection of men he once trusted, both in Missouri and in Illinois, Joseph treasured those who remained faithful. He took comfort in the promise the Lord had made to him during the harsh months he spent in Liberty Jail: "Thy friends do stand by thee, and they shall hail thee again with warm hearts and friendly hands" (D&C 121:9). During this tense period of religious turmoil and legal distraction, he felt the spiritual buoyancy that love and loyalty could produce, and he chose to record the names of the faithful in his history. "These," he wrote, "I have met in prosperity, and they were my friends; and I now meet them in adversity, and they are still my warmer friends. These love the God that I serve; they love the truths that I promulgate; they love those virtuous, and those holy doctrines that I cherish in my bosom with the warmest feelings of my heart, and with that zeal which cannot be denied. I love friendship and truth; I love virtue and law."[50]

The members of the Relief Society, more than one thousand by the time of Joseph's martyrdom in 1844, provided an arsenal of female friends, ready to follow, honor, and defend him.[51] "The Society has done well," he declared on August 31. "Their principles are to practice holiness." Though he would not attend another meeting, he was confident that the Relief Society was firmly established and that it would follow the course on which it had been launched. His last words to the Society bespoke the burden he shouldered in combating the forces so persistently marshaled against him and the Church. But he also prophetically proclaimed that the Church would survive and surmount all opposition. "It will be but a little season," he reassured the women on that warm August day, "and all these afflictions will be turn'd away from us inasmuch as we are faithful and are not overcome by these evils. By seeing the blessings of the endowment rolling on, and the kingdom increasing and spreading from sea to sea; we will rejoice that we were not overcome by these foolish things."[52] These words would be remembered when the Church, once again, was forced to move by intolerant neighbors, this time a thousand miles to the west, where it would finally establish a permanent home.

During that one brief season in 1842, Joseph laid the foundation for women's responsibility in the mission of the Church. Moreover, for Joseph, the Relief Society had been not only a venue for religious instruction but also a respite from the barrage of disparagement that constantly plagued him. His message to the women was always one of inclusiveness; they were integral to the Church and its mission of salvation to humankind. In the twenty-three-year hiatus until 1867, when the Relief Society began to be reinstated Churchwide in Utah,[53] that conviction remained steady and became the kingpin on which the Relief Society functioned for decades thereafter. The symbiotic relationship between the Relief Society and the temple, which Joseph had established, was evident in the appointment of the next three Relief Society presidents—Eliza R. Snow, Zina D. H. Young, and Bathsheba W. Smith—to serve simultaneously as both Relief Society president and head of female temple workers.[54]

The Nauvoo minutes were sacred to the Relief Society and were read in women's conferences and repeatedly printed in the *Woman's Exponent*. A symbolic rendering of the "key" graced Relief Society halls at the fiftieth commemoration of its organization. And no one kept alive the spirit of Joseph's ennobling words more than Eliza R. Snow, the secretary who had carefully recorded his sermons to women and preserved the minutes on the trek to Utah: "The Relief Society is at the head of all womanhood upon the earth," she declared to the women of the Smithfield, Utah, Relief Society in 1878. "We are laying the foundation for the salvation of all women," she reminded them, "and if you are faithful you will be over all women. . . . Let us live up to the missions we took upon ourselves before we came here."[55]

Joseph's teachings to the Relief Society during that summer of 1842 vitalized a whole generation of Latter-day Saint women and provided a pattern for religious expression that reached well into the future and far beyond the design of other religious and charitable societies. He did indeed have "something better" for them. Affording a text for the development of the organization and a record of Joseph's counsel, the Nauvoo minutes also provide valued insight into the character of the Prophet himself. During that year of stress and anxiety he was yet able to remain calm and continue in his mission to establish the kingdom. Nothing thwarted this commitment. He created a unified body of Latter-day Saints, who were firm in their own convictions but merciful to the wayward or uncommitted, underscoring all his teachings to the Relief Society. He not only taught the members principles that would lead to their exaltation in the life to come but also gave them a pattern of living in this one. Moreover, as one account asserts, "under his trials the Prophet seem[ed] to have grown more tender-hearted, more universal in his sympathies."[56] The challenges he faced, instead of agitating or dismaying him, seemed to transmit a calm and reflective mood in which he expressed deeply felt affection for the friends and family who had been loyal to him under all the trying circumstances. The minutes of the Female Relief Society of Nauvoo are a fruitful document, offering evidence of the extraordinary purpose of the Relief Society, additional understanding of Joseph's teachings and deeper insight into his character. It is little wonder that this record was regarded with such reverence and preserved with such foresight.

NOTES

1. Portions of the text and notes for this article will be expanded in a forthcoming edition of "A Record of the Organization and Proceedings of the Female Relief Society of Nauvoo" and other Relief Society documents, edited and annotated by the authors.

2. "A Record of the Organization and Proceedings of the Female Relief Society of Nauvoo," holograph (hereafter cited as Female Relief Society of Nauvoo, Minutes), Archives of the Family and Church History Department, The Church of Jesus Christ of Latter-day Saints, Salt Lake City, hereafter cited as Church Archives.

3. Excerpts from Joseph Smith's sermons to the women were edited and published in Joseph Smith, *History of the Church of Jesus Christ of Latter-day Saints,* ed. B. H. Roberts, 2nd ed. rev. (Salt Lake City: Deseret Book, 1948–57), 4:570–71, 602–7. *The Words of Joseph Smith: The Contemporary Accounts of the Nauvoo Discourses of Joseph Smith,* comp. and ed. Andrew F. Ehat and Lyndon W. Cook (Provo, UT: Religious Studies Center, Brigham Young University, 1980) reproduces the six sermons from the original record. Jill Mulvay Derr, Janath Russell Cannon, and Maureen Ursenbach Beecher, *Women of Covenant: The Story of Relief Society* (Salt Lake City: Deseret Book, 1992), 23–58, includes a lengthy discussion of the sermons and much recent scholarship on Mormon women quotes from the sermons. For example, see Carol Cornwall Madsen, "Mormon Women and the Temple: Toward a New Understanding," in *Sisters in Spirit: Mormon Women in Historical and Cultural Perspective,* ed. Maureen Ursenbach Beecher and Lavina Fielding Anderson (Urbana and Chicago: University of Illinois Press), 80–110.

4. Female Relief Society of Nauvoo, Minutes, March 17, 1842.

5. Sarah M. Kimball, Reminiscence, March 17, 1882, National Women's Relief Society Record, 1880–1892, Church Archives.

6. Smith, *History of the Church,* 4:492.

7. Sarah M. Kimball, Reminiscence, March 17, 1882, National Women's Relief Society Record, 1880–1892. "Sarah M. Kimball," in Augusta Joyce Crocheron, *Representative Women of Deseret, A Book of Biographical Sketches* (Salt Lake City: J. C. Graham & Co., 1884): 27. See also Derr, Cannon, and Beecher, *Women of Covenant,* 26–27.

8. Some official histories indicate that only eighteen women attended the initial meeting. However, as Maureen Ursenbach has shown, the names of two women have been crossed out in the original record: Athalia Rigdon Robinson and Nancy Rigdon, daughters of

Sidney Rigdon (Female Relief Society of Nauvoo, Minutes, March 17, 1842). Apparently their names were "blotted out" when they followed their father out of the Church (Alma 5:57; 6:3; see Maureen Ursenbach Beecher and James L. Kimball Jr., "The First Relief Society: A Diversity of Women," *Ensign*, March 1979, 25–29; also Derr, Cannon, and Beecher, *Women of Covenant*, 27–28). News of the woman's society traveled quickly through Nauvoo largely due to women who urged their neighbors and family members to join. See Beecher and James L. Kimball Jr., "The First Relief Society: A Diversity of Women," and Maurine Carr Ward, "'This Institution Is a Good One': The Female Relief Society of Nauvoo, 17 March 1842 to 16 March 1844," *Mormon Historical Studies* 3, no. 2 (Fall 2002): 86–203, which includes a list of members and describes family connections.

9. Joseph Smith explained that this was the office to which Emma had already been ordained twelve years earlier when she had received a blessing by revelation at his hands, later canonized as section 25 of the Doctrine and Covenants. Joseph read the revelation to the assembled women and explained that Emma's election to preside was a manifestation of her calling in the revelation as an "elect lady" (see D&C 25:3). Joseph Smith's journal, written by his scribe Willard Richards, indicates: "[I] shewed that *Elect* meant to be *Elected to a certain work* &,& and that the revelation was then fulfilled by Sister Emma's Election to the Presidency of the Soc[i]ety, having previously been ordained to expound the scriptures. her councillors were ordained by Elder J<ohn> Taylor & Emma <was> Blessed by the same" (Dean C. Jessee, *Papers of Joseph Smith*, vol. 2, "Journal, 1832–1842" [Salt Lake City: Deseret Book, 1992], 371).

10. The women's collectivized humanitarian efforts far exceeded unorganized individual aid in scope and regularity and became a primary conduit of social welfare during the two years the Relief Society functioned in Nauvoo. At the end of the first year Eliza R. Snow, elected secretary of the Society at its first meeting, compiled a report of the Society's operations, which showed that $507 had been collected in donations and $306 spent in charitable work, leaving a balance of $200, only $29 of which was cash ("Female Relief Society," Annual Report, from March 16 [*sic*], 1842, to March 16, 1843, *Times and Seasons*, August 1, 1843, 287).

11. Female Relief Society of Nauvoo, Minutes, March 30, 1842.

12. The endowment, bestowed only to the elders in the Kirtland Temple, was partial or preliminary; the full endowment, for all worthy members, was revealed and introduced in Nauvoo. See Alma P. Burton, "Endowment," in *Encyclopedia of Mormonism*, 2: 454–56.

13. Female Relief Society of Nauvoo, Minutes, March 30, 1842. In a

sketch of the Relief Society organization, Eliza R. Snow wrote: "The Society soon became so popular that even those of doubtful character in several instances applied for admission, and to prevent imposition by extending membership to such ones inadvertently, stricter rules were adopted than seemed requisite at first. Each one wishing to join the Society was required to present a certificate of her good moral character, signed by two or more responsible persons" ("The Female Relief Society: A Brief Sketch of Its Organization and Workings in the City of Nauvoo, Hancock Co., Ill.," *Woman's Exponent*, June 15, 1872, 8). The need for such a "recommendation" prefigures the recommendation later required for temple admittance.

14. Female Relief Society of Nauvoo, Minutes, March 30, 1842. See also Doctrine and Covenants 38:37; 105:104–5.

15. Female Relief Society of Nauvoo, Minutes, March 30, 1842.

16. Ezra Taft Benson, "What I Hope You Will Teach Your Children about the Temple," *Ensign*, August 1985, 9.

17. Victor L. Ludlow, "Priesthood in Biblical Times," in *Encyclopedia of Mormonism*, ed. Daniel H. Ludlow (New York: Macmillan, 1992), 3:1138–40.

18. Smith, *History of the Church*, 4:492–93.

19. Female Relief Society of Nauvoo, Minutes, March 30, 1842.

20. "Relief Society Reports" [Pioneer Stake], *Woman's Exponent*, July and August 1905, 14. See also "Relief Society Conference," *Woman's Exponent*, October 1 and 15, 1902, 37. Bathsheba Smith was one of a number of men and women who received their temple endowments from Joseph Smith before the Nauvoo Temple was completed (Andrew F. Ehat, "Joseph Smith's Introduction of Temple Ordinances and the 1844 Mormon Succession Question" [MA thesis, Brigham Young University, 1981], 107).

21. By this time the Society numbered more than two hundred members. All, however, following Joseph's injunction, had to be admitted by recommend attesting to their faithfulness and good character. As young Talitha Garlick explained, "There was no Society for the young people at that time, so I, as did all the other girls, who wanted and were *worthy*, joined the Relief Society" ("Talitha [Talitha Cumi Garlick Avery Cheney]," in "Eight Pioneer Autobiographies," *Our Pioneer Heritage*, ed. Kate B. Carter [Salt Lake City: Daughters of Utah Pioneers, 1971], 15:118).

22. From the diary of Wilford Woodruff, as quoted in Jessee, *The Papers of Joseph Smith*, 2:378–79. See also Smith, *History of the Church*, 4:602–8, wherein some modifications occur. Reaffirming Joseph Smith's intent, Elder Bruce R. McConkie of the Quorum of the Twelve declared in 1978 at the dedication of the Nauvoo

Monument to Women: "Where spiritual things are concerned, as pertaining to all of the gifts of the Spirit, with reference to the receipt of revelation, the gaining of testimonies, and the seeing of visions, in all matters that pertain to godliness and holiness and which are brought to pass as a result of personal righteousness—in all these things men and women stand in a position of absolute equality before the Lord." ("Our Sisters from the Beginning," *Ensign* 9 [January 1979]:61.)

23. See Derr, Cannon, and Beecher, *Women of Covenant,* 44; and Kathryn H. Shirts, "Priesthood and Salvation: Is D&C 84 a Revelation for Women Too?" *Sunstone* 15 (September 1991): 20-27.

24. Female Relief Society of Nauvoo, Minutes, April 28, 1842. Joseph Smith made frequent allusions, during this period, to his impending death (see Ronald K. Esplin, "Joseph Smith's Mission and Timetable: 'God Will Protect Me until My Work Is Done,'" in *The Prophet Joseph: Essays on the Life and Mission of Joseph Smith,* ed. Larry C. Porter and Susan Easton Black [Salt Lake City: Deseret Book, 1988], 280–319).

25. He was an experienced mentor. Even as he had languished in Missouri's Liberty Jail, aching from the betrayal of so many of his "friends," his charitable nature had not failed him. He wrote to the Church during those dark days in Missouri, "Let thy bowels also be full of charity towards all men, and to the household of faith" (D&C 121:45).

26. Female Relief Society of Nauvoo, Minutes, April 28, 1842. Joseph Smith had first enunciated this principle just a month earlier in two of the Articles of Faith he had written in answer to a request by newspaper editor John Wentworth. The second Article states that "men will be punished for their own sins and not for Adam's transgression" and the third, that "through the Atonement of Christ, all mankind may be saved by obedience to the laws and ordinances of the Gospel" ("Church History," *Times and Seasons,* March 1, 1842, 709).

27. Spring City [Utah] Ward, Sanpete North Stake, Relief Society Minutes, 1878-1901, vol. 2, June 23, 1878, Church Archives.

28. Female Relief Society of Nauvoo, Minutes, April 28, 1842.

29. Joseph Smith joyfully greeted the proliferation of spiritual gifts. "To witness and feel with our own natural senses, the like glorious manifestations of the power of the priesthood; the gifts and blessings of the Holy Ghost; and the good and condescension of a merciful God . . . combined to create within us sensations of rapturous gratitude, and inspire us with fresh zeal and energy, in the cause of truth," he wrote of spiritual manifestations experienced at the first Church conference in June 1830. The next month he found his "faith

much strengthened, concerning dreams and visions in the last days, foretold by the ancient Prophet Joel [2:28]" ("History of Joseph Smith," *Times and Seasons,* December 1, 1842, 23, and February 1, 1843, 92). See Steven C. Harper, "'A Pentecost and Endowment Indeed': Six Eyewitness Accounts of the Kirtland Temple Experience," in *Opening the Heavens: Accounts of Divine Manifestations, 1820–1844,* ed. John W. Welch (Provo, UT: Brigham Young University; Salt Lake City: Deseret Book, 2005), 327–71. For accounts of women exercising spiritual gifts, see Derr, Cannon, and Beecher, *Women of Covenant,* 13, 45, 68, 90, and 219–22, 429–30.

30. Female Relief Society of Nauvoo Minutes, April 28, 1842.

31. Three weeks earlier, Joseph had written a lengthy editorial for the *Times and Seasons* on the gift of discernment, and three days after this meeting Joseph Smith spoke to a public gathering in Nauvoo "on the keys of the kingdom," and stated, "The keys are certain signs and words by which false spirits and personages may be detected from true, which cannot be revealed to the Elders till the Temple is completed" (*History of the Church,* 4:608; see also *The Words of Joseph Smith,* 119).

32. "Recollections of the Prophet Joseph Smith," *Juvenile Instructor,* June 1892, 345. Female Relief Society of Nauvoo, Minutes, April 28, 1842, read: "That according to his prayers God had appointed him elsewhere."

33. Esplin discusses Joseph Smith's sense of urgency in "Joseph Smith's Mission and Timetable, 'God Will Protect Me until My Work Is Done.'"

34. Derr, Cannon, and Beecher, *Women of Covenant,* 46–50, discusses some interpretations of the statement. In later years many Latter-day Saints maintained that Joseph Smith's 1842 "turning the key" to women opened opportunities for secular knowledge and advancement and that the proximity between the first woman's rights convention in Seneca Falls, New York, in 1848, and the organization of the Relief Society six years earlier was no coincidence.

35. Quoted in Lyndon W. Cook and Milton V. Backman Jr., eds., *Kirtland Elders' Quorum Record, 1836–1841* (Provo, UT: Grandin Books, 1985), 6–7.

36. "Kirtland Conference Minutes," *Times and Seasons,* November 15, 1841, 589. In a later effort toward clarification, the 1854 Church history compilation project, headed by Church Historian George A. Smith, a member of the Quorum of the Twelve, renders the phrase from the Relief Society minutes, "I now turn the key *in your behalf*" (*History of the Church,* 4:607; emphasis added; see Derr, Cannon, and Beecher, *Women of Covenant,* 74).

37. Female Relief Society of Nauvoo, Minutes, April 28, 1842.

38. "Incidents, Travel, and Life of Nancy Naomi Alexander Tracy," 24–25, Church Archives.

39. Mercy Thompson, "Recollections of the Prophet Joseph Smith," *Juvenile Instructor,* July 1892, 399.

40. Female Relief Society of Nauvoo, Minutes, May 27, 1842. Newel K. Whitney (1795–1850) was a Presiding Bishop of the Church and the husband of Relief Society counselor Elizabeth Ann Whitney. Both had joined the Church in Kirtland, Ohio, and developed a close, loving friendship with Joseph and Emma Smith. Bishop Whitney had been a successful merchant in Kirtland, and managed Joseph Smith's store in Nauvoo.

41. Joseph instructed that group of men "in the principles and order of the Priesthood, attending to washings, anointings, endowments and the communication of keys pertaining to the Aaronic Priesthood, and so on to the highest order of the Melchisedek Priesthood. . . . In this council was instituted the ancient order of things for the first time in these last days." Bishop Whitney and others in the first group were aware that "there was nothing made known to these men but what will be made known to all the Saints of the last days, so soon as they are prepared to receive and a proper place is prepared to communicate them" (*History of the Church,* 5:2). The circle of those who received the ordinance through Joseph Smith gradually expanded and was known as the "Holy Order." Emma Smith received her endowment September 23, 1843, the first woman to enter the "Holy Order" (see Madsen, "Mormon Women and the Temple," 85–88, from Andrew F. Ehat, "Joseph Smith's Introduction of Temple Ordinances and the 1844 Mormon Succession Question," Master's thesis, Brigham Young University, 1981, 107).

42. The ancient or patriarchal order of the Melchizedek Priesthood is "an order of family government" (Benson, "What I Hope You Will Teach Your Children about the Temple," 9). According to Elder James E. Talmage, through "the ordinances pertaining to the House of the Lord, woman shares with man the blessings of the Priesthood . . . seeing and understanding alike, and cooperating to the full in the government of their family kingdom" (*Young Woman's Journal,* October 1914, 602–3). The blessings of this order of the priesthood are given only to husbands and wives together, as explained by Lynn A. McKinlay, "Patriarchal Order of the Priesthood," in *Encyclopedia of Mormonism,* 3:1067. In 1839 Joseph Smith admonished his apostles to "go to and finish the temple, and God will fill it with power, and you will then receive more knowledge concerning this priesthood" (*History of the Church,* 5:555; see D&C 107:18–20). As Bruce R. McConkie explained, men and women who are married in the temple "in the new and everlasting

covenant of marriage . . . enter into the patriarchal order . . . [and] reap the full blessings of patriarchal heirship in eternity where the patriarchal order will be the order of government and rule" (*Mormon Doctrine*, 2nd ed. [Salt Lake City: Bookcraft, 1966], 559).

43. Female Relief Society of Nauvoo, Minutes, August 13, 1843.

44. Bathsheba W. Smith, Diary, typescript, Church Archives. She also made a number of other public statements about her involvement in this endowment group. Some can be found in *Blood Atonement and the Origin of Plural Marriage* (Independence, MO: Zion's Printing and Publishing, n.d.), 87–88; N. B. Lundwall, comp., *Temples of the Most High* (Salt Lake City: Bookcraft, 1941), 246; "Latter-day Temples," *Relief Society Magazine*, April 1917, 185–86; Augusta Joyce Crocheron, *Representative Women of Deseret: A Book of Biographical Sketches* (Salt Lake City: J. C. Graham, 1884), 45; and Nauvoo Endowment Record, 1, Church Archives.

45. Nauvoo, as noted by historians Lyndon Cook and Andrew Ehat, was the final setting for this expansive teaching, producing "a quantum increase of light" (*The Words of Joseph Smith*, 84).

46. Relief Society of Nauvoo, Minutes, June 9, 1842; see D&C 121, especially verses 37–46.

47. Relief Society of Nauvoo, Minutes, June 9, 1842.

48. For details of the events plaguing Joseph during this time see Smith, *History of the Church*, 5:67–108. In response to the writs of extradition to Missouri on charges of complicity in the murder of former governor Lilburn Boggs, the City Council, the Relief Society, Joseph's wife Emma, and other individuals had all sent petitions to Illinois governor Thomas Carlin asking for his protection. Only dismissal of the case kept Joseph in Illinois.

49. Relief Society of Nauvoo, Minutes, August 31, 1842.

50. Smith, *History of the Church*, 5:108. Joseph writes specific words of tribute to several of his friends and lists the names of others, as recorded in *History of the Church*, 5:108–9.

51. According to Maurine Ward's careful examination of the names recorded, membership numbered 1,331 (Ward, "The Female Relief Society of Nauvoo," 88).

52. Relief Society of Nauvoo, Minutes, August 31, 1842.

53. The last meeting of the Female Relief Society of Nauvoo was on March 16, 1844. Activity resumed briefly in Utah from 1854 to 1858 but waned when ward organizations were disrupted by the coming of Johnston's Army to Utah. The Relief Society was permanently reestablished after Brigham Young's call to bishops to organize ward societies in December 1867, and Eliza R. Snow's work with local bishops to bring ward organizations to pass, beginning

in April 1868 (see Derr, Cannon, and Beecher, *Women of Covenant,* 59–126).

54. The fifth general president, Emmeline B. Wells, was a veteran of Nauvoo but arrived in that city too late to join the Relief Society. She was, nonetheless, well versed in the minutes, which she copied into her own notebook, and its activities, as related by Elizabeth Ann Whitney, Emma Smith's counselor.

55. Smithfield Ward Relief Society, Minutes, "Minutes of a Special Meeting Held in the School House, 12 May 1878," Church Archives; see also Smithfield Ward Relief Society, Minutes, October 26, 1885, Church Archives. Snow recorded all of Joseph Smith's sermons to the women, though other women, such as Phebe M. Wheeler and Hannah Ells, penned minutes after the Relief Society began meeting in ward units in July 1843. Relief Society of Nauvoo, Minutes.

56. Some of these characteristics are enumerated in Smith, *History of the Church,* 5:xxviii.

CHAPTER NINE

"NOW THIS CAUSED US TO MARVEL": THE BREADTH OF GOD'S HEAVEN AND THE DEPTH OF HIS MERCY

GUY L. DORIUS

The dawning of this dispensation had as its catalyst Joseph Smith's yearnings to know where he stood in the sight of God. His desires came from both his family heritage and the religious environment of his youth. As with most of us, no doctrine had a more powerful pull upon him than the understanding of how to get to heaven, or at least how to improve one's standing with God. There is ample evidence that the Restoration instilled in Joseph an understanding of the Atonement and its reach, which caused him to marvel not only for himself and his family but for all mankind. These new insights reversed the sectarian notions of his day and substantiated many of the ideas that he and his forefathers had about the eternal heavens. As we come to understand the fertile soil in which the doctrines of the Restoration were planted, none of the doctrines blossom more beautifully than those of the Atonement and the salvation offered to all people.

A RELIGIOUS ENVIRONMENT

Joseph Smith found himself in a religious environment that was fueled by a contest for adherents to the various sects. As Joseph himself stated:

Guy L. Dorius is an associate professor of Church history and doctrine at Brigham Young University.

> There was in the place where we lived an unusual excite-
> ment on the subject of religion. . . . Indeed, the whole dis-
> trict of country seemed affected by it, and great multitudes
> united themselves to the different religious parties, which
> created no small stir and division amongst the people, some
> crying, "Lo, here!" and others, "Lo, there!" Some were con-
> tending for the Methodist faith, some for the Presbyterian,
> and some for the Baptist.
>
> For, notwithstanding the great love which the converts
> to these different faiths expressed at the time of their con-
> version, and the great zeal manifested by the respective
> clergy, who were active in getting up and promoting this
> extraordinary scene of religious feeling, in order to have
> everybody converted, as they were pleased to call it, let them
> join what sect they pleased; yet when the converts began to
> file off, some to one party and some to another, it was seen
> that the seemingly good feelings of both the priests and the
> converts were more pretended than real; for a scene of great
> confusion and bad feeling ensued—priest contending against
> priest, and convert against convert; so that all their good feel-
> ings one for another, if they ever had any, were entirely lost
> in a strife of words and a contest about opinions. (Joseph
> Smith—History 1:5–6)[1]

These contests included rhetoric about the nature of heaven and
hell. Most of these sects subscribed to teachings at least colored by
the prolific writings of Jonathan Edwards. Although he was an
eighteenth-century theologian, the effect of his writings dominated
nineteenth-century thought, especially in New England.[2] His doctrine invited very few to heaven. Man was considered fallen and
detestable. The very notion of someone being saved was so miraculous that it was almost impossible to conceive of it.[3] In a sermon
specifically aimed at children, Edwards stated, "You are so sinful and
wicked a creature that none of your righteousness is worthy to be
accepted."[4] The odds of entering heaven were not good, even for children who had been baptized. The overall influence these philosophies had on the religious thought of the early nineteenth century
created a feeling of wretchedness and despair that invited listeners to
look for any promised remedy among the religionists offering such.

The religions that Joseph Smith's family would have been associated with sought to make sense of Edwardian ideas (those based on

the teachings of Jonathan Edwards) of the depraved nature of man and his quest for salvation. The Calvinist response perpetuated the idea of the sinfulness of man but suggested that because of the Fall of Adam, all of his posterity came into the world with a sinful nature. This nature led to man's sinful acts. Edwardian thought suggested that sin was simply an act of will, whereas Calvinists suggested that the Fall corrupted all human faculties and that depravity was universal and led to sinful choices.[5] Presbyterianism was closely aligned with Calvinist theology. Out of this religious thought came slightly more hope for sinners because they could come to understand why they chose to sin, and through prescribed worship they could attempt to approach God.

While still promoting the idea of the depravity of human beings, Methodists took their message to common people such as farmers and shopkeepers. They sought to teach a more practical theology that was not tainted by the philosophies of the educated elite. The message was carried by mostly uneducated preachers and contained a healthy dose of hellfire and damnation. According to the upper class, this seemed especially well suited for the uneducated, who needed a constant reminder of their perilous state before God.[6]

A FAMILY CONTEXT

The idea of a very crowded hell caught the attention of young Joseph Smith. He was likely aware of the beliefs of his grandfather, through his father, which stood in stark contrast to a message of hellfire and damnation. Asael Smith was known for his liberal views on religion and apparently would have nothing to do with the concept of eternal hell. He aligned himself more with the teachings of the Universalists. In stark contrast to both Edwardian and Calvinist theology stood the Universalist belief that it was not in the nature of God to eternally damn His children. They promoted the doctrine of a universal salvation, which logically followed the concept of a universal atonement.[7] Proponents of this belief taught that the love of God revealed through Jesus Christ would restore the whole family of mankind to holiness and happiness.

Although most of Asael's children aligned themselves with the Congregationalists and Presbyterians, his son Joseph did not.[8] Joseph Smith Jr. noted, "My father's family was proselyted to the

Presbyterian faith, and four of them joined that church, namely, my mother, Lucy; my brothers Hyrum and Samuel Harrison; and my sister Sophronia," but that he leaned toward the Methodist sect (Joseph Smith—History 1:7–8).

PRAYERS ANSWERED

Finding no rest among the different religionists, Joseph petitioned the Lord in a stand of hardwood trees adjacent to his home. On that early spring day of 1820, he was told to join none of the sects, and that answer tends to be highlighted in the story of the First Vision. However, Joseph was told something that reveals a far deeper yearning. Of some eight contemporary accounts of the First Vision, five of them reveal that Joseph had a concern for the state of his soul and his future status, and that he longed for a forgiveness of his sins.[9] Elder Henry B. Eyring of the Quorum of the Twelve commented on this fact after studying different versions of the vision: "I read an account that I had not seen before in which he emphasized that he went to the grove, not simply to know which church to join. In fact, in that particular account, that's hardly mentioned. It was that he felt overcome by the need to be forgiven and to have his sins washed away and a sense that there was no way he knew how to do that. In the visitation, he was told that his sins were forgiven."[10] This very personal quest by young Joseph coupled with his search for a religion that could offer such peace were the very fuel of restoration. After returning from the grove, he remarked to his mother, "Never mind, all is well—I am well enough off" (Joseph Smith—History 1:20). It is easy to understand how "well enough off" he must have felt after having the Savior of the world declare his sins forgiven.

After the vision, Joseph was left to ponder for more than three years. He joined no sect and suffered persecution because of it. He again mentioned, "I was left to all kinds of temptations; and, mingling with all kinds of society, I frequently fell into many foolish errors, and displayed the weakness of youth, and the foibles of human nature; which, I am sorry to say, led me into divers temptations, offensive in the sight of God. In making this confession, no one need suppose me guilty of any great or malignant sins. A disposition to commit such was never in my nature" (Joseph Smith—History 1:28). Being again concerned about his sins, he stated: "In consequence of these things, I often felt condemned for my weakness and imperfections; when, on the evening of the above-mentioned twenty-first of September, after I had retired to my bed for the night, I betook myself to prayer and supplication to Almighty God for forgiveness of all my sins and follies, and also for a manifestation to me, that I might know of my state and standing before him; for I had full confidence in obtaining a divine manifestation, as I previously had one" (Joseph Smith—History 1:29). As a result of this petition, Moroni appeared to teach the Prophet and start his preparation to receive the plates containing the Book of Mormon. Joseph must have again felt approved of by the Lord. This forgiveness and approval would be extended to the Prophet throughout his life (see D&C 29:3; 60:7; 62:3; 110:5).

Adding to Joseph's discontent about the sectarian doctrines concerning salvation was the tragic death of his older brother Alvin in November of 1823. Alvin was well-loved by the community and his family for his good nature. His final admonition to Joseph was to follow through with the work of the Restoration. Mother Smith wanted a proper Christian burial for Alvin, so she secured a Presbyterian minister to give the funeral sermon. Joseph's younger brother William reported the following: "Rev. Stockton had preached my brother's funeral sermon and intimated very strongly that he had gone to hell, for Alvin was not a church member, but he was a good boy, and my father did not like it."[11] This declaration must have had a chilling effect on the Smiths, particularly Joseph Sr. and the Prophet Joseph. Other personal experiences, including the death of Joseph and Emma's firstborn son, Alvin, would continue to fuel the Prophet's questions about salvation and the remission of sins.

DOCTRINE IN THE BOOK OF MORMON

Joseph's first assignment as prophet was to translate the Book of Mormon, and in that effort he was given further insight into the reaching effects of Christ's Atonement. Of particular personal interest for Joseph were the book's teachings on the salvation of children. In a reversal of the sectarian teachings of Joseph Smith's day, the Book of Mormon prophet King Benjamin declared: "Behold he judgeth, and his judgment is just; *and the infant perisheth not that dieth in his infancy;* but men drink damnation to their own souls except they humble themselves and become as little children, and believe that salvation was, and is, and is to come, in and through the atoning blood of Christ, the Lord Omnipotent" (Mosiah 3:18; emphasis added). Abinadi's teachings on the Atonement and the Resurrection make reference to the salvation of little children. He stated, "And little children also have eternal life" (Mosiah 15:25).

The strongest Book of Mormon passages about the salvation of children occur in the book of Moroni. Mormon taught his son Moroni this doctrine by the word of the Lord, stating: "Listen to the words of Christ, your Redeemer, your Lord and your God. Behold, I came into the world not to call the righteous but sinners to repentance; the whole need no physician, but they that are sick; wherefore, little children are whole, for they are not capable of committing sin; wherefore the curse of Adam is taken from them in me, that it hath no power over them" (Moroni 8:8). Mormon went on to indict the practice of infant baptism, calling it a "mockery" and suggesting that it was their parents who needed to "humble themselves as their little children" and repent and be baptized in order to be saved with them (see Moroni 8:9–12). He suggested that anyone "that supposeth that little children need baptism is . . . in the bonds of iniquity; . . . wherefore, should he be cut off while in the thought, he must go down to hell" (Moroni 8:14). These Book of Mormon verses instilled in Joseph an understanding that there was a generous and just God who would not limit the salvation of children to the narrow definitions of the religious sects of his day. These scriptures clearly illuminated principles and doctrine, but there was still a need for clarification. What of those who never heard the gospel? What would the outcome be for the good and honest people of the earth? These were questions yet to be answered.

JOSEPH'S PERSONAL EXPERIENCE

The Lord's generosity was evident in Joseph's early experiences in his work in restoring the kingdom of God to the earth. In the process of translating the Book of Mormon, Joseph experienced some challenges which demonstrated the balance of justice and mercy. At the request of Martin Harris and after petitioning the Lord, Joseph let Martin take the original transcript of the book of Lehi, and it was lost. The Lord strongly chastened Joseph, stating: "And behold, how oft you have transgressed the commandments and the laws of God, and have gone on in the persuasions of men. For, behold, you should not have feared man more than God. Although men set at naught the counsels of God, and despise his words—yet you should have been faithful; and he would have extended his arm and supported you against all the fiery darts of the adversary; and he would have been with you in every time of trouble" (D&C 3:6–8).

After this chastening, the Lord again rekindled hope when He offered: "Behold, thou art Joseph, and thou wast chosen to do the work of the Lord, but because of transgression, if thou art not aware thou wilt fall. But remember, God is merciful; therefore, repent of that which thou hast done which is contrary to the commandment which I gave you, and thou art still chosen, and art again called to the work" (D&C 3:9–10).

Having experienced a withdrawal of the Spirit and the reproof of the Lord, Joseph again felt the Lord's invitation to repent and return. These very personal experiences were preparing the young prophet to receive more extensive doctrine.

In a revelation that referred to the punishment issued at the time of the lost manuscript, the Savior revealed further insights as He taught Joseph and Martin the reality of the Atonement. The revelation teaches an important doctrine concerning the punishment received by those who disobey. The Lord revealed to Joseph: "Surely every man must repent or suffer, for I, God, am endless. Wherefore, I revoke not the judgments which I shall pass, but woes shall go forth, weeping, wailing and gnashing of teeth, yea, to those who are found on my left hand. Nevertheless, it is not written that there shall be no end to this torment, but it is written *endless torment*" (D&C 19:4–6; emphasis in original).

In issuing this punishment, the Lord makes an interesting observation that endless torment does not mean there would be no end to it. He further clarifies by saying, "For, behold, I am endless, and the punishment which is given from my hand is endless punishment, for Endless is my name. Wherefore, Eternal punishment is God's punishment. Endless punishment is God's punishment" (D&C 19:10–12).

This type of punishment was then defined when Joseph and Martin were taught: "Wherefore I command you to repent—repent, lest I smite you by the rod of my mouth, and by my wrath, and by my anger, and your sufferings be sore—how sore you know not, how exquisite you know not, yea, how hard to bear you know not. For behold, I, God, have suffered these things for all, that they might not suffer if they would repent; but if they would not repent they must suffer even as I; which suffering caused myself, even God, the greatest of all, to tremble because of pain, and to bleed at every pore, and to suffer both body and spirit—and would that I might not drink the bitter cup, and shrink" (D&C 19:15–18).

After this graphic description of the kind of suffering the rebellious must go through, the offer was again given to Joseph and Martin to "repent, lest I humble you with my almighty power; and that you confess your sins, lest you suffer these punishments of which I have spoken, of which in the smallest, yea, even in the least degree you have tasted at the time I withdrew my Spirit" (D&C 19:20).

These revelations to Joseph illustrate that there were divine expectations but that there was also an allowance made for mercy through repentance. More important was the reality that punishment had an end. The Lord was preparing Joseph to receive in more detail the doctrine of heaven. As ordinances and priesthood were revealed to him, he was also receiving numerous revelations with regard to the reach of the Atonement.

THE VISION OF CELESTIAL WORLDS

In February of 1832, Joseph Smith and Sidney Rigdon were involved in the translation of the New Testament. The Prophet recorded: "Upon my return from Amherst conference, I resumed the translation of the Scriptures. From sundry revelations which had been received, it was apparent that many important points touching the salvation of man, had been taken from the Bible, or lost before it was compiled. It appeared self-evident from what truths were left, that if God rewarded every one according to the deeds done in the body the term 'Heaven,' as intended for the Saints' eternal home must include more kingdoms than one. Accordingly, on the 16th of February, 1832, while translating St. John's Gospel, myself and Elder Rigdon saw the following vision."[12] The vision that followed was again due to the Prophet's concern over the nature of heaven and the salvation of man.

In the revelation now found in section 76 of the Doctrine and Covenants, the Lord revealed to Joseph and Sidney the eternal heavens in exquisite detail. Of greatest importance was the revelation concerning the reach of the Atonement. After seeing God the Father and the Son in the vision, they were taught about the fall of Lucifer and the state of those who follow him. Because of the nature of the sin the sons of perdition would commit and the knowledge they would have to obtain in order to commit such a sin, Joseph and Sidney recorded that sons of perdition "are they who shall go away into the lake of fire and brimstone, with the devil and his angels—and the only ones on whom the second death shall have any power" (D&C 76:36–37). They learned that these were the only children of God who would go to the traditional "hell" that they had been brought up to believe was more encompassing.

The vision further revealed to them that these were "the only ones who shall not be redeemed in the due time of the Lord, after the sufferings of his wrath. For all the rest shall be brought forth by the resurrection of the dead, through the triumph and the glory of the Lamb, who was slain, who was in the bosom of the Father before the worlds were made" (D&C 76:38–39).

Instead of limiting the accessibility of the Atonement, this revelation declared that almost all God's children would experience the reach of divine love through the administration of an infinite Atonement. Joseph and Sidney declared: "And this is the gospel, the glad tidings, which the voice out of the heavens bore record unto us—that he came into the world, even Jesus, to be crucified for the world, and to bear the sins of the world, and to sanctify the world, and to cleanse it from all unrighteousness; that through him all might be saved whom the Father had put into his power and made by him; who glorifies the Father, and saves all the works of his hands, except those sons of perdition who deny the Son after the Father has revealed him. Wherefore, he saves all except them" (D&C 76:40–44).

Joseph and Sidney were then permitted to see the different kingdoms that people would be redeemed to dependent on their choices in life. The vision was an expansion of what Paul taught the Saints in Corinth when he stated: "There are also celestial bodies, and bodies terrestrial: but the glory of the celestial is one, and the glory of the terrestrial is another. There is one glory of the sun, and another glory of the moon, and another glory of the stars: for one star differ-eth from another star in glory" (1 Corinthians 15:40–41). They beheld the celestial, terrestrial, and telestial kingdoms and the nature of those who inherit each. In revelation received later, Joseph would come to understand more clearly that "they who are not sanctified through the law which I have given unto you, even the law of Christ, must inherit another kingdom, even that of a terrestrial kingdom, or that of a telestial kingdom. For he who is not able to abide the law of a celestial kingdom cannot abide a celestial glory. And he who can-not abide the law of a terrestrial kingdom cannot abide a terrestrial glory. And he who cannot abide the law of a telestial kingdom can-not abide a telestial glory; therefore he is not meet for a kingdom of glory. Therefore he must abide a kingdom which is not a kingdom of glory" (D&C 88:21–24).

Through these revelations, the Prophet Joseph Smith was given an expanded understanding of what it meant to be saved. The reality of a very large heaven became evident. But it was a different heaven than Universalist doctrine taught. Our Heavenly Father's children, through their use of agency, would determine where in heaven they would go. There was a place prepared even for the sinners after suf-fering God's wrath, which was "the glory of the telestial, which sur-passes all understanding" (D&C 76:89). Elder Dallin H. Oaks of the Quorum of the Twelve Apostles taught:

> The theology of the restored gospel of Jesus Christ is comprehensive, universal, merciful, and true. Following the necessary experience of mortal life, all sons and daughters of God will ultimately be resurrected and go to a kingdom of glory. The righteous—regardless of current religious denomi-nation or belief—will ultimately go to a kingdom of glory more wonderful than any of us can comprehend. Even the wicked, or almost all of them, will ultimately go to a marvelous—though lesser—kingdom of glory. All of that will occur because of God's love for his children and because of the atonement and resurrection of Jesus Christ, "who glori-fies the Father, and saves all the works of his hands." (D&C 76:43)[13]

A VERY PERSONAL VISION

Joseph Smith continued to receive instruction concerning the salvation of mankind. Years after having the vision of the degrees of glory, a very personal vision was unfolded before him. On January 21, 1836, in the office of the presidency on the third floor of the nearly completed Kirtland Temple, Joseph received a blessing from his aged father. The Prophet then received a vision in which he saw the celestial kingdom and its beauty. He viewed the throne of God and saw the Father and the Son. Joseph then recorded:

> I saw Father Adam and Abraham; and my father and my mother; my brother Alvin, that has long since slept;
> And marveled how it was that he had obtained an inheritance in that kingdom, seeing that he had departed this life before the Lord had set his hand to gather Israel the second time, and had not been baptized for the remission of sins.
> Thus came the voice of the Lord unto me, saying: All who have died without a knowledge of this gospel, who would have received it if they had been permitted to tarry, shall be heirs of the celestial kingdom of God;
> Also all that shall die henceforth without a knowledge of it, who would have received it with all their hearts, shall be heirs of that kingdom;
> For I, the Lord, will judge all men according to their works, according to the desire of their hearts.
> And I also beheld that all children who die before they arrive at the years of accountability are saved in the celestial kingdom of heaven. (D&C 137:5–10)

One can imagine the joy of father and son as they marveled over the vision of their beloved son and brother Alvin, who had been declared lost. Joseph now knew that not only was heaven a large place that would accept almost all of God's children but also that accommodation had been made for everyone to have the opportunity to accept the fulness of the gospel and return to God in the celestial kingdom. Even little children would be taken care of in this all-encompassing plan.

Further instructions from Joseph Smith would teach the Saints of their duty in doing work for the dead. In the years following these revelations, baptisms for the dead would be performed; eventually temple ordinances would be offered for their salvation.

CONCLUSION

Recognizing the inconsistency and intolerance of the prevalent Edwardian and Calvinist thinking of his day, the Prophet Joseph searched for the truth. He was driven by his own feelings of inadequacy and unworthiness as well as his desire to understand the nature of God and the salvation of man. In response to his humble prayer, the Restoration of the fulness of the gospel ensued. The restored doctrine refutes the narrow doctrines of exclusion and offers a more generous invitation. The gospel is that Christ's Atonement is a ubiquitous offering to all of God's children. This is the good news. Through that offering, all mankind will be saved and for those who choose to obey the fulness of the celestial law, they will be in the company of God. Little children are alive in Christ, and those who die in infancy will return to the Father of their spirits. As the gospel sweeps across the worlds of the living and the dead, all will have the opportunity to accept whatever they are willing to accept and will receive that which the Father has prepared for them in His kingdom. This is the expanded vision of heaven that Joseph Smith witnessed and testified of. It is the very thing that caused him "to marvel." These beautiful and sublime doctrines in turn invite us to marvel at the reach and breadth of the offering of the Son of God.

NOTES

1. For a detailed examination of the religious excitement in Joseph Smith's region, see Milton V. Backman, "Awakenings in the Burned-over District: New Light on the Historical Setting of the First Vision," *Brigham Young University Studies* 9, no. 3 (Spring 1969): 301–20.

2. See Norman Fiering, *Jonathan Edwards's Moral Thought and Its British Context* (Chapel Hill: University of North Carolina Press, 1981), 13.

3. Jonathan Edwards, *The "Miscellanies" (Entry Nos. 501–832)*, vol. 18 of *The Works of Jonathan Edwards*, ed. Ava Chamberlain (New Haven and London: Yale University Press, 2000), 64–66.

4. Jonathan Edwards, *Sermons and Discourses, 1739–1742*, vol. 22 of *The Works of Jonathan Edwards*, ed. Harry S. Stout and others (New Haven and London: Yale University Press, 2003), 177.

5. E. Brooks Holifield, *Theology in America: Christian Thought from the*

Age of the Puritans to the Civil War (New Haven and London: Yale University Press, 2003), 152.

6. Holifield, *Theology in America,* 261.

7. Holifield, *Theology in America,* 147.

8. Richard Lloyd Anderson, *Joseph Smith's New England Heritage* (Salt Lake City: Deseret Book, 2003), 133.

9. James B. Allen, "Eight Contemporary Accounts of Joseph Smith's First Vision: What Do We Learn from Them?" *Improvement Era,* April 1970, 12.

10. From the transcript of remarks made at the unveiling of *The Vision* statue in the Joseph Smith Building, Brigham Young University, on October 17, 1997.

11. J. S. Peterson interview with William Smith, 1893, *Zion's Ensign,* January 13, 1894; this section was reprinted in *Latter-day Saints' Millennial Star,* February 26, 1894, 133.

12. Joseph Smith, *History of the Church of Jesus Christ of Latter-day Saints,* ed. B. H. Roberts (Salt Lake City: The Church of Jesus Christ of Latter-day Saints, 1951), 1:245.

13. Dallin H. Oaks, "Apostasy and Restoration," *Ensign,* May 1995, 87.

CHAPTER TEN

ELIJAH'S MISSION, MESSAGE, AND MILESTONES OF DEVELOPMENT IN FAMILY HISTORY AND TEMPLE WORK

CYNTHIA DOXEY

The last verses of the Old Testament record the prophecy given by Malachi that Elijah the prophet would return to the earth before the coming of the "great and dreadful day of the Lord" to "turn the heart of the fathers to the children, and the heart of the children to their fathers" (Malachi 4:5–6). Although these are just two verses of scripture, the prophecy and its fulfillment have had a lasting impact on the lives of people throughout the world. Elijah restored priesthood keys to Joseph Smith and Oliver Cowdery in the latter days to carry out his mission of turning the hearts of fathers and children toward each other.

The restoration of Elijah's keys and the associated temple ordinances have influenced the Church and people throughout the world as they now seek to join their families together. Joseph Smith's role in the restoration of temple and family history work laid the foundation for further developments to take place. The focus of this paper will first be on the prophecies and fulfillment of Elijah's mission in the latter days and the teachings of Joseph Smith regarding the redemption of the dead. Second, attention will be given to the effects of Elijah's coming on record keeping, family history, and temple work in the past two centuries.

Cynthia Doxey is an associate professor of Church history and doctrine at Brigham Young University.

Prophecies of Elijah's Return

The prophecy about Elijah's coming and the resulting turning of the hearts of fathers and children is one of the few that is found in all the standard works: the Bible (see Malachi 4:5–6), the Book of Mormon (see 3 Nephi 25:5–6), the Doctrine and Covenants (see D&C 2:1–3; 110:13–16; 128:17–18), and the Pearl of Great Price (see Joseph Smith—History 1:38–39). Prophecies of Elijah's return to the earth appear to be prevalent in the scriptures and in traditional folklore. For example, a custom is still observed during the Jewish Passover where a cup of wine is placed on the table but is not drunk, and the door is opened in the expectation that Elijah will return to unify the people and bring deliverance from oppression.[1]

Although many people expect Elijah to return, they do not understand why or what he will do when he comes. Without the Restoration and the further understanding that Joseph Smith provided in this dispensation, the purpose and fulfillment of Elijah's return would not be accessible to us. In 1964 President N. Eldon Tanner said he had read a Christian commentary on the passage in Malachi and noted that the scripture was not well explained. He stated, "The full meaning and impact of this prophecy and promise could in no wise be understood until Elijah himself actually appeared to Joseph Smith and Oliver Cowdery in 1836."[2]

Joseph Smith related that when Moroni visited him on the evening of September 21, 1823, he spoke about the ancient record found on the gold plates and also taught him from the Bible. Some of the first scriptures that Moroni quoted were verses from Malachi 4, but Joseph said Moroni quoted them "with a little variation from the way it reads in our Bibles" (Joseph Smith—History 1:36). Interestingly, this passage is the only one from all those quoted by Moroni that was chosen to be included in the Doctrine and Covenants as section 2. Similar emphasis was given by the Savior in 3 Nephi 25:5–6. He restated the prophecy of Malachi for the Nephites because they did not have it in the plates of brass. Some of the "variation" that is found between Moroni's quotation and Malachi's original found in the Bible helps Latter-day Saints understand Elijah's mission in the latter days more fully.

SCRIPTURAL COMPARISONS

In Malachi 4:5–6, we read, "Behold, I will send you Elijah the prophet before the coming of the great and dreadful day of the Lord: and he shall turn the heart of the fathers to the children, and the heart of the children to their fathers, lest I come and smite the earth with a curse." Malachi's prophecy states that Elijah will come back at some time before the Second Coming of the Lord Jesus Christ, with the purpose of turning the hearts of fathers and children to each other. If this scripture were all that we had to go on, however, we might wonder what Elijah would be doing when he returned. Would he just come to visit people and bring love to families? Why would the earth be cursed if he did not come?

Latter-day scriptures and the words of the Prophet Joseph Smith significantly augment our understanding. The words of Moroni read: "Behold, I will reveal unto you the Priesthood, by the hand of Elijah the prophet, before the coming of the great and dreadful day of the Lord. And he shall plant in the hearts of the children the promises made to the fathers, and the hearts of the children shall turn to their fathers. If it were not so, the whole earth would be utterly wasted" (D&C 2:1–3).

We learn from Moroni's words that Elijah is not just coming for a visit at the Passover meal; he actually will reveal the priesthood or confer priesthood authority having to do with uniting families for eternity. The Prophet Joseph Smith taught that the reason Elijah had that assignment was because he "was the last Prophet that held the keys of the Priesthood," and thus he was to "restore the authority and deliver the keys of the Priesthood, in order that all the ordinances may be attended to in righteousness."[3] These keys bind or seal parents to each other and children to their parents for time and all eternity, allowing all the ordinances of the gospel to be ratified and in effect both on earth and in heaven.[4] Joseph Smith further commented on Elijah's mission of redeeming the dead by teaching, "What is this office and work of Elijah? It is one of the greatest and most important subjects that God has revealed. . . . Now was this merely confined to the living, to settle difficulties with families on earth? By no means. It was a far greater work. . . . This is the spirit of Elijah, that we redeem our dead, and connect ourselves with our fathers which are in heaven."[5] The restoration of these priesthood keys to the Prophet Joseph Smith and his teachings about the work of redeeming the dead help us recognize the importance of Elijah's work and why it is so important to the Lord's work to "bring to pass the immortality and eternal life of man" (Moses 1:39).

Moroni used different wording than Malachi's phrase, "turn the hearts of the fathers." Joseph Smith recorded that Moroni said, "Plant in the hearts of the children the promises made to the fathers." This language emphasizes that the children of the latter days will be blessed with the fulness of the gospel, including the blessings of the Abrahamic covenant. The covenant given to Abraham and his seed includes the promise of "the continuation of seed or the continuation of the family unit."[6] As those promises of eternal family life enter the hearts of the children through the temple ordinances they perform in their own behalf, they should gain a desire to turn to their fathers and seek them out to perform ordinances vicariously. We often refer to that desire as the Spirit of Elijah. Elder Bruce R. McConkie taught: "We are the children, and after we receive these blessings for ourselves, our attention turns almost by instinct to the well-being of our ancestors who died without a knowledge of the gospel. . . . It thus becomes our privilege, on the basis of salvation for the dead, to search out our ancestors—to whom the same blessings have been promised as have come to us—and to make these blessings available to them through the vicarious ordinances of the house of the Lord."[7]

Joseph Smith taught that "the word *turn* . . . should be translated *bind,* or *seal,*"[8] meaning that Elijah's mission was not only to help families love one another but also to create eternal families through covenants and ordinances that bind individuals as families throughout eternity. That the responsibility of doing this work is laid on the children of this generation is again evidenced as we read in D&C 98:16, "Seek diligently to turn the hearts of the children to their fathers." The teachings of the Prophet and the revelations he received from the Lord greatly enhance our understanding of what it means to turn our hearts. The priesthood keys Joseph received from Elijah make it possible for Latter-day Saints to fulfill our obligation to bind our families together for eternity.

As we further analyze differences between these two passages from Malachi and Moroni, we find that the last statement from

Moroni sounds much stronger than that from Malachi. Moroni says that if Elijah were not to come, "the whole earth would be utterly wasted at [the Lord's] coming" (D&C 2:3) rather than that the earth would be smitten with a curse (see Malachi 4:6). Although being smitten with a curse does not sound good, being "utterly wasted" sounds devastating. The whole purpose of the earth would be a total waste without Elijah's coming, because the earth was created to provide a place for Heavenly Father's children to experience mortality and to make and keep covenants that would help them return to Him as eternal families. Furthermore, our own lives would be a waste because without performing temple ordinances to seal our families together, we would not have roots and branches (see Malachi 4:1), or eternal family units with ancestry and posterity. McConkie and Ostler state it another way: "If we do not accomplish the primary purpose for which we came to mortality, namely the forming of an eternal family unit, we have wasted our lives on matters that are not of eternal importance."[9]

Fulfillment of the Prophecy

Without the additional scriptural revelations and the teachings of the Prophet Joseph Smith, we would not have this understanding of the important work of Elijah. Although scriptural comparison is interesting, the more important thing to remember is that the prophecy of Elijah's return was fulfilled! One of the great blessings of this dispensation is that Elijah *did* come during the latter days to reveal the keys of the sealing power to Joseph Smith and Oliver Cowdery. He came during the time of the Passover while the Jews were waiting for him.[10] Instead of coming to them, however, Elijah revealed himself to others of the house of Israel who were organized under the authority and direction of the Lord Jesus Christ in the latter days.

The restoration of the sealing keys is recorded in Doctrine and Covenants 110, where Joseph Smith and Oliver Cowdery described a series of angelic visitations in the Kirtland Temple, namely, the appearance of the Savior, Moses, Elias, and Elijah on April 3, 1836, one week after the dedication of the temple. The scripture states that Elijah told them the time had "fully come" for Malachi's prophecy to be fulfilled and that he committed the "keys of this dispensation" into Joseph Smith's and Oliver Cowdery's hands (see D&C 110:14–16). Through the Holy Ghost, all people can gain their own testimonies that Elijah actually came. But there are other evidences that the hearts of children have been turned to their fathers.

In 1972 Elder Mark E. Petersen of the Quorum of the Twelve Apostles wrote that a further witness of Elijah's appearance comes as we answer the following question: "Is there a recently developed and widespread interest among living persons regarding their fore-fathers?"[11] Elder Petersen responded with a number of facts about the development and increase of family history interest since the nine-teenth century. He suggested there is ample evidence to show the effects of Elijah's visit as we see the development of family history, records, research, and temple work both in the Church and through-out the world.[12] Since Elder Petersen's statement, the continued growth and development of family history and temple work has demonstrated further evidence of Elijah's visit to Joseph Smith.

FAMILY HISTORY AND RECORD KEEPING THROUGHOUT THE WORLD

Before the visit of Elijah, the general population in Western soci-ety showed little interest in family history. Genealogies were kept and recorded in the Bible as evidence that people had the lineage to be rightful heirs to the blessings of Abraham. Royalty and nobility could produce evidence of their heritage in order to claim their rights to the inheritance of thrones and estates. However, only a handful of people beyond these groups were interested in their own family his-tories, and there were no organized societies in the United States solely devoted to the study of genealogy.[13]

One of the milestones with which to measure the beginning of the interest in family history is the establishment of the United States' (and perhaps the world's) oldest genealogical society: the New England Historic Genealogical Society in 1845. Other genealogical societies such as the New York Genealogical and Biographical Society (founded in 1869), the National Genealogical Society (organized in 1903), and the Society of Genealogists in London (beginning in 1911) soon followed and have multiplied to the point where there are now literally thousands of genealogical-oriented societies throughout the world.[14]

Not only was there a growing interest in genealogy research in the mid-nineteenth century, but governments also began placing a greater emphasis on keeping record of their citizens. It may not be coincidence that beginning in January 1837, the year after Elijah appeared to Joseph Smith and Oliver Cowdery, England and Wales began civil registration of records of births, marriages, and deaths. Scotland began their civil registration in 1855. Similarly, in the United States, the mid-nineteenth century was the time when many states began to pass laws requiring the registration of vital records, with Massachusetts leading the way in 1841.[15]

Another evidence of how records have changed since Elijah's visit is the type of information that was required in records maintained by governments. Two good examples are the British Census, which began in 1841 to ask for names, ages, and birthplaces, and the United States Census, which changed in 1850 to ask for names, ages, and birthplaces for everyone living in the household, and in 1880 added the categories of "relationship to head" and "parents' birthplaces." Before 1850, the census asked only for the name of the head of household and the approximate age and gender for everyone else. The Spirit of Elijah may well have had an effect on government records throughout the world.

DEVELOPMENT OF FAMILY HISTORY AND TEMPLE WORK IN THE CHURCH

Joseph Smith built the foundation for the process of redeeming the dead which has moved forward at an ever-increasing pace to the current time. Joseph taught the doctrines associated with the redemption of the dead, and every prophet in this dispensation has continued to emphasize this great work.[16] In addition, through the years since Joseph Smith, the Church has promoted a rapid expansion of family history and temple work with the building of temples and the development of family-history research tools such as microfilmed records and automated databases now available on the Internet.

It was some years after Elijah's coming that Joseph Smith began to teach about baptism for the dead. On August 10, 1840, while preaching at the funeral of Seymour Brunson, Joseph Smith first mentioned this concept. Later, he gave the following instructions:

"The Saints have the privilege of being baptized for those of their relatives who are dead, whom they believe would have embraced the Gospel, if they had been privileged with hearing it, and who have received the Gospel in the spirit, through the instrumentality of those who have been commissioned to preach to them while in prison."[17] President Wilford Woodruff taught that Joseph Smith recognized the eternal significance and urgency of redeeming the dead: "When the Prophet Joseph had this revelation from heaven, what did he do? . . . He never stopped till he got the fulness of the word of God to him concerning the baptism for the dead."[18] President Woodruff described how Joseph Smith and many of the Saints in Nauvoo performed baptisms for the dead in the Mississippi River before there was a baptismal font in the Nauvoo Temple.[19] In January 1841, the Lord taught the Saints that the ordinance of baptism for the dead belongs in the temple and commanded them to build a temple for baptisms and for the further ordinances that would be revealed (see D&C 124:28–41).

The other ordinances of the temple were restored through the Prophet during the Nauvoo period as well, with the endowment first being given to Church leaders in May 1842 in the upper room of Joseph Smith's general store.[20] Prior to leaving Nauvoo in 1846, many members received these sacred ordinances in the temple, their anxiety being very great to receive the blessings of the endowment.[21] Although proxy endowments and sealings were not carried out in Nauvoo, Joseph Smith laid the groundwork for the work to go forward when the Saints were established in the Great Basin.[22] He also received revelations that brought further understanding of God's eternal plan for His children. For example, Joseph Smith received a vision of the celestial kingdom in January 1836, learning that individuals who die without a knowledge of the gospel, but who would have accepted it, will be heirs to that kingdom (see D&C 137:5–7).

Since Joseph Smith's day, the Church has spent much time, effort, and money in providing resources to further the work of redemption of the dead. The first temple to be completed in Utah was the St. George Temple in 1877. Today, temples are found throughout the world. In 1994, President Gordon B. Hinckley, then First Counselor in the First Presidency, stated, "This is the great season of temple building and temple activity. . . . I am confident that the Lord will permit us and direct us to go on building these sacred structures as we become worthy of them."[23] During his tenure as the president of the Church, the number of temples that have been dedicated or announced has grown from 50 to 130 as of October 2004.[24] This large increase in temples demonstrates a fulfillment of the words he spoke in 1994 and shows the importance of temple work in the Church today and in the future. President Brigham Young prophesied that the time would come when there will be "thousands" of temples on the earth.[25]

Many Latter-day Saints in the nineteenth century turned their hearts to their fathers as they pursued their own family history research, but it was not a priority for all Church members. At the April general conference in 1894, President Wilford Woodruff put a new emphasis on the doctrine of sealing families together as he taught, "We want the Latter-day Saints from this time to trace their genealogies as far as they can, and to be sealed to their fathers and mothers. Have children sealed to their parents, and run this chain through as far as you can get it. . . . This is the will of the Lord to this people."[26] This focus on searching out our own genealogies led Church leaders and members to formally organize their family history efforts by creating the Genealogical Society of Utah (GSU) on November 14, 1894. The goals for the society were to establish and maintain a library, to educate members about how to do genealogical research, and to acquire records of the dead that could be used in temple work.[27] With the organization of the GSU, family history research went forward and increased in importance in the Church and has become well known throughout the world.

Much has happened since the organization of the Genealogical Society of Utah that makes the Church a leader in genealogical record keeping, storage, and dissemination. The library began with a small collection of 300 books in 1894 but has grown to include more than 360,000 books, 2.5 million rolls of microfilmed genealogical records, and 742,000 microfiche records, along with many electronic databases and resources.[28] In the limitations of this paper, it is not possible to go into detail about all these events.[29] Therefore, the attached table mentions only a few of the major milestones that have had a great impact on family history research.

TABLE—MILESTONES OF FAMILY HISTORY IN THE CHURCH

1927—Temple Records Index Bureau (TIB)	The TIB indexes the names of individuals who received their endowments either for themselves or by proxy since 1842. It was the primary method for clearing names for temple work until 1969 when the International Genealogical Index began.[1]
1938—Microfilming	Microfilming both preserves and makes available the records found in many archives and libraries.[2]
1963—The Granite Mountain Records Vault	The Vault was constructed to house the burgeoning collection of microfilms and to preserve them from damage. Inside the mountain, the vault has proper temperatrues, humidity, and security for keeping the microfilms in good condition.[3] While the master films stay in the vault, they can be copied and sent to any Family History Centers for patron use.
1969—International Genealogical Index (IGI)	As computer technology became available, the Church created the IGI as a computer database for the purpose of indexing all of the temple ordinances for deceased individuals, replacing the TIB's original card catalog system.
1984—Personal Ancestral File (PAF)	With personal computers becoming the norm for many households, this computerized method of storing and organizing genealogical data became available for families' research.[4] This program is used extensively throughout the world because it can be downloaded for free from the www.familysearch.org website.
1990—Family Search™	This program had several databases for searching family history information, including the lineage-linked Ancestral File with millions of names, a searchable IGI, the Social Security Death Index, Military Index, and the automated Family History Library Catalog.[5]

1993—TempleReady	The method for preparing names for the temple became more accessible to Church members as TempleReady was automated at a Family History Center. The previous approval process took several weeks, but could now be completed in a matter of minutes.[6]
1999—www.familysearch.org	This Internet website has databases such as Ancestral File, the IGI, and the Family History Library Catalog. SInce its launching in May 1999, more databases such as censuses from Canada, Britain, and the U.S., have been added to the site. The site is one of the most popular genealogy sites on-line, with millions of hits per day.[7]

[1] Allen, et al., 101.

[2] Ibid., 218, 223; R. Scott Lloyd, "A Century of Progress in Family History Work," *Church News*, June 26, 1995, 5.

[3] Allen, et al., 239–240.

[4] Ibid., 324.

[5] Ibid., 330; Sperry, 296.

[6] R. Scott Lloyd, 5.

[7] R. Scott Lloyd, "Today we are taking a historic step," *Church News*, May 29, 1999, 8.

The advances in technology in the past ten years have made genealogy research quite different than what it was before. Computerized databases and Internet resources with digital images of original records make it possible for people to carry out their family history research from their homes. The Church has continued to be a leader in making resources available to the public with more than four thousand Family History Centers scattered across the earth, along with the free Internet access to many of its computerized databases. In 1994 President Howard W. Hunter said that the Lord's hand had guided the development of technology to accelerate the work of redeeming the dead. Looking toward the future, President Hunter declared, "We stand only on the threshold of what we can do with these tools. I feel that our most enthusiastic projections can capture only a tiny glimpse of how these tools can help us—and of the eternal consequences of these efforts."[30] A partial fulfillment of that prophecy can be seen by the use of the Internet for family history work. It has made the research process much less arduous and has also provided rapid and accurate results. No doubt there will continue to be great advances in the work of collecting and providing access to records and in the building of temples, all to hasten the salvation of the dead.

TURNING OUR OWN HEARTS TO OUR FATHERS

From the first visit of the angel Moroni to the visit of Elijah in the Kirtland Temple and continuing throughout his life, Joseph Smith laid the foundation of this great work of turning the hearts of children to their fathers. Referring to Moroni's visit, President Gordon B. Hinckley said, "It is tremendously significant to me that this declaration, this repetition of the wondrous words of Malachi concerning the work for the dead, was given to the boy Joseph four years before he was allowed to take the plates from the hill . . . and well before the Church was organized. It says much concerning the priority of this work in the plan of the Lord."[31] Joseph Smith emphasized the doctrines and practices related to redeeming the dead, including temple work and baptism for the dead (see D&C 127 and 128). He recognized the importance of this work as he told the Church, "Let me assure you that these are principles in relation to the dead and the living that cannot be lightly passed over" (D&C 128:15), and "the Saints have not too much time to save and redeem their dead."[32]

If the Latter-day Saints of this generation are to build upon the foundation laid by the Prophet Joseph Smith, we must work to fulfill our responsibility to research our ancestors and provide temple ordinances for them so that "they might be judged according to men in the flesh, but live according to God in the spirit" (D&C 138:34). President Woodruff taught that if Latter-day Saints could see the labors of the missionaries in the spirit world, they "would lose all interest in the riches of the world, and instead thereof their whole desires and labors would be directed to redeem their dead."[33] Other prophets have taught that "this work must hasten,"[34] and that "it matters not what else we have been called to do, or what position we may occupy, or how faithfully in other ways we have labored in the Church, none is exempt from this great obligation."[35]

Clearly, today we have the responsibility to turn our hearts and seal our families together for all eternity, just as the Saints in Joseph Smith's day had. Perhaps we may have an even greater obligation because it is now so much easier for us to access records and attend temples than it was for the Saints in the earlier days. Joseph Smith encouraged the Saints of his day (and ours) by saying: "Brethren, shall we not go on in so great a cause? Go forward and not backward. Courage, brethren; and on, on to the victory! Let your hearts rejoice, and be exceedingly glad. Let the earth break forth into singing. Let the dead speak forth anthems of eternal praise to the King Immanuel, who hath ordained, before the world was, that which would enable us to redeem them out of their prison; for the prisoners shall go free" (D&C 128:22).

Surely the Church and its people must build upon the foundation of the Restoration begun by Joseph Smith to do our part in setting the prisoners free.

NOTES

1. Ralph L. Smith, *Word Biblical Commentary* (Waco, TX: Word Books, 1984), 342.
2. Nathan Eldon Tanner, "The Heavens are Open," *Improvement Era,* June 1964, 461.
3. Joseph Smith, *Teachings of the Prophet Joseph Smith,* comp. Joseph Fielding Smith (Salt Lake City: Deseret Book, 1976), 172.
4. Joseph Fielding Smith, *Doctrines of Salvation,* comp. Bruce R. McConkie (Salt Lake City: Bookcraft, 1955), 2:119.
5. Smith, *Teachings,* 337–38.
6. Joseph Fielding McConkie and Craig J. Ostler, *Revelations of the Restoration: A Commentary on the Doctrine and Covenants and Other Modern Revelations* (Salt Lake City: Deseret Book, 2000), 24.
7. Bruce R. McConkie, *A New Witness for the Articles of Faith* (Salt Lake City: Deseret Book, 1985), 509.
8. Smith, *Teachings,* 330.
9. McConkie and Ostler, *Revelations of the Restoration,* 24.
10. Smith, *Doctrines of Salvation,* 2:101.
11. Mark E. Petersen, "Why Mormons Build Temples," *Ensign,* January 1972, 49.
12. Petersen, "Why Mormons Build Temples," 52–53.

13. James B. Allen, Jessie L. Embry, and Kahlile B. Mehr, *Hearts Turned to the Fathers: A History of the Genealogical Society of Utah, 1894–1994* (Provo, UT: BYU Studies, 1995), 24.

14. Kip Sperry, "From Kirtland to Computers: The Growth of Family History Record Keeping," in *The Heavens Are Open: The 1992 Sperry Symposium on the Doctrine and Covenants,* comp. Byron R. Merrill and others (Salt Lake City: Deseret Book, 1993), 293–94.

15. Sperry, "From Kirtland to Computers," 292.

16. Howard W. Hunter, "We Have a Work to Do," *Ensign,* March 1995, 64.

17. Joseph Smith, *History of the Church of Jesus Christ of Latter-day Saints,* ed. B. H. Roberts, 2nd ed. rev. (Salt Lake City: Deseret Book, 1960), 4:179, 231.

18. Wilford Woodruff, *The Discourses of Wilford Woodruff,* ed. G. Homer Durham (Salt Lake City: Bookcraft, 1946), 153.

19. Woodruff, *Discourses,* 153.

20. Smith, *History of the Church,* 5:1–2.

21. More than five thousand endowments were given in the temple from December 10, 1845, to February 7, 1846. The *History of the Church,* 7:541–80, gives reference to how many individuals received their endowments each day. The Nauvoo Temple records contain all the names and dates of endowments and sealings.

22. Proxy endowments and sealings began in the St. George Temple in 1877.

23. Gordon B. Hinckley, "A Century of Family History Service," *Ensign,* March 1995, 62. This talk was originally given on November 13, 1994, on the one hundredth anniversary of the organization of the Genealogical Society of Utah.

24. Gordon B. Hinckley, "Condition of the Church," *Ensign,* November 2004, 5.

25. Brigham Young, *Discourses of Brigham Young,* John A. Widtsoe (Salt Lake City: Deseret Book, 1954), 394.

26. Woodruff, in *Discourses,* 157.

27. Allen, Embry, and Mehr, *Hearts Turned to the Fathers,* 45–46.

28. "110 Years of Progress, with More to Come," *Church News,* February 5, 2005, 5. Information on the Family History Library's holdings can be found at its Internet site: *www.familysearch.org.*

29. The most comprehensive description of the progress of family history research in the Church can be found in Allen, Embry, and Mehr's history of the Genealogical Society of Utah.

30. Hunter, "We Have Work to Do," 65.

31. Gordon B. Hinckley, "A Century of Family History Service," *Ensign*, March 1995, 61.

32. Smith, *Teachings*, 330.

33. Woodruff, in *Discourses*, 152.

34. Hunter, "We Have Work to Do," 64.

35. Smith, *Doctrines of Salvation*, 2:14.

CHAPTER ELEVEN

"MILLIONS SHALL KNOW BROTHER JOSEPH AGAIN": JOSEPH SMITH'S PLACE AMONG THE PROPHETS

SCOTT C. ESPLIN

Interpretations of Joseph Smkith's role in the latter-day doctrinal restoration vary greatly with time and perspective. As early in this dispensation as 1833, opponents such as the Reverend Diedrich Willers of the German Reformed Church announced: "The greatest imposter of our times in the field of religion is no doubt a certain Joseph Smith. . . . This new sect should not cause the Christian Church great astonishment. The past centuries have also had religious off-shoots. But what has become of them all? . . . They have all been absorbed in the Sea of the Past and marked with the stamp of oblivion. This will also be the lot of the Mormonites."[1] After the Martyrdom, Illinois governor Thomas Ford likewise wrote, "Thus fell Joe Smith, the most successful imposter in modern times; a man who, though ignorant and coarse, had some great natural parts which fitted him for temporary success, but which were so obscured and counteracted by the inherent corruption and vices of his nature that he never could succeed in establishing a system of policy which looked to permanent success in the future."[2]

Though negative at times, some non-LDS remembrances sense more in Joseph's mission. Josiah Quincy, recalling his association with the Prophet, concluded, "Of the multitudinous family of Smith,

---

Scott C. Esplin is a doctoral candidate in educational leadership and a part-time instructor of Church history and doctrine at Brigham Young University.

from Adam down (Adam of the 'Wealth of Nations,' I mean), none had so won human hearts and shaped human lives as this Joseph. His influence, whether for good or for evil, is potent today, and the end is not yet. . . . If the reader does not know just what to make of Joseph Smith, I cannot help him out of the difficulty. I myself stand helpless before the puzzle."[3]

The Prophet himself offered a different perspective on his mission. In his 1838 account of early Church history, Joseph characterized himself as "an obscure boy . . . of no consequence in the world, . . . doomed to the necessity of obtaining a scanty maintenance by his daily labor" (Joseph Smith—History 1:22–23). Six months later, when visited by a woman who inquired "whether [he] professed to be the Lord and Savior," he reported, "I replied, that I professed to be nothing but a man, and a minister of salvation, sent by Jesus Christ to preach the Gospel."[4]

Joseph's self-deprecating style masks his true role in the Restoration. The sweep of prophetic world history reveals the description "an obscure boy . . . of no consequence" as a gross understatement. Contrast it with Moroni's depiction of the same seventeen-year-old boy. On the eve of their first visit, the ancient Nephite record-keeper prophesied that "God had a work for [Joseph] to do; and that [his] name should be had for good and evil among all nations, kindreds, and tongues, or that it should be both good and evil spoken of among all people" (Joseph Smith—History 1:33). Fifteen years later, while Joseph was in an obscure Missouri jail, the Lord Himself summarized Joseph's mission: "The ends of the earth shall inquire after [his] name, and fools shall have [him] in derision, and hell shall rage against [him]; while the pure in heart, and the wise, and the noble, and the virtuous, shall seek counsel, and authority, and blessings constantly from under [his] hand" (D&C 122:1–2). How do the "pure in heart, and the wise, and the noble, and the virtuous" of all ages view Joseph Smith's mission? What doctrinal "counsel, and authority, and blessings" do they hope to receive at his hand?

"ART THOU THAT PROPHET?": JOSEPH SMITH AS KNOWN BY THE ANCIENTS

Ancient prophets, emphasizing Joseph Smith's role in religious history, focus on the blessing of a doctrinal restoration. Even apostate

Judaism in New Testament times had some expectation of a prophet
with this mission. Answering the Jews who questioned John the
Baptist, the prophet "confessed, and denied not that he was Elias; but
confessed, saying; I am not the Christ. And they asked him, saying;
How then art thou Elias? And he said, *I am not that Elias who was to
restore all things.* And they asked him, saying, Art thou that prophet?
And he answered, No" (Joseph Smith Translation, John 1:21–22).
Further questioning him, the Jews asked, "Why baptizest thou then,
if thou be not the Christ, *nor Elias who was to restore all things, neither
that prophet?*" (Joseph Smith Translation, John 1:26; emphasis added).

A second New Testament reference to this prophet of restoration
comes from the Mount of Transfiguration, where the discussion of
Elias, John the Baptist, and a prophet to restore all things continued.
Matthew recorded the Savior's declaration, "But I say unto you, Who
is Elias? Behold, this is Elias, whom I send to prepare the way before
me. Then the disciples understood that he spake unto them of John
the Baptist, *and also of another who should come and restore all things,* as
it is written by the prophets" (Joseph Smith Translation, Matthew
17:13–14; emphasis added).

Different interpretations of these passages exist. Some interpret
the Messiah Himself as this restorer of all things.[5] Others describe
him as a Messiah, son of Joseph, destined to precede the Christ.[6] Still
others portray the Elias of restoration as a composite individual,
"having in mind all the prophets who came to restore the fulness of
the gospel."[7] Elder Bruce R. McConkie observed, "John's questioners
were familiar with some ancient Messianic prophecy, unknown to us,
which foretold the coming of Elias to perform a mighty work of
restoration."[8] George Laub, recording a sermon by Joseph Smith,
reports the Prophet's use of the verse, saying, "Brother Joseph Smith
was chosen for the last dispensation or seventh dispensation. [At] the
time the grand council [sat] in heaven to organize this world, Joseph
was chosen for the last and greatest prophet, to lay the foundation
of God's work of the seventh dispensation. Therefore the Jews asked
John the Baptist if he was Elias or Jesus or that great prophet that was
to come."[9] From this statement, authors Robert L. Millet and Joseph
Fielding McConkie conclude, "Joseph Smith was the final great Elias
before the Messiah; he was an Elias of restoration."[10]

As Matthew characteristically noted in his account, these traditions of a prophet to "restore all things" were "written by the prophets." They begin as early as Genesis. Nearly four thousand years before Joseph Smith's birth, his namesake, Joseph in Egypt, prophesied that in the latter days, the Lord's people would be "scattered again," that "a branch shall be broken off, and shall be carried into a far country" where the people would be in "hidden darkness . . . [and] captivity" (Joseph Smith Translation, Genesis 50:25). To remedy these conditions, Joseph the patriarch declared, "A seer shall the Lord my God raise up, who shall be a choice seer unto the fruit of my loins. . . . He shall bring them to the knowledge of the covenants which I have made with thy fathers" (Joseph Smith Translation, Genesis 50:26, 28). Joseph in Egypt also prophesied that the latter-day seer would be great in God's eyes, would bring forth His word, would have power to convince others of its truthfulness, and would ultimately restore the house of Israel (Joseph Smith Translation, Genesis 50:29–30, 32). Furthermore, this seer, sharing the same name as ancient Joseph, would likewise share his mission: to bring salvation to the suffering family of Israel.

Isaiah also possessed an Old Testament understanding of the mission of Joseph Smith. After describing the millennial day, he stated, "And in that day there shall be a root of Jesse, which shall stand for an ensign of the people; to it shall the Gentiles seek: and his rest shall be glorious" (Isaiah 11:10). In March of 1838, the Lord answered the Prophet's query concerning the identity of this "root of Jesse," stating that "it is a descendant of Jesse, as well as of Joseph, unto whom rightly belongs the priesthood, and the keys of the kingdom, for an ensign, and for the gathering of my people in the last days" (D&C 113:6). Just two short years before this response, in the Kirtland Temple, Joseph had received, under the hands of Moses, the "keys of the gathering of Israel" (D&C 110:11). Nine years before, he received "the keys of the kingdom" under the hands of Peter, James, and John (D&C 27:12–13). While the exact identification of "the root of Jesse" is unknown, Elder Bruce R. McConkie observed: "Are we amiss in saying that the prophet here mentioned is Joseph Smith, to whom the priesthood came, who received the keys of the kingdom, and who raised the ensign for the gathering of the Lord's people in our dispensation? And is he not also the 'servant in the hands of Christ, who is partly a descendant of Jesse as well as of Ephraim, or of the house of Joseph, on whom there is laid much power'? (D&C 113:4–6.) Those whose ears are attuned to the whisperings of the Infinite will know the meaning of these things."[11]

Old and New Testament prophets, with their eyes focused on the scattering of their beloved Israel, naturally saw and emphasized Joseph Smith's role as gatherer and restorer of all things. Book of Mormon prophets, covering the same time period, likewise taught of the mission of Joseph Smith, emphasizing his role in relation to them. Father Lehi used an account of Joseph in Egypt's prophecy when teaching his own son Joseph of his namesake's future mission. He tied Joseph Smith to the ancients, stating, "He shall be great like unto Moses" (2 Nephi 3:9). To this latter-day seer, the Lord would "give power to bring forth my word . . . and not to the bringing forth my word only, saith the Lord, but to the convincing them of my word, which shall have already gone forth among them" (3:11). Citing Joseph in Egypt, he continued the link, "And his name shall be called after me; and it shall be after the name of his father. *And he shall be like unto me;* for the thing, which the Lord shall bring forth by his hand, by the power of the Lord shall bring my people unto salvation" (3:15; emphasis added).

Joseph Smith's mission in preserving and restoring scripture is emphasized by other Book of Mormon prophets. To his son Helaman, Alma taught, "The Lord said: I will prepare unto my servant Gazelem, a stone, which shall shine forth in darkness unto light, that I may discover unto my people who serve me, that I may discover unto them the works of their brethren" (Alma 37:23). The servant *Gazelem* mentioned by Alma is unidentified, but *Gazelam* was one of the names used in early printings of the Doctrine and Covenants as a code name for Joseph Smith.[12] Of it, Elder McConkie wrote, "With reference to the name Gazelam, it is interesting to note that Alma in directing Helaman to preserve both the Urim and Thummim and the plates containing the Book of Ether, says that such record will be brought to light by the Lord's servant *Gazelem,* who will use 'a stone' in his translation work. . . . It may be that *Gazelem* is a variant spelling of *Gazelam* and that Alma's reference is to the Prophet Joseph Smith who did in fact bring forth part at least of the Ether record."[13] Later, in the book of Ether itself, Moroni seems to speak directly to Joseph Smith, instructing him again on his role in restoring the truths of scripture (see Ether 5:1–4).

Christ, speaking to the Nephites during his visit, further prophesied of Joseph Smith and his mission of restoration and clarification. Describing a marred servant in His hands doing "a great and a marvelous work" in the latter days, the Savior stated, "It shall come to pass that whosoever will not believe in my words, who am Jesus Christ, which the Father will cause *him* to bring forth unto the Gentiles; . . . they shall be cut off from among my people who are of the covenant" (3 Nephi 21:9, 11; emphasis added; see also D&C 135:1; 10:43).

In addition to his role in preserving the Nephite record, other Book of Mormon references describe Joseph's role in illuminating the doctrinal darkness of ages past. Lehi taught, "Out of the fruit of [Joseph of Egypt's] loins the Lord God would raise up a righteous branch unto the house of Israel; not the Messiah" (2 Nephi 3:5). Like the Messiah, this branch would be instrumental "in the latter days, in the spirit of power, unto the bringing of them out of darkness unto light—yea, out of hidden darkness and out of captivity unto freedom" (2 Nephi 3:5).

"THE BEST BLOOD": THE UNDERSTANDING OF JOSEPH'S MISSION IN HIS OWN DAY

While ancient prophets labored to describe a man they had never met, Joseph Smith's contemporaries may have struggled to appreciate the mission of a man they knew so well. Good friend Benjamin F. Johnson recalled, "While with him in such fraternal, social, and sometimes convivial moods, we could not then so fully realize the greatness and majesty of his calling, which, since his martyrdom, has continued to magnify in our lives, as the glories of this last dispensation more fully unfold to our comprehension."[14] In spite of this challenge, some sensed the depth of his mission. Elder John Taylor called Joseph and his brother, Hyrum, "the best blood of the nineteenth century" (D&C 135:6). Linking Joseph's mission to that of the Savior, he continued, "Joseph Smith, the Prophet and Seer of the Lord, has done more, save Jesus only, for the salvation of men in this world, than any other man that ever lived in it" (D&C 135:3).

Latter-day revelation highlights many of the contributions of

Joseph Smith. Early in the dispensation, the Doctrine and Covenants emphasized his role in producing scripture, stating, "This generation shall have my word through you" (D&C 5:10). Elder Gerald N. Lund analyzed the fulfillment of this prophecy. Using the term *producer* rather than *author* of scripture to better reflect the combined efforts of writing, translating, transcribing, and abridging, he credits Mormon with producing 338 pages of scripture, Moses with 308, and Jeremiah with 170.[15] By comparison, Joseph Smith, in his contributions of the Book of Mormon, Doctrine and Covenants, Pearl of Great Price, and Joseph Smith Translation of the Bible, is responsible for nearly 900. In fact, "before Joseph Smith, the world had only the 1,590 pages of the Bible; through this one man, the Lord increased our scriptural library by more than half."[16]

Not only did the Prophet Joseph add breadth to the scriptural canon but he also added depth. His contributions are responsible for our understanding of the purpose of life, God's eternal plan for the destiny of His children, the nature of God, the importance of family, and countless other previously unknown truths. Contemporaries emphasize this doctrinal clarity from his teaching. President Brigham Young declared: "What is the nature and beauty of Joseph's mission? You know that I am one of his Apostles. When I first heard him preach, he brought heaven and earth together; and all the priests of the day could not tell me anything correct about heaven, hell, God, angels, or devils: they were as blind as Egyptian darkness. When I saw Joseph Smith, he took heaven, figuratively speaking, and brought it down to earth; and he took the earth, brought it up, and opened up, in plainness and simplicity, the things of God; and that is the beauty of his mission."[17] Defending him in the trying days of the Kirtland apostasy, Elder John Taylor emphasized Joseph's role in restoring doctrinal knowledge, "From whence do we get our intelligence, and knowledge of the laws, ordinances and doctrines of the kingdom of God? Who understood even the first principles of the doctrines of Christ? Who in the Christian world taught them? If we, with our learning and intelligence, could not find out the first principles, which was the case with myself and millions of others, how can we find out the mysteries of the kingdom? It was Joseph Smith, under the Almighty, who developed the first principles, and to him we must look for further instructions."[18]

Some outside the general councils of the Church also recognized in Joseph a source of doctrinal clarity. Daniel Tyler called Joseph "a great reconciler of discrepancies in passages of scripture which were or seemed to be in conflict with each other."[19] Wandle Mace recalled, "I have felt ashamed myself sometimes, having studied the scriptures so much, that I had not seen that which was so plain when he touched them. He as it were turned the key, and the door of knowledge sprang wide open, disclosing precious principles, both new and old. . . . He would unravel the scriptures and explain doctrine as no other man could. What had been mystery he made so plain it was no longer mystery."[20] James Palmer summarized, "He could hand out to all mankind God's divine law and make it so plain to the understanding of the people, that on reflection one would think he had always known it, whereas you had only just been taught it."[21]

In addition to his doctrinal clarity, others recognized in Joseph the return of doctrinal authority. Mary Elizabeth Rollins Lightner observed, "We all felt that he was a man of God, for he spoke with power, and as one having authority in very deed."[22] Upon watching Joseph address a conference, Rhoda Richards declared, "It appeared to me as if the whole sectarian world must fall before him as if it was the God of heaven spake."[23] Latter-day scriptures emphasize Joseph's role in restoring this authority. The preface to the Doctrine and Covenants states, "I the Lord . . . called upon my servant Joseph Smith . . . that every man might speak in the name of God the Lord, even the Savior of the world" (D&C 1:17, 20). President Joseph Fielding Smith linked this to priesthood, defining it as "the authority of God delegated to man, by which he is given power to officiate in all the ordinances of the Gospel [and] speak in the name of the Lord."[24] Joseph Smith, as the instrument through whom the priesthood was restored, fulfilled this mission, causing men to again authoritatively "speak in the name of the Lord." Other latter-day scriptures emphasize Joseph's holding these keys forever (see D&C 28:7; 90:2–3; 112:15). Brigham Young declared, "The *keys* of the *Priesthood* were committed to Joseph, to build up the *Kingdom of God* on the *earth,* and were not to be taken from him in time or in eternity."[25]

"Mingling with Gods": Joseph Smith's Mission as Understood by His Successors

Highlighting the continued role Joseph Smith plays in the Lord's latter-day work, congregations around the world sing, "Mingling with Gods, he can plan for his brethren."[26] After his death, Joseph's successors continued to emphasize the eternal nature of his mission. Brigham Young taught:

> Joseph Smith holds the keys of this last dispensation, and is now engaged behind the veil in the great work of the last days. . . . No man or woman in this dispensation will ever enter into the celestial kingdom of God without the consent of Joseph Smith. From the day that the Priesthood was taken from the earth to the winding-up scene of all things, every man and woman must have the certificate of Joseph Smith, junior, as a passport to their entrance into the mansion where God and Christ are—I with you and you with me. I cannot go there without his consent. He holds the keys of that kingdom for the last dispensation—the keys to rule in the spirit-world; and he rules there triumphantly.[27]

President George Q. Cannon further declared: "If we get our salvation we shall have to pass by him; if we enter into our glory it will be through the authority that he has received. We cannot get around him."[28]

Joseph himself prophesied of his laboring for the kingdom beyond the grave. On his last visit to Ramus, Illinois, the Prophet hinted at his pending death. Benjamin Johnson, questioning him, exclaimed, "Oh! Joseph, what could we, as a people do without you? and what would become of the great Latter-day work if you should leave us?"[29] Joseph responded, "Benjamin, I should not be far away from you, and if on the other side of the veil I should still be working with you, and with a power greatly increased, to roll on this kingdom."[30]

Several of Joseph's successors have testified from personal experience of his continued work beyond the veil. President Brigham Young reported being visited by the Prophet on several occasions, receiving counsel on how to guide the Saints.[31] President Wilford Woodruff stated, "Joseph Smith visited me a great deal after his death, and taught me many important principles."[32] The Vision of

the Redemption of the Dead reports President Joseph F. Smith's seeing the Prophet in the spirit world, where he, along with the faithful
elders, "continue their labors" (see D&C 138:52–57). President Heber
J. Grant described a heavenly dream in which Joseph, counseling
with the Savior, "mentioned . . . and requested" that young Heber be
chosen as an Apostle.[33]

These statements of Joseph's continued influence after his death
on the work of the Restoration match the principle outlined by
Presidents George Q. Cannon and Joseph F. Smith at the death of
President John Taylor: "Though we have lost his presence here, his
influence will still be felt. Such men may pass from this life to
another, but the love which beats in their hearts for righteousness
and for truth cannot die. They go to an enlarged sphere of usefulness.
Their influence is extended and more widely felt, and Zion will feel
the benefit of his labors."[34]

The Prophet's continued interest in the work of this dispensation
is characteristic of another role emphasized by his successors. Joseph
Smith, as a dispensation head, stands unique among men called in
our day. "There is an order and a hierarchy even among those called
as chosen oracles and mouthpieces of the Almighty."[35] Elder
McConkie emphasized: "You start out with the Lord Jesus, and then
you have Adam and Noah. Thereafter come the dispensation heads.
Then you step down, appreciably, and come to prophets and
apostles, to the elders of Israel. . . . Every prophet is a witness of
Christ; every dispensation head is a revealer of Christ for his day; and
every other prophet or apostle who comes is a reflection and an echo
and an exponent of the dispensation head. All such come to echo to
the world and to expound and unfold what God has revealed
through the man who was appointed for that era to give his eternal
word to the world. Such is the dispensation concept."[36]

The principle of a dispensation head is evident in temple recommend interviews, where testimonies of the current prophet and of
Joseph Smith as the dispensation head are required. It is also apparent in general conference, where speakers frequently bear testimony
of the current prophet and the dispensation head. Few trace their testimonies back through every intervening prophet. President Gordon
B. Hinckley's testimony is characteristic of the principle. Highlighting
Joseph Smith's place in the plan, he wrote, "I worship the God of

heaven, who is my Eternal Father. I worship the Lord Jesus Christ, who is my Savior and my Redeemer. I do not worship the Prophet Joseph Smith, but I reverence and love this great seer through whom the miracle of this gospel has been restored. I am now growing old, and I know that in the natural course of events, before many years, I will step across the threshold to stand before my Maker and my Lord and give an accounting of my life. And I hope that I shall have the opportunity of embracing the Prophet Joseph Smith and of thanking him and of speaking of my love for him."[37]

A RESTORATION OF COUNSEL, AUTHORITY, AND BLESSINGS

Based on prophetic commentary by the "pure in heart, and the wise, and the noble, and the virtuous" of all ages, Joseph's mission centers on "counsel, and authority, and blessings" (D&C 122:2). Old and New Testament prophets looked to Joseph Smith for the blessing of a restored posterity. Book of Mormon prophets looked to him for the blessing of a restored record. His contemporaries and successors turn to him for doctrinal counsel and priesthood authority. Eliza R. Snow summarized the feelings of many in a poetic tribute shortly following Joseph's death:

> We mourn the Prophet, from whose lips have flow'd
> The words of life, thy spirit has betow'd—
> A depth of thought, no human art could reach
> From time to time, roll'd in sublimest speech,
> From the celestial fountain, through his mind,
> To purify and elevate mankind:
> The rich intelligence by him brought forth,
> Is like the sun-beam, spreading o'er the earth. . . .
> The noble martyrs now have gone to move
> The cause of Zion in the courts above.[38]

With help from his prophetic peers and insights from others who knew him, we begin to see the mission of the "obscure" New York farm boy. Someday, we may fully understand one of Joseph's final comments about himself. At the conclusion of his April 1844 King Follett discourse, he told those assembled in Nauvoo, "You don't know me; you never knew my heart. No man knows my history. I cannot tell it: I shall never undertake it. I don't blame any one for not believing my history. If I had not experienced what I have, I would not have believed it myself. . . . When I am called by the trump of the archangel and weighed in the balance, you will all know me then."[39] Someday, millions really shall know him again.[40]

NOTES

1. Diedrich Willers, "Church Book of the Reformed Church of Christ in Fayette Township, Seneca County in State of New York, 1833," cited in Larry C. Porter, Milton V. Backman Jr., and Susan Easton Black, eds., *Regional Studies in Latter-day Saint Church History: New York* (Provo, UT: Department of Church History and Doctrine, Brigham Young University, 1992), 161.

2. Thomas Ford, *A History of Illinois, From Its Commencement as a State in 1818 to 1847* (Chicago: S. C. Griggs, 1854), 354–55, cited in Mark L. McConkie, *Remembering Joseph: Personal Recollections of Those Who Knew the Prophet Joseph Smith* (Salt Lake City: Deseret Book, 2003), 29–30.

3. Josiah Quincy, *Figures of the Past from the Leaves of Old Journals* (Boston: 1883), 399–400; cited in McConkie, *Remembering Joseph,* CD-ROM.

4. Joseph Smith, *History of the Church of Jesus Christ of Latter-day Saints,* ed. B. H. Roberts, 2nd ed. rev. (Salt Lake City: Deseret Book, 1980), 3:201.

5. Bruce R. McConkie, *Doctrinal New Testament Commentary, Volume 1: The Gospels* (Salt Lake City: Bookcraft, 1965), 1:129; see also Robert J. Matthews, *A Burning Light: The Life and Ministry of John the Baptist* (Provo, UT: Brigham Young University Press, 1972), 68–73.

6. Commentaries on noncanonical references to the Messiah, son of Joseph, include: "'Messiah the son of Joseph': a forerunner of the Messiah the son of David who will fight against Israel's enemies at the end-time and fall in battle. In earlier texts he is a rather nebulous figure, but he is treated fully in the late apocalypses: See b.Sukk 52a/b; TarJon to Ex 40:11 ('Messiah son of Ephraim . . . at whose hand Israel will triumph over Gog and his allies at the end of days')" (3 Enoch 45:5, in James H. Charlesworth, ed., *Old Testament Pseudepigrapha* (Garden City, NY: Doubleday, 1983), 1:298, note t; also, "The Jews looked for a 'faithful prophet' (I Macc. xiv:41) who was to terminate the prophetic period and usher in the Messianic reign. But after Peter, as recorded in Acts iii:22, applied the prophecy of Deut. to Christ, the Christian Church adopted this interpretation" (W. Robertson Nicoll, *The Expositor's Greek Testament* [Grand Rapids, MI: Eerdmans, 1960], 1:693). *The Theological Dictionary of the New Testament* observes, "The Messiah [ben] Joseph

. . . is first attested in literature in the 2nd cent. A.D. . . . In contrast to the Messiah [ben] David, who is anointed for kingly rule, the Messiah [ben] Joseph is anointed for military action. . . . After his manifestation he will lead his armies from Upper Galilee to Jerusalem where he will rebuild the temple and defeat the peoples surrounding Israel. After forty years of peace he will be killed in battle against his enemies. . . . The people will lift up a lament for him. . . . The Messiah [ben] David, whose coming is contemporary with or just after that of the Messiah [ben] Joseph, will finally conquer the enemies of Israel. . . . It is perhaps a proof that Messianic ideas were much more complicated in the time of Jesus than we can show from the written sources at our disposal" (Gerhard Friedrich, ed., *Theological Dictionary of the New Testament* [Grand Rapids, MI: Eerdmans, 1974], 9:526–27).

7. Joseph Fielding Smith, *Doctrines of Salvation* (Salt Lake City: Bookcraft, 1954), 1:174. See also Bruce R. McConkie, *Mormon Doctrine*, 2nd ed. (Salt Lake City: Bookcraft, 1979), 221.

8. Bruce R. McConkie, *Doctrinal New Testament Commentary, Volume 1: The Gospels* (Salt Lake City: Bookcraft, 1965), 1:130.

9. George Laub, in Andrew F. Ehat and Lyndon W. Cook, comps., *The Words of Joseph Smith* (Provo, UT: Religious Studies Center, 1980), 370; spelling and punctuation modernized. It should be noted that "Laub did not transcribe his original notes of this discourse in his journal until a year after the death of Joseph Smith; thus, this reference to John 1:21 may be Laub's interpolation" (see Ehat and Cook, *Words of Joseph Smith*, 405 n. 50).

10. Joseph Fielding McConkie and Robert L. Millet, *Joseph Smith: The Choice Seer* (Salt Lake City: Bookcraft, 1996), xviii; see also Joseph Fielding Smith, *Answers to Gospel Questions* (Salt Lake City: Deseret Book, 1963), 4:194.

11. Bruce R. McConkie, *The Millennial Messiah: The Second Coming of the Son of Man* (Salt Lake City: Deseret Book, 1982), 339–40; see also Kent P. Jackson, "Revelations Concerning Isaiah," in Robert L. Millet and Kent P. Jackson, *Studies in Scripture: Volume One, The Doctrine and Covenants* (Sandy, UT: Randall Book, 1984), 331–32.

12. See section heading for Doctrine and Covenants 78 and 82. In editions prior to 1981, Joseph Smith was identified as *Gazelam* in Doctrine and Covenants 78:9; 82:11; 104:26, 43, 45, 46.

13. McConkie, *Mormon Doctrine*, 307–8.

14. Benjamin F. Johnson, "Benjamin F. Johnson to George S. Gibbs, 1903," cited in E. Dale LeBaron, "Benjamin F. Johnson: Colonizer, Public Servant, and Church Leader" (master's thesis, Brigham Young University, 1966), 328.

15. Gerald N. Lund, "A Prophet for the Fulness of Times," *Ensign,* January 1997, 52.

16. Lund, "A Prophet," 52.

17. Brigham Young, in *Journal of Discourses* (London: Latter-day Saints' Book Depot, 1854–86), 5:332.

18. John Taylor, in B. H. Roberts, *The Life of John Taylor* (Salt Lake City: Bookcraft, 1963), 40–41.

19. Daniel Tyler, "Recollections of the Prophet Joseph Smith," *Juvenile Instructor,* May 15, 1893, 332.

20. Wandle Mace, "Autobiography of Wandle Mace," typescript copy, L. Tom Perry Special Collections, Harold B. Lee Library, Brigham Young University, 46–49, 100–101; cited in McConkie, *Remembering Joseph,* CD-ROM.

21. James Palmer, "Reminiscences," Church Archives, The Church of Jesus Christ of Latter-day Saints, Salt Lake City, 69–70; spelling and grammar have been modernized; cited in McConkie, *Remembering Joseph,* CD-ROM.

22. Mary Lightner, "Mary Elizabeth Rollins Lightner," *Utah Genealogical and Historical Magazine,* July 1926, 194–95, cited in McConkie, *Remembering Joseph,* CD-ROM.

23. Rhoda Richards, Diaries, 1784–1879, April 7, 1844, Church Archives, in Richard Neitzel Holzapfel and Jeni Broberg Holzapfel, *Women of Nauvoo* (Salt Lake City: Bookcraft, 1992), 89.

24. Joseph Fielding Smith, *The Way to Perfection* (Salt Lake City: Deseret News Press, 1931), 70.

25. Brigham Young, in *Journal of Discourses,* 1:133; emphasis in original.

26. William W. Phelps, "Praise to the Man," *Hymns* (Salt Lake City: The Church of Jesus Christ of Latter-day Saints, 1985), no. 27.

27. Brigham Young, in *Journal of Discourses,* 7:289; spelling modernized.

28. George Q. Cannon, in *Journal of Discourses,* 23:361.

29. "Benjamin F. Johnson to George S. Gibbs, 1903," cited in LeBaron, "Benjamin F. Johnson," 332–33.

30. Joseph Smith, in "Benjamin F. Johnson to George S. Gibbs, 1903," 333.

31. Brigham Young, Manuscript History of Brigham Young, 1846–1847, comp. Elden J. Watson (Salt Lake City: n.p., 1971), 528–30; see also Ronald W. Walker, "Brigham Young: Student of the Prophet," *Ensign,* February 1998, 51.

32. Wilford Woodruff, *The Discourses of Wilford Woodruff,* ed. G. Homer Durham (Salt Lake City: Bookcraft, 1946), 288.

33. Heber J. Grant, in Conference Report, April 1941, 5.

34. Roberts, *Life of John Taylor,* 415–16.

35. Joseph Fielding McConkie and Robert L. Millet, *Joseph Smith: The Choice Seer* (Salt Lake City: Bookcraft, 1996), xxi.

36. Bruce R. McConkie, "This Generation Shall Have My Word through You," in *Hearken, O Ye People: Discourses on the Doctrine and Covenants* (Sandy, UT: Randall Book, 1984), 4–5.

37. Gordon B. Hinckley, "As One Who Loves the Prophet," in *The Prophet and His Work: Essays from General Authorities on Joseph Smith and the Restoration* (Salt Lake City: Deseret Book, 1996), 13.

38. Eliza R. Snow, *Times and Seasons,* July 1, 1844, 575.

39. Smith, *History of the Church,* 6:317.

40. William W. Phelps, "Praise to the Man," *Hymns,* no. 27.

CHAPTER TWELVE

SALVATION OF LITTLE CHILDREN: COMFORTING DOCTRINE RESTORED

J. PETER HANSEN

One of the greatest blessings of all mortality is having a body that can produce children. A desire of most men and women is to bring forth young ones, to raise up their own, basking in the warmth of the unique love shared between parents and child. From time to time, however, tragedy strikes. A little child is lost to death, and grief-stricken parents plead, "Where is my baby? Who is taking care of her? Will I ever be permitted to see my little one again?" Restored truth reveals comforting answers.

Unfortunately, many saddened parents, confounded by false doctrine about the fate of children after death, fear that their children are condemned by tradition-bound philosophies of men that provide no hope of heaven for children taken by early death. Such dark teachings cannot be part of Heavenly Father's great plan of happiness. They leave the grieving parents as cold as the tomb itself. Such was the case of Louise Graehl.

Louise and George Graehl, who were not yet members of the Church, married in 1844 and operated a confectionary store in Geneva, Switzerland. Louise wrote: "Ten years had passed since our marriage when we lost a sweet little girl, Emma, just fifteen months old. At the funeral I had a visit from the minister of the [church] in which we lived and another minister of the Christian Church, who

J. Peter Hansen is an institute director at the Pleasant Hill (California) Institute of Religion.

came to comfort us, but they could not tell me if my sweet baby was saved, for *they said there was no provision in the Bible for the salvation of children,* but that we may hope that the Lord would take care of them. This time I felt indignant at their speech for in my heart I was sure that my little angel was all right and that those ministers knew nothing."[1]

The Prophet Joseph Smith and his beloved wife, Emma, suffered through similar experiences. The couple gave birth to nine children and adopted the infant twins of John and Julia Murdock after Julia died during childbirth. Six of the Smith's children suffered infant death.[2] The couple's hearts must have nearly burst. What could be more difficult for a mother and father? In the face of these tragic events, traditional religions of their day could not balm the wounded heart but instead deepened the wound. False doctrines of annihilation, original sin, and infant baptism prevailed.

ANNIHILATION, ORIGINAL SIN, AND INFANT BAPTISM

To be annihilated is "the act of reducing to nothing, or nonexistence . . . so that the name can no longer be applied to it."[3] According to a theological commentary published in 1830, annihilation is "the act of reducing any created being into nothing. . . . It requires the infinite power of God to effect it."[4] Annihilation doctrine finds its roots in an incomplete interpretation of the biblical passage "Except a man be born of water and of the Spirit, he cannot enter into the kingdom of God" (John 3:5). Many other scriptures sustain that truth (see Mark 16:16; Matthew 3:15; Luke 7:30; 2 Nephi 31:4–11). The philosophies of men allege that *everyone* born to man must be baptized. Their logic follows that when a child is born and dies without having been baptized, the gates of heaven slam shut. This was the message of the ministering religious leaders to Louise Graehl at the death of her little Emma. In this view, the unbaptized, irrespective of age, are eternally expelled from the presence of Heavenly Father, and they may subjected to something worse—annihilation.

The belief was controversial. To believe in annihilation one must also uphold the theory of creation *ex nihilo*—to create something out of nothing—which Reverend Baden Powell of Oxford University taught "is not a doctrine of scripture."[5] Conventional theology held that someone who was not baptized was annihilated or returned to the nothing from which God created him.

Joseph Smith explained away ex nihilo theory. He revealed that "man was also in the beginning with God. Intelligence, or the light of truth, was not created or made, neither indeed can be" (D&C 93:29). Annihilation doctrine is preceded by, and predicated upon, the widely accepted doctrine of original sin—a major contributor to the suggestion that unbaptized children are lost for eternity.

Original sin philosophy is a painful and condemning fiery dart in the quiver of most Christian religions. It is one that President Joseph Fielding Smith called "as *damnable a doctrine* as was ever taught among the children of men, for little children are not tainted with sin."[6] Original sin doctrine proposes that because of the transgression of Adam and Eve, babies are born wounded and scarred with the sins of their first parents, whose sins exclude them from attaining salvation.

"Original sin," according to Catholic theology, is "the hereditary stain with which we are born on account of our origin or descent from Adam," "the privation of sanctifying grace in consequence of the sin of Adam," and "the privation of justice that each child contracts at its conception."[7] Further, "those who die in original sin, without ever having contracted any *actual sin,* are deprived of the happiness of heaven."[8] Protestant doctrine agrees.

John Calvin wrote that sin is inherited. "We believe that all the posterity of Adam is in bondage to original sin, which is a hereditary evil."[9] One religion applied the doctrine to a universal scale: "The Church of England, for instance, teaches that original sin 'is the fault and corruption of the Nature of every man, that naturally is ingendered of the offspring of *Adam;* whereby man is very far gone from original righteousness, and is of his own nature inclined to evil, so that the flesh lusteth always contrary to the spirit; and therefore in every person born into this world, it deserveth God's wrath and condemnation.'"[10]

Judaism also accepts inherited sin doctrine, but prescribes an antidote. In some Jewish sects, the rite of "circumcision [provides] a means of escaping damnation"[11] from hereditary sin.[12] Coupled together, the tenets of annihilation and original sin beget a troubling and controversial doctrine, a practice that purports to be the cure-all for original sin and a sure protection from annihilation. The idea of infant baptism undermines Heavenly Father's plan of salvation by placing restrictive boundaries on the infinite Atonement of Jesus Christ.

For centuries, babies have been baptized in an effort to save them from the effect of original sin. William H. W. Fanning explains the position of the Roman Catholic Church. "Christ makes no exception to this law [baptism] and it is therefore general in its application, embracing both adults and infants. . . . St. Augustine (III, *De Anima*) says: 'If you wish to be a Catholic, do not believe, nor say, nor teach, that infants who die before baptism can obtain the remission of original sin.'"[13] Most religions of Joseph Smith's day agreed that when a child died without baptism, it was doomed. The unsettling teachings that disheartened Louise Graehl in 1854 continued into the twentieth century, when Joseph Fielding Smith served as a missionary. He said:

> I remember when I was in the mission field in England, there was an American family there. . . . One evening as we sat in their home, the man's wife turned to me and said: "Elder Smith, I want to ask you a question." Before she could ask her question, she began to cry. I did not know what the matter was. She sobbed, and when she had composed herself enough to ask the question, she told me this story:
>
> When they went over to England, they had the misfortune of losing a little baby. They were attending the Church of England. They went to the minister and wanted to have that baby laid away with a Christian burial, as they had been attending the church. The minister said to her: "We can't give your child a Christian burial because it was not christened. Your baby is lost." That was a rather blunt way to put it, but that is the way she told the story; and that woman's heart had been aching and aching for two or three years. So she asked the question of me: "*Is my baby lost? Will I never see it again?*"[14]

Sister Graehl, along with the good sister whom Elder Smith met and perhaps millions of other mothers and fathers of deceased children, kneel in need of comfort. They need the sure comfort that only the plan of happiness can provide.

Truth restored to Joseph Smith holds that every mortal inherits seeds of mortality as a result of the Fall (see 2 Nephi 2:21). Every one of Heavenly Father's spirit children departs from His presence some time between conception and mortal birth (see Abraham 3:22–23; D&C 138:55–56; D&C 93:29). Each life experience will include temptation, pain, illness, trials, and tribulations (see 1 Nephi 12:17; Alma 7:11; Ether 12:6). Within a lifetime, each mortal being will violate a law of heaven or earth (see Alma 12:14). Eventually, all men will die (see 2 Nephi 9:6). Because of the original sin of Adam, all mankind experience both the pangs and the blessings of mortality (see Moses 5:1, 10–11). This, however, is not the "damnable doctrine" to which President Smith referred. His reference is to the false precept that each child born to man is sullied by the sin of Adam. The Prophet taught, "We believe that men will be punished for their own sins, and not for Adam's transgression" (Articles of Faith 1:2). Thankfully, the heavens are open (see Joseph Smith—History 1:17). The Savior restored one of heaven's most soothing doctrines to His prophet of the dispensation of the fulness of times—the comforting doctrine of the salvation of little children.

The Salvation of Children Taught by the Book of Mormon

The Prophet Joseph and Emma Smith were no strangers to the grief of laying children in the grave. They lost five of their own flesh and one adopted son to early death. One can only imagine the relief the Smiths must have felt as they read from the Book of Mormon the restored words of an angel who spoke to King Benjamin. The angel taught the king about the certainty of the birth, death, and resurrection of Jesus Christ. Then he applied this saving doctrine to little children: "His blood atoneth for the sins of those who have fallen by the transgression of Adam. . . . And even if it were possible that little children could sin they could not be saved; but I say unto you they are blessed; for behold, as in Adam, or by nature, they fall, even so the blood of Christ atoneth for their sins. . . . For behold he judgeth, and his judgment is just; and the infant perisheth not that dieth in his infancy. . . . [They are saved] in and through the atoning blood of Christ, the Lord Omnipotent" (Mosiah 3:11–18).

What a magnificent revelation! Restored doctrine, new to Joseph Smith, was revealed to the world. Three important doctrines taught by King Benjamin directly oppose the false doctrines of original sin, infant baptism, and annihilation.

First, because of the Atonement, no baptism is required to remit any effect Adam's transgression could possibly have on his progeny. The Atonement covers all sins of the repentant, and Adam certainly was repentant (see Moses 5:4–9). Parents can be assured that when a child dies, he or she is sanctified by the Atonement. The little one will not perish. Truth revealed to the world by King Benjamin through the Prophet Joseph is that there is no original sin in effect.

Second, Joseph Smith directly struck down the devilish but prevalent doctrine that infants are not redeemable without baptism. In addition, the doctrine of the age of accountability is foreshadowed. "If it were *possible* that little children could sin," spoke the angel, the Atonement covers the sin (Mosiah 3:16; emphasis added). Since the Atonement cancels out original sin, and because children *cannot* sin, infant baptism is unnecessary. In fact, the Prophet additionally taught, "The doctrine of baptizing children, or sprinkling them, or they must welter in hell, is a doctrine not true, not supported in Holy Writ, and is not consistent with the character of God. All children are redeemed by the blood of Jesus Christ, and the moment that children leave this world, they are taken to the bosom of Abraham."[15] This stands alone as doctrine unique to the Restoration. In an earlier revelation, Joseph instructed further, "Little children are holy, being sanctified through the atonement of Jesus Christ" (D&C 74:7). He taught that there is simply no accountability assigned to children because of the atoning sacrifice of the Savior. Therefore, infant baptism is not a ritual recognized by heaven.

Finally, the restored doctrine destroys the frightening theory of annihilation. "The infant perisheth not that dieth in his infancy" (Mosiah 3:18) because of the sacrifice of the Lamb of God. If there is no original sin, there is no need for infant baptism, and annihilation is annihilated. The Book of Mormon does not stop there.

The ancient prophet Abinadi stood before wicked King Noah. He testified of the Redeemer and of the first resurrection, or the resurrection of the just. These are they who will be exalted, or who will receive eternal life, which is living with God. Abinadi stated simply, "Little children also have eternal life" (Mosiah 15:25). Even though Book of Mormon people had the words of King Benjamin and

Abinadi available to them, it appears that some disputed about infant baptism. Joseph Smith found supporting evidence in the last of the plates of gold, "from which fact we infer that disputation upon this subject had arisen among the Nephites."[16] The prophet Mormon wrote on this subject at great length to his son Moroni.

> There have been disputations among you concerning the baptism of your little children.
>
> And now, my son, I desire that ye should labor diligently, that this gross error should be removed from among you. . . .
>
> Listen to the words of Christ, your Redeemer, your Lord and your God. . . . Little children are whole, for they are not capable of committing sin; wherefore the curse of Adam is taken from them in me, that it hath no power over them; and the law of circumcision is done away in me. . . .
>
> I know that it is solemn mockery before God, that ye should baptize little children. . . .
>
> And their little children need no repentance, neither baptism. . . .
>
> But little children are alive in Christ, even from the foundation of the world; . . . they are all alike and partakers of salvation. . . . Little children cannot repent; wherefore, it is awful wickedness to deny the pure mercies of God unto them, for they are all alive in him because of his mercy.
>
> And he that saith that little children need baptism denieth the mercies of Christ, and setteth at naught the atonement of him and the power of his redemption. . . .
>
> For behold that all little children are alive in Christ, and also all they that are without the law. For the power of redemption cometh on all them that have no law; wherefore, he that is not condemned, or he that is under no condemnation, cannot repent; and unto such baptism availeth nothing—
>
> But it is mockery before God, denying the mercies of Christ, and the power of his Holy Spirit, and putting trust in dead works. (Moroni 8:5–6, 8–9, 11–12, 17, 19–20, 22–23)

True doctrine was now restored. The words of Mormon are consistent with those of King Benjamin. We learn that little children are not capable of committing sin (8:8); that original sin is removed through the atoning sacrifice (8:8); that children should be baptized when they are accountable for their actions (8:10); that all little children are alive in Christ (8:12); and that infant baptism is a solemn mockery before God and denies the tender mercies of Christ (8:23).

Having translated the Book of Mormon, the Prophet went to work on restoring lost scripture in the Bible. Abraham, like Mormon, fought against the practice of infant baptism. Furthermore, he knew the age of accountability.

THE AGE OF ACCOUNTABILITY IN THE BIBLE

The Lord told Abraham, "My people have gone astray from my precepts, and have not kept mine ordinances, which I gave unto their fathers." They were not observing the law of baptism and had "taken unto themselves the washing of children, and the blood of sprinkling." Finally, they believed that "the blood of the righteous Abel was shed for sins," as though Abel were the Messiah (see Joseph Smith Translation, Genesis 17:3–7).

After Jehovah bound Abraham to Him by covenant, He revealed that "children are not accountable before me until they are eight years old" (Joseph Smith Translation, Genesis 17:11). The age of accountability and the age for children to be baptized was now deeply rooted in the mind and heart of the Prophet of the Restoration. Restored doctrine flowered into official Church doctrine when he taught the Saints that "parents [who] have children in Zion, or in any of her stakes which are organized, that teach them not to understand the doctrine of repentance, faith in Christ the Son of the living God, and of baptism and the gift of the Holy Ghost by the laying on of the hands, when *eight years old,* the sin be upon the heads of the parents" (D&C 68:25; emphasis added; see also 18:42 and 20:71 and Joseph Smith Translation, Genesis 17).[17]

TEACHINGS FROM THE DOCTRINE AND COVENANTS

For at least 3,800 years the Lord has spoken directly to man about the fate of children after death. He spoke to Abraham in about 2000 B.C., having previously spoken to his fathers before him. He taught King Benjamin about this doctrine in 124 B.C. Between A.D. 400 and 421, He spoke to the prophet Mormon. On September 26, 1830, the resurrected Christ again revealed the correct doctrine of the salvation of little children through the Prophet Joseph: "Behold, I say unto you, that little children are redeemed from the foundation of the world through mine Only Begotten; wherefore, they cannot sin, for power is not given unto Satan to tempt little children, until they begin to become accountable before me" (D&C 29:46–47). Furthermore, He revealed additional comforting doctrine regarding those who are not accountable because of mental handicap, saying, "And he that hath no understanding, it remaineth in me to do according as it is written" (D&C 29:50; see also Mosiah 3:11). But where will these precious ones reside?

From a truly remarkable vision, Joseph Smith described the place of highest redemption, the celestial kingdom, and some of its inhabitants. That which Joseph saw was not the celestial kingdom as it existed the day the vision was received; it was a vision of how the lives of the Prophet's family members would be after the resurrection. He saw God the Father and the Son, streets of gold, Father Adam, Abraham, his own father and mother, and his *unbaptized* brother Alvin, who had been dead for twelve years (see D&C 137:1–6).[18] Next, Joseph learned how it was possible that this twenty-five-year-old adult, Alvin, who was well beyond the age of accountability at the time of his death, could be in the holiest place in all creation: "All who have died without a knowledge of this gospel, who would have received it if they had been permitted to tarry, shall be heirs of the celestial kingdom of God; also all that shall die henceforth without a knowledge of it, who would have received it with all their hearts, shall be heirs of that kingdom; for I, the Lord, will judge all men according to their works, according to the desire of their hearts" (D&C 137:7–9).

The doctrine of comfort continues in the following verse: "I also beheld that all children who die before they arrive at the years of accountability are saved in the celestial kingdom of heaven" (D&C 137:10). This truth was revealed again—children are saved, not just in a mysterious heavenly place but in the celestial kingdom!

Armed with the good news of the restored gospel, the Prophet preached at several funerals and ministered to his faithful friends.

MINISTERING BY APPLYING TRUE DOCTRINE

Eleven years had passed since the death of their adopted son, one-year-old Joseph Smith Murdock. During that time, Joseph and Emma lost other children. They would lose yet another to stillbirth. Nine months before the stillborn son was delivered, the Prophet delivered a Sabbath-day address in Nauvoo. In the sermon he spoke to the parents of deceased three-year-old toddler Marian Lyon, explaining why some children die in infancy.

> In my leisure moments I have meditated upon the subject, and asked the question, why it is that infants, innocent children, are taken away from us, especially those that seem to be the most intelligent and interesting. The strongest reasons that present themselves to my mind are these: This world is a very wicked world; and it is a proverb that the "world grows weaker and wiser;" if that is the case, the world grows more wicked and corrupt. In the earlier ages of the world a righteous man, and a man of God and of intelligence, had a better chance to do good, to be believed and received than at the present day: but in these days such a man is much opposed and persecuted by most of the inhabitants of the earth, and he has much sorrow to pass through here. The Lord takes many away, even in infancy, that they may escape the envy of man, and the sorrows and evils of this present world; they were too pure, too lovely, to live on earth; therefore, if rightly considered, instead of mourning we have reason to rejoice as they are delivered from evil, and we shall soon have them again.[19]

Two years later at the funeral of King Follett, Joseph taught that parents of deceased children will have the privilege of raising their children to full stature in the Resurrection: "'Will mothers have their children in eternity?' Yes! Yes! Mothers, you shall have your children; for they shall have eternal life, for their debt is paid. There is no damnation awaiting them for they are in the spirit. But as the child dies, so shall it rise from the dead, and be forever living in the learning of God. It will never grow [in the grave]; it will still be the child, in the same precise form [when it rises] as it appeared before it died out of its mother's arms."[20]

Sister Isabella Horne reported that she witnessed the Prophet ministering to the wife of John Taylor, a future president of the Church.

> In conversation with the Prophet Joseph Smith once in Nauvoo, the subject of children in the resurrection was broached. I believe it was in Sister Leonora Cannon Taylor's house. She had just lost one of her children, and I had also lost one previously. The Prophet wanted to comfort us, and he told us that we should receive those children in the morning of the resurrection just as we laid them down, in purity and innocence, and we should nourish and care for them as their mothers. He said that children would be raised in the resurrection just as they were laid down, and that they would obtain all the intelligence necessary to occupy thrones, principalities and powers. The idea that I got from what he said was that the children would grow and develop in the Millennium, and that the mothers would have the pleasure of training and caring for them, which they had been deprived of in this life.[21]

The doctrine that little children inherit salvation stretches from eternity to eternity. The worthy in Christ "shall receive a crown in the mansions of my Father, which I have prepared for them" (D&C 59:2), which the Lord spoke to Joseph Smith. This truth lived in the days of Adam, and it is true today. True principles find application across generations of time.

Mike Stanley was a high-school-aged intern who worked at a hospital in Provo, Utah, in 1985. He relates an experience that demonstrates the stark, contrasting realities of those who have the blessings of restored truth and those who are deprived of them.

> One afternoon an infant was rushed into the emergency room. Unfortunately, the child had already passed away as a victim of sudden infant death syndrome (SIDS). The parents came in to view the body of their baby. Their grief was obvious and justified. A dark and gloomy feeling prevailed in the hospital room. The family's preacher was summoned to the hospital to console the parents. They chatted first at the bedside and then in a nearby conference room for a lengthy period of time. The weeping continued, and the family was inconsolable. As I pondered the events, I realized why they were so distraught. According to their understanding,

because the child had not been baptized, he was now a child of the devil. Their hopes and dreams for their baby would be left unfulfilled not only in this life but also in the life beyond.

Later the same day, another infant was brought into the emergency room. A similar scene unfolded. This child, also a victim of SIDS, was pronounced dead by the attending physician. The parents were brought into the room. Tears of grief accompanied sorrow. But even in that moment of tragedy, theirs was a feeling not limited to loss but also of hope and light. The feeling was not tangible but was vividly real and comforting, especially when contrasted with the earlier events of the day. A short time later, this Latter-day Saint family's bishop arrived. I do not know or recall the content of their conversations with this priesthood leader. I do know, however, that the feeling in the room was vastly different than what I had witnessed before, for theirs was an understanding of a merciful plan. Even as a teenager, I recognized the comforting spirit that can accompany and console the aching heart.[22]

Family bonds stretch and grow far beyond death. "Families can be together forever,"[23] the hymn proclaims. That is Heavenly Father's plan. His little children are eternally a part of it. They shall live and shall inherit celestial glory! This doctrine stands as one of the sweetest, most comforting of all restored doctrines. It stands as a witness of the divine mission of Joseph Smith.

NOTES

1. Carol Cornwall Madsen, *Journey to Zion: Voices from the Mormon Trial* (Salt Lake City: Deseret Book, 1997), 508–9; emphasis added. Louise Charlotte Leuba Graehl claimed to have been the first female convert baptism in Geneva. She continued to write of that experience. "Sometime after this [the passing of little Emma] Mr. Roulst, one of our acquaintances, came and spoke to me about a new religion that he had just embraced. He seemed to be full of joy and said many things about the great light he had received; but I must confess that I paid very little attention to all that he said for I had known him only as a man of the world and I thought it very funny to have him speak that way about religion. At that time I did not care for any religion anyhow. However, he continued to talk and one day he brought me some pamphlets to read. They were on

the first principles of the Gospel, and I was astonished in reading them, for they threw a new light on the Scriptures that I had read so often, but not understood before. I was baptized into the Latter-day Saint Church on the 7th of June, 1853, being the first woman in Geneva to join the church, and my husband was baptized one month later."

2. Robert J. Matthews, "A Walk through the Bible with the Prophet Joseph Smith," in *Thirty-first Annual Joseph Smith Memorial Sermon, Logan Institute of Religion* (Logan, UT: Logan LDS Institute of Religion, 1973), 1–2. Only five of eleven of Joseph and Emma Smith's children survived to the age of accountability. This is a brief summary of the chronology of their children which is taken largely from Matthews's paper.

   Alva (or Alvin) born and died on June 15, 1828, Harmony, Pennsylvania.

   Louisa, born April 30, 1831, Kirtland, Ohio—a fraternal twin, lived about three hours.

   Thaddeus, born April 30, 1831, Kirtland, Ohio—a fraternal twin, lived about three hours.

   Joseph Smith Murdock, born April 30, 1831, Kirtland; adopted; died a few days after March 25, 1832.

   Julia Murdock, born April 30, 1831, Kirtland; adopted; died in 1880 at the age of forty-nine near Nauvoo, Illinois.

   Joseph Smith III, born November 6, 1832, at Kirtland. This was the first of the Prophet's natural children to live to maturity. He died in 1914 at the age of eighty-two.

   Frederick Granger Williams, born June 20, 1836, at Kirtland; died April 13, 1862.

   Alexander Hale Smith, born June 2, 1838, at Far West, Missouri; died in 1909.

   Don Carlos Smith, born June 13, 1840, at Nauvoo; died in 1841 at the age of fourteen months.

   "A boy," born December 26, 1842. He did not survive his birth.

   David Hyrum Smith, born November 17, 1844 at Nauvoo, five months after the Prophet's martyrdom. He died in 1904 at the age of sixty.

3. Noah Webster, *An American Dictionary of the English Language,* Facsimile Edition (New York: S. Converse, 1828; reprint, republished in Facsimile Edition by Foundation for American Christian Education, San Francisco, Thirteenth Printing, August 2000).

4. Charles Buck, "Annihilation," in *A Theological Dictionary,* Woodward's New Edition.

5. Rev. Baden Powell of Oxford University wrote these thoughts for

Kitto's *Cyclopaedia of Biblical Literature,* according to Joseph Fielding Smith in *Teachings of the Prophet Joseph Smith,* comp. Joseph Fielding Smith (Salt Lake City: Deseret Book, 1969), 350–51n5.

6. Joseph Fielding Smith, *Doctrines of Salvation, Volume Two,* ed. Bruce R. McConkie (Salt Lake City: Bookcraft, 1955), 2:49; emphasis in the original.

7. S. Harent, "Original Sin," in *Catholic Encyclopedia,* ed. Charles G. Herbermann and others (New York: Robert Appleton, 1911), 11:312–15. Harent further explained that original sin is "the hereditary stain that is dealt with here" and that "Adam by his fault transmitted to us not only death but also sin." According to conclusions of the Council of Trent, "original sin is described not only as the death of the soul (Sess. V, can. ii), but as a 'privation of justice that each child contracts at its conception' (Sess. VI, cap. iii). But the council calls 'justice' what we would call sanctifying grace (Sess. VI). . . . St. Augustine already cited, 'the deliberate sin of the first man is the cause of original sin.' This principle is developed by St. Anselm: 'the sin of Adam was one thing but the sin of children at their birth is quite another, the former was the cause, the latter is the effect' (De conceptu virginali, xxvi)." Harent continued his own commentary, declaring, "The crime of a father brands his yet unborn children with shame, and entails upon them a share of his own responsibility. . . . Original sin is a real sin which deprives the soul of sanctifying grace. It has the same claim to be a sin as has habitual sin."

8. William H. W. Fanning, "Baptism," in *Catholic Encyclopedia,* ed. Charles G. Herbermann and others (New York: Robert Appleton, 1907), 2:266; emphasis added.

9. Byron R. Merrill, "Original Sin," in *Encyclopedia of Mormonism,* ed. Daniel H. Ludlow (New York: Macmillan, 1992), 1052; from R. Reed, *The Gospel as Taught by Calvin* (Grand Rapids, MI, 1979), 33.

10. Bruce R. McConkie, *Mormon Doctrine,* 2nd ed. rev. (Salt Lake City: Bookcraft, 1966), 550. Herein, Elder McConkie references the *Book of Common Prayer,* The Anglican Church of Canada, 662–63; emphasis in original.

11. Merrill, "Original Sin," 1052; from Samuel Cohon, *Essays in Jewish Theology* (Cincinnati, OH, 1987), 265.

12. Circumcision might absolve male children from original sin, but how does one deal with the female infant? The practice and procedure has been modified over the years. "The ceremony is clearly a male ritual, and has become more and more so through the years. Originally the [male] child was held by his mother during the operation. . . . It was the practice for centuries . . . [to offer] a prayer for the mother's recovery from childbirth. . . . But by the sixteenth cen-

tury, at the very latest, the mother had been relegated to a back room, or even to a different building, her home, while the men attended the ceremony at the synagogue.

"The result of all this is a certain ambivalence about the ritual today, especially among circles of liberal Jews who value gender equality. On the one hand, it is nearly unthinkable after all these centuries not to have your son circumcised. But on the other hand, the fact that only boys can be circumcised and the evolution of the ritual into a men-only affair make it equally impossible for these modern Jews to go through the rite as it has come down to us.

"Some liberal Jews, therefore, have altered the traditional rite. The Reform movement, for example, emphasizes the *brit* (the covenant aspect) and plays down the *milah* (the actual operation of circumcision). There is a single eighth-day liturgy for boys and for girls, a common 'Covenant Ceremony' in which boys and girls are inducted into the 'covenant of Abraham and Sarah.' The only difference is that in the boy's rite, as the liturgical words are recited, a mohel or physician performs the operation" (Rabbi Morris N. Kertzer, *What Is a Jew?* First Touchstone Edition [New York: Touchstone, 1993], 241–42).

13. Fanning, "Baptism," 2:258–74. Fanning continues, "St. Ambrose (II De Abraham., c. xi) speaking of the necessity of baptism, says: 'No one is excepted, not the infant, not the one hindered by any necessity.'" He goes on, saying, "Catholic theologians are unanimous, consequently, in declaring that infants dying without baptism . . . are certainly excluded from heaven." One of authority must perform baptism. "The Roman Ritual declares: 'The legitimate minister of baptism is the parish priest.'" But, so unforgiving is the belief that infants must be baptized that "the Ritual also says that the father or mother should not baptize their own child, except in danger of death when no one else is at hand who could administer the sacrament [baptism]. . . . The authoritative decision of the Church, however, is plain. Pope Urban II (c. Super quibus, xxx, 4) writes: 'It is true baptism if a woman in case of necessity baptizes a child in the name of the Trinity.' The Florentine decree for the Armenians says explicitly: 'In case of necessity, not only a priest or a deacon, but even a layman or woman, nay *even a pagan or heretic may confer baptism.*' The main reason for this extension of power as to the administration of baptism is of course that the Church has understood from the beginning . . . the absolute necessity of baptism for the salvation of souls" (emphasis added).

14. Smith, *Doctrines of Salvation,* 2:52; emphasis in original.

15. Joseph Smith, *History of the Church of Jesus Christ of Latter-day Saints,* ed. B. H. Roberts, 2nd ed. rev. (Salt Lake City: Deseret News, 1908),

4:554; emphasis added. This address was delivered in the grove west of the Nauvoo Temple on March 20, 1842. The body of the deceased child of Windsor P. Lyon was lying in a coffin before the congregation. The Prophet felt inspired to depart from his prepared remarks and spoke the foregoing.

16. James E. Talmage, *Articles of Faith*, 12th ed. (Salt Lake City: The Church of Jesus Christ of Latter-day Saints, 1924), 127. Also, "The Nephite prophet Mormon denounced the practice of infant baptism, which had apparently crept in among his people, and declared that anyone who supposed that little children need baptism would deny the mercies of Christ, setting at naught the value of his atonement and the power of his redemption" (Carl S. Hawkins, "Baptism," in *Encyclopedia of Mormonism*, 1:93–94).

17. "Genesis Chapter 17, of the Inspired Version [Joseph Smith Translation] explains that the age of accountability is set at 8 years. This was made known in the Inspired Version at a date earlier than it is recorded in D&C 68:25. It seems unmistakable, that this important principle was revealed to Joseph Smith while translating Genesis 17, in connection with the 8 days of age when circumcision was performed" (Matthews, "Walk through the Bible," 7).

18. Section 137 was given to Joseph by vision on January 21, 1836. It was truly a vision of the future. Joseph Smith Sr. was in the upper room of the Kirtland Temple with the younger Joseph when he received the vision. Lucy Mack Smith, Joseph's mother, was also alive and was elsewhere in the village. Alvin had not yet received ordinances by proxy. (Baptism for the dead was introduced at Nauvoo in 1840.) Yet all three were shown in the celestial kingdom, surrounded in glory (see Joseph Fielding McConkie and Craig J. Ostler, *Revelations of the Restoration* [Salt Lake City: Deseret Book, 2000], 1138–39).

19. Smith, *History of the Church*, 4:553. This paragraph is taken from the same address referenced in footnote 18.

20. Joseph Smith, *Discourses of the Prophet Joseph Smith*, ed. Alma P. Burton (Salt Lake City: Deseret Book, 1956), 138–39.

21. Smith, *History of the Church*, 4:556.

22. This account is paraphrased from a personal letter dated December 23, 2004, to the author from Michael D. Stanley, director of the LDS Institute of Religion in Visalia, California. It is his story and is used and edited with his permission.

23. "Families Can Be Together Forever," *Hymns* (Salt Lake City: The Church of Jesus Christ Latter-day Saints, 1985), no. 300.

CHAPTER THIRTEEN

A Prophet "as in Days of Yore"

BRETT L. HOLBROOK

From humble beginnings in a quiet grove in 1820, a marvelous flood of light burst into the world in a grand restoration of truth. According to the dictionary, the word *restore* means "to bring back into existence or use; re-establish" or "to bring back to an original condition."[1] One of the greatest parts of the doctrinal restoration in this dispensation under Joseph Smith was the "bringing back" of an understanding of the role of a true prophet. In each dispensation on this earth, prophets have been called to do the Lord's will and impart His word to His children (see Amos 3:7). After the Great Apostasy, the role and function of prophets had been lost to mankind. Part of the restoration under Joseph Smith was to restore how God communicates and works through His anointed servants, the prophets. Even as this dispensation began to unfold, the need for a prophet was sorely felt. Brigham Young lamented that, before he found the gospel, he "would be willing to crawl around the earth on [his] hands and knees, to see such a man as was Peter, Jeremiah, [or] Moses."[2] As done anciently, the Lord would anoint a prophet like Moses to usher in this dispensation. The calling of Joseph Smith as a prophet was accompanied by the necessary signs and symbols to support, sustain, and define his role.

The Lord had foretold the restoration of prophets and declared

Brett L. Holbrook is director of the Costa Mesa California Institute of Religion.

in this dispensation, "I will raise up unto my people a man, who shall lead them like as Moses" and "My servant Joseph Smith, Jun., is the man" (D&C 103:16, 21; see also 28:2; Moses 1:41; 2 Nephi 3:7, 9). In January of 1836 in Kirtland, Joseph Smith received a blessing from his father, wherein Joseph stated that he "sealed upon me the blessings of Moses, to lead Israel in the latter days, even as Moses led him in days of old."[3] Joseph had been ordained as "President of the High Priesthood" at a conference in January of 1832.[4] His role as prophet was further revealed in 1835, as "the duty of the President of the office of the High Priesthood is to preside over the whole church, and to be like unto Moses—Behold, here is wisdom; yea, to be a seer, a revelator, a translator, and a prophet, having all the gifts of God which he bestows upon the head of the church" (D&C 107:91–92).

Those four specific functions of the President of the High Priesthood were reiterated in 1841, as the Lord stated He had given His "servant Joseph to be a presiding elder over all [the] church, to be a translator, a revelator, a seer, and prophet" (D&C 124:125). To restore the meaning of those four titles, the Lord prepared symbolic evidence to sustain Joseph Smith as the prophet of God.[5] John Taylor compared the preservation of the symbols Moses had in the ark of the covenant[6] with others likewise preserved on the American continent in the Book of Mormon: "As ancient Israel preserved in the Ark of the Covenant memorials of God's power, goodness and mercy, manifested during the exodus from Egypt, in the two tablets of stone and the pot of manna; and of the recognition of the Aaronic Priesthood in Aaron's rod that budded; and as the sword of Laban, the sacred plates already revealed, as well as numerous others yet to be made manifest, and a Urim and Thummim were preserved on this continent; so will there be an exhibition an evidence, a memorial . . . preserved and manifested in the dispensation that the Lord in His loving kindness has now inaugurated."[7] The Liahona was added to the sacred collection of the sword of Laban, the plates, and the Urim and Thummim to make up a group of symbols that would be an "exhibition of evidence" in the latter days of the Prophet's role. As Moses led the children of Israel anciently with the ark and sacred objects, Joseph Smith would be the Moses of the last dispensation with the sacred symbols preserved for his role.

THE SACRED COLLECTION OF SYMBOLS

These sacred symbols were passed down among those who were in authority as the Lord's representatives in the Book of Mormon.[8] From the history of the Church, we find that all four parts of the sacred collection of symbols were preserved, and their coming forth as part of the Restoration under Joseph Smith helps to testify of his role as the prophet to head up this last dispensation. Just prior to the publication in 1829 of the Book of Mormon, the Lord warned Joseph Smith, "Behold, if they will not believe my words, they would not believe you, my servant Joseph, if it were possible that you should show them all these things which I have committed unto you. . . . Behold, verily I say unto you, I have reserved those things which I have entrusted unto you, my servant Joseph, for a wise purpose in me, and it shall be made known unto future generations" (D&C 5:7, 9). Echoing the words of Alma and Mormon (see Alma 37:3; Words of Mormon 1:7), the Lord promised that three others would be called and ordained, "unto whom I will show these things," and their testimony would be added to Joseph's (D&C 5:11). Three months later those three witnesses—Oliver Cowdery, David Whitmer, and Martin Harris—were told in a revelation that they would "have a view of the plates, and also of the breastplate, the sword of Laban, the Urim and Thummim, . . . and the miraculous directors" (D&C 17:1). They would be witnesses to the sacred symbols and were to "testify of them, by the power of God." The Lord continued, "And this you shall do that my servant Joseph Smith, Jun., may not be destroyed, that I may bring about my righteous purposes unto the children of men" (D&C 17:3–4).

In the Restoration of the Church of Jesus Christ and His gospel to the earth, the sacred collection of items appears as an additional witness to the calling of a prophet in the latter days. The three witnesses later testified that they saw all four of the items, even as the Lord had promised they would.[9] It is thought that the sacred symbols Joseph possessed were eventually returned to the angel, but there were many of the early Saints for whom the power of the symbols in connection with Joseph remained. All four items came forth in this dispensation as testimonies to the office and calling of Joseph Smith as "a seer, a revelator, a translator, and a prophet." The conferring of those four titles upon Joseph Smith in this dispensation corresponds to the four sacred items the Lord preserved as a testament of the role of Joseph Smith, that he "may not be destroyed, that I may bring about my righteous purposes unto the children of men" (D&C 17:4).

Joseph as Seer—the Urim and Thummim

Elder Orson F. Whitney explained that "a seer is one who sees. But it is not the ordinary sight that is meant. The seeric gift is a supernatural endowment. Joseph was 'like unto Moses;' and Moses, who saw God face to face, explains how he saw him in these words: 'Now mine own eyes have beheld God; yet not my natural, but my spiritual eyes; for my natural eyes could not have beheld; for I should have withered and died in his presence; but his glory was upon me; and I beheld his face, for I was transfigured before him.' [Moses 1:11.]"[10] One with the seeric gift, to see or perceive the things of God, was considered to be "greater than a prophet" (Mosiah 8:15). Ammon further taught, "A seer can know of things which are past, and also of things which are to come, and by them shall all things be revealed, or, rather, shall secret things be made manifest, and hidden things shall come to light, and things which are not known shall be made known by them" (Mosiah 8:17). In the development of a seer, the Lord has bestowed blessings to help in the process. Elder Widtsoe remarked: "A seer is one who sees with spiritual eyes. He perceives the meaning of that which seems obscure to others; therefore he is an interpreter and clarifier of eternal truth. He foresees the future from the past and the present. This he does by the power of the Lord operating through him directly, or indirectly with the aid of divine instruments such as the Urim and Thummim."[11]

The Urim and Thummim[12] were also "called interpreters. . . . And whosoever is commanded to look in them, the same is called a seer" (Mosiah 8:13). They were a gift given to many of the Lord's servants, such as Abraham (see Abraham 3:1), Noah,[13] Moses and Aaron (see Exodus 28:30),[14] the brother of Jared (see Ether 2:23), and Mosiah (see Mosiah 8:13). Joseph Smith received the Urim and Thummim with the plates for the purpose of translation in 1827 (see Joseph Smith—History 1:59, 62; Ether 3:23, 24, 28).[15] In addition to translation, the Urim and Thummim served as an instrument for Joseph to see with spiritual eyes and receive other revelations and inspiration. The early revelations in the Doctrine and Covenants Joseph received through the Urim and Thummim.[16] His mother, Lucy Mack Smith, wrote, "That of which I spoke, which Joseph termed a key, was indeed, nothing more nor less than the Urim and Thummim, and it was by this that the angel showed him many things which he saw in vision." She continued by saying, "He could ascertain, at any time, the approach of danger, either to himself or the Record, and on account of which he always kept the Urim and Thummim about his person."[17] It was through the Urim and Thummim that Joseph received the command for him and Oliver Cowdery to be baptized, and by this same instrument Joseph was told to write to David Whitmer for assistance so he could complete the translation of the plates.[18]

As a seer, Joseph had the privilege of using the Urim and Thummim, but he did not always need it. As Joseph developed as the Lord's anointed servant, so did his ability to receive communication from the Lord. Joseph explained in 1831 to Orson Pratt while working on his inspired translation of the Bible that "the Lord gave him the Urim and Thummim when he was inexperienced in the Spirit of inspiration. But now he had advanced so far that he understood the operations of that Spirit, and did not need the assistance of that instrument."[19] Revelations after section 17 of the Doctrine and Covenants were apparently received without them. President Joseph Fielding Smith held that the Urim and Thummim were returned with the plates to the angel and that the Prophet Joseph never used them after the organization of the Church. Any mention of the Urim and Thummim after that was most likely referring to a seer stone that Joseph was known to possess.[20] On December 27, 1841, Elder Wilford Woodruff and the rest of the Twelve met with the Prophet Joseph. On that date he recorded, "I had the privilege of seeing for the first time in my day the Urim and Thummim."[21] Elder Brigham Young recorded on the same day that Joseph "explained to us the Urim and Thummim which he found with the plates" and "he showed us his seer stone."[22] For the purposes of our examination, whether these statements about the Urim and Thummim refer to the original, a new set of interpreters, or a seer stone doesn't matter. The fact that the symbolism of the Urim and Thummim stayed connected with the Prophet Joseph Smith and his role as seer among the early Saints is what does.

Some of Joseph Smith's closest associates years later continued to view him as having the Urim and Thummim and the seeric gift. Edward Stevenson first met the Prophet in 1834, and his family loaned Joseph their copy of *Book of Martyrs* by John Fox. When Joseph returned it, he stated, "I have, by the aid of the Urim and Thummim, seen those martyrs."[23] In July of 1843, Joseph and Hyrum Smith were discussing the revelation on plural marriage. Hyrum "very urgently requested Joseph to write the revelation by means of the Urim and Thummim, but Joseph in reply, said he did not need to, for he knew the revelation perfectly from beginning to end."[24] After the death of the Prophet Joseph, Elder Heber C. Kimball testified that this divine instrument passed on to the next leader of the Church: "'Has brother Brigham Young got the Urim and Thummim?' Yes, he has . . . everything that is necessary for him to receive the will and mind of God to this people. Do I know it? Yes, I know all about it."[25] Joseph Smith was a seer as in ancient times, and the Urim and Thummim was a symbol that testified of the restoration of that role in this dispensation.

JOSEPH AS REVELATOR—THE LIAHONA

An understanding of revelation is one of the wonderful doctrines restored by the Prophet Joseph Smith. As Amos declared, "Surely the Lord God will do nothing, until he revealeth the secret unto his servants the prophets" (Joseph Smith Translation, Amos 3:7; see also Daniel 2:28). Using an example of an ancient prophet, Joseph Smith was told, "This is the spirit of revelation; behold this is the spirit by which Moses brought the children of Israel through the Red Sea on dry ground" (D&C 8:3). Moses was a revelator for the children of Israel by receiving revelation to help them cross the Red Sea and escape the Egyptians. Elder John A. Widtsoe stated: "A revelator makes known, with the Lord's help, something before unknown. It may be new or forgotten truth, or a new or forgotten application of known truth to man's need."[26] While anyone may qualify to receive revelation of truth for oneself, only the President of the High Priesthood can receive it on behalf of all the people. Among the sacred symbols passed on to Joseph Smith, the Liahona testified of his role as revelator.

In the Book of Mormon, the prophet Lehi was given "a round

ball of curious workmanship" that "pointed the way whither [he] should go into the wilderness" (1 Nephi 16:10). Not only would it point Lehi and his family to the most fertile parts of the wilderness, but it also worked "according to the faith and diligence and heed" that was given it (1 Nephi 16:16, 28). In addition, "there was also written upon [its spindles] a new writing, which was plain to be read, which did give us understanding concerning the ways of the Lord; and it was written and changed from time to time" (1 Nephi 16:29). From this sacred instrument they received direction and new revelation that would guide them in the wilderness. Alma tells us this ball or director was also called the Liahona, or compass, and it was a type or shadow of the words of Christ that will lead us to eternal bliss if we heed them (see Alma 37:38–45).

The function of the Liahona was an example of how the words of Christ are revealed. The Apostle John recorded that because of apostasy, the Church "fled into the wilderness, where she hath a place prepared of God" (Revelation 12:6). It was revealed to Joseph Smith that Satan did "drive the church into the wilderness" (D&C 86:3), and the opening of this dispensation was "the beginning of the rising up and the coming forth of [the] church out of the wilderness" (D&C 5:14; see also 33:5; 109:73). To be led out, the Lord said, the Church needed to hear "the voice of one crying in the wilderness—in the wilderness, because you cannot see him—my voice, because my voice is spirit; my spirit is truth" (D&C 88:66). Joseph heard that voice in the wilderness when in the grove in 1820 the word of Christ was revealed to him (see Joseph Smith—History 1:14–20). Joseph Smith was the revelator of the Lord's word in this dispensation and was called as His servant. In that role as revelator Joseph was told, "This generation shall have my word through you" (D&C 5:10; see also 21:5; 43:3). Like the Liahona, Joseph was to reveal the word of Christ to guide the church through the wilderness.

Those who knew Joseph saw him as the director and guide, the revelator of the will of God. Edward Partridge, the first bishop in this dispensation, understood that role when he said the Lord would "give unto his people a prophet, through whom they can have the word of the Lord from time to time, to lead them along from the wilderness in which they have been lost."[27]

Brigham Young suggested, "A guide is what we want—a guide for our actions on the earth. God has given us one—he revealed a guide through Joseph Smith, the Prophet, and others who have lived in modern times, and they have revealed the will of the Almighty unto the people."[28]

Joseph Murdock wrote in 1844, a few months before Joseph's martyrdom, "He is a prophet of God and as much called to guide the people in this day as Moses was in his day."[29] President George Q. Cannon testified that the Apostles have the keys "necessary to obtain revelation from God, and to lead and guide this people in the path that leads to the celestial glory; but there is only one man at a time who can hold the keys, who can dictate, who can guide, who can give revelation to the Church. The rest must acquiesce in his action, the rest must be governed by his counsels, the rest must receive his doctrines. It was so with Joseph."[30]

Not only did Joseph exemplify the role of Revelator, he restored our understanding of revelation. Even as the writing on the Liahona was "changed from time to time" according to their faith, Joseph taught that this was "the principle on which the government of heaven is conducted—by revelation adapted to the circumstances in which the children of the kingdom are placed."[31] Joseph Smith showed that the heavens are indeed open, and the Liahona testified of his role as revelator to guide the Church out of the wilderness to the promised land.

JOSEPH AS TRANSLATOR—THE PLATES

The role of translator is very similar to that of seer, but the Lord lists the two roles separately in three different revelations (see D&C 21:1; 107:92; 124:125). Even though the title "translator" is not in use today, "should records appear needing translation, the President of the Church may at any time be called, through revelation, to the special labor of translation."[32] What exactly does it mean to "translate"? The most basic understanding is "to express in another language, systematically retaining the original sense." But is it always to render something from one language to another? Not necessarily, as "translate" is further defined as "to put in simpler terms, explain" or "to convey from one form or style to another; convert."[33] A translator's responsibility, then, is to make something more understandable, whether through other words or different languages. The prophetic office of translator is different in that it requires the gift of translation, which is one of the gifts of the Spirit (see Alma 9:21). Through the translation process, knowledge would be revealed and one would gain greater understanding.

As part of the sacred collection, the angel Moroni entrusted the plates to Joseph Smith, and the Lord said Joseph would "have power to translate through the mercy of God, by the power of God, the Book of Mormon" (D&C 1:29; see also 20:8). The plates were obviously the prominent part of the sacred collection and held specific significance. When Alma passed the records on to his son Helaman, he noted that "these things should be preserved; for behold, they have enlarged the memory of this people, yea, and convinced many of the error of their ways, and brought them to the knowledge of their God unto the salvation of their souls" (Alma 37:8). The record they kept, in addition to the plates of brass, "brought them to the knowledge of the Lord their God, and to rejoice in Jesus Christ their Redeemer" (Alma 37:9). The plates revealed knowledge, knowledge of the gospel and of God, and without that knowledge one could not know God.[34] The Lord stated in this dispensation, "For this very purpose are these plates preserved, which contain these records—that the promises of the Lord might be fulfilled, which he made to his people; and that the Lamanites might come to the knowledge of their fathers, and that they might know the promises of the Lord, and that they may believe the gospel and rely upon the merits of Jesus Christ" (D&C 3:19–20). The plates contained the knowledge of God and would give the reader greater understanding of the gospel.

Joseph was given the gift to translate (D&C 5:4) and revealed to Oliver Cowdery that through this gift one "may translate and receive knowledge from all these ancient records which have been hid up, that are sacred." (D&C 8:11) After the translation of the Book of Mormon, we know that Joseph returned the plates to the custody of the angel Moroni.[35] However, the role of translator, the symbol of revealed knowledge and understanding from the Book of Mormon plates, continued in Joseph Smith. In addition to the Book of Mormon, Joseph received commandments to translate the Old and New Testaments (see D&C 35:20; 45:60–61; 90:13; 93:53) and other records. In his short time in mortality, Joseph Smith restored large volumes of knowledge by translation and revelation. Elder Jeffrey R.

Holland said, "More books or pages of scripture have come to us through Joseph Smith than from any other prophet—more even than from Moses, Luke, Paul, and Mormon combined!"[36] Just what the Prophet Joseph produced by way of translation filled most of his adult life.[37] The knowledge restored by Joseph Smith as translator has shed greater light on ancient prophets and their teachings.

Those who knew Joseph understood the supernal gifts that he had for divinely restoring knowledge. Brigham Young declared that "Joseph Smith, the Prophet of the last days, had a happy faculty of . . . throwing a flood of light into the gloom of ages, . . . connecting the heavenly and the earthly together—in one blending flood of heavenly intelligence."[38] Benjamin F. Johnson records that "the Lord began through the Prophet Joseph to turn the Keys of Knowledge to flood the world with new Light and Life."[39] As a translator, Joseph restored that lost knowledge. Other records have been promised by the Lord to come forth (see D&C 6:26),[40] and the office of translator will again be needed to bring back lost truth and knowledge. Elder Orson Pratt stated that we "will behold other books come forth and other records translated" by one "that God will raise up by which these ancient records will be brought to light."[41] Joseph Smith was the translator to open this dispensation, and he brought the first of those ancient records to light.

JOSEPH AS PROPHET—THE SWORD OF LABAN

The term *prophet* can be used in a variety of ways. In a generic sense, a prophet is one who has the spirit of prophecy, and "the testimony of Jesus is the spirit of prophecy" (Revelation 19:10). Anyone who has that testimony "is a prophet within the sphere of responsibility and authority given him."[42] But in a specific sense, those with the calling or office of a prophet differ in their sphere of responsibility than those generally with that testimony. President Anthony W. Ivins taught: "A careful study of the etymology of the word and of the lives, works and character of the prophets of old makes clear the fact that a prophet was, and is, one called to act as God's messenger. He is to teach men the character of God, and define and make known to the people, his will."[43] President Harold B. Lee testified, "A prophet is one who speaks, who is inspired of God to speak in his name."[44] As one with divine authority, he becomes a legal administrator for God's kingdom on earth and, like Moses, he is "to preside over the whole church" (D&C 107:91). As a prophet would officially declare the word of God, he is also a teacher of it. Elder Widtsoe explains: "A prophet is a teacher. That is the essential meaning of the word. He teaches the body of truth, the gospel, revealed by the Lord to man; and under inspiration explains it to the understanding of the people. He is an expounder of truth. . . . He becomes a warrior for the consummation of the Lord's purposes with respect to the human family. The purpose of his life is to uphold the Lord's plan of salvation."[45] As a "warrior" for the Lord and defender of the faith, the role of the prophet is to be his spokesman invested with divine authority to teach the word of the Lord.

The word of the Lord is often symbolized in the scriptures as a double-edged sword,[46] and the Lord declared that his "sword is bathed in heaven" (D&C 1:13). For many, the sword is a symbol of divine authority and power,[47] and the sword of Laban held that prominence in the Book of Mormon.[48] The Saints early in this dispensation also understood that symbol,[49] and the sword of Laban was known to be associated with the Prophet Joseph Smith. In 1831 there were many spiritual phenomena and false visions in the Church that prompted the Lord to reveal section 50 of the Doctrine and Covenants. John Whitmer recorded that "some would fancy to themselves that they had the sword of Laban, and would wield it as expert as a light dragoon."[50]

The Saints looked upon Joseph Smith as a leader fighting for their cause with the sword symbolic of the authority of God. In the October 1838 journal of Albert P. Rockwood, which was sent in installments as letters, he wrote to his family about the Mormon militia at Far West and the Battle of Crooked River. He implored to his father, "Come to Zion and fight for the religion of Jesus[.] many a hoary head is engaged here, the Prophet goes out to the battle as in days of old. he has the sword that Nephi took from Laban. is not this marvellous? well when you come to Zion you will see <& learn> many marvellous things, which will strengthen your faith, and which is for the edification of all the saints."[51]

Even as some felt that Joseph possessed the sword of Laban, his strongest association with the sacred symbol comes from the famous "cave story" mentioned in a discourse by Brigham Young in 1877. In the middle of his sermon about the treasures that the Lord has stored up in the earth, Brigham related a story from the life of Oliver Cowdery:

> When Joseph got the plates, the angel instructed him to carry them back to the hill Cumorah, which he did. Oliver says that when Joseph and Oliver went there, the hill opened, and they walked into a cave, in which there was a large and spacious room. . . . They laid the plates on a table; it was a large table that stood in the room. Under this table there was a pile of plates as much as two feet high, and there were altogether in this room more plates than probably many wagon loads; they were piled up in the corners and along the walls. The first time they went there the sword of Laban hung upon the wall; but when they went again it had been taken down and laid upon the table across the gold plates; it was unsheathed, and on it was written these words: "This sword will never be sheathed again until the kingdoms of this world become the kingdom of our God and his Christ." I tell you this as coming not only from Oliver Cowdery, but others who are familiar with it.[52]

President Heber C. Kimball delivered an earlier discourse in 1856 that mentioned the same event, noting, "How does it compare with the vision that Joseph and others had, when they went into a cave in the hill Cumorah, and saw more records than ten men could carry?"[53] Here it is declared a vision, but the authenticity of it is strengthened by many other accounts mentioning it with some variations.[54] Whether it was a vision or a physical event, the meaning was real, and the principles in it just as relevant.

The symbolic meaning of the words written on the sword is what was associated with Joseph Smith. It is reminiscent of the words of the Lord to Ezekiel: "Seeing then that I will cut off from thee the righteous and the wicked, therefore shall my sword go forth out of his sheath against all flesh from the south to the north: that all flesh may know that I the Lord have drawn forth my sword out of his sheath: it shall not return any more" (Ezekiel 21:4–5). In 1838 Albert P. Rockwood wrote, "The Prophet has unsheathed his sword and in the name of Jesus declares that it shall not be sheathed again untill [sic] he can go unto any County or state in safety and in peace."[55] The Saints connected the wording on the sword of Laban with Joseph as the prophet. Years later in Nauvoo, Joseph Smith repeated the same language on the sword that declared it will never be sheathed again.

Joseph was mayor and lieutenant general of the Nauvoo Legion and had the three roles of prophet, military leader, and civil administrator. On June 18, 1844, close to his death and with enemies on all sides, Joseph assembled the Nauvoo Legion. In full uniform, he gave his last public address to the troops, during which he drew his sword, presented it to heaven, and said: "I call God and angels to witness that I have unsheathed my sword with a firm and unalterable determination that this people shall have their legal rights."[56] Other witnesses recorded the event, saying that the Prophet stated: "The sword is unsheathed and shall never return to its sheath again until all those who reject the truth and fight against the kingdom of God are swept from the face of the earth."[57] The sword Joseph used at this time was not the sword of Laban, but language similar to what was on the sword of Laban in the cave was used in conjunction with his Nauvoo military blade. Like some of the other sacred items, it was the symbolism that was important, not whether it was still the original object or not. As Joseph stood before his troops as their military leader, the sword had the same symbolic meaning as the sword of Laban, and the people rallied around him as their authorized leader. The sword of Laban was a symbol of divine authority that testified of Joseph as a prophet who speaks the word of God.

CONCLUSION

Joseph Smith was called as a prophet of God, a prophet as "in days of yore."[58] To testify of the restored understanding of the role of a prophet, the Lord preserved a collection of sacred items "for future generations." As part of the doctrinal restoration through the Prophet Joseph Smith, these symbols bore witness of his calling and restored to the world an understanding of how God works with his official representatives here on earth. As one like unto Moses, Joseph was to be called "a seer, a revelator, a translator, and a prophet" (D&C 107:92), the meaning of which had been lost to the world. Each sacred object symbolized one of these aspects. The Urim and Thummim testified of Joseph's role as seer, that he would see with spiritual eyes and bring vision to his people. The Liahona bore witness of the revelator receiving the word of God to guide the Church out of the wilderness. The plates showed forth the gift as translator that had been given to Joseph, to bring knowledge and understanding back to light. Finally, the sword of Laban was a symbol of divine authority and power that had been placed upon Joseph as the prophet to speak the word of God. In time still to come the role of translator will again be needed, but today we sustain the President of the High Priesthood as "prophet, seer, and revelator." Through the Restoration, the Lord has brought "back to an original condition" His spokesmen and witnesses here upon the earth.

NOTES

1. *The American Heritage Dictionary,* 2nd ed., s.v. "restore."

2. Brigham Young, in *Journal of Discourses* (London: Latter-day Saints Book Depot, 1854–86), 8:228.

3. Joseph Smith, *History of the Church of Jesus Christ of Latter-day Saints,* ed. B. H. Roberts, 2nd ed. rev. (Salt Lake City: Deseret Book, 1974), 2:380.

4. Smith, *History of the Church,* 1:267.

5. Symbols are a type of universal language, defined as "something that represents something else by association, resemblance or convention, especially a material object used to represent something invisible" (*The American Heritage Dictionary,* 2nd ed., s.v. "symbol"). Even when the objects are removed or lost, the power of the association remains as the symbolism becomes more important to the people than the object, and the symbolism can even be transferred to other objects (H. J. T. Johnson, "Regalia," in *Encyclopedia of Religion and Ethics,* ed. James Hastings [New York: Charles Scribner's Sons, 1951], 10:632).

6. For Moses and the children of Israel, a collection of symbols went before them in the form of the ark of the covenant (see Numbers 10:33). Not only did the mercy seat on top of the ark represent the presence of the Lord (Exodus 25:22), but the items contained therein were symbols of the Lord's providence, guidance, and authority. The Apostle Paul tells us that within the ark of the covenant "was the golden pot that had manna, and Aaron's rod that budded, and the tables of the covenant" (Hebrews 9:4). All three of these items were preserved by direct command of the Lord, "to be kept for a token" and "to be kept for your generations" (Numbers 17:10; Exodus 16:32–34; 25:16; 40:20).

7. John Taylor, *The Mediation and Atonement* (Salt Lake City: Deseret News, 1882), 122–23.

8. Great care was taken to pass these items down (see 2 Nephi 5:12–14; Mosiah 1:15–16; 28:20; Alma 37:3, 14; 50:38).

9. See, for example, Lyndon W. Cook, ed., *David Whitmer Interviews* (Orem, UT: Grandin Book, 1991), 11, 15, 20, 86, 127, 192, 198, 213.

10. Orson F. Whitney, *Cowley & Whitney on Doctrine,* comp. Forace Green (Salt Lake City: Bookcraft, 1963), 233–34.

11. John A. Widtsoe, *Evidences and Reconciliations,* arr. G. Homer Durham (Salt Lake City: Bookcraft, 1960), 258.

12. "In other terms, communicating light perfectly, and intelligence perfectly, through a principle that God has ordained for that purpose" (John Taylor, in *Journal of Discourses,* 24:263).

13. Orson Pratt, in *Journal of Discourses,* 16:50.

14. Orson Pratt, in *Journal of Discourses,* 19:206.

15. Smith, *History of the Church,* 4:537.

16. See Doctrine and Covenants sections 3, 6, 7, 10, 11, 12, 14, 15, 16, and 17.

17. Lucy Mack Smith, *History of Joseph Smith* (Salt Lake City: Bookcraft, 1958), 110.

18. Smith, *History of Joseph Smith,* 142, 147.

19. Orson Pratt, *Millennial Star,* August 11, 1874, 498–99; Widtsoe, *Evidences and Reconciliations,* 89–90.

20. Joseph Fielding Smith, *Doctrines of Salvation,* ed. Bruce R. McConkie (Salt Lake City: Bookcraft, 1954), 3:223–24.

21. Wilford Woodruff, *Waiting for World's End: The Diaries of Wilford Woodruff,* ed. Susan Staker (Salt Lake City: Signature Books, 1993), 50.

22. Brigham Young, *Millennial Star,* February 20, 1864, 118–19.

23. Edward Stevenson, *Reminiscences of Joseph, the Prophet* (Salt Lake City: Edward Stevenson, 1893), 5–6.

24. Smith, *History of the Church,* 5:xxxii.

25. Heber C. Kimball, in *Journal of Discourses,* 2:111.

26. Widtsoe, *Evidences and Reconciliations,* 258.

27. Edward Partridge, in *Messenger and Advocate,* January 1835, 61.

28. Brigham Young, in *Journal of Discourses,* 15:192.

29. "Joseph Stacey Murdock to John Dougless, East Hamilton, N.Y., Jan. 24, 1844," in Mark L. McConkie, *Remembering Joseph* (Salt Lake City: Deseret Book, 2003), 66.

30. George Q. Cannon, in *Journal of Discourses,* 19:234.

31. Smith, *Teachings,* 256.

32. Widtsoe, *Evidences and Reconciliations,* 256.

33. *The American Heritage Dictionary,* 2nd ed., s.v. "translate."

34. This was the case with the Mulekites, whose "language had become corrupted; and they had brought no records with them; and they denied the being of their Creator; and Mosiah, nor the people of Mosiah, could understand them" (Omni 1:17).

35. Smith, *History of the Church,* 1:18–19.

36. Quoted in Neal A. Maxwell, *A Wonderful Flood of Light* (Salt Lake City: Bookcraft, 1990), 18.

37. Chronologically, Joseph translated the following: the Book of Mormon between 1828 and 1829; the Parchment of John (D&C 7) April 1829; the Joseph Smith Translation of the Bible between 1830 and 1833; the book of Abraham between 1835 and 1842; and the Papyrus Scroll of Joseph in Egypt in 1835 (see Robert J. Matthews, "Joseph Smith—Translator," in *Joseph Smith: The Prophet, the Man,* ed. Susan Easton Black and Charles D. Tate Jr. [Salt Lake City: Bookcraft, 1993], 77–79).

38. Brigham Young, in *Journal of Discourses,* 9:310.

39. Quoted in Dean R. Zimmerman, *I Knew the Prophets* (Bountiful, UT: Horizon, 1976), 52.

40. These records include the sealed portion of the Book of Mormon (2 Nephi 27:7, 22), those of the lost tribes of Israel (2 Nephi 29:13), an account of the mount of transfiguration (D&C 63:20–21), the record of John the Baptist (93:18), and the book of Enoch (D&C 107:57).

41. Orson Pratt, in *Journal of Discourses,* 19:216.

42. Harold B. Lee, *Stand Ye in Holy Places: Selected Sermons and Writings of President Harold B. Lee* (Salt Lake City: Deseret Book, 1975), 155.

43. Anthony W. Ivins, in Conference Report, October 1925, 20. A prophet was one who was an official representative of God, who would deliver the word of God as a messenger (see Malachi 1:13; 2 Chronicles 36:15–16). As the authorized messenger, a prophet was sent because he "hath stood in the counsel of the Lord, and hath perceived and heard his word" (Jeremiah 23:18).

44. Lee, *Stand Ye in Holy Places,* 153.

45. Widtsoe, *Evidences and Reconciliations,* 257.

46. Some of these references are Revelation 1:16; 19:15; 1 Nephi 21:2; D&C 6:2; 11:2; 12:2; 14:2; 33:1.

47. Brett L. Holbrook, "The Sword of Laban as a Symbol of Divine Authority and Kingship," *Journal of Book of Mormon Studies* 2, no. 1 (Spring 1993): 41–48.

48. Originally taken by Nephi around 600 B.C. from Laban, who was slain by it, this sword of "exceedingly fine" (1 Nephi 4:9) workmanship was passed down among the sacred items in Nephite history. Once it was brought to the new world, Nephi "did take the

sword of Laban, and after the manner of it did make many swords" (2 Nephi 5:14). Held by the Nephite kings as a symbol of authority, the people said Nephi "was a great protector for them, having wielded the sword of Laban in their defense" (Jacob 1:10). Nearly four hundred years later, against the Lamanites, King Benjamin "did fight with the strength of his own arm, with the sword of Laban" (Words of Mormon 1:13).

49. Joseph Smith on occasion saw the formation of stars in the night sky as a sword or a stream of light in the heavens in the form of a broadsword that was witnessed by others (John J. Stewart, *Joseph Smith the Mormon Prophet* [Salt Lake City: Hawkes Publishing, 1966], 154–155; *History of the Church*, 4:439; Joseph Grant Stevenson, ed., *Autobiography of Edward Stevenson, 1820–1897* [Provo, UT: Stevenson's Genealogical Center, 1986], 90).

50. F. Mark McKiernan and Roger D. Launis, eds., *An Early Latter-day Saint History: The Book of John Whitmer* (Independence, MO: Herald House, 1980), 62.

51. D. C. Jessee and D. J. Whitaker, "The Last Months of Mormonism in Missouri: The Albert P. Rockwood Journal," *BYU Studies* 28 (Winter 1988): 25.

52. Brigham Young, in *Journal of Discourses,* 19:38.

53. Heber C. Kimball, in *Journal of Discourses,* 4:105. David Whitmer also spoke of "the caves [that] hold other records that will not come forth till all is peace" (Cook, *David Whitmer Interviews,* 7, 22, 127).

54. See Alexander Baugh, "The Visions of Joseph Smith," *BYU Studies* 38, no. 1 (1999): 33–34, 52–53.

55. Jessee and Whitaker, "The Albert P. Rockwood Journal," 25.

56. Smith, *History of the Church*, 6:497–99.

57. George Morris, "Autobiography," L. Tom Perry Special Collections, Harold B. Lee Library, Brigham Young University, 17. Others recorded it as follows: "I can see him now, as he stood with his sword drawn and lifted toward heaven, as he declared the things which should take place on the earth, that the sword should not be sheathed until the earth was cleansed from wickedness" (Wandle Mace, "Journal [1809–1890]," L. Tom Perry Special Collections, Harold B. Lee Library, Brigham Young University, 134); "(Drawing his sword out of its scabbard and raised it above his head,) I will call upon the Gods to bear witness of this. I will draw my sword and it shall never be sheathed again until vengeance is taken upon all your enemies" (William Bryam Pace, "Diary," L. Tom Perry Special Collections, Harold B. Lee Library, Brigham Young University, 6); "Then, Said He, I will die for you. Drew his sword and raised it up to heaven and said it should never be sheathed

again until Zion was redeemed" (Larson, *Diary of Charles Lowell Walker*, 2:524).

58. Joseph S. Murdock, "Come, Listen to a Prophet's Voice," *Hymns* (Salt Lake City: The Church of Jesus Christ of Latter-day Saints, 1985), no. 21.

CHAPTER FOURTEEN

THE SCRIPTURAL RESTORATION

KENT P. JACKSON

Much of the Restoration of the gospel through Joseph Smith involved scripture. As a significant branch of his calling, the Prophet restored the Bible to earlier purity and brought forth new holy books that no one living in his day had ever heard of. Although a book of the modern Church was revealed (the Doctrine and Covenants), most of the scriptural restoration involved records from the past. The coming forth of scriptural truths and sacred volumes formed a crucial part of the Lord's latter-day work.

Among the important events of the Restoration was a series of encounters Joseph Smith had with scripture, most often involving the Bible. Each of those encounters contributed in its way to the bringing forth of gospel light, and each continues to bless the Church today, in some ways even more so now than in the early days of the Restoration. We shall examine those scriptural encounters in the order in which they happened, highlighting the contributions each makes to our understanding of the Bible or of biblical teachings. The intent is not to analyze these contributions but simply to list and summarize them. Again and again, we will see that modern revelation confirms, clarifies, and explains the teachings of the Old and New Testaments. Even more to the point, the Restoration not only

Kent P. Jackson is a professor of ancient scripture at Brigham Young University.

221

touches on every biblical doctrine but also dramatically improves upon the Bible's presentation of every doctrine.

ENCOUNTER 1: JOSEPH SMITH'S QUEST FOR TRUTH

Young Joseph Smith grew up in the home of "goodly parents who spared no pains to instructing [him] in the Christian religion."[1] Part of that instruction was to believe in the Bible and trust it to provide answers for life's most important questions. In the search that ultimately led to his prayer in the Sacred Grove, he sought an answer in the Bible to his question regarding which of all the churches was right. Yet because "the teachers of religion of the different sects understood the same passages of scripture so differently," he finally lost confidence in "settling the question by an appeal to the Bible" (Joseph Smith—History 1:12). As good and as important as the Bible is—an assessment Joseph Smith maintained throughout his life—it alone is not sufficient to answer all gospel questions. That was perhaps the first revealed lesson of the Restoration, coming even before the First Vision.

ENCOUNTER 2: THE FIRST VISION

The First Vision was part of the scriptural restoration because it teaches us important things about the Bible. Joseph Smith was motivated by Bible passages to pray in his quest for truth (James 1:5; see Joseph Smith—History 1:11–12). By doing so, he learned the truth of the promise in the scriptures: "Ask, and it shall be given you; seek, and ye shall find; knock, and it shall be opened unto you" (Matthew 7:7). The Prophet noted in his 1835 account that his prayer in the Sacred Grove tested the truth of that scripture.[2] But he also learned from the First Vision that not all truth is in the Bible, because the fulness of the gospel was not then on earth, yet it would "at some future time be made known" to him.[3]

Although the First Vision shows that not all truth is in the Bible, it nonetheless bears confirming testimony to important biblical teachings. From the First Vision, we learn that Satan, as the Bible tells us, is real and is not an imaginary force but an "actual being from the unseen world" (Joseph Smith—History 1:16). We learn that the God of the Bible exists, that Jesus Christ is God's Son, and that the Bible is true in its teaching that we are indeed created in God's physical image. From the First Vision we also learn the truthfulness of the biblical teaching that God and Jesus are separate, individual beings. In the Sacred Grove, those truths were revealed in plainness, unencumbered by the ancient creeds that distorted their meaning for most of Christianity. The First Vision, as part of the scriptural restoration, confirms those truths and thus bears testimony that the Bible is true.

ENCOUNTER 3: MORONI'S TEACHING OF JOSEPH SMITH

On the night of September 21–22, 1823, the angel Moroni appeared to Joseph Smith to begin the process of preparing him for his life's mission. In addition to informing him about the Book of Mormon, Moroni quoted scripture after scripture to teach Joseph Smith about the work that God would soon undertake through him. In the account in the Joseph Smith—History in the Pearl of Great Price, the Prophet mentioned only five passages that Moroni quoted and discussed, but he stated that the angel also "quoted many other passages" (Joseph Smith—History 1:41).[4] In 1835 Oliver Cowdery published three articles in the Church's newspaper, the *Messenger and Advocate,* in which he gave greater detail about Moroni's visits, undoubtedly based on what he had learned from Joseph Smith.[5] Those articles mention thirty passages that Moroni quoted or discussed, and like the list the Prophet himself provided, almost all were from the Old Testament.[6] Moroni's scriptures combine to give a coherent message about the great work that was then beginning, as can be seen in the topics covered in those verses: (1) the scattering of Israel and apostasy, (2) the calling of Joseph Smith, (3) the opening of the heavens and gifts of the Spirit, (4) the coming forth of the Book of Mormon, (5) the restoration of the priesthood and its keys, (6) the gathering and restoration of Israel, (7) the destruction and the purification of the earth, (8) the deliverance of the faithful, (9) the Second Coming of Jesus, and (10) the millennial blessings of the Saints.[7] Moroni's teaching of Joseph Smith from the Bible provided nothing less than a panoramic introduction to the dispensation of the fulness of times and the work of the Lord's Saints in it.

It is not insignificant that Moroni chose to teach Joseph Smith by citing, quoting, and commenting on the words of earlier prophets in scripture. Indeed, his doing so was part of the scriptural restoration, not only because he clarified and contextualized the words of biblical writers but also because he confirmed their truth.

ENCOUNTER 4: TRANSLATING THE BOOK OF MORMON

The coming forth of the Book of Mormon is a great tangible sign that God was doing a marvelous work in the latter days (see 3 Nephi 21:1–7). Joseph Smith's translation of the Book of Mormon is perhaps the most profound miracle of the Restoration. An uneducated young man who had spent his entire life in an obscure corner of the earth brought forth a book with such an amazing message that it is changing the world. Critics have tried for over a century and a half to destroy it, but its assertions become more and more credible the more they are scrutinized.[8]

Recent research into the original manuscript of the Book of Mormon has led to a greater understanding of how it was produced. Joseph Smith did not translate the Book of Mormon by using expertise in an original language to convey its meaning into a target language. Instead, evidence suggests that the English translation was *revealed* to Joseph Smith visually and that he dictated to his scribes the English words that he saw.[9] The text was revealed in Joseph Smith's dialect of English, but at the same time it contained vocabulary and usage that were foreign to his time and place.[10] Thus in the most technical sense, Joseph Smith was not the "translator" of the Book of Mormon any more than he was its "author," as he was identified for copyright purposes on the title page of the 1830 edition.

ENCOUNTER 5: THE BOOK OF MORMON

The Book of Mormon is a keystone of the Restoration that reveals in plainness fundamental truths that are central to the gospel. The following are some important doctrines that are found in the Bible but for which the Book of Mormon makes indispensable contributions.

Jesus and the Atonement. The Atonement is at the core of the Book of Mormon, and no book in the world teaches it better. In addition to clear and masterful presentations on the first principles and ordinances (see 3 Nephi 11:31–39; 27:13–21), the Book of Mormon contains profound teachings on salvation through the merits of Christ (see 2 Nephi 2:8), the relationship between grace and works (see

2 Nephi 25:23; 31:19), and what it means to be born again (see Mosiah 5:6–9).

Satan. The Bible says nothing about Satan's origin and little of his objectives. Lehi taught that Satan was once "an angel of God" who fell from heaven. Because he knew he would be "miserable forever," Satan "sought also the misery of all mankind," "that all men might be miserable like unto himself" (2 Nephi 2:17–18, 27).

The Fall of Adam and Eve. Lehi taught that if Adam and Eve had not fallen, they would have had no children (see 2 Nephi 2:22–23). In contrast to the traditional Christian view, the Book of Mormon teaches that the Fall was a positive step in the progress of the human family. "Adam fell that men might be; and men are, that they might have joy" (2 Nephi 2:25).

The antiquity of the gospel. The Book of Mormon begins with a colony of Christians six hundred years before Jesus' birth and informs us of another such group perhaps two thousand years earlier. Those groups had the gospel revealed to them in plainness, and they knew, even centuries before Jesus' coming, that His gospel was the only way to salvation (see Jacob 4:4–5; Mosiah 5:8).

The house of Israel. The authors of the Book of Mormon conveyed to us a clearer understanding of the house of Israel and its role in God's plan than can be found in any other book. Israel's restoration includes the restoration of the knowledge that Jesus is Israel's Redeemer (see 1 Nephi 10:14; 22:11–12), that the promised gathering of scattered Israelites will follow their conversion to Christ (see 2 Nephi 10:7–8; 3 Nephi 20:30–33), and that the Gentiles will save scattered Israel in the last days by bringing them Jesus' word (see 1 Nephi 13:38–40; 15:13–14).

The law of Moses. The Book of Mormon teaches the meaning and the intent of the law of Moses far better than does the Old Testament. The law and its observances "were types of things to come" (Mosiah 13:31).

Prophets and scripture. The Book of Mormon models processes by which revelation is received, including appearances (see Alma 8:14–18), dreams (see 1 Nephi 2:1), visions (see 1 Nephi 11–14), and quiet promptings (see 2 Nephi 32:7; Alma 14:11). In the Book of Mormon we learn that the message of all God's prophets, even in the Old Testament, is Jesus Christ (see Jacob 4:4; 3 Nephi 20:24).

The Bible. Nephi learned in a vision that "many plain and precious things" would be "taken away" from the Bible, causing people to "stumble" because of the omissions (1 Nephi 13:28–29, 32). Other books would come forth in the latter days to restore "the plain and precious things which have been taken away" from the Bible (1 Nephi 13:39–40).

One of the purposes of the Book of Mormon is to establish the truth of the Bible (see 1 Nephi 13:39–40). To do so is part of the scriptural restoration. Indeed, the Book of Mormon stands as a witness for the biblical prophets and writers, "proving to the world that the holy scriptures are true" (D&C 20:11).

ENCOUNTER 6: TRANSLATING THE BIBLE

In June 1830 Joseph Smith began working through the Bible to revise it by inspiration. In an intense biblical encounter that took about three years, he restored to the Bible "precious things" that been lost from it (see 1 Nephi 13:23–29) and revealed many important truths pertaining to biblical passages, people, and events.[11] The Prophet made changes, additions, and corrections in hundreds of verses. Collectively, these are called the "Joseph Smith Translation" (JST) or, as Joseph Smith and others in his day referred to it, the "New Translation."[12] In some parts of the Bible, much new material was added, as in the Genesis chapters that are included in the Pearl of Great Price, called "Selections from the Book of Moses." As far as can be determined, every book in the Bible was examined, but no changes were made in thirteen of them.[13] On some of the manuscript pages, the Prophet made a later pass (or passes) to revise his original dictation or to add further information until he felt the text was as the Lord wanted it to be.[14]

Joseph Smith's encounter with the Bible during the process of the New Translation was a unique part of the scriptural restoration. He was not revealing new scripture from ancient texts in his possession, as with the Book of Mormon and the book of Abraham. His "original manuscript" was the King James Version—already in English, already in print for more than two centuries, and already in the hands of members of the Church. Thus the work on the JST was a unique revelatory experience. Its importance was not limited to what is found in the final product, however. In addition to the New

Translation itself, including the book of Moses and Joseph Smith—Matthew in the Pearl of Great Price, the translation project yielded much fruit in educating the Prophet. It was an important means by which he gained knowledge of the Bible and knowledge of the Spirit that he used throughout his life.

Encounter 7: The Joseph Smith Translation of the Bible

Most changes the Prophet made to the biblical text were small rewordings or modernizations of King James language to make the text more clear and understandable for today's readers.[15] But the most significant changes are the revisions and additions that shed new light on history and doctrine. The following are some important topics that are taught in the JST with greater clarity and precision than they are in the Bible.

The nature of God. The Joseph Smith Translation testifies to the literal reality that God has a body (see Moses 6:9; 7:4; Exodus 33:20; John 1:18; 1 Timothy 6:15–16; 1 John 4:12).[16]

The extent and purpose of the Father's work. In the Joseph Smith Translation, we learn that God has created "worlds without number" inhabited by His children (Moses 1:33), with the purpose "to bring to pass the immortality and eternal life of man" (Moses 1:39).

The mission of Jesus Christ. From the New Translation we learn that Jesus was divine in the premortal world. He cast Satan out for rebellion (see Moses 4:2–3) and was the Creator (see Moses 1:32–33).

The plan of salvation. The Lord's plan of happiness is revealed clearly in the JST, even in the Old Testament. In the earliest generations, men learned that Jesus Christ is "the only name which shall be given under heaven, whereby salvation shall come unto the children of men" and that redemption is "unto all men, through the blood of [the] Only Begotten" (Moses 6:52, 62).

Satan. In the JST we read that Satan proposed his own desires in contrast to the plan of the Father: he would be God's son, he would "redeem all mankind, that one soul shall not be lost," and the Father would give him His honor. Now it is his goal "to deceive and to blind men, and to lead them captive at his will, even as many as would not hearken unto [God's] voice" (Moses 4:1–4).

The Fall of Adam and Eve. Eve said, "Were it not for our transgression we never should have had seed, and never should have known good and evil, and the joy of our redemption, and the eternal life which God giveth unto all the obedient" (Moses 5:11). These and other teachings from the New Translation are foreign to the Bible as we have received it, and they contradict traditional Christian beliefs.

The antiquity of the gospel. The JST teaches that the gospel of Jesus Christ was revealed in the beginning of human history. Adam and Eve were Christians (see Moses 5:9–12; 6:51–62, 64–66), as were their righteous descendants (see Moses 7:10–11; 8:23–24).

Enoch and the establishment of Zion. Even though Enoch is mentioned in the Bible, if we did not have the New Translation, we would not know anything about his life, his righteous people, or his people's translation because none of these details is in the Bible (see Moses 6–7).

Melchizedek and his priesthood. The JST teaches that Adam held what we call the Melchizedek Priesthood (see Moses 6:67), and it informs us of the ministry of Melchizedek and of the priesthood that bears his name (see Genesis 14).

The house of Israel. The New Translation teaches of the descendants of Joseph of antiquity taking the gospel to the rest of Israel (see Genesis 48). Joseph foretold the ministry of a choice seer who would bring Israel the Lord's word. The records of Joseph and Judah would grow together to establish the truth (see Genesis 50).

The purpose of animal sacrifice. The JST teaches the origin of animal sacrifice. An angel told Adam that it was "a similitude of the sacrifice of the Only Begotten of the Father, which is full of grace and truth" (Moses 5:7).

The law of Moses. The New Translation shows that after the golden calf incident, the Lord withdrew from Israel His sacred law—"my holy order, and the ordinances thereof" (JST, Exodus 34:1), "the everlasting covenant of the holy priesthood" (JST, Deuteronomy 10:2). In place of the higher law and the blessings that pertain to it, the law of Moses was instituted, governed by the Aaronic Priesthood. None of this is found in the Bible.

The Second Coming of Jesus Christ. Joseph Smith—Matthew in the Pearl of Great Price, an excerpt from the JST, is one of the great revelations concerning the last days, and it makes sense of Matthew 24, a very difficult biblical chapter that otherwise cannot be fully understood.

Degrees of glory. While translating John 5, Joseph Smith and his scribe received a vision of the degrees of glory that clarifies and expands on biblical teachings. In the revelation itself we read this explanation: "While we were doing the work of translation, which the Lord had appointed unto us, we came to the twenty-ninth verse of the fifth chapter of John, which was given unto us as follows. . . . And while we meditated upon these things, the Lord touched the eyes of our understandings and they were opened, and the glory of the Lord shone round about" (D&C 76:15, 19).

ENCOUNTER 8: THE DOCTRINE AND COVENANTS

The Doctrine and Covenants is a scriptural book unlike any of the others already discussed, being not a restored book but a truly modern scripture. At the same time, however, it is a significant part of the restoration of ancient scripture. For Joseph Smith, the revelations in the Doctrine and Covenants were another encounter with the Bible because most of the revelations, in one way or another, expound on principles, doctrines, or themes already present in the Old and New Testaments. Consider the following Doctrine and Covenants topics, among many others that could be listed: God the Father, Jesus Christ, and the Holy Ghost; or faith, repentance, baptism, the gift of the Holy Ghost, justice, mercy, the Fall, the Atonement, the Resurrection, and the last judgment; or covenants, temples, ordinances, spiritual gifts, tithing, the Church, missionary work, angels, Satan, temptation, the last days, the Second Coming, and the Millennium. All of these are biblical concepts, and none of them was introduced to the world for the first time in the Doctrine and Covenants. Yet the revelations in the Doctrine and Covenants add significant understanding to each of them, with clarifying words in the voice of the Lord Himself that teach us more—in many cases much more—than can be found in the Bible.

The Doctrine and Covenants contributes to the scriptural restoration in more direct ways as well. Some of the revelations deal explicitly with passages or events from the Bible. Section 45 is a new account of the Olivet Discourse from Matthew 24. Section 86 provides a needed explanation to Jesus' parable of the wheat and the tares in Matthew 13, and it also expounds on words of the Old Testament prophet Isaiah. Section 77 is a question-and-answer session concerning the book of Revelation, and section 113 is a question-and-answer session concerning Isaiah. Section 132 responds to questions about marriage raised during the Bible translation. In section 65, we learn that the stone that Daniel saw cut out of the mountain without hands is The Church of Jesus Christ of Latter-day Saints. Section 7 is a revelation concerning the mission of the Apostle John, and section 74 is an explanation of a passage in 1 Corinthians. Section 46 expands some verses from the same New Testament book. Section 76 is a grand enlargement of a statement of Jesus in John 5. Section 84 provides new insights into the lives of Moses and Jethro (among others), and it sheds dramatic new light on the history of the priesthood in Old and New Testament times. Similarly, section 107 reveals things about Adam, Enoch, Melchizedek, and other patriarchs that are entirely unknown in the Bible. And section 110 records the actual visits to Joseph Smith of three persons whose lives are known and discussed in the Bible—Jesus, Moses, and Elijah.

To these lists can be added many examples in which the Doctrine and Covenants uses biblical phrases or biblical images in such a way as to explain and clarify them, thus enabling us to understand the Bible better. Indeed, the Doctrine and Covenants is one of the great keys to understanding the Bible, an indispensable companion and guide to the records of ancient Israel and the early Church. Without it, the scriptural restoration would not be complete.

ENCOUNTER 9: THE BOOK OF ABRAHAM

Starting in 1835, Joseph Smith had another revelatory encounter with a previously unknown ancient scripture when the record of Abraham came into his hands. In early 1842, the first installments were published, with the anticipation that more would come at a later date.[17] The book of Abraham restores much gospel light to the world. Consider the following topics in which this book reveals in plainness things sometimes only hinted at in the Bible:

God and Jesus Christ. In the book of Abraham, we learn that there is order among the citizens of the universe, with God the Father being the greatest of all (see Abraham 3:1–24). Abraham learned that Jesus Christ was among "the intelligences that were organized before the world was." Even then, he was already "like unto God" (Abraham 3:22, 24).

The premortality of humankind. The book of Abraham gives us our best scriptural view into our premortal existence (see Abraham 3:22–28). In the presence of the Father and the Son, humans had agency, the capacity to make rational choices and be accountable for them. There some were foreordained to be the Lord's chief servants on earth (see Abraham 3:22–28).

The reason for life on earth. The book of Abraham gives us the scriptures' clearest statement concerning a fundamental purpose of our mortal existence. The Father's children would be tested on earth to see if they would "do all things whatsoever the Lord their God shall command them." Those who would be faithful in their mortal estate would "have glory added upon their heads for ever and ever" (Abraham 3:25–26).

Satan. From the book of Abraham, we learn things about Satan that are not preserved in the Bible. He was our spirit sibling before the creation of the earth. When the Father chose Christ instead of him, Satan became "angry, and kept not his first estate." He rebelled, and "many followed after him" (Abraham 3:27–28).

The Creation. The book of Abraham teaches the doctrine that the earth would be made of already existing materials: "We will go down, . . . and we will take of these materials, and we will make an earth whereupon these may dwell" (Abraham 3:24). This doctrine expands on what is contained in the Bible and refutes the basic belief of traditional Christianity that the world was created *ex nihilo*—out of nothing.

Abraham's life and priesthood. The book of Abraham contains historical material not found in Genesis or elsewhere in the Bible. The account of Abraham's father's efforts to offer him as a human sacrifice helps us view his history in the Bible in an entirely new light (see Abraham 1:5–15; Genesis 22:1–18). Abraham and his ancestors had true priesthood: "It came down from the fathers, from the beginning of time, yea, even from the beginning, or before the foundation of the earth" (Abraham 1:3).

The Abrahamic covenant. The book of Abraham provides important insights into the Abrahamic covenant, the mission of Abraham's descendants, the future of the house of Israel, and the principle of adoption (see Abraham 2:9–10).

ENCOUNTER 10: JOSEPH SMITH'S BIBLE SERMONS

During the last five years of his life, the Prophet Joseph Smith gave frequent sermons in which he taught from, and expounded on, Bible passages. Those Bible-based sermons were among the most important aspects of his ministry, because they were the primary means by which he taught doctrine to the Saints during that time. The Prophet discussed, quoted, and paraphrased from the Bible with ease, apparently without having a Bible with him as he spoke. Yet he discussed many passages, and as he did so he opened new meanings to the minds of his hearers, often going far beyond the teachings in the Bible. Following are some of the things that we learn:

The Father, the Son, and the Holy Ghost are three separate beings. "I have always declared God to be a distinct personage. Jesus Christ [is] a separate and distinct person from God the Father; the Holy Ghost is a distinct personage or spirit."[18] This doctrine is evident in the Bible, but it stands in sharp contrast to fundamental beliefs of most other Christians.

The Father and the Son have bodies of flesh and bones. This doctrine is another dramatic departure from traditional Christian doctrine (see D&C 130:22). Because God has a material body, "the idea that the Father and the Son dwell in a man's heart is an old sectarian notion, and is false" (D&C 130:3).

The Holy Ghost has a body of spirit. "The Son has a tabernacle and so has the Father. But the Holy Ghost is a personage of spirit without a tabernacle."[19] "There is no such thing as immaterial matter. All spirit is matter, but it is more fine or pure, and can only be discerned by purer eyes; we cannot see it; but when our bodies are purified we shall see that it is all matter" (D&C 131:7–8).

God is an exalted man. "God, that sits enthroned, is a man like one of yourselves. That is the great secret. . . . If you were to see him today you would see him in all the person, image, [and] very form of man."[20] This is a dramatic departure from the beliefs of most other Christians, but it is consistent with the actual doctrine of the Bible.

We are eternal beings. "The spirit of man is not a created being. It existed from eternity and will exist to eternity."[21] Some part of us, described as "the spirit," "the soul," "the immortal spirit," "the mind of man," "the intelligent part," and "intelligence," is eternal. According to Joseph Smith, God did not make it; it always existed.[22]

We may become as God is. "What was the design of the Almighty in making man? It was to exalt him to be as God."[23] "God himself, . . . because he was greater, saw proper to institute laws whereby the rest could have a privilege to advance like himself."[24]

In his sermons and instructions, often centered in passages from the Bible seen in the new light of the Restoration, Joseph Smith was making known to us the answers to life's most universal questions—questions that are evoked in the Bible but are answered fully only through modern revelation: Who am I? Where did I come from? Why am I here? Where am I going? Although these are biblical questions, it is the scriptural restoration that provides answers to them and to many more like them.

Assessing the Scriptural Restoration

Three concluding thoughts are in order concerning the scriptural restoration:

First, Joseph Smith produced more scripture than anyone else in history. We cannot say with certainty that there never was a time in which there were more pages of scripture available than we have now. But I give it as my opinion that we have more revelation publicly available to us today than anyone else in the history of the world has ever had. The scriptural restoration not only touched every dispensation of the gospel, but it also restored vital knowledge concerning each one. Moreover, it shed light on virtually every important scriptural person who ever lived prior to our day. Joseph Smith said: "The dispensation of the fulness of times will bring to light the things that have been revealed in all former dispensations, also other things that have not been before revealed."[25]

Second, we get our doctrine from modern revelation. The Lord made this matter clear when he told Joseph Smith, "This generation shall have my word through you" (D&C 5:10). I know of no doctrine for which we would turn first to the Bible for the clearest and best answers or explanations. President Marion G. Romney taught:

> In each dispensation, from the days of Adam to the days
> of the Prophet Joseph Smith, the Lord has revealed anew the

principles of the gospel. So that while the records of past dispensations, insofar as they are uncorrupted, testify to the truths of the gospel, still each dispensation has had revealed in its day sufficient truth to guide the people of the new dispensation, independent of the records of the past. I do not wish to discredit in any manner the records we have of the truths revealed by the Lord in past dispensations. What I now desire is to impress upon our minds that the gospel, as revealed to the Prophet Joseph Smith, is complete and is the word direct from heaven to this dispensation. It alone is sufficient to teach us the principles of eternal life.[26]

Finally, the Restoration is bigger and greater than most Latter-day Saints have imagined. Most of us undervalue it and do not appreciate what it has done. It was with good reason that the future founder of the Disciples of Christ, Alexander Campbell, complained in 1831 that the Book of Mormon dealt with, and provided answers for, all the important gospel controversies of his generation.[27] If Campbell lived today, he would find that the Book of Mormon and the other revealed sources also answer questions that were not even thought of in his time but are important issues now. The work of the Restoration is "one of vast magnitude and almost beyond the comprehension of mortals," a work "worthy of arch-angels; a work which will cast into the shade the things which have heretofore been accomplished."[28] As Joseph Smith said, the people whose names and lives are recorded in the Bible foresaw our day. "They have looked forward with joyful anticipation to the day in which we lived; and fired with heavenly and joyful anticipations, they have sung, and [written], and prophesied of this our day. . . . We are the favored people that God has made choice of to bring about the Latter Day glory. It is left for us to see, participate in, and help to roll forward the Latter Day glory, 'the dispensation of the fulness of times, when God will gather together all things that are in heaven, and all things that are upon the earth, even in one.'"[29]

NOTES

1. Dean C. Jessee, ed., *The Papers of Joseph Smith* (Salt Lake City: Deseret Book, 1989–97), 1:3; capitalization standardized.
2. See Jessee, *Papers of Joseph Smith*, 2:69.
3. *Times and Seasons*, March 1, 1842, 707.

4. See Joseph Smith—History 1:36–41: Malachi 3 ("part"); Malachi 4:1–6; Isaiah 11:1–16; Acts 3:22–23; Joel 2:28–32.

5. The articles are in the form of letters addressed to W. W. Phelps; "Letter IV. To W. W. Phelps, Esq.," *Latter Day Saints' Messenger and Advocate,* February 1835, 77–80; "Letter VI. To W. W. Phelps, Esq.," April 1835, 108–12; "Letter VII. To W. W. Phelps, Esq.," July 1835, 156–59.

6. For a list, see Kent P. Jackson, *From Apostasy to Restoration* (Salt Lake City: Deseret Book, 1996), 103–4, 114–15 nn. 2–7.

7. See the discussion and references in Jackson, *From Apostasy to Restoration,* 105–13.

8. Despite what opponents of the Book of Mormon claim, the historical sources overwhelmingly confirm Joseph Smith's account of its coming forth. A recent attack on the Book of Mormon in Grant H. Palmer, *An Insider's View of Mormon Origins* (Salt Lake City: Signature Books, 2002), depends on a bias of disbelief in the miraculous and repeats many of the same criticisms that have been attempted unsuccessfully since 1830.

9. See Royal Skousen, "How Joseph Smith Translated the Book of Mormon: Evidence from the Original Manuscript," *Journal of Book of Mormon Studies* 7, no. 1 (1998): 22–31.

10. Royal Skousen, personal communication.

11. See Scott H. Faulring, Kent P. Jackson, and Robert J. Matthews, eds., *Joseph Smith's New Translation of the Bible: Original Manuscripts* (Provo, UT: Religious Studies Center, Brigham Young University, 2004); and Robert J. Matthews, *"A Plainer Translation": Joseph Smith's Translation of the Bible—A History and Commentary* (Provo, UT: Brigham Young University Press, 1975).

12. See Doctrine and Covenants 124:89; *Times and Seasons,* July 1840, 140. See also Joseph Smith, *History of the Church of Jesus Christ of Latter-day Saints,* ed. B. H. Roberts, 2nd ed. rev. (Salt Lake City: Deseret Book, 1957), 1:341, 365; 4:164. The title *Inspired Version* refers to the edited, printed edition, published in Independence, Missouri, by the Community of Christ.

13. Esther, Ecclesiastes, Song of Solomon, Lamentations, Obadiah, Micah, Nahum, Habakkuk, Zephaniah, Haggai, Malachi, 2 John, and 3 John.

14. The evidence suggests that his final word revisions were in place by the summer of 1833, or not long thereafter. From then on, the Prophet endeavored to see to its publication, but that effort did not prove successful in his lifetime (see Robert J. Matthews, "Joseph Smith's Efforts to Publish His Bible Translation," *Ensign,* January 1983, 57–64).

15. Latter-day Saints are generally unaware of those changes, because, for the most part, only changes with doctrinal significance were selected for the footnotes in the Church's publication of the Bible.

16. Bible references are to the biblical passage at which the JST change is made, not to the Community of Christ Inspired Version.

17. *Times and Seasons,* March 1, 1842, 703–6; March 15, 1842, 719–22; May 16, 1842, 783. Elder John Taylor wrote the next year: "We had the promise of Br. Joseph, to furnish us with further extracts from the Book of Abraham. These with other articles that we expect from his pen . . . we trust will make the paper sufficiently interesting" (*Times and Seasons,* February 1, 1843, 95).

18. Joseph Smith, *The Words of Joseph Smith: The Contemporary Accounts of the Nauvoo Discourses of the Prophet Joseph,* comp. and ed., Andrew F. Ehat and Lyndon W. Cook (Provo, UT: Religious Studies Center, Brigham Young University, 1980), 378. In quotations from this source, capitalization, punctuation, and spelling have been standardized when necessary.

19. Smith, *Words of Joseph Smith,* 64.

20. Smith, *Words of Joseph Smith,* 357.

21. Smith, *Words of Joseph Smith,* 9.

22. Smith, *Words of Joseph Smith,* 346, 360; see also 345, 351–52, 359.

23. Smith, *Words of Joseph Smith,* 247.

24. Smith, *Words of Joseph Smith,* 360.

25. *Times and Seasons,* October 15, 1841, 578.

26. Marion G. Romney, "A Glorious Promise," *Ensign,* January 1981, 2.

27. Alexander Campbell, *Millennial Harbinger,* February 7, 1831, 93.

28. *Times and Seasons,* October 1840, 178–79.

29. *Times and Seasons,* May 2, 1842, 776.

CHAPTER FIFTEEN

THE RESTORATION OF THE NEW AND EVERLASTING COVENANT OF MARRIAGE

SHERRIE MILLS JOHNSON

"Herein is the work of my Father continued, that he may be glorified" (D&C 132:63).

When God placed Adam and Eve upon the earth, He established a system of family government patterned after celestial government—the patriarchal order, or, as it is called in the Doctrine and Covenants, "the new and everlasting covenant of marriage" (D&C 131:2). We lived under this priesthood order in our premortal existence.[1] This type of government is a perfect system of organization; however, as apostasy occurred on the earth, men neglected and counterfeited the patriarchal order of God. When Joseph Smith restored the gospel to the earth, he reestablished the patriarchal order and a correct understanding of what God intended the new and everlasting covenant of marriage to be.

Speaking of this new and everlasting covenant of marriage, President Ezra Taft Benson explained that this "order of priesthood spoken of in the scriptures is sometimes referred to as the patriarchal order because it came down from father to son. . . . But this order is otherwise described in modern revelation as an order of family government where a man and woman enter into a covenant with God—just as Adam and Eve—to be sealed for eternity, to have posterity, and to do the will and work of God throughout their mortality."[2] In the

Sherrie Mills Johnson is an instructor of ancient scripture at Brigham Young University.

patriarchal order, power resides with God the Eternal Father, who shares—through covenants—that power with men and women upon conditions of righteousness so that they can assist in His work upon the earth. And what is His work? "To bring to pass the immortality and eternal life of man" (Moses 1:39).

"I HAVE ENDOWED HIM WITH THE KEYS OF THE POWER OF THIS PRIESTHOOD" (D&C 132:59).

Since the patriarchal order is an order of the priesthood, a definition of priesthood is important before we proceed. Elder Bruce R. McConkie defined priesthood thus: "As pertaining to eternity, priesthood is the eternal power and authority of Deity by which all things exist."[3] Joseph Smith explained priesthood by saying that it is "a perfect law of theocracy, and stands as God to give laws to the people, administering endless lives to the sons and daughters of Adam."[4] The prophet further explained that the Melchizedek Priesthood "is the channel through which all knowledge, doctrine, the plan of salvation, and every important matter is revealed from heaven."[5]

The problem in understanding priesthood is that our finite minds have trouble comprehending anything so encompassing, so magnificent. Usually when speaking of priesthood we make reference to only parts of the priesthood. As Joseph Smith explained, the priesthood has "parts, ramifications, powers and blessings belonging to the same," and "all Priesthood is Melchizedek, but there are different portions or degrees of it."[6] Elder John A. Widtsoe explained that "motherhood is an eternal part of Priesthood."[7] Another part of priesthood consists of the offices to which men are ordained. Often, when we speak of priesthood within a cultural context, it is these offices of the priesthood to which we refer. But it should always be remembered that priesthood is much more than the offices that belong to it. As Elder Bruce R. McConkie explained, "The priesthood is greater than any of its offices. No office adds any power, dignity, or authority to the priesthood. All offices derive their rights, prerogatives, graces, and powers from the priesthood."[8]

The priesthood of God, then, is the power of God. This is the power by which the immortality and eternal life of man will be brought about. By sharing this power, thereby empowering His children, God desires to make us like He is. One of the major efforts of

His work includes organizing worlds and peoples and preparing places for them to eternally abide in His power. As the Lord revealed to Joseph Smith, "If you will that I *give unto you a place* in the celestial world, you must prepare yourselves by doing the things which I have commanded you and required of you" (D&C 78:7; emphasis added). Shortly before performing the Atonement, which enables this priesthood power in our lives, Jesus comforted the people by saying, "In my Father's house are many mansions; if it were not so, I would have told you. *I go to prepare a place* for you. And when I go, I will prepare a place for you, and come again, and receive you unto myself; that where I am, ye may be also" (Joseph Smith Translation, John 14:2–3; emphasis added). Preparing a place is an act of organization and implies that in the eternal scheme of things everyone has a place or that there is a proper order in which we should and will abide.

"MY HOUSE IS A HOUSE OF ORDER, SAITH THE LORD GOD" (D&C 132:18).

One of the major functions of the priesthood is to bring about this order—to organize mankind into the proper eternal arrangement. As Joseph Smith said, "The spirits of men are eternal . . . they are organized according to that Priesthood which is everlasting, 'without beginning of days or end of years.'"[9] Many of the words we use in conjunction with priesthood illustrate this concept. The correct name of the Melchizedek Priesthood itself includes the word *order*. As Joseph Smith explained, before being called Melchizedek, the priesthood "was called *the Holy Priesthood, after the Order of the Son of God*. But out of respect or reverence to the name of the Supreme Being, to avoid the too frequent repetition of his name, they, the church, in ancient days, called that priesthood after Melchizedek, or the Melchizedek Priesthood" (D&C 107:3–4). In the Book of Mormon, this priesthood is referred to as "the order of his Son" (Alma 13:2), or "the holy order of God" (Alma 4:20), or simply the "holy order" (2 Nephi 6:2).

An *order* is a group of people united or organized in a formal way.[10] In addition to being part of its title, the concept of organization is further emphasized by the fact that a man receives the priesthood by being ordained to it. *Ordain* comes from the Latin root *ordinare*, which means to put in order. Once ordained with priesthood power, a man has the authority to officiate in *ordinances*. This English word originates from the same Latin root, *ordinare*, as did *ordain*, but also comes to us through the Middle French *ordenance*, which means an act of arranging.[11] Thus we see that the very titles and vocabulary of the priesthood help us understand the significance of order within the gospel and allow us to define priesthood government on earth as a system by which every righteous individual is united within the proper order—the family order—and empowered to function and progress within the plan of salvation.

"ALL WHO WILL HAVE A BLESSING AT MY HANDS SHALL ABIDE THE LAW WHICH WAS APPOINTED FOR THAT BLESSING" (D&C 132:5).

Once we understand the importance of priesthood order, we are in a position to begin to understand the patriarchal order, or the new and everlasting covenant of marriage, because in the restored gospel of Jesus Christ, marriage is part of the priesthood—an actual order within the priesthood (see D&C 131:2). That is why a man and a woman must declare themselves worthy to be eligible to enter the patriarchal order. It is a holy priesthood order, and only those committed to obey God are eligible to receive this power. In addition to being worthy, the man and the woman must have received the prerequisite ordinances intended to prepare them for this order. A man must also have been ordained to an office within the Melchizedek Priesthood. In other words, he must have "taken his place" or have "been arranged" within the offices of the priesthood. When a man and woman are married in the new and everlasting covenant of marriage, they are *sealed* together and in the eyes of God are considered "one flesh" (Genesis 2:24), or one unit—a family unit. As one unit, they now take their place within the patriarchal order of the priesthood—the man and woman together. This does not mean that the woman holds priesthood office with the man. As Elder Bruce R. McConkie explains, "Women do not have the priesthood conferred upon them and are not ordained to offices therein, but they are entitled to all priesthood blessings. Those women who go on to their exaltation, ruling and reigning with husbands who are kings and priests, will themselves be *queens* and *priestesses*. They will hold positions of power, authority, and preferment in eternity."[12]

When entering the patriarchal order, a man and a woman do not covenant with each other. Instead, each of them covenants with God—the Eternal Patriarch.[13] Therefore, marriage in the gospel of Jesus Christ is not a dyad but a triad with God as the head, and it establishes a partnership with God the Father, His Son Jesus Christ, and the Holy Ghost. It is also interesting to note that the patriarchal order is entered into at an altar. Under the law of Moses, an altar is the place of sacrifice.[14] It is also the designated place for God's children to make covenants with Him. As such, the altar represents Jesus Christ and His great Atonement. In the temple sealing ceremony, the man and the woman kneel, the altar between them, to sacrifice their aloneness, their selfishness, their separateness. At that altar they make their covenants with God and are given the authority to perform the sacred rites that pertain to marriage that will make them one with each other—one flesh. As they remain worthy, they also become one with God. As one with Him, they do God's work upon the earth. Together, then, they continue (upon conditions of worthiness) as part of this priesthood order known as the patriarchal order, which is preparatory to and prerequisite for them to enter the highest degree of the celestial kingdom, where, if they are faithful, they will eventually inherit all that God has.

It is important to note here that *all* worthy people will have the opportunity to at some point enter this order. This is a promise from a God, who cannot lie (see Ether 3:12). Although not everyone has this opportunity in mortality, every worthy person will eventually be given the opportunity to enter the patriarchal order. Therefore, it is imperative that all of God's children understand the patriarchal order and how it operates in the eternal scheme of their lives.

"THIS IS ETERNAL LIVES—TO KNOW THE ONLY WISE AND TRUE GOD, AND JESUS CHRIST, WHOM HE HATH SENT" (D&C 132:24).

The goal of the gospel of Jesus Christ is to establish God's order and bring as many people who have a desire to a knowledge of and unity with God, a unity that is possible only through the power of the priesthood. Because of the Fall, mortal beings were cut off from the presence of God. The priesthood provides the ordinances that, through the Atonement of Jesus Christ, allow us to reunite with God or to be brought into "at-one-ment" with Him. This uniting process can be considered a healing process whereby we are made whole or healed from the effects of the Fall and from the effects of our own sins. It is also a progression, and becoming one flesh with another human being is a necessary step in this process of being made whole. The absolute intimacy and selfless sharing of life that is intended as part of the new and everlasting covenant of marriage is not only made possible by priesthood power but can also only be achieved through priesthood power.

As Lehi explained to his son Jacob, "I know that thou art redeemed, *because of the righteousness of thy Redeemer;* for thou hast beheld that in the fulness of time he cometh to bring salvation unto men" (2 Nephi 2:3; emphasis added). Neither Jacob nor you nor I will be saved solely because of our own efforts, our own righteous acts. We are saved because of the righteousness of Jesus Christ. Neither are our natures and hearts changed because of our self-discipline or knowledge of psychological techniques. They are changed through the blood of Jesus Christ (see Mosiah 4:3, 11; Moses 6:59–60). Likewise, our marriage relationships are not made strong and eternal because we are good at loving each other or meeting one another's needs. They are made eternal because of the Atonement of Jesus Christ. Too often we speak of the difference between a temple marriage and a civil marriage as simply a matter of duration. More important, however, they differ in the amount of divine power available to enhance the quality of the relationship. When worthily entered, the new and everlasting covenant of marriage means that priesthood power can operate in the relationship, making the union celestial now—not just in the next life. By that I mean it has the potential of possessing qualities that characterize celestial existence, such as extreme happiness and joy.

At a Brigham Young University Education Week lecture many years ago, Chauncey Riddle said something I have never forgotten: "Right now the Church is known for its large families. It will become a light to the world . . . only when it becomes known for its good marriages."[15] The first step to achieving a celestial marriage is to understand the power available and then to use it. Perhaps this is part of what Joseph Smith had in mind when he said that the devil "will so transform things as to make one gape at those who are doing the will of God."[16] Obviously evil is becoming more pronounced. But I think that in the latter days, righteousness is also becoming more pronounced. Thus the gap is widening, causing people to "gape" at those who are striving after righteousness. For us to do the will of God, we must study and understand this amazing gift of priesthood that Joseph Smith restored to the earth, be worthy to use it, and invoke its powers in our daily lives and in our family relationships.

"I . . . WILL GIVE UNTO THEE THE LAW OF MY HOLY PRIESTHOOD, AS WAS ORDAINED BY ME AND MY FATHER BEFORE THE WORLD WAS" (D&C 132:28).

In order to participate in this patriarchal order and to help men and women progress within it, each of us has duties to perform. Men are to preside in the home in the physical stead of God, in the same way that Christ presides over the Church (see 1 Corinthians 11:3; Ephesians 5:21–33). Men are also to administer the life-giving ordinances of the priesthood to their family and to others as called upon to do so. Women are to give life. They are also to assist in the work of the priesthood—to help bring to pass the immortality and eternal life of God's children. What becomes clear as one ponders this is that neither of them can do what they need to do alone. Neither man nor woman is complete without the other, and alone neither can fully help in bringing about the work and glory of God. To participate fully in His work, both men and women must be united in the Lord. This relationship was clearly defined in the Garden of Eden before the Fall.

In the beginning God declared, "It is not good that the man should be alone; I will make him an help meet for him" (Genesis 2:18). The adjective *meet* is seldom used in English anymore, but Webster's 1828 *American Dictionary of the English Language* defines it as "fit; suitable; proper; qualified."[17] The Hebrew word translated as "help" in this verse is *ezer,* which is used twenty-one times in the Old Testament. Of those twenty-one occurrences, sixteen refer to God. Two examples are "O God: thou art my help and my deliverer" (Psalm 70:5), and "our soul waiteth for the Lord: he is our help and our shield" (Psalm 33:20). Some have thought the word "help" indicates that women are subordinate to men; but *subordinate* as a translation of the word *ezer* is a misuse of the word. There is no way man can conceive of God as his subordinate. Instead, Adam was incomplete and needed Eve in order to be complete.[18] President Joseph Fielding Smith explained that "neither the man nor the woman were capable of filling the measure of their creation alone. The union of the two was required to complete man in the image of God."[19] As a pair, then, man and woman are completed in the image of God (see Genesis 1:26–27; Moses 2:26–27) and are trusted and empowered to do the work of God. According to Genesis, the woman is the qualified and necessary help needed to accomplish the work of the priesthood.[20]

The earliest revelation recorded in the Doctrine and Covenants that speaks of the importance of priesthood and its organizing and uniting power is section 2: "Behold, I will reveal unto you the Priesthood, by the hand of Elijah the prophet, before the coming of the great and dreadful day of the Lord. And he shall plant in the hearts of the children the promises made to the fathers, and the hearts of the children shall turn to their fathers. If it were not so, the whole earth would be utterly wasted at his coming." This revelation, delivered by Moroni to the Prophet Joseph Smith, occurred during the night of September 21, 1823. Almost six years later, on May 15, 1829, John the Baptist appeared to Joseph Smith and Oliver Cowdery and began the restoration of the offices of the priesthood when he ordained them to the Aaronic Priesthood (see D&C 13). Shortly after that Peter, James, and John restored the Melchizedek Priesthood. But the 1823 revelation stated that the priesthood would be revealed by Elijah. It was not until thirteen years later, on April 3, 1836, that Elijah appeared to Joseph Smith and Oliver Cowdery in the newly finished Kirtland Temple. On that occasion, Jesus Christ first appeared to accept the temple (see D&C 110:7). Immediately afterward, Moses appeared to restore the "keys of the gathering of Israel" (110:11). Elias next appeared and "committed the dispensation of the gospel of Abraham" (110:12), and finally Elijah appeared to bestow upon Joseph Smith the keys of the sealing powers (see 110:13–16). This was the culmination of priesthood power—the restoration of the power by which the family system of government that existed in heaven could operate on the earth and the power to seal these family units so they would be valid through all eternity.

In 1843 the revelations concerning the new and everlasting

covenant of marriage (D&C 131 and 132) were recorded, but as the heading to section 132 explains, "The doctrines and principles involved in this revelation had been known by the Prophet since 1831." A few of the early Church leaders and their wives had received the temple ordinances beginning in May of 1842.[21] But for the body of the Church to receive these blessings, there needed to be a temple. In 1842, Joseph explained to the Relief Society that "the Church is not now organiz'd in its proper order, and cannot be until the Temple is completed."[22] Then again in 1843 Joseph said, "Go to and finish the [Nauvoo] temple, and God will fill it with power, and you will then receive more knowledge concerning this priesthood."[23]

It is difficult to describe in one or two sentences how this power of the priesthood empowers men and women in the patriarchal order. Part of the reason for the difficulty occurs because one cannot understand the new and everlasting covenant of marriage until one understands the gospel within which the Lord through Joseph Smith situated the patriarchal order. Paradoxically, it was during the time Joseph Smith experienced abuses of worldly power in Liberty Jail that the Lord revealed to him that the "rights of the priesthood are inseparably connected with the powers of heaven, and that the powers of heaven cannot be controlled nor handled only upon the principles of righteousness" (D&C 121:36). When we analyze how God uses priesthood power, we see that He doesn't use it to dominate or coerce His children; instead, He allows them to be "agents unto themselves" (D&C 29:39). He uses power to edify, heal, encourage, teach, create, and bless. That is the only way priesthood power can be used. The powers of heaven are "controlled" and "handled" only by means of righteousness. This emphasis on righteousness helps us understand that the only thing priesthood power should be used to dominate is our own nature. As Joseph Smith said, "A man can do nothing for himself unless God direct him in the right way; and the priesthood is for that purpose."[24]

"FOR I HAVE CONFERRED UPON YOU THE KEYS AND POWER OF THE PRIESTHOOD, WHEREIN I RESTORE ALL THINGS, AND MAKE KNOWN UNTO YOU ALL THINGS IN DUE TIME" (D&C 132:45).

As part of the increase in knowledge that Joseph Smith promised, he established the Relief Society, explaining that "the Church was never perfectly organized until the women were thus organized"[25] and that "the society should move according to the ancient Priesthood."[26] This statement has great meaning when understood within the gospel framework. The work of the ancient priesthood (as it is today) was to establish God's kingdom on the earth, and the sisters were to be involved in that work. During the first year the Relief Society was organized, 1842, seventeen meetings were held, six of which the Prophet Joseph attended and spoke at. In the manuscript history of the Church dated April 28, 1842, Joseph wrote, "I . . . gave a lecture on the Priesthood shewing how the sisters would come in possession of the privileges, blessings, and gifts of the Priesthood . . . and that they might attain unto these blessings by a virtuous life and conversation and diligence in keeping all the commandments."[27] This and other messages indicate how Joseph intended the sisters to help in the work of the priesthood and enlightens us as to what the work of the priesthood entails. More importantly, however, it provides a pattern that shows us how priesthood power can and should operate for both men and women within the new and everlasting covenant of marriage.

In the very first meeting of what would become known as the Relief Society, Joseph instructed the sisters that they were to "provoke the brethren to good works in looking to the wants of the poor . . . to assist by correcting the morals and strengthening the virtues of the community, and save the Elders the trouble of rebuking."[28] Later, on April 28, 1842, he amended this by instructing as to how they were to provoke the brethren: "You must put down iniquity and by your good example provoke the Elders to good works."[29] He also said, "Let the weight of innocence be felt which is more mighty than a millstone hung about the neck. Not war, not jangle, not contradiction, but meekness, love purity, these are the things that should magnify us."[30] He encouraged them "to expound scriptures to all."[31] He told them that "there should be a select society, separate from all the evils of the world, choice, virtuous and holy." He encouraged them to repent by saying, "All hearts must repent—be pure and God will regard them and bless them in a manner that could not be bless'd in any other way."[32] If this advice were heeded by all husbands and wives, divorce would never occur.

In addition to words encouraging righteousness, Joseph warned them, "Do not injure the character of anyone,"[33] and he "commended them for their zeal but said some times their zeal was not according to knowledge. One principal object of the institution was to purge out iniquity."[34] He added that an "aspiring disposition will be in this Society, and must be guarded against—that every person should stand and act in the place appointed, and thus sanctify the Society and get it pure." He then promised them that "if you will be pure, nothing can hinder."[35]

At this sixth meeting of the newly organized Relief Society, Joseph also "read the Chap [1 Corinthians 12] and give instructions respecting the different offices, and the necessity of every individual acting in the sphere allotted him or her; and filling the several offices to which they were appointed."[36] After this he said, "I now turn the key to you in the name of God and this Society shall rejoice and knowledge and intelligence shall flow down from this time."[37] It was six days after this pronouncement that the endowment was administered to men and women for the first time in this dispensation.[38]

The word *key* was often used by the Prophet Joseph Smith. In this instance, it refers to a means of unlocking revelation whereby "knowledge and intelligence shall flow." It is this knowledge and intelligence that empowers men and women to become like Christ, and by becoming more like Christ they are in turn unified with each other. In other words, the magnificent "key" that was given was the key to the knowledge that allows the blessings and power of the priesthood to change us—to allow us to be born again. In this born-again state, we are pure and sanctified and empowered by the Holy Spirit, who guides and direct us in all things (see 2 Nephi 32:5)—including our marital and family relationships. Priesthood power that is obtained through the covenants and through righteous living binds relationships, enhances us spiritually, and makes us one with each other and with God. As Mormon explains, "In Christ there should come every good thing" (Moroni 7:22). Thus, turning to Christ allows priesthood power to operate in our lives, which not only ensures that our marital relationships will be eternal but allows celestial happiness to be part of our relationships here in mortality.

As we read the teachings of Joseph Smith, it becomes clear that he understood he was restoring a way of life that would help men and women overcome the carnal, sensual tendencies that keep us from receiving the power God wants us to have. Wilford Woodruff records hearing the Prophet teach some "precious principles" to the people: "Ever keep in exercise the principles of mercy & be ready to forgive our brother on the first intimations of repentance & asking forgiveness. . . . Beware of pride & not seek to excel one above another but act for each others good & honorably make mention of each others name in our prayrs before the Lord & before our fellow men, & not backbite & devour our brother."[39] To the Relief Society the Prophet said, "It is by union of feeling we obtain pow'r with God."[40] And to a council of high priests and elders he explained, "No man is capable of judging a matter, in council, unless his own heart is pure; and that we frequently are so filled with prejudice, or have a beam in our own eye, that we are not capable of passing right decisions."[41]

"I WILL MAGNIFY MY NAME UPON ALL THOSE WHO RECEIVE AND ABIDE IN MY LAW" (D&C 132:64).

It is this righteous way of life that allows priesthood power to be part of our marital relationships. In its splendor, the patriarchal order, or new and everlasting covenant of marriage, is both a means by which we obtain this power from God and the laboratory in which we practice and become proficient in using it. For those who succeed in this endeavor, the patriarchal order also becomes the crowning blessing whereby the marital relationship in its most magnificent form is allowed to continue for all eternity.

Those who understand the power that can be theirs and who use it are greatly blessed. A friend told me that at one point in her marriage, she and her husband realized they no longer loved each other. "He was leaving on a business trip, and it occurred to me that I didn't care if he ever came home," she explained. "Before he left, I confronted him with my feelings and he told me he felt the same. We decided to think about it while he was gone. When he returned, I expected him to say that since we didn't love each other any more we should divorce, but instead he told me that we needed to repent. I was surprised, but willing to try. We mapped out a course whereby we studied the scriptures more, determined to serve better in our Church callings, analyzed our lives to see where we needed to change actions and habits, held more honest and sincere fasts, and attended the temple more often. I can't say how or when it happened, but just as inexplicably as our love had faded, it was back. Only it was better, richer, and more joyful than it had ever been before. Since that time, when we begin to grow apart, we know what to do. We repent, and our marriage just keeps getting better and better."

In his autobiography, Parley P. Pratt expressed his feelings after Joseph explained the new and everlasting covenant of marriage to him: "I had loved before, but I knew not why. But now I loved—with a pureness—an intensity of elevated, exalted feeling, which would lift my soul from the transitory things of this groveling sphere and expand it as the ocean. I felt that God was heavenly Father indeed; that Jesus was my brother, and that the wife of my bosom was an immortal, eternal companion; a kind of ministering angel, given to me as a comfort, and a crown of glory for ever and ever. In short, I could now love with the spirit and with the understanding also."[42] Obviously, Elder Pratt was seeing and understanding the patriarchal order of marriage from within the context of the whole gospel of Jesus Christ. That is the only way it can be properly understood.

Joseph Smith restored the gospel of Jesus Christ and with it the new and everlasting covenant of marriage, which is an order of the priesthood, or, in other words, an order of God's power. When entered into with this understanding, both parties know that they are taking their place in God's eternal order and by so doing are being called upon to live by a higher law. They also know that by abiding that higher law of righteousness they not only assist in the work and the glory of God, but they also allow God to be part of and empower their marriage relationship. "For where two or three are gathered together in my name, there am I in the midst of them" (Matthew 18:20). With God in their midst, those living in the new and everlasting covenant of marriage will be blessed with enabling priesthood power. Such a union will not only be eternal; it will also be happy, rewarding, and strong enough to endure the adversity and challenges of mortality.

NOTES

1. Bruce R. McConkie, *Mormon Doctrine*, 2nd ed. (Salt Lake City: Bookcraft, 1966), 559.
2. Ezra Taft Benson, "What I Hope You Will Teach Your Children about the Temple," *Ensign*, August 1985, 7.

3. McConkie, *Mormon Doctrine*, 594.

4. Joseph Smith, *Teachings of the Prophet Joseph Smith*, comp. Joseph Fielding Smith (Salt Lake City: Deseret Book, 1976), 322.

5. Joseph Smith, *History of the Church of Jesus Christ of Latter-day Saints*, ed. B. H. Roberts, 2nd ed. rev. (Salt Lake City: The Church of Jesus Christ of Latter-day Saints, 1950), 4:207.

6. Smith, *Teachings*, 167, 180.

7. John A. Widtsoe, *Evidences and Reconciliations* (Salt Lake City: Bookcraft, 1960), 308.

8. McConkie, *Mormon Doctrine*, 595.

9. Smith, *Teachings*, 208.

10. Order seems to be very important to the Lord. Much of the Mosaic law was characterized by order. The temple furniture was arranged in a specific order, and rituals were performed in exact ways, which were to be routinely followed in daily life. There is so much pre-scribed order that, while some say its only function was to keep society organized, it appears to be pointing to more important things—to remind the people of eternal order.

11. C. S. Lewis points out that certain elements of mortal life con-stantly surprise us. Says Lewis, "We are so little reconciled to time that we are even astonished at it" (*Reflections on the Psalms* [Orlando: Harcourt, 1958], 138). We are startled to see how through time someone has grown, or we are surprised at how fast or slow time goes by on differing occasions. If time were the only thing we had ever known, the passage of it shouldn't surprise us. It would be like water to a fish—unnoticeable. In the same way, most mortals possess a longing for order that seems strange in a world of chaos. How could we long for something we never knew existed? Order is an eternal principle that feels like home and is part of what we knew in our premortal existence. Thus I consider the longing for order that most of us experience a form of homesickness.

12. McConkie, *Mormon Doctrine*, 594.

13. I am aware that some consider the marriage covenant to be a covenant between a man and a woman. However, Elder McConkie defines a covenant as "a binding and solemn compact, agreement, contract, or mutual promise between God and a single person or a group of chosen persons" (*Mormon Doctrine*, 166). In addition, our beginning definition of patriarchal order from President Benson states that the patriarchal order is "an order of family government where a man and woman enter into a covenant with God" (see note 2). He said nothing about them covenanting with each other. In a private conversation on March 10, 2005, with Robert Matthews, past temple president of the Mount Timpanogos Temple, he told me that he had carefully studied the wording of

the marriage sealing ceremony and found no indication that any of the promises were made with anyone but God. In his book *Approaching Zion* (Salt Lake City: Deseret Book, 1989), 385, Hugh Nibley claims that Heber C. Kimball taught that "there are no covenants made between individuals in the church. All promises and agreements are between the individual and our Father in Heaven; all other parties, including the angels are present only as witnesses." I have been unable to find Kimball's original teaching on the subject, but it is consistent with the teachings concerning gospel covenants. By definition a covenant entails eternal promises that only God has the power to bestow.

14. Today altars are still places of sacrifice. Each Sunday we appear before the altar of the sacrament to renew our covenant to sacrifice our sins and to remember Jesus Christ.

15. Quoted in Sherrie Johnson, *Man, Woman, and Deity* (Salt Lake City: Bookcraft, 1991), 5.

16. Joseph Smith, *The Words of Joseph Smith,* comp. and ed. Andrew F. Ehat and Lyndon W. Cook (Provo, UT: Religious Studies Center, Brigham Young University, 1980), 117.

17. Noah Webster, *American Dictionary of the English Language* (San Francisco: Foundation for American Christian Education, 1987), s.v. "meet." The current definition for the word *meet* is "necessary" or "precisely adapted to a particular situation, need, or circumstance" (*Merriam-Webster's Collegiate Dictionary,* 11th ed., s.v. "meet").

18. Sherrie Mills Johnson, "It Is Not Good That the Man Should Be Alone," in *Living a Covenant Marriage,* ed. Douglas E. Brinley and Daniel K. Judd (Salt Lake City: Deseret Book, 2004), 253–66.

19. Joseph Fielding Smith, *Doctrines of Salvation,* comp. Bruce R. McConkie (Salt Lake City: Bookcraft, 1954), 2:70.

20. Johnson, *Man, Woman, and Deity.*

21. Smith, *History of the Church,* 5:1–2.

22. Smith, *Words of Joseph Smith,* 115.

23. Smith, *Teachings,* 323; see also D&C 107:18, 20.

24. Smith, *History of the Church,* 6:363.

25. Sarah M. Kimball, "Autobiography," *Woman's Exponent,* September 1, 1883, 51.

26. Smith, *Words of Joseph Smith,* 110.

27. Smith, *Words of Joseph Smith,* 119.

28. Smith, *Words of Joseph Smith,* 104.

29. Smith, *Words of Joseph Smith,* 117.

30. Smith, *Words of Joseph Smith,* 117.

31. Smith, *Words of Joseph Smith,* 105.

32. Smith, *Words of Joseph Smith,* 115.

33. Smith, *Words of Joseph Smith,* 105.

34. Smith, *Words of Joseph Smith,* 110.

35. Smith, *Words of Joseph Smith,* 116–17.

36. Smith, *Words of Joseph Smith,* 115.

37. Smith, *Words of Joseph Smith,* 118.

38. Smith, *History of the Church,* 5:1–2; see also Smith, *Teachings,* 137.

39. Smith, *Words of Joseph Smith,* 7.

40. Smith, *Words of Joseph Smith,* 123.

41. Smith, *Teachings,* 69.

42. Parley P. Pratt, *Autobiography of Parley P. Pratt* (Salt Lake City: Deseret Book, 1976), 298.

CHAPTER SIXTEEN

"THAT THY DAYS MAY BE PROLONGED": ATTEMPTS ON THE LIFE OF JOSEPH SMITH

CRAIG K. MANSCILL AND DEREK R. MOCK

In March of 1829, in Harmony, Pennsylvania, the Lord spoke to Joseph Smith Jr. in revelation, saying, "There are many that lie in wait to destroy thee from off the face of the earth; and for this cause, that thy days may be prolonged, I have given unto thee these commandments" (D&C 5:33). Previous to this revelation, Joseph had experienced several instances in which his life was in danger; and from the point of this revelation to the end of his life in 1844, Joseph experienced escalating instances of brutality and potential harm. Indeed, the thirty-eight-year life of Joseph Smith Jr. provides a significant collection of attempts to end the Prophet's life from a variety of different sources. The attempts on the life of the Prophet are not often sequentially considered within the context of Joseph's life. A sample of attempts demonstrates that these provided an important catalyst for Joseph's personal growth. Experiencing repeated attempts on his life from a very young age and through manhood taught Joseph that God would preserve him until his work was completed. This is not to say that Joseph knew when his life would be over any better than we know when ours will be over. At times, it seems that he did not see how he could be spared. However, he did know, as we

Craig K. Manscill is an associate professor of Church history and doctrine at Brigham Young University. Derek R. Mock is a graduate student in political science at Brigham Young University.

can come to know, that God would preserve, protect, and provide a way as he continued with faith.

A look at the plotted attempts against Joseph's life reveals plots ranging from solo schemes to coordinated group efforts. Along with the growing number of individuals and organizations trying to end the Prophet's life, the frequency and intensity of these attempts increased. As Joseph could handle more, he was tried with more. With his development into manhood, Joseph came to view the trials he endured as important catalysts to his personal process of becoming. Becoming often holds a high price. For Joseph, a man who loved his fellows, a painful part of being a prophet must have been that some of the conspirators against his life were his professed friends, suspecting neighbors, and past associates.

Although the plots eventually culminated in his death, Joseph's escape from a plethora of direct threats points to either uncanny good luck or the hand of a higher power actively preserving his life. Joseph often claimed the latter of these as his benefactor. His belief in his calling from God provided him with the strength and will to continue. His determination was bolstered by his faith. Regarding those who often opposed him, he simply reaffirmed that "it was nevertheless a fact that I had beheld a vision."[1]

From the time he began to relate his heavenly visitation, Joseph's life was in near-constant danger. Joseph would be the first to profess the belief that divine protection had shielded him from what must have sometimes seemed to be unmitigated certainty of destruction. In many cases, Joseph's life was spared by some small change in circumstance: the timely arrival of a neighbor coming to help, the softened heart of a sheriff, or the blatant refusal of a military officer's order.

Representative segments of history are selected to show that the attempts against the Prophet's life became progressively better coordinated, more vehement, and more specifically intentioned as Joseph grew into his calling as a prophet of God.

ATTEMPTS ON THE LIFE OF THE PROPHET

Joseph experienced his first major multiperson organized attempt against his life as he went about moving the plates to his home. After four years of waiting and instruction, Joseph was allowed to take the plates from their resting place in the Hill Cumorah on September 22, 1827.[2] As he received the plates, he received very strict instruction from the angel Moroni that he was to do all he could to protect the plates. Word that Joseph had the plates quickly spread. Joseph said: "I soon found out the reason why I had received such strict charges to keep them safe and why it was that the messenger had said that when I had done what was required at my hand, he would call for them, for no sooner was it known that I had them than the most strenuous exertions were used to get them from me. Every stratagem that could be invented was resorted to for that purpose."[3]

Hearing reports of a group of between ten and twelve men "clubbed together, with one Willard Chase, a Methodist class leader, at their head," Joseph Sr. went to the neighbors to discover what he could.[4] Hearing of their strong desire to find the plates, Joseph Sr. subsequently sent Emma to inform Joseph.[5] With news of collaborations to get the plates, Joseph set out to retrieve the plates from their temporary hiding place in an old birch log.[6]

When Joseph arrived at the log, he retrieved the plates and wrapped them in his linen frock. He then "placed them under his arm and started for home."[7] After traveling for only a short distance, Joseph considered it safer to move from the road to the woods. Joseph traveled in the woods for some distance. Joseph's mother gives the following account of what happened next:

> He came to a large windfall, and as he was jumping over a log, a man sprang up from behind it and gave him a heavy blow with a gun. Joseph turned around and knocked him down, then ran at the top of his speed. About half a mile farther he was attacked again in the same manner as before; he knocked this man down in like manner as the former and ran on again; and before he reached home he was assaulted the third time. In striking the last one, he dislocated his thumb, which, however, he did not notice until he came within sight of the house, when he threw himself down in the corner of the fence in order to recover his breath. As soon as he was able, he arose and came to the house. He was still altogether speechless from fright and the fatigue of running.[8]

Of this time, Joseph recounts that "the persecution became more bitter and severe than before, and multitudes were on the alert continually to get [the plates] from me if possible. But by the wisdom of God, they remained safe in my hands."[9]

As the Church grew in numbers in the New York area, the enemies of Joseph and the Church grew as well. In Colesville, New York, near the Knights' residence, on June 28 and 29, 1830, Joseph and the Saints performed several baptisms. As they were thus engaged, they were persecuted by a mob rallied by local religious leaders. Eventually, he was arrested by a constable for disorderly preaching of the Book of Mormon.[10]

Although the constable was required to enact his duty, he was not allowed to give Joseph into the hands of those who had plotted to take his life. A short distance from the Knights' residence, the wagon in which Joseph and the constable were traveling was surrounded by a group of men. Joseph sensed that they thought he had fallen into their hands, seeming "to await some signal from the constable" to take him.[11] However, as Joseph states, "to their great disappointment, [the constable] gave the horse the whip, and drove me out of their reach."[12]

The mob chased the wagon "in close pursuit."[13] As Joseph and the constable fled, one of the wheels on the wagon became detached, which event "left [them] once more very nearly surrounded by [the mob]."[14] Joseph writes that they "managed to replace the wheel and again left" the mobbers behind them.[15]

Once in the town of South Bainbridge, Chenango County, where Joseph's trial was to take place on the following day, the constable put Joseph up in the top-floor room of a tavern. And in order to protect Joseph through the night, the constable slept on the floor with his feet to the door and his firearm at his side, while Joseph slept in the bed provided with the room.[16]

It is amazing to think through the range of emotions that Joseph must have felt as he worked his way through the experience. His emotions must have ranged from the possible surprise of being surrounded in the constable's wagon to the adrenaline-filled moment of replacing the detached wagon wheel. The deepest moment of them all must have been when Joseph noted the constable asleep against the door. There must have been in Joseph's heart a realization that God would not leave him until he had finished his work.

Another instance in which Joseph saw the hand of the Lord

protecting and preserving his life came with his experiences at Far West and the resulting stay in Liberty Jail. On October 27, 1838, Governor Boggs ordered that the Saints be driven from the state. "The Mormons must be treated as enemies. . . . Their outrages are beyond all description," he wrote.[17] With the Saints surrounded, Joseph and other leaders of the Church were betrayed into the hands of the militia led by General Lucas—a known enemy of the Church. Joseph describes the scene as follows: "The officers would not converse with us, and the soldiers, almost to a man, insulted us as much as they felt disposed, breathing out threats against me and my companions. I cannot begin to tell the scene which I there witnessed. The loud cries and yells of more than one thousand voices, which rent the air and could be heard for miles, and the horrid and blasphemous threats and curses which were poured upon us in torrents, were enough to appall the stoutest heart."[18]

On the stand of a friend to the Saints, General Doniphan, Joseph was spared death by firing squad. Not willing to release the prisoners, their captors sent Joseph, Hyrum, and others on to Liberty Jail. Their petitions for redress went unheeded. Poison was administered to them from time to time. The dosages were concentrated to the point that their bodies could not even absorb the poison. After vehemently vomiting, they "would lie some two or three days in a torpid, stupid state, not even caring or wishing for life."[19]

At times in this condition, Joseph cried out: "O God, where art thou? And where is the pavilion that covereth thy hiding place?" (D&C 121:1). He was cut off from the comfort that home and family provide. He was illegally held by the state because of fallacious reports. As anyone in this situation would, Joseph had a choice. He chose wisely and allowed himself to be schooled through these experiences. Realizing the inescapable need to be totally contrite, he chose to submit his will to God: "[And] when the heart is sufficiently contrite, then the voice of inspiration steals along and whispers, My son, peace be unto thy soul; thine adversity and thine afflictions shall be but a small moment."[20]

In Liberty Jail, Joseph received Doctrine and Covenants sections 121 through 123. Verses from these sections have come to be a standard to those who suffer under the weight of affliction. After telling Joseph all the things that could happen, the Lord—as the master instructor—points out that "the Son of Man hath descended below them all. Art thou greater than he?" (D&C 122:8). And with words of reassuring love, Joseph was given the knowledge that he would be guaranteed the time to finish his mission on the earth (see D&C 122:9). Remarkably, this faith is quickly transferred by way of exhortation to those who were afflicted along with Joseph: "Let us cheerfully do all things that lie in our power; and then may we stand still, with the utmost assurance, to see the salvation of God, and for his arm to be revealed," he wrote (D&C 123:17).

Including his experiences in Far West, Joseph experienced many different types of attempts on his life: bands hunting him, mobs harassing him, the state sentencing him, among many other types of attempts (see appendix). In Nauvoo, Joseph experienced attempts on his life from within his circle of friends. On December 29, 1842, he said that his life was "more in danger from some little dough-head of a fool in this city than from any numerous and inveterate enemies abroad."[21] To protect himself, Joseph commissioned the city's police force to protect him not only against enemies from the outside but from enemies on the inside as well. Along with the city's police force Joseph also appointed bodyguards, which he named his "life guard." Even with these protections, one may sense the surprise that Joseph had at learning that treachery was closer to home than he suspected: "Can it be possible that the traitor whom Porter Rockwell reports to me as being in correspondence with my Missouri enemies, is one of my quorum?"[22]

On May 7, 1842, Joseph was to participate in a sham battle by the Nauvoo Legion. Dr. John C. Bennett was a man of considerable rank, holding the positions of mayor, chancellor of the university, and major general of the Nauvoo Legion. As such, Bennett requested that Joseph command one of the cohorts in the sham battle. When Joseph refused, Bennett further persisted that Joseph should "take a position in the rear of the cavalry without his staff during the engagement."[23] To this request the chief of Joseph's life guard, Captain A. P. Rockwood, objected.

Joseph and his staff chose their own position during the sham battle.[24] These events left Joseph with strong suspicions: "Why did [Bennett] request me to command one of the cohorts, and also to take my position without my staff, during the sham battle on the seventh of May, 1842, where my life might have been forfeited and no man have known who did the deed?"[25]

The threats from within the Church continued to grow. On one occasion Joseph said that "were it not for enemies within the city, there would be no danger from foes without,"[26] adding that "if it were not for a Brutus, I might have lived as long as Caesar would have lived."[27]

In the final months of his life, Joseph worked diligently to preserve his life and to continue helping the Church accomplish its God-appointed agenda; that is, the building of the temple and the endowing of members with power, among others. However, as the Church grew in Nauvoo, so did the number of those who opposed the Church. Apostates from within mingled with anti-Mormon leagues without. During the later Nauvoo period, opinions gathered in the two opposing camps of opinion: Joseph was either a fallen prophet, needing to be replaced; or he remained a strong leader of the Saints, still receiving direct revelation from God. Outside Nauvoo, similar polarizations developed. Those who tried to remain neutral were branded jack Mormons by those who were against the Mormons, and they also received threats.

Although Joseph and the city council guarded their reactions against threats and persecutions in order to ward off a reason for an assault on the city, they had their limits. The Mormons had at their disposal two papers in which they circulated news and doctrinal commentary. These papers also played another important role. As the primary means of mass communication, the papers acted as the medium through which public opinion (in Nauvoo and the surrounding regions) was both informed and affected. In the midst of mounting political struggles between the lawless bands surrounding Nauvoo and the Saints, great efforts were made by those who violently opposed the Church to stop the circulation of these two papers outside of Nauvoo. In this they were somewhat successful.

Brigham Young states that their success emboldened them, becoming a type of impetus for setting up a press that intended to print slanderous comments.[28] The result of this effort was the *Nauvoo Expositor*, which printed "the most libelous, false, and infamous reports concerning citizens of Nauvoo, and especially the ladies."[29] Most of the Nauvoo populace were outraged. Sensing that some of the public might take things into their own hands, Joseph, as mayor, convened the city council to discuss this matter. After some discussion, they realized that action against the press would be a powerful motivation for the mobs to take action against the Saints in Nauvoo.

At this important point of decision, the Prophet addressed the council. Brigham Young remembers the following about the Prophet's discourse: "He exhibited in glowing colors the meanness, corruption and ultimate designs of the anti-'Mormons'; their despicable characters and ungodly influences, especially of those who were in our midst. He told of the responsibility that rested upon us, as guardians of the public interest, to stand up in the defense of the injured and oppressed, to stem the current of corruption, and as men and saints, to put a stop to this flagrant outrage upon this people's rights."[30]

Through entirely lawful means, the city council ordered that the press be destroyed. The press was destroyed and the type scattered. With the destruction of the press, the enemies of Joseph and the Church organized themselves to move Joseph from Nauvoo to Carthage. With an eventual mandate from the governor of Illinois, Governor Thomas Ford, Joseph went to Carthage to answer the warrants against himself.

On June 23, 1844, at 6:30 in the morning, Joseph and some colleagues, among whom was his brother Hyrum, set out for Carthage. On his way out of Nauvoo, as Joseph passed the temple, he hinted at his understanding that the coming events would culminate with his death: "This is the loveliest place and the best people under the heavens; little do they know the trials that await them."[31] He also commented to Daniel H. Wells how he wished to be remembered, saying, "I wish you to cherish my memory, and not think me the worst man in the world either."[32]

Once in Carthage, Joseph was harassed by the mobs. Statements from those in Carthage indicated that Governor Ford knew the plans of those whom he had adopted into the state militia. It was well understood that Joseph was being held on false charges. Rumors circulated that Joseph and his companions "should not go out of Carthage alive," and "that the law cannot touch them, but that powder and ball will."[33]

At 5:16 P.M. on June 27, 1844, a mob rushed past the guards who were charged to watch Joseph. The mob fired into the room through the window and through the door. A shot through the door hit Hyrum in the face, to the side of the nose. Another shot through the window hit him right after the first. A final two shots hit him as he fell to the floor. Seeing his brother falling, "Joseph exclaimed, 'Oh, dear brother Hyrum!'"[34] After firing his revolver down the hall, Joseph was hit by one or two shots. He ran to the window in an attempt to escape. He cried out, "O Lord, my God!" and either fell or jumped from the window. In the process, he was hit by more balls from beneath.[35]

IN RETROSPECT: ATTEMPTS ON THE PROPHET'S LIFE EXAMINED

Perhaps the most extraordinary thing about Joseph's life is the way that he handled his trials. He viewed his trials as important catalysts to his personal process of becoming, even though he did not always understand how his life could be spared. Also, as Joseph gained experience, he felt that his life would be spared until his work was completed.

As is natural for anyone who repeatedly faces seemingly insurmountable challenges, Joseph was obliged to contemplate why he was repeatedly persecuted. From a very young age, Joseph illustrates his deep introspection on the matter. After the First Vision, he said, "While they were persecuting me, reviling me, and speaking all manner of evil against me falsely for so saying, I was led to say in my heart, Why persecute me for telling the truth?"[36] As time passed and Joseph matured, his perspective of the barrage of persecutions focused on his personal growth:

> I am like a huge, rough stone rolling down from a high mountain; and the only polishing I get is when some corner gets rubbed off by coming in contact with something else, striking with accelerated force against religious bigotry, priestcraft, lawyer-craft, doctor-craft, lying editors, suborned judges and jurors, and the authority of perjured executives, backed by mobs, blasphemers, licentious and corrupt men and women—all hell knocking off a corner here and a corner there. Thus I will become a smooth and polished shaft in the quiver of the Almighty, who will give me dominion over all and every one of them, when their refuge of lies shall fail, and their hiding place shall be destroyed, while these

smooth-polished stones with which I come in contact become marred.[37]

Given the burden some of the trials placed on him, Joseph's conclusion is impressive. Surely, Joseph's perspective of his trials must have resulted from an application of great humility, though at times such humility must have been very difficult to apply. This is well illustrated in the tarring and feathering of Joseph on March 24, 1832. On the following day, Sunday, he preached to a congregation among which were some of those who had attempted to take his life the night before.[38] Still, the more poignant trial came for Joseph when his infant son Joseph died of complications that likely resulted from exposure to the cold on the 24th. This trial required real application of humility. Joseph the man applied in his heart what Joseph the Prophet had taught, which, of course, is the real test of discipleship. Joseph had little choice but to learn from these refining experiences he constantly faced.

At his lowest times, a very human side of Joseph can be seen. Joseph knew that God could preserve his life. He had seen God the Father and the Son—he knew of their reality and transcendent power. Still, as we all are, Joseph's knowledge was tested. Could he repeatedly transform his knowledge into action, into choice? On one occasion, Joseph Smith Sr. gave the Prophet a patriarchal blessing in which he promised Joseph that he would accomplish all the work the Lord had for him to do. At this time enemies surrounded Joseph from within the Church and from without. Joseph cried out: "'Oh! my father, shall I?' 'Yes,' said his father, 'you shall live to lay out the plan of all the work which God has given you to do.'"[39] Within the context of his life at the time, Joseph's interrogatory shows great faith.

Although Joseph at times searched for faith to deal with situations, in every struggle we see a hero emerging from the trials. He stood ever strong in his faith, fortitude, and courage to do what he knew to be right. This is perhaps best seen in the case of the *Nauvoo Expositor*.

The men of the Nauvoo City Council knew that the press was a way to strike at the Saints as a whole and at Joseph individually where it was the most damaging—next to heart and home. Writing especially scandalous reports about the women of the Church, the press sought to bring an act against itself, which would provide the impetus to drive the Saints from the area. Knowing this, the council was very cautious. Driven from Far West, they had rebuilt their homes; indeed, they wanted to stay. Joseph acutely understood this. Repeatedly he had pled with the Lord over the Saints as he sat in Liberty Jail. Furthermore, he understood his position among the Saints well enough to know that his life would be directly affected by the decision of the council.

Setting all this aside, he stood up for the right. Brigham Young recalls that at this important time Joseph swayed the vote. He did not always see how his life could be spared. Yet with faith he moved forward, declaring the truth, even when his own health, comfort, and life were at stake.

Joseph did not know exactly what the whole of his earthly ministry entailed. Although he knew that God could preserve his life, he also understood that such promises were forfeit once his mission was complete. His understanding of the scope and specifics of his mission often took on new meaning as he might have thought, and as others certainly thought, his life was over. It was in the confines of Liberty Jail that he came to understand that much more was still required of him.[40] An understanding of exactly what God wanted him to do became increasingly clear to the Prophet as the momentum of the work increased.[41] With time, it became evident to him that his life's mission was coming to a close—the window of time in which he had to complete his mission was shrinking. He pled with the Saints to lend him the power that came through their prayers for him that he might "be enabled to escape every stratagem of Satan, surmount every difficulty, and bring this people to the enjoyment of those blessings which are reserved for the righteous."[42] Indeed, Joseph felt an urgency to finish the work he had to do.

Joseph Smith came to understand his mission "line upon line, precept upon precept" (D&C 98:12). This understanding was conditional and depended upon his faithfulness. Performance of duty one day was a prerequisite for more complete understanding the next. The mission of Joseph Smith was a great and marvelous work that included bringing forth the Book of Mormon, restoring the priesthood and priesthood keys, revealing precious gospel truths, organizing the true Church, and establishing temple work. The nearer

Joseph Smith came to fulfilling his mission the more intense the attempts on his life became.

An integral part of his finishing his work was passing on the keys of the kingdom to the Twelve so that if he was taken, the Church would remain intact. Joseph worked diligently to ready the Twelve to hold those keys. Publicly he gave the Saints a vision of the place the Twelve would hold in the kingdom of God: in a conference he said that the time had come "for the Twelve 'to stand in their place next to the First Presidency.'"[43]

After adequate preparation, Joseph conferred the keys of the kingdom on the Twelve—"every key and every power that he ever held himself before God."[44] This done, a major part of his work was completed; one might say this was the step before his final testimony. Joseph said, "Some have supposed that Brother Joseph could not die; but this is a mistake: it is true there have been times when I have had the promise of my life to accomplish such and such things, but, having now accomplished those things, I have not at present any lease of my life, I am as liable to die as other men."[45]

Joseph's faith in God's power to deliver was repeatedly tried over the course of his life as attempts on his life increased in both number and intensity. At the beginning of his ministry, Joseph was shot at and chased by a few men. Later, he was tarred and feathered by an organized group of men whose intent was to seriously harm and even kill him. Eventually, armies gathered against him. Each of these assaults he survived. However, the final days of his life revealed organized and desperate groups of adversaries from within the Church and without who attempted to take his life. These were men close to him, men whom he took to be his friends.

The opposition against Joseph that motivated these attempts stemmed from the political ambitions of his adversaries, general misconceptions held by the residents of neighboring areas, and differences in political aims between the Saints and a group of residents in the area. In a closer and more personal sense, the opposition came from those who Joseph had once thought were his friends. At the beginning of his ministry, Joseph's life was in danger for the sake of money when three, possibly of a much larger group, tried to take the plates from Joseph as he moved them from an old birch log to his parents' residence. Later in his life, Joseph's life was nearly extinguished because of religious bigotry in New York, when he was tarred, feathered, and nearly poisoned. Eventually, in Carthage, Joseph's life was taken because of internal enemies motivated by jealousy and the desire for power. Joseph was subjected to the blunt end of jealousies, the deleterious effects of lies and false stories, the misinformed opinions of those around him that it was time for new leadership, and the outright hatred of those whom he had bested at one thing or another.

The attempts on Joseph's life reinforced his belief that God was the master architect of his life. Ranging in emotions from total confidence that he would escape from the hands of his enemies to heartfelt concern that the way was too narrow to traverse, Joseph moved forward, one step at a time. Orson Hyde reported that when Joseph's work was completed, the Prophet said it was "but little matter what becomest of me." Orson Hyde added, "From many things which he said and did it is evident that he [k]new an eventful period had arrived, that his exit was at hand, for he said, 'I will die for this people' and he has gone."[46]

As Joseph's life is viewed in retrospect, a great man emerges from the fires of trial. Having his life threatened through every major phase of his life, the Prophet did not falter in his declaration of truth. One need not wonder if his mission was completed. Joseph's life was not cut short. Joseph "lived great, and," when his mission was completed and God called him home, "he died great." Indeed, "in the eyes of God and his people," Joseph was a prophet preserved by the hand of the Lord (D&C 135:3).

NOTES

1. Joseph Smith, *History of the Church of Jesus Christ of Latter-day Saints*, ed. B. H. Roberts, 2nd ed. rev. (Salt Lake City: Deseret Book, 1951), 1:7–8.
2. Joseph Smith, *The Personal Writings of Joseph Smith*, comp. and ed. Dean C. Jessee (Salt Lake City: Deseret Book, 1984), 207–8.
3. Smith, *Personal Writings*, 208.
4. Lucy Mack Smith, *History of Joseph Smith by His Mother* (Salt Lake City: Stevens & Wallis, 1945), 107.
5. Smith, *History of Joseph Smith*, 107.
6. Smith, *History of Joseph Smith*, 107.
7. Smith, *History of Joseph Smith*, 107.

8. Smith, *History of Joseph Smith,* 108.

9. Smith, *History of the Church,* 1:18–19.

10. Donna Hill, *Joseph Smith: The First Mormon* (Garden City, NY: Doubleday, 1977), 111.

11. Smith, *History of the Church,* 1:88–89.

12. Smith, *History of the Church,* 89.

13. Smith, *History of the Church,* 89.

14. Smith, *History of the Church,* 89.

15. Smith, *History of the Church,* 89.

16. Smith, *History of the Church,* 89. Joseph's scribe uses the language "in order that all might be right with himself and with me also, he slept during the night with his feet against the door," indicating that the constable was also worried for his own safety in consideration of the mob that must have reached the town that night.

17. Smith, *History of the Church,* 3:175.

18. Smith, *History of the Church,* 2:239.

19. Smith, *History of the Church,* 3:420.

20. Smith, *History of the Church,* 3:293.

21. Hill, *First Mormon,* 388.

22. Hill, *First Mormon,* 389 n. 6.

23. B. H. Roberts, *The Rise and Fall of Nauvoo* (Salt Lake City: Bookcraft, 1965), 135.

24. Roberts, *Rise and Fall,* 135.

25. Roberts, *Rise and Fall,* 135.

26. Quoted in Smith, *History of Joseph Smith,* 320.

27. Quoted in Smith, *History of Joseph Smith,* 320.

28. Smith, *History of the Church,* 7:61–62.

29. Smith, *History of the Church,* 7:61–62.

30. Smith, *History of the Church,* 7:61–62.

31. Smith, *History of the Church,* 6:554.

32. Smith, *History of the Church,* 6:554.

33. Smith, *History of the Church,* 6:566–68.

34. Smith, *History of the Church,* 6:616–22.

35. Smith, *History of the Church,* 6:616–22.

36. Smith, *History of the Church,* 1:7–8.

37. Smith, *History of the Church,* 6:401.

38. Smith, *History of Joseph Smith,* 221; see also Smith, *History of the Church,* vol. 1.

39. Smith, *History of Joseph Smith,* 309–10.

40. Ronald K. Esplin, "Joseph Smith's Mission and Timetable: 'God Will Protect Me until My Work Is Done,'" in *The Prophet Joseph: Essays on the Life and Mission of Joseph Smith,* ed. Larry C. Porter and Susan Easton Black (Salt Lake City: Deseret Book, 1988), 299.
41. See Esplin, "Joseph's Mission and Timetable," 280–319.
42. Smith, *History of the Church,* 4:230.
43. Esplin, "Joseph's Mission and Timetable," 302.
44. Esplin, "Joseph's Mission and Timetable," 309.
45. Smith, *History of the Church,* 4:587.
46. Orson Hyde, in Esplin, "Joseph's Mission and Timetable," 310.

APPENDIX

BRIEF DESCRIPTIONS OF SELECTED ATTEMPTS ON
THE LIFE OF THE PROPHET

ATTEMPT BY THREE MEN TO GET THE PLATES AS JOSEPH MOVED THEM
Date: September 1827
Place: Palmyra, New York, en route from retrieving the plates from an old birch log to his parents' home.[1]
Brief description: After Joseph received the plates from the angel Moroni, he hid them in an old birch log at a distance about three miles from his parents' home. Later he went to retrieve the plates from the log. Going home under cover of a forest trail, he was attacked at three different points by different men.

SEVERAL SHOOTING ATTEMPTS
Date: September 1827–April 1830[2]
Place: In and around the area between Palmyra and Fayette, New York.[3]
Brief description: Shortly after Joseph received the plates at the hands of the angel Moroni, many attempts were made to get the plates from him and to take his life. Joseph stated that as part of these attempts he was shot at on several occasions.

AFTERMATH OF RETRIEVING THE PLATES: ARMED
MEN ON THE SMITH FARM
Date: Sometime shortly after September 22, 1827
Place: Smith family farm, Palmyra, New York

Brief description: Joseph brought home the Urim and Thummim. He set about working on his father's farm in order to be near the plates—to watch over and protect them. His mother recounted that one day in the afternoon Joseph rushed into the house asking if a mob had come in search of the plates. When she said no, he informed her that a mob would be there that night to find the plates. With this, and in consultation with one Mr. Braman, the Smiths decided to place the plates under one of the hearthstones. They finished their work of secluding the plates as an armed mob rode up to the house.[4]

FORTY MEN SEEK TO WAYLAY THE PROPHET JOSEPH SMITH[5]

Date: The day that the contract for the printing of the Book of Mormon was signed.

Place: Between Manchester and Palmyra, New York.

Brief description: A mob gathered and lay in wait for Joseph as he was en route from Manchester to Palmyra. These forty intended to do Joseph some harm as he took his journey.

A KIND CONSTABLE

Date: June 28–29, 1830

Place: Colesville and South Bainbridge, New York.

Brief description: A writ of arrest was served to Joseph on spurious charges. A plan to ambush Joseph on his way to trial was thwarted by a kind-hearted constable.

PASSING BY HIS BITTEREST ENEMIES UNHARMED

Date: August 1830

Place: A short distance from the home of Mr. Knight in Colesville, New York.

Brief description: Joseph and a group of elders went to visit the Saints in Colesville. Praying for divine intervention, they passed by their enemies unseen.

TARRING AND FEATHERING IN HIRAM, OHIO

Date: March 24, 1832

Place: Hiram, Ohio

Brief description: Joseph was up late caring for one of his adopted twins, Joseph, who had the measles. A mob of men broke into his home and pulled him outside. They tarred and feathered his body to such an extent that when Emma, his wife, saw him later that night she fainted thinking that he was covered with blood. As his attackers tried to pour poison down his throat, Joseph resisted and had his tooth broken as a consequence.

Mr. Porter's Inn—Greenville Poisoning

Date: Between May 6 and June 1832

Place: Greenville, Indiana

Brief description: Joseph Smith Jr., Newel K. Whitney, and Sidney Rigdon traveled from Independence, Missouri, on their way back to Kirtland. Up to the point of Greenville, Indiana, they traveled by stage. For an unmentioned reason, the horses bolted and Newel K. Whitney broke his leg. Joseph stayed with him at an inn. An attempt was made to poison the two. They were miraculously preserved and left as soon as Whitney could travel.

Man Feigning Sickness

Date: April 18, 1834

Place: In between Newburg and New Portage, Ohio (heading toward New Portage)

Brief description: Joseph Smith, in company with a few other elders of the Church, was traveling to a conference in New Portage. Midcourse, the small group was approached by someone who said he was sick and wanted a ride. They refused him the ride as directed by the Spirit and continued on their journey. The man was joined by two others, who chased Joseph and his party.

Gallatin Elections

Date: After August 6 and probably before October 1838.

Place: Home of Lucy Mack Smith in Far West, Missouri

Brief description: Rumors resulting from a previous struggle between the Mormons and the standing voting body brought an armed body of militia to the home of Lucy Mack Smith. This group's stated intention was to "kill Joseph Smith and all the 'Mormons.'"[6] After meeting the Prophet, the men chose not only to leave him alone but also some went so far as to guard him on his way home.[7]

EXTRADITION FROM FAR WEST (I of III)

Date: November 1, 1838

Place: Far West, Missouri

Brief description: Subsequent to the horrific scenes that unfolded at Far West, the governor called out a militia that eventually numbered as many as 2,500 men. The Saints in Far West had six hundred armed men.[8] Joseph and several other Church leaders were taken captive as they went to speak with the commanding officer under a flag of truce. After being mocked and ridiculed, the prisoners were made to sleep on the bare ground.[9] After a night-long court martial, the prisoners were sentenced to be shot. Defying the orders of his commander, General Alexander Doniphan removed his brigade and marched from Far West.[10]

EXTRADITION FROM FAR WEST (II of III)

Date: November 2, 1838

Place: Far West, Missouri

Brief description: As Joseph and his companions climbed into a wagon with the purpose of moving to Jackson County, five men stepped forward and fired on them. Luckily, not one of the weapons fully discharged.

FAILED HEARINGS—A SECRET PLOT

Date: April 16, 1839

Place: En route from Daviess County to Boon County, Missouri

Brief description: Joseph and his fellows were moved from Daviess County to Boon County. The guards who moved them were given instructions not to let the prisoners arrive in Boon County. After the guards became purposefully intoxicated, Joseph and company made their escape.

CATACLYSMIC EVENTS AT CARTHAGE

Date: Thursday, June 27, 1844 (5:16 P.M.)

Place: Carthage Jail, Carthage, Illinois

Brief description: After being given a mandate by Governor Thomas Ford to come to Carthage, Joseph, Hyrum, and a few others went to have an interview with the governor and to await their trial. Unruly mobs had been integrated into the state-collected militia; among these were the Carthage Greys—sworn enemies of Joseph and the Church. Having exerted considerable energy to get Joseph into their hands, this mob gathered in the guise of state authority and waited for an opportunity to kill Joseph. On the evening of June 27, an assault took place, which left the Prophet and his brother Hyrum dead.

NOTES

1. Lucy Mack Smith, *History of Joseph Smith by His Mother* (Salt Lake City: Stevens & Wallis, 1945), 109.

2. Between September 1827, when Joseph got the plates, and April 6, 1830, when the Church was officially organized and "several began to believe" (Joseph Smith, *History of the Church of Jesus Christ of Latter-day Saints,* ed. B. H. Roberts, 2nd ed. rev. [Salt Lake City: Deseret Book, 1951], 4:53). We are here assuming that Joseph is associating several believing on his name with the official organization of the Church. Note that there were many that started to really believe on his word from the beginning. For example, see Doctrine and Covenants sections 14–18 for some of those who began to believe in Joseph's word and calling.

3. Specific locations are not documented for these shootings. This projected area is extrapolated from the location of the events that Joseph indicates as surrounding the shootings.

4. Smith, *History of Joseph Smith,* 14.

5. Lucy seems to be the only one that references this specific attempt. Because of the details that she gives concerning the attempt, the historical setting in which she places the attempt, and the people that she names in regards to the attempt, it seems that she places the attempt accurately in the context of the coming forth of the Book of Mormon. Why major writers on the life of Joseph have not made reference to this attempt in detail is unknown.

6. Smith, *History of Joseph Smith,* 238.

7. See Smith, *History of Joseph Smith,* 237–38.

8. Donna Hill, *Joseph Smith: The First Mormon* (Garden City, NY: Doubleday, 1977), 242.

9. This exposure to the weather caused some of them to be sick for some time.

10. See Smith, *History of the Church,* 4:19–38.

CHAPTER SEVENTEEN

"THE ESTABLISHED ORDER OF THE KINGDOM OF GOD"

ROBERT J. MATTHEWS

I have taken the title "The Established Order of the Kingdom of God" from a statement by the Prophet Joseph Smith as he was discussing the purpose of the ministration of angels and of spirits to men and women on the earth. His explanation was that heavenly messengers converse with mortals to teach them "the established order of the kingdom of God" and to bring those mortals "up to the standard of their [the angels'] knowledge."[1] The "established order" is that which already exists in heaven. By their ministering, heavenly messengers raise the cultural, spiritual, and intellectual level of the mortals to a higher plane so that the order of heaven will become the order on earth.

Explanations by the Prophet Joseph Smith and by other prophets, along with many scriptural passages, shape and mold our understanding about the purpose of revelation and tell of the lifestyle and society of celestial culture. They give us a peek into what is meant by the salvation of mankind. The Lord is making it possible for us to become like Him. Salvation is an attainment—not alone what we *know* or what we *do* but what we *become*.

COMPLETENESS OF THE ETERNAL PLAN

Revelation gives us a feeling for the exactness and completeness as well as the ancient nature of the plan of salvation. It is called the

---

Robert J. Matthews, who has served as dean of Religious Education, is professor emeritus of ancient scripture at Brigham Young University.

new and everlasting covenant. The plan is eternal and thus is very old and everlasting, but each one of us learns it individually, and thus to us it is "new." The plan of salvation, with its promises and blessings, is not only what our Heavenly Father requires us to live by but also the same plan and system that He and other celestial persons live by. That gives particular meaning to the scripture in which the Lord says, "Be ye holy; for I am holy" (1 Peter 1:15–16; see Leviticus 11:45; 19:2; 20:26). If we are to be comfortable in God's presence, then we must be as much like Him as possible. The revealed plan of redemption that we have in the Church, and which is spoken of in the scriptures, reflects the life and environment of the celestial kingdom.

EXALTATION AND REDEMPTION

Our Heavenly Father is infusing into our mortal, fallen environment the kind of life that He has as rapidly as we can absorb it. He has revealed the authority of the holy priesthood and the laws, ordinances, and family organization that exist in heaven. He does not force it upon us, but as we taste of the joy, the testimony, and the knowledge of the gospel, and of the Holy Spirit, we want more. It is natural to thirst for more knowledge. The transition from our mortal condition into celestial glory and holiness is so huge that it will take much time and effort. The change cannot be made casually or by osmosis. It is not accomplished by intellectuality or education alone. The change can come only through the Atonement of Jesus Christ and by our faith, repentance, and obedience to the ordinances. It requires a mighty change of heart brought about by the cleansing power of the Holy Ghost upon us. Exaltation in the presence of God is redemptive—spiritual, intellectual, and physical. We are commanded to serve God with all our heart, might, mind, and strength. The gospel of Jesus Christ, with all its powers of change and upward mobility, is the only way that we can be prepared to return home and stand comfortably in the presence of God.

A DIVINE ORIENTATION

The plan of salvation, with its ordinances, commandments, and priesthood authority, is actually a divine pattern of celestial society superimposed upon our mortal condition. When the Lord calls a great prophet or seer, He generally gives him a vision of the universe and of eternity to orient him so that he will know what is in heaven and can thus teach with conviction and authority. Adam, Enoch, the brother of Jared, Abraham, Moses, Peter, Paul, Nephi, and Joseph Smith had this orientation, as did many others. We receive an orientation, on a smaller scale, in the endowment of the temple. It shows us what God's plans are, and we receive some secrets of the universe. The principles and ordinances that saved and exalted the ancient prophets will save and exalt us.

Establishing a Heavenly Colony on Earth

Heavenly messengers planting the gospel on the earth through conferring heavenly priesthood, doctrines, ordinances, and covenants upon mortal men, are establishing a colony, so to speak. It is like settlers coming from the old world of Europe to America, bringing their customs, ideas, and lifestyle with them. Thus we have *New* York, *New* Jersey, *New* Hampshire, *New* England, and *New* Holland; and in the South Pacific, *New* Zealand, *New* South Wales, and *New* Guinea, named and patterned after their origins. In like manner the Lord began a "colony" from heaven when he came to Joseph Smith in the Sacred Grove and later sent Moroni, John the Baptist, Peter, Moses, Elijah, and other heavenly representatives to establish the dispensation of the fulness of times. The little stone was cut out of the mountain, without human hands, and will eventually fill the whole earth (see Daniel 2:45).

The Grand Rule of Heaven

One of the firmly established orders of heaven is taught in the Joseph Smith Translation of Amos 3:7: "Surely the Lord God will do nothing, until he revealeth his secret unto his servants the prophets." In explaining this matter, the Prophet Joseph Smith said, "The grand rule of heaven was that nothing should ever be done on earth without revealing the secret to his servants the prophets."[2] He added, "The prophet says that God will do nothing but what he will reveal unto his Servants the prophets consequently if it is not made known to the Prophets it will not come to pass."[3]

AN OPPORTUNITY TO BECOME LIKE GOD

In the King Follett Discourse, the Prophet Joseph Smith said that until we know something about the character of God, we do not comprehend ourselves. When God proposed to save His children, He proposed to make them precisely like Himself, in character, attributes, glory, and happiness. Complete salvation is for each person to be clothed in a perfect, resurrected, physical body, organized into a family with eternal increase of children, kingdoms, and worlds.

KNOWING OUR HEAVENLY FATHER

President Ezra Taft Benson tells of our closeness to God because of our pre-earth life: "Nothing is going to startle us more when we pass through the veil to the other side than to realize how well we know our Father and how familiar His face is to us."[4]

If we connect that with Doctrine and Covenants 130:1–2, we get a clear picture: "When the Savior shall appear we shall see him as he is. We shall see that he is a man like ourselves. And that same sociality which exists among us here will exist among us there, only it will be coupled with eternal glory, which glory we do not now enjoy."

In our mortality we have temporarily forgotten what we once knew, but by the revelations from heaven we learn again that our earth life is an extension of the sociality we knew in heaven, before we were born on earth.

President Joseph F. Smith explained: "Things upon the earth, so far as they have not been perverted by wickedness, are typical of things in heaven. Heaven was the prototype of this beautiful creation when it came from the hand of the Creator, and was pronounced 'good.'"[5]

ONE DIVINE PLAN

Everything in the gospel of Jesus Christ, from premortal life, to earth life, to postmortal life, to resurrection and eternal judgment, is one package; each segment is based and built upon the same format, the same goals, the same plan, and the same purposes as every other segment. And every human being will go through all of these steps. A man who had served a mission in Australia seventy years ago told me that to cross the continent of Australia by rail in those days required three different railroad companies. Each went only part of the distance, and each one had a different width of track, so one company's train could not run on another company's track. You could ride one train as far as it went, then change to the other company, and so forth. No unity, no continuity. Contrast that with the plan of salvation that God has for the human family. One plan comprehends the entire trip from newborn spirit child to exaltation. One plan fits all places, all persons, all conditions. It is correlated, unified, and divine, and is the plan of God our Father, made available to us through the Atonement of Jesus Christ. It is adapted to the needs of every person through the love, mercy, and grace of God. It is the new and everlasting covenant, and everything in the plan is done in the name of Jesus Christ.

The reason we have an established order in the Church is that this great, eternal plan was worked out and established before the foundations of the earth were laid. In fact, this earth, and all the other planets and stars and moons, were created in harmony with, and because of, the more ancient plan of salvation. We learn much about the system from the explanation by the Lord in Doctrine and Covenants 132:5, 6, 8–11:

> All who will have a blessing at my hands shall abide the law which was appointed for that blessing, and the conditions thereof, as were instituted from before the foundation of the world.
>
> And as pertaining to the new and everlasting covenant, it was instituted for the fulness of my glory; and he that receiveth a fulness thereof must and shall abide the law, or he shall be damned, saith the Lord God. . . .
>
> Behold, mine house is a house of order, saith the Lord God, and not a house of confusion.
>
> Will I accept of an offering, saith the Lord, that is not made in my name?
>
> Or will I receive at your hands that which I have not appointed?
>
> And will I appoint unto you, saith the Lord, except it be by law, even as I and my Father ordained unto you, before the world was?

FIXED AND IMMOVABLE PRINCIPLES

The Prophet Joseph Smith taught that "God has made certain decrees which are fixed and immovable." He went on to say that one of those fixed principles is that baptism by immersion is the only way to obtain remission of sins; another fixed principle is that after baptism, the gift of the Holy Ghost can be obtained only by the laying on of hands. He said that God will not acknowledge any other way and that these principles were decreed before the world was made.[6] The Prophet further explained: "We are only capable of comprehending that certain things exist, which we may acquire by certain fixed principles. If men would acquire salvation, they have got to be subject, before they leave this world, to certain rules and principles, which were fixed by an unalterable decree before the world was."[7] In like manner the holy priesthood existed before the world was. It is called the "holy order after the order of the Son of God" and has existed forever and will exist forever. What we have on earth in the Church is a little twig of the priesthood tree that exists in heaven. I quote from Elder Orson Pratt:

> There are authorities in heaven as well as upon the earth, and the authorities in heaven are far greater in number than the few who are upon the earth. This is only a little branch of the great tree of the Priesthood—merely a small branch receiving authority from heaven, so that the inhabitants of the earth may be benefited as well as the inhabitants of the eternal world; but the great trunk of the tree of the Priesthood is in heaven. There you will find thousands and millions holding the power of the Priesthood.[8]

The Prophet Joseph Smith said marvelous things about priesthood and described it as a "channel":

> [The Melchizedek Priesthood is the] grand head, and holds the highest authority which pertains to the priesthood, and the keys of the Kingdom of God in all ages of the world to the latest posterity on the earth; and is the channel through which all knowledge, doctrine, the plan of salvation and every important matter is revealed from heaven.
>
> Its institution was prior to "the foundation of this earth," . . . and is after the order of the Son of God. . . . It is the channel through which the Almighty commenced revealing His glory at the beginning of the creation of this earth, and through which He has continued to reveal Himself to the children of men to the present time, and

through which He will make known His purposes to the end of time.[9]

He added, "Ordinances, instituted in the heavens before the foundation of the world, in the priesthood, for the salvation of men, are not to be altered or changed. All must be saved on the same principles."[10]

"A HOUSE OF ORDER"

The Prophet Joseph Smith proclaimed, "The great thing for us to know is to comprehend what God did institute before the foundation of the world."[11] This declaration places much importance on the pre-earth decisions of God. From Joseph Smith's teachings we learn that not only were pre-earth appointments and foreordinations placed upon various persons, such as Jesus Christ and the prophets, but also that there were decrees and directions concerning every necessary factor in the salvation of the human family. Included in those pre-earth councils were decrees concerning priesthood powers, keys, ordinances, covenants, dispensations, the gathering, revelation, Church organization, salvation for the dead, the restoration of all things, the Fall of Adam, the Atonement of Jesus Christ, resurrection, final judgment, the laws governing blessings, and every important matter.[12] In addition, the Lord has held certain things in reserve, keeping them hidden and secret, to be revealed only in the dispensation of the fulness of times, such as the details regarding the Second Coming of Jesus Christ, the Millennium, the New Jerusalem, and related things. These secrets are yet to be revealed in this dispensation.

The Lord decreed that every dispensation should be governed by the same priesthood law, and that "all things pertaining to [the dispensation of the fulness of times] should be conducted precisely in accordance with the preceding dispensations."[13] Thus, there is an established order in the Church and kingdom because all these things are set up and governed by provisions decreed by the Father and the Son before the world was.

Among the explanations by the Prophet Joseph Smith are the following:

1. The Lord revealed the entire gospel plan to Adam and set him

to be at the head, and Adam "presides over the spirits of all mankind."[14]

2. The Lord decreed that salvation in every age of the world could only be administered in the name of Christ and through the gospel and ordinances of Christ.[15]

3. Therefore, the Lord "set the ordinances to be the same forever and ever, and set Adam to watch over them, to reveal them from heaven to man, or to send angels to reveal them. . . . These angels are under the direction of Michael or Adam, who acts under the direction of the Lord."[16] "Whenever [priesthood keys and ordinances] are revealed from heaven, it is by Adam's authority."[17]

4. "There are no angels who minister to this earth except those who do belong or have belonged to it" (D&C 130:5).

5. "There has been a chain of [priesthood] authority . . . from Adam to the present time."[18]

6. The law of common consent must apply to all administrative operations in the Church.[19] There are to be no secret ordinations. A man must "come in at the gate" (D&C 43:7) and be regularly ordained by those who are known to have authority in the Church.

7. The president may receive revelation for the Church, and every person may receive revelation for his or her responsibility and personal guidance, but none receive revelation or direction from God for those higher in authority than themselves.[20]

8. "There is a law, irrevocably decreed in heaven before the foundation of this world, upon which all blessings are predicated—and when we obtain any blessing from God, it is by obedience to that law upon which it is predicated" (D&C 130:20–21).

All of the foregoing, and more, reflect the established order, and show that the Lord's "house is a house of order . . . and not a house of confusion" (D&C 132:8).

Absolute Truths

When we find in the scriptures, and in the teachings of the prophets, phrases and terms such as "the holy order of God," "new and everlasting covenant," and "before the foundation of the world," we are talking about *absolute truths* revealed from God to us because He wants to bring us up to His standard. I know that some things are relative, but fundamental gospel truths are absolute because they were decreed in the grand council before the world was organized. I heard a person declare with great finality that there are no absolute truths, and that everything is relative. If that were so, then his own statement could not be true, because he was making an absolute statement. Be assured that there *are* absolute truths: they come from God, are the "fixed principles" that are essential to our eternal progress, and were in existence before this world was formed. There is comfort in knowing that salvation operates on the basis of permanent truth.

AN ABSOLUTE TRUTH

The great plan that God has revealed for us to follow is absolute and is the same plan that enabled Him to become who He is. The Prophet Joseph Smith said:

> God himself was once as we are now, and is an exalted man, and sits enthroned in yonder heavens! That is the great secret. If the veil were rent today, and the great God who holds this world in its orbit, and who upholds all worlds and all things by his power, was to make himself visible,—I say, if you were to see him today, you would see him like a man in form—like yourselves in all the person, image, and very form as a man; for Adam was created in the very fashion, image and likeness of God.[21]

INHERITANCE OF REAL ESTATE IN ETERNITY

Another vital factor of the established order of the kingdom of God is the *reality* of *physical things* in eternity. Elder Lorenzo Snow said: "[If the Saints will consecrate] they will eventually be exalted to possess all that is desirable—the land, the houses, the vineyards, the cattle, the gold, the silver, and all the riches of the heavens and of the earth. The Lord says, All these things are mine; and because of the willingness of my people, all will be restored back to me; and then I will put them in possession of all the riches of eternity."[22]

And Elder Orson Pratt explained: "Heavenly riches and earthly riches are of the same nature; only one is glorified and made immortal, and the other is in a fallen, unglorified state. If we are not willing to be governed by the law of equality in regard to that which is of the least value, who shall entrust us with all the riches of eternity?"[23]

Both of these Brethren used the phrase "riches of eternity" in speaking of physical things. This phrase is used three times in the Doctrine and Covenants. Look at Doctrine and Covenants 38:18–20, 39, and notice that the Lord is talking about real substance—actually it is real estate, a land inheritance—both on earth and also in heaven. Here are the words:

> And I hold forth and deign to give unto you greater riches, even a land of promise, a land flowing with milk and honey, upon which there shall be no curse when the Lord cometh;
> And I will give it unto you for the land of your inheritance, if you seek it with all your hearts.
> And this shall be my covenant with you, ye shall have it for the land of your inheritance, and for the inheritance of your children forever, while the earth shall stand, and ye shall possess it again in eternity, no more to pass away. . . .
> And if ye seek the riches which it is the will of the Father to give unto you, ye shall be the richest of all people, for ye shall have the riches of eternity; and it must needs be that the riches of the earth are mine to give.

The *physical nature* of eternity is one of the riches of eternity. It is the established order of heaven that the Saints will possess landed property. Jesus said, "The meek . . . shall inherit the earth" (Matthew 5:5; see also D&C 88:17). He really meant it.

Gender Is an Eternal and Absolute Principle

Another of the great realities of eternity, both on earth and in heaven, is that gender—maleness and femaleness—is an eternal principle. In the "Proclamation to the World" about the family, we read the following in paragraph two: "All human beings—male and female—are created in the image of God. Each is a beloved spirit son or daughter of heavenly parents, and, as such, each has a divine nature and destiny. Gender is an essential characteristic of individual premortal, mortal, and eternal identity and purpose."[24] You notice that the proclamation states that every human being "is a beloved spirit son or daughter of heavenly parents." The scope of the family in the proclamation includes God's extensive *family*, as well as our individual earthly families. The proclamation says that gender is an *eternal identification* and an *essential characteristic* and has an *eternal purpose.* This is a very sacred doctrinal declaration and lays the groundwork for eternal marriage, for a mother in heaven and everlasting families. Gender is the established order of the kingdom of God.

In the seventh paragraph of the proclamation we read: "The family is ordained of God. Marriage between man and woman is essential to His eternal plan."[25] It is basic doctrine of the gospel of Jesus Christ that eternal marriage, as performed in the temple, is necessary for us to obtain a fulness of God's glory. The logic is unmistakable. We have in the Church the *pattern* of the celestial family—to enable us to become precisely as our heavenly parents are. If marriage for eternity is necessary for *us* to become like our heavenly parents, it must have been necessary for them also. The physical nature of eternity requires a literal bodily physical resurrection of flesh and bone (see D&C 93:33–34). Hence, God has a body of flesh and bone.

A Material Existence

The plan of salvation is the established order of heaven transferred to the earth. Elder Orson Pratt said it well:

> A Saint who is one in deed and in truth, does not look for an immaterial heaven, but he expects a heaven with lands, houses, cities, vegetation, rivers, and animals; with thrones, temples, palaces, kings, princes, priests, and angels; with food, raiment, musical instruments, etc., all of which are material. Indeed, the Saints' heaven is a redeemed, glorified, celestial, material creation, inhabited by glorified material beings, male and female, organized into families, embracing all the relationships of husbands and wives, parents and children, where sorrow, crying, pain, and death will be no more. Or to speak still more definitely, this earth, when glorified, is the Saints' eternal heaven. On it they expect to live, with body, parts, and holy passions; on it they expect to move and have their being; to eat, drink, converse, worship, sing, play on musical instruments, engage in joyful, innocent, social amusements, visit neighboring towns and neighboring worlds; indeed, matter and its qualities and properties are the only beings or things with which they expect to associate.[26]

Elder Pratt also said:

> The dealing of God towards his children from the time they are first born in Heaven, through all their successive stages of existence, until they are redeemed, perfected, and made Gods, is a pattern after which all other worlds are dealt with. . . . The creation, fall, and redemption of all future worlds with their inhabitants will be conducted upon the same general plan. . . .
>
> The Father of our spirits has only been doing that which His Progenitors did before Him. Each succeeding generation of Gods follow the example of the preceding ones. . . . [The same plan is carried out] by which more ancient worlds have been redeemed.[27]

If we believe these statements, we will see that earth life is a reflection of what exists in heaven. Our Heavenly Father and our Savior Jesus Christ have given us the divine pattern to enable us to become like them. Because it exists in heaven, it is therefore the established order in the Church on earth, which is the training ground. Because we belong to a church that practices the heavenly pattern, it is almost like having one foot already in heaven. It was possibly this relationship that prompted President Brigham Young to say that "the Latter-day Saints have the most natural faith and belief of any people on the face of the earth."[28]

Mortals cannot comprehend all the things of God. We scarcely understand the system, but the Holy Spirit tells us that the gospel plan foreshadows our eternal progress.

INDEBTEDNESS TO THE PROPHET JOSEPH SMITH

President Brigham Young expressed great appreciation for the Prophet Joseph:

> I never saw any one, until I met Joseph Smith, who could tell me anything about the character, personality and dwelling-place of God, or anything satisfactory about angels, or the relationship of man to his Maker.[29]

> What is the nature and beauty of Joseph's mission? You know that I am one of his Apostles. When I first heard him

preach, he brought heaven and earth together; and all the priests of the day could not tell me anything correct about heaven, hell, God, angels, or devils; they were as blind as Egyptian darkness. When I saw Joseph Smith, he took heaven, figuratively speaking, and brought it down to earth; and he took the earth, brought it up, and opened up, in plainness and simplicity, the things of God; and that is the beauty of his mission.[30]

What a delight it was to hear Brother Joseph talk upon the great principles of eternity; he would bring them down to the capacity of a child, and he would unite heaven with earth, this is the beauty of our religion.[31]

And President Gordon B. Hinckley eloquently testified:

How great indeed is our debt to [Joseph Smith]. His life began in Vermont and ended in Illinois, and marvelous were the things that happened between that simple beginning and tragic ending. It was he who brought us a true knowledge of God, the Eternal Father, and His Risen Son, the Lord Jesus Christ. During the short time of his great vision he learned more concerning the nature of Deity than all of those who through centuries had argued the matter in learned councils and scholarly forums. . . . Through him were restored the keys of the holy temples, that men and women might enter into eternal covenants with God and that the great work for the dead might be accomplished to open the way for eternal blessings.[32]

LIFE WITH A VIEW

Several years ago I visited Niagara Falls and marveled at the size and the noise of that spectacle. We had reservations in a very tall hotel on the river's edge, and many in the group hoped for a room with a view of the falls. Executives, moguls, and schoolteachers all want offices and homes with a view. Even in the scriptures, "upper rooms" have priority. Most of us will probably not have a home on a hilltop or an office or penthouse with a view of the city. The Book of Mormon describes the earth as "a dark and dreary wilderness" (1 Nephi 8:4). That is the lonely world we live in if we do not have the light of the gospel of Jesus Christ. If we participate in the ordinances of salvation, we become acquainted with the established order of heaven. We have a light for our path, we get a glimpse of eternity while still on earth, and we have more than just a room but a *life* with a view, and we begin to see the established order of the kingdom of God.

NOTES

1. Joseph Smith, *Teachings of the Prophet Joseph Smith,* comp. Joseph Fielding Smith (Salt Lake City: Deseret Book, 1976), 320, 325.

2. *Times and Seasons,* September 1, 1842, 905.

3. Joseph Smith, *The Words of Joseph Smith,* comp. and ed. Andrew F. Ehat and Lyndon W. Cook (Provo, UT: Religious Studies Center, 1980), 181.

4. Ezra Taft Benson, "Jesus Christ—Gifts and Expectations," *Ensign,* December 1988, 6.

5. Joseph F. Smith, *Gospel Doctrine,* 7th ed. (Salt Lake City: Deseret Book, 1946), 21.

6. Smith, *Teachings,* 197–99.

7. Smith, *Teachings,* 324.

8. Orson Pratt, "Elijah's Latter-day Mission," in *Masterful Discourses and Writings of Orson Pratt,* ed. N. B. Lundwall (Salt Lake City: N. B. Lundwall, 1946), 259.

9. Smith, *Teachings,* 166–67.

10. Smith, *Teachings,* 308.

11. Smith, *Teachings,* 320.

12. From unpublished research in which I identified seventeen topics that are declared to have been decreed before the world was created.

13. Smith, *Teachings,* 168.

14. Smith, *Teachings,* 157–58, 167.

15. Smith, *Teachings,* 168.

16. Smith, *Teachings,* 168.

17. Smith, *Teachings,* 157.

18. Smith, *Teachings,* 191.

19. Smith, *Teachings,* 75, 108; see D&C 28:13.

20. Smith, *Teachings,* 111.

21. Smith, *Teachings,* 345.

22. Lorenzo Snow, in *Journal of Discourses* (London: Latter-day Saints' Book Depot, 1854–86), 5:65.

23. Orson Pratt, "The Equality and Oneness of the Saints," in *Masterful Discourses*, 596–97.

24. "The Family: A Proclamation to the World," *Ensign*, November 1995, 102.

25. "The Family: A Proclamation to the World," 102.

26. Pratt, *Masterful Discourses*, 60.

27. Orson Pratt, "The Pre-existence of Man," in *The Seer*, September 1853, 134–35.

28. Brigham Young, *Discourses of Brigham Young*, ed. John A. Widtsoe (Salt Lake City: Deseret Book, 1946), 125.

29. Young, *Discourses*, 458.

30. Young, *Discourses*, 458–59.

31. Young, *Discourses*, 459.

32. Gordon B. Hinckley, "A Season for Gratitude," *Ensign*, December 1997, 2.

CHAPTER EIGHTEEN

JOSEPH SMITH ON THE BODY AS A FALLEN OR BLESSED VESSEL

DANIEL B. McKINLAY

One of the bewildering issues of mortal life is the mystery of our embodiment. Throughout time, as humans have matured, they have been intrigued by their bodies and wondered why they exist and what their role is. Acknowledging the marvel that the body is, many have nevertheless concluded that it is a nuisance and is necessarily transitory. Viewing it as the prison of the soul or otherwise observing its inevitable destiny of decay and dissolution, it has commonly been disparaged. On the subject of the body, its purpose and potential destiny, Joseph Smith stands as a colossus. His explanation as a revelator of answers to these perplexities offers enlightenment, reassurance, and exhilaration for those who grasp and appreciate his teachings.

As early as February 16, 1832, in the vision of the degrees of glory, the Prophet taught that there is something inherently divine in our beings: he and Sidney Rigdon affirmed that our spirits are begotten sons and daughters unto God (see D&C 76:24). We as Church members have responded most warmly to that concept. In fact, that view usually predominates when we discuss the aspects of our spirit-body composition. But frankly, our welcome reception of that encouraging doctrine has sometimes deflected our attention

Daniel B. McKinlay is resident scholar at the Institute for the Study and Preservation of Ancient Religious Texts.

from a parallel concept equally emphasized by the Prophet, namely, that our mortal state is a genuinely fallen one.

With reference to his assessment of our mortal condition, I begin with the Prophet's view of the body at the start of our sojourn in our fallen world, and then I consider its potential ascent to divinely sanctioned fulfilment. The result will indicate the Prophet's unique proposition in our day about the nature of the physical body in its various stages. In addition to the teachings of the Prophet, including revelations he received in the Restoration scriptures, I will draw on supplementary comments that have been made by some of the brethren who were taught by him, as well as by a few who lived quite a while after his martyrdom in 1844 but who built on his anchor teachings.

The Prophet Saw Distinct Personages

When we think of the various facets of wonder the boy Joseph perceived from his First Vision, we note with great interest his report that he saw two personages. The 1828 *American Dictionary of the English Language* defines a personage as "a man or woman of distinction; as an illustrious *personage*," and as an "exterior appearance; stature; air; as a tall *personage*; a stately *personage*."[1] The knowledge of God that Joseph derived from his vision provided him with a concrete catalyst for his view of the embodiment of men and women.

The announcement that Joseph saw the Father and the Son in the form of personages would be surprising to adherents of traditional Christianity, who believed God to be unembodied. They may have forgotten that Stephen claimed that he saw the Son of Man standing on the right hand of God (see Acts 7:56). Stephen saw something that he was able to identify with the shape of the historical Jesus. Presumably, the Being by whom the Son of Man stood was also in human shape. But because of metaphysical claims in Christendom that spanned back to early councils, God had been relegated to a static abstraction, an amorphous "essence" of some kind. In one sense this was to be expected, since the doctrine of God had become wedded with some forms of Greek philosophy.[2]

Inherent Human Weakness

Joseph would naturally have been awestricken as he contemplated the grandeur of Deity. Yet at the same time he would have recognized the limitations of the mortal body, which functions within earthly time and space. A sweeping observation would reveal to him that the newborn, if lucky, would be healthy and robust, and with growth would continue in that way, and would possibly even attain beauty, however that might be defined;[3] but in time its body would decline. If it reached old age, it would inevitably lose its smoothness and soundness. But in any case, for everyone, the body would lose its animation and die. Given that observation, it would be preposterous to claim that God could share such a decaying existence with humanity. He must be an other-than-human being. By the time the Prophet came to the world, that assumption had pervaded the Christian world for centuries.

There were at least two ways a person could view the body in antiquity, and the legacy continues today: it was perceived as either a toy, a plaything, naturally designed with the properties for sensual gratification, which could and should be realized; or it was considered a bother and an irritant because of the ravages afflicted by continued experience in the natural world. In both instances, it could be scorned and denigrated. It has been called a nasty shack, a prison of the soul, a tomb, a mud heap, and a host of other degrading epithets.[4] Throughout history many have yearned for the release of the soul from the impediment of the body that hosts it. Salvation for many has been regarded as a liberation from the frustrations of mortality.

In contrast, the Prophet encapsulated his view of the body in this impressively concise statement on the purpose for our existence in the world: "We came to this earth that we might have a body and present it pure before God in the celestial kingdom." He added what some would consider, in light of the preceding views, to be an astonishing proposition: "The great principle of happiness consists in having a body."[5] This magnificently succinct declaration is pivotal in coalescing what is said about the body in both the Book of Mormon and the Bible.

CHRIST'S BODY AS MODEL

The Prophet learned by revelation that "every spirit of man was innocent in the beginning" (D&C 93:38). This was advanced frequently by President Brigham Young when he proclaimed that our spirits came to the earth pure and holy.[6] That concept and the

Prophet's discovery from the First Vision and many other divine encounters that testify that the risen Lord is still embodied may have influenced his optimistic attitude toward the body. But his insight does not negate the biblical and Book of Mormon notions of fallen flesh, which we all witness in our sojourn in life.[7] The body of Jesus serves as the great archetype for that part of humanity that searches for sanctification.

The hymn "Jesus, Once of Humble Birth,"[8] by one of the Prophet's treasured associates, Elder Parley P. Pratt, teaches in terms of contrasts that were likely influenced by the "Christological hymn" by Paul in Galatians 2:5–11. In those verses we learn that the pre-mortal Jesus chose to "empty" (*ekenosen*) Himself of His godly stature and come to the earth in the form of a slave or servant, in the likeness of men. This indeed corroborates the view that in one sense of quality, Jesus took a humble step downward. To strengthen that idea, Romans 8:3 tells us almost in passing that God sent "his own Son in the likeness of sinful flesh." I know of no statement by the Prophet that challenges Paul's wording. I do not believe that these verses cheapen the importance of the body, since there is more to the matter of Christ's and our embodiment than what these verses directly communicate. In coming to the earth embodied, Jesus was able to identify thoroughly with the human race. In the likeness of sinful flesh, He was able vicariously to empathize with the totality of our human experiences (even our downward propensities) as they take place in the body. He was also able to effect the great Atonement as it relates to our mortal condition.

The Prophet's translation of King Benjamin's address, complementing Paul's words, gives us a marvelous glimpse of what Jesus' Incarnation means for us: "And lo, he shall suffer temptations, and pain of body, hunger, thirst, and fatigue, even more than man can suffer, except it be unto death; for behold, blood cometh from every pore, so great shall be his anguish for the wickedness and the abominations of his people" (Mosiah 3:7).

Likewise, the Prophet's translation of Alma 7:11–13, containing the profound comment of Alma to the Saints in the city of Gideon, says:

> And he shall go forth, suffering pains and afflictions and
> temptations of every kind; and this that the word might be

fulfilled which saith he will take upon him the pains and the sicknesses of his people.

And he will take upon him death, that he may loose the bands of death which bind his people; and he will take upon him their infirmities, that his bowels may be filled with mercy, according to the flesh, that he may know according to the flesh how to succor his people according to their infirmities.

Now the Spirit knoweth all things; nevertheless the Son of God suffereth according to the flesh that he might take upon him the sins of his people, that he might blot out their transgressions according to the power of his deliverance.

My point in citing these excerpts is that with His body, Christ identified with our weaknesses and did something for us that affects the whole of us, including our bodies. Implicit in this is that the lovely effect of Christ's Atonement is relevant to us here and now, but it also is intended to exceed the events pertaining to the earth on which we now live.

We are to reverence Christ's body, both in its preresurrected and glorified states. The poignancy of this opportunity is reflected in the words of institution at the Last Supper as preserved by Paul.[9] Jesus said to the disciples when He was on the verge of entering Gethsemane and the cross, "Take, eat: this is my body, which is broken for you: this do in remembrance of me" (1 Corinthians 11:24). In a perfect blending with these words, God revealed to the Prophet that when we bless the bread portion of the sacrament, we do it "in remembrance of the body of [His] Son" (Moroni 4:3). We thus call to mind the sacrifice wrought for us through Jesus' preresurrected body. Perhaps we may also view the Lord's body as the perfect model for our own beings, which engenders gratitude for Him on our part.[10]

When we deal with the spectrum of Christ's role as Savior and archetype for us, His entry into the world in "the likeness of sinful flesh" and His identification with us in our bodily ordeals comprise only the first part of the overall plan. We learn, continuing further in the Christological hymn in Philippians, that having prevailed in His decrepit condition analogous to a slave, He has become "highly exalted" (Philippians 2:9). Certainly in His exalted condition, He is gloriously embodied. But He does not stand in isolation in that sphere. Paul tells us later in Philippians that the Savior "shall change our vile [*tapeinoseus*, humble or lowly] body, that it may be fashioned like unto his glorious body, according to the workings whereby he is able even to subdue all things unto himself" (3:21). Thus, the promise to us is not only a resurrection but also potentially a qualitative adjustment that will imitate in grandeur the body of the Master. This correlates naturally with the Prophet's statement that we have a body to "present it pure before God in the celestial kingdom."[11]

THE BODY IN OUR PRESENT TELESTIAL WORLD

Aside from our anticipated glorious resurrection, what are we to think of our fleshly instruments in the sordid world we live in at present? Should we renounce it with contempt as some of the ancients did? In his exposition on the dichotomy between the works of the flesh and the fruits of the Spirit, Paul says that "they that are Christ's have crucified the flesh with the affections and the lusts" (Galatians 5:24). And as noted above, he associates our bodies with "sinful flesh." I suggest that Paul speaks as he does for at least two reasons: (1) our fallen condition makes us vulnerable to "the fiery darts of the wicked" (Ephesians 6:16; D&C 27:17) and to our inherent selfishness; (2) the adversary and his hosts are permitted to "send forth . . . his shafts in the whirlwind" and "his hail and his mighty storm" (Helaman 5:12), which can penetrate us and all too often succeed.[12]

Granted, the body is not inherently evil; it is susceptible to sin, and that is precisely the point of our experiencing a probation in this world—to see what choices we will make that relate to our body and character. Hugh Nibley points out the view in early Christian apocryphal literature that "the soul is not sent down as punishment nor imprisoned in the flesh . . . ; rather it is sent to be tried and tested in 'the blessed vessel' of the flesh whose immortality is guaranteed by the resurrection."[13] Again, this gestures toward the statement by the Prophet that our purpose in having a body is to "present it pure before God in the celestial kingdom." It was all arranged in the premortal plan, as the Prophet taught in the King Follett discourse: "God himself, finding he was in the midst of spirits and glory, because he was more intelligent, saw proper to institute laws whereby the rest could have a privilege to advance like himself."[14] The pathway for advancement required the taking of a physical body.

PREMORTAL ANTICIPATION

Beginning with the Prophet's teaching that we existed as spirit children of our Father in Heaven as a point of departure, Elder Russell M. Nelson says that "we eagerly anticipated the possibility of coming to earth and obtaining a physical body. Knowingly we wanted the risks of mortality, which would allow the exercise of agency and accountability."[15] While we Latter-day Saints accept this proposition, sometimes in the heat of mortal experience it can be astonishing! Yet the Prophet taught that obtaining a body was absolutely indispensable to our ultimate fulfilment. Hence, "the devil has no body, and herein is his punishment."[16]

It was common for American religionists in the Prophet's day to distinguish between the characteristics of body and spirit, as Joseph noted: "The body is supposed to be organized matter, and the spirit, by many, is thought to be immaterial, without substance. With this latter statement we should beg leave to differ, and state that the spirit is a substance; that it is material, but that it is more pure, elastic and refined matter than the body; that it existed before the body, can exist in the body; and will exist separate from the body, when the body will be mouldering in the dust; and will in the resurrection, be again united with it."[17]

The Prophet learned another germane principle about the spirit when he inquired about certain aspects of the Revelation of John. The Lord revealed in Doctrine and Covenants 77:2 that "that which is temporal [is] in the likeness of that which is spiritual; the spirit of man in the likeness of his person" (compare Moses 3:5). Commenting on this doctrine, Elder Erastus Snow said that "our spirits are the express image of our tabernacles, and, united together, the Scriptures inform us, are the express image of God."[18] Elder Parley P. Pratt more explicitly tells us that our "organized spirit we call a body, because, although composed of the spiritual elements, it possesses every organ after the pattern and in the likeness or similitude of the outward or fleshly tabernacle it is destined to eventually inhabit. Its organs of thought, speech, sight, hearing, tasting, smelling, feeling, etc., all exist in their order as in the physical body; the one being the exact similitude of the other."[19]

The Fallen Body, the Spirit, and the Atonement

In spite of the existential unity of body and spirit, virtually all of us have been touched by the tensions that exist between both components of our being when it comes to the choices with which we are confronted. President Brigham Young warned that "the body is of the earth, and is subject to the power of the devil, and is under the mighty influence of that fallen nature that is of the earth. If the spirit yields to the body, the devil then has power to overcome both the body and spirit of that man, and he loses both."[20]

Like President Young, I believe that Elder Erastus Snow, who likewise was taught by the Prophet, understood what Paul was getting at in the fifth chapter of Galatians when he spoke of the war between the flesh and the spirit. Said Elder Snow:

> The body does not control the spirit, but the spirit controls the body. Still the Apostle Paul says that there is a law of the flesh—that wars against the spirit; and, says Paul, "to be carnally minded is death; but to be spiritually minded is life and peace" [Romans 8:6]. He further says that this law of the flesh—that is in our members and the lusts thereof—that wars against the law of the spirit brings our bodies into bondage, even the bondage of sin, but it is made the duty of the spirit to subdue the flesh and the lusts and desires thereof [Galatians 5:24], and to bring it into subjection to the law of the spirit. This is the warfare and the struggle of our lives.[21]

Inferring from the Prophet's position that the body is pertinent to our happiness and fulfillment, Elder Hugh B. Brown averred "that matter is not essentially evil but that its purpose is to serve spirit, while spirit controls and glorifies matter. There is a beneficent and eternal relationship between spirit and element."[22]

Elder John A. Widtsoe, a scientist, was always interested in the relationship between the spirit and the body, and he discussed it in this general conference excerpt: "Man is an eternal spirit inhabiting a body of this earth, a perishable body, which some day we believe will be made imperishable. By means of that body, given by our Father in heaven, we are able to accomplish the great mission known as earth life. Through the body the spirit speaks, and through the body the experiences of earth are made the possession of the spirit. It is well that we give due care and consideration to the welfare of the body, which is the one great characteristic of this epoch in our eternal journey."[23]

Heber C. Kimball encouraged the Saints:

> If we seek him with all our hearts, and observe those things that pertain to righteousness, working diligently in his kingdom, he will feel after us and inspire our hearts with his Holy Spirit, and the influence thereof will rest upon us continually; it will enter into every muscle, sinew, and fibre of the body, in proportion to our fitness to receive it. If we render ourselves susceptible of the nourishment that is imparted by the Spirit of God to the spirits that dwell within these mortal bodies, we shall have sufficient light and power to enable our spirits to dictate our bodies and lead them unto eternal life.[24]

Our goal is to temper our vulnerable but blessed bodies with the sanctifying influence of the Atonement, and certainly that sanctifying power is transmitted through the ordinances. The Lord revealed to the Prophet that "in the ordinances thereof [referring to the priesthood], the power of godliness is manifest. And without the ordinances thereof, and the authority of the priesthood, the power of godliness is not manifest unto men in the flesh" (D&C 84:20–21).

I would say that our bodies can indeed become blessed through two intertwining factors: (1) we can exert our agency to rebuke Satan-inspired attacks on our flesh. In the process we demonstrate respect for our bodies.[25] President Spencer W. Kimball made the inspiring declaration that "the highest achievement of spirituality comes as we conquer the flesh."[26] But (2) the subduing of our bodies in preparation for a celestial resurrection cannot come about unless we call upon the refining empowerment of the Atonement with its offer of repentance and ordinances.

As we ponder over the various levels of physical delight, we recognize that they are not necessarily equal in long-term satisfaction. Elder Adam S. Bennion made this thoughtful observation:

> In ordinary language we talk as if joy, pleasure, gladness, and happiness were all synonymous. But in this passage from the Book of Mormon ["men are, that they might have joy"] joy has a far richer meaning. Pleasure, in my mind, is essentially a gratification of one of the senses. Happiness seems to

center in a kind of contentment born of good fortune or of
some fortuitous circumstance. But joy reveals a certain spiritual exaltation. . . . As I have been thinking about it, joy
seems to me to be essentially spiritual and has an abiding
quality with a hint of eternal bliss.[27]

Perhaps the surpassing sensation that Elder Bennion speaks of
was intimated by the resurrected Lord when he said to a group of
Lehites in a spiritually-consuming setting with parents, children, and
angels, "My joy is full" (3 Nephi 17:20).

I believe that we can experience a level of joy in our bodies in
this life, yet anticipate a heightening of it in the Resurrection. It is
not necessary or even appropriate to mortify the body in an attempt
to have dominion over it. But spiritual discipline is requisite.
President John Taylor stated the nobility of our prospects on earth:
the object of man is not the gratification of sensual appetites but "to
soar like the eagle" and "to rise in the scale of being."[28] With a slight
but significant qualification, President David O. McKay added, "The
body with its five or more senses, with its appetites and passions, is
essential to life and happiness, but in the ultimate analysis it is only
a means to a higher end. When man makes its gratification an end
in itself, he frustrates the purpose and descends to sensuality."[29] What
Presidents Taylor and McKay say here correlates well with a commandment given to Adam by an angel. He declared, "Thou shalt do
all that thou doest in the name of the Son" (Moses 5:8). We can and
should *enjoy* but *consecrate* our doings while in the body. In such circumstances we, while we are in our bodies, stand approved before
God.

THE BODY OF GOD AND THE BODIES OF HIS CHILDREN

Seeing in vision the glorious bodies of the Father and the Son
must have been pivotal for Joseph's understanding of the human
body, as demonstrated by the fact that He utterly rejected the God of
the creeds when he stated, "That which is without body, parts, and
passions is nothing."[30] Elder Parley P. Pratt, in his *Key to the Science of
Theology*, elaborated on this thesis.[31]

Taking, I believe, the embodiment of God as his foundational
point, the Prophet explained why we are embodied: "The design of
God before the foundation of the world was that we should take

tabernacles, that through our faithfulness we should overcome & thereby obtain a resurrection from the dead."[32]

THE BODY IN THE RESURRECTION

In the general conference in April 1843, the Prophet explained a portion of the mystery of the Resurrection. One of the Twelve, Orson Pratt, who had a gifted scientific mind made a comment based on the understanding of his day. The following response of the Prophet is recorded: "There is no fundamental principle belonging to a human system that ever goes into another in this world or in the world to come; I care not what the theories of men are. We have the testimony that God will raise us up, and he has the power to do it. If anyone supposes that any part of our bodies, that is, the fundamental parts thereof, ever goes into another body, he is mistaken."[33]

This notion was elaborated upon a number of times by President Brigham Young, who often spoke of the "component parts" of the body that would somehow survive death and be called together and united at the time of resurrection.[34] The idea accords perfectly with what the Prophet learned from Amulek in his ministry to the inhabitants of Ammonihah (see Alma 11:43), and Alma in his interview with Corianton (see Alma 40:23): all parts of the body will be restored and reunited with their spirit counterparts. But in the Resurrection, the elements of the body will no longer be structured in the gross or corrupt condition that characterizes life in mortality. The Prophet taught that in the Resurrection, "all will be raised by the power of God, having spirit in their bodies, and not blood."[35]

President Spencer W. Kimball noted that at the appointed time, "the spirit will be housed eternally in a remodeled body of flesh and bones."[36] Elder Russell M. Nelson, with the expertise of a physician, explained further: "The Lord who created us in the first place surely has power to do it again. The same necessary elements now in our bodies will still be available—at His command. The same unique genetic code now embedded in each of our living cells will still be available to format new ones then."[37] This has intriguing application to the Prophet himself. Even though he suffered a bullet-riddled death, he will be gloriously resurrected, and his body will be devoid of any mortal impediments.[38]

Although all those who have taken mortal tabernacles will be resurrected, there will be qualitative variations in the finished products. President John Taylor begins the track of this thought with the following summary:

> It is the design of God, as I understand it, in our coming here, to give unto us bodies, that the spirits that were created before might have tabernacles wherein they might live and exist, and move and act, as corporeal substances, if you please; and that according to certain inscrutable laws of God pertaining to the human family and the future destiny of man, and the world in which we live; that through the union of the body and spirit, and their obedience to certain laws which the great Eloheim has given for the guidance of His people, that they might be more exalted, more dignified, more glorious than it would be possible for them to be, had they not come here to sojourn in these tabernacles, and combat with the various evils to which the flesh is heir.[39]

In Doctrine and Covenants 88 the Lord tells us that there are levels of resurrection that correspond to the telestial, terrestrial, and celestial kingdoms (see D&C 88:20–31). Elder Melvin J. Ballard described the ultimate outcome of this future event for us all when he said that those who are resurrected with "the glory of the celestial [kingdom] shall have a body whose very fineness and texture, the composition of it, the quality of the flesh shall be superior" to that of a lower degree of glory.[40]

MARITAL UNION OF BODIES

Closely connected to the fall of humankind and our acquisition of a fallen body is the opportunity to participate in marriage. For the Prophet, this was a sacrament consisting of the union of two souls, male and female, each of which is composed of spirit and body. Through the approved sexual union of the two souls, a new house for a spirit is formed in the world. In some branches of Christendom, the notion has arisen, again from the Greek aversion to the physical world and the assumption that the physical joining of the sexes is at best a necessary evil, that celibacy is a holier condition than that of marriage, in spite of the fact that in the prototypical marriage of Adam and Eve they were blessed (as well as commanded) to multiply and replenish the earth. That marvelous blessing has never been rescinded. In the restored Church, the Lord revealed to the Prophet that the sealing of husband and wife in marriage, with the prospect of loving a noble embodied posterity, can be the ultimate joy in eternal existence. Hence the counsel that we show reverence and respect for our bodies as we anticipate marriage and parenthood in this world to prepare for an intensification of joy in eternity.

Springing from this insight are two related exalting principles at work. First is the loveliness of the Resurrection. The Prophet, who knew whereof he spoke through visionary experience, simply stated that no one can describe the beauty of the Resurrection.[41] One of his trusted friends, who was also one of his successors in the Presidency, Lorenzo Snow, informed a general conference audience in the twilight of his life that nothing is more beautiful to look upon than a resurrected body.[42] And what President Snow said in the last session of the conference leads to the other great principle: The joy of resurrected beings is enhanced by the presence of resurrected loved ones.[43] Embodied now, we can take great delight in our associations with family members and dear friends here and hereafter.[44] As the Prophet Joseph said:

> So plain was the vision, that I actually saw men, before they had ascended from the tomb, as though they were getting up slowly. They took each other by the hand and said to each other, "My father, my son, my mother, my daughter, my brother, my sister." And when the voice calls for the dead to arise, suppose I am laid by the side of my father, what would be the first joy of my heart? To meet my father, my mother, my brother, my sister; and when they are by my side, I embrace them, and they me.[45]

Although we experience a certain level of love in this world, a fondness for many with whom we associate, President Young was of the understanding that in the resurrection of those who abide a celestial law there is a dimension of love that exceeds what we are entitled to here. Apparently, this more profound love is tied in with worthiness to experience it.[45]

In a celestial resurrection, the parameters of divine love shared by a married couple may be increased, as explained by Elder Parley P. Pratt:

> The eternal union of the sexes, in and after the resurrection, is mainly for the purpose of renewing and continuing the work of procreation. In our present or rudimental state, our offspring are in our own image and partake of our natures, in which are the seeds of death. In like manner will the offspring of immortal and celestial beings be in the likeness and partake of the nature of their divine parentage. Hence, such offspring will be pure, holy, incorruptible and eternal. They will in no wise be subject unto death, except by descending to partake of the grosser elements, in which are the inherent properties of dissolution or death.[47]

In summary, through the Prophet we know that our embodiment on this telestial earth, while fraught with misery at times, is part of the plan for our ultimate joy. The body begins in a fallen environment and can become debilitated and defiled as a result of foolish choices on our part. But by applying the merciful option of repentance and priesthood ordinances offered through the Atonement, and by recognizing the body as a superb vessel of expression and acting accordingly, it can become a sanctified instrument that will someday dwell in the society of celestial beings and our Heavenly Father.

The Prophet's revelations on the role of the body in time and eternity was unique in his generation. These revelations can be most exhilarating to us as we experience the perplexities of earth life, and they can ennoble our appreciation for the gift that our body really is. The Prophet gives full life to the famous dictum of the Apostle Paul that, for the Christian, the body is a temple (see 1 Corinthians 6:19).

NOTES

1. Noah Webster, *An American Dictionary of the English Language* (Foundation for American Christian Education: San Francisco, 1995), s.v. "personage."

2. Because the creedal dogma on God took such potent root, the meaning of the statement in Genesis 2:27 that man was created in the image of God was obscured and lost its original reference to the kindred relationship of Deity and humanity.

3. According to many who knew and loved the Prophet, he was a specimen of the ideal of beauty (see Truman G. Madsen, *Joseph Smith Among the Prophets* [Salt Lake City: Deseret Book, 1965], 1–2;

Matthew B. Brown and Val W. Brinkerhoff, *Joseph Smith: The Man, the Mission, the Message* [American Fork: Covenant, 2004], 10–14).

4. For example, Shakespeare referred to the body as "this muddy vesture of decay" in *The Merchant of Venice*, 5.1.64.

5. Joseph Smith, *Teachings of the Prophet Joseph Smith*, comp. Joseph Fielding Smith (Salt Lake City: Deseret Book, 1938), 181.

6. Brigham Young, in *Journal of Discourses* (London: Latter-day Saints' Book Depot, 1854–86), 8:138; 6:291; 18:258; *Millennial Star*, supplement 1853, 56. Elder Boyd K. Packer, "Little Children," *Ensign*, November 1986, 17, has noted that "each time a child is born, the world is renewed in innocence."

7. Elder Delbert L. Stapley, "Our Responsibility: To Save the World," *Ensign*, December 1971, 97, gives a vivid analogy: "Many rivers have their beginning from springs of pure, crystal-clear water gushing forth from a mountainside. As the water wends its way to the sea, there are side tributaries that join the main stream. Some of these tributaries are polluted and contaminate the main stream, which started pure at its source. By the time the river reaches the sea, pollution has occurred in the body of the stream. How much like life this symbolic representation is! . . . In the beginning of mortal life all mankind is innocent before God and, therefore, is like the beginning river of water, pure and undefiled. As the polluted tributaries of water enter the main stream, our lives too become polluted when we allow tributaries of evil and wickedness to enter."

8. Parley P. Pratt, "Jesus, Once of Humble Birth," *Hymns* (Salt Lake City: The Church of Jesus Christ of Latter-day Saints, 1985), no. 196.

9. The words of institution are recorded in each of the synoptic Gospels and by Paul. It is generally recognized that the earliest version is that of Paul.

10. Notice the comment of the premortal Jesus to the brother of Jared: "Behold, this body, which ye now behold, is the body of my spirit; and man have I created after the body of my spirit; and even as I appear unto thee in the spirit will I appear unto my people in the flesh" (Ether 3:16).

11. Smith, *Teachings*, 181. The Prophet's views on the resplendent resurrected body cohere nicely with Paul's statement. Other Christians from upstate New York to Nauvoo probably did not attribute such grandeur to Joseph's interpretation of the Resurrection as stated here by Paul.

12. Taking this into consideration, Elder Joseph B. Wirthlin, "Being Righteous in Our Hearts," *Speeches of the Year, 1996–97* (Provo, UT:

Brigham Young University, 1997), 161, makes the jolting observation that the natural man craves fulfilment in the telestial order.

13. Hugh Nibley, *Mormonism and Early Christianity* (Salt Lake City and Provo, UT: Deseret Book and FARMS, 1987), 16. To call the body a "vessel" (*skeuos*) suggests a temple connection, since many of the instruments in the Jerusalem Temple were called by that name. The imperative "Be ye clean, that bear the vessels of the Lord" (Isaiah 52:11) brings added meaning to temple associations.

14. Smith, *Teachings,* 354.

15. Russell M. Nelson, "Doors of Death," *Ensign,* May 1992, 72. In the view of Elder Hugh B. Brown, "What Is Man and What He May Become," *Brigham Young University Speeches of the Year*, March 25, 1958, 5, "When [the] plan was first presented to us we were not deterred by the fact that the journey would be dangerous. We, with millions, shouted for joy at the prospect of earth life, even though we doubtless had some warning that problems and perils lay ahead."

16. Smith, *Teachings,* 181.

17. Smith, *Teachings,* 207.

18. Erastus Snow, *Millennial Star,* May 13, 1878, 295. More recently, Elder Mark E. Petersen, "We Believe in God, the Eternal Father," *Speeches of the Year, 1973,* 241, teaches that "our spirit resembles our body, or rather our body was tailored to fit our spirit. The spirit bears the image and likeness of God, and the body, if it's normal, is in the image and likeness of the spirit."

19. Parley P. Pratt, *Key to the Science of Theology* (Salt Lake City: George Q. Cannon, 1891), 51–52.

20. Brigham Young, in *Journal of Discourses,* 2:256.

21. Erastus Snow, in *Journal of Discourses,* 26:216.

22. Hugh B. Brown, Conference Report, April 1957, 104.

23. John A. Widtsoe, in Conference Report, April 1926, 108.

24. Heber C. Kimball, in *Journal of Discourses,* 9:126–27.

25. In an oft-repeated statement, David O. McKay, "Spirituality: The Goal in Life," *Improvement Era,* December 1956, 914, affirmed that "man's earthly existence is but a test, whether he will concentrate his efforts, his mind, his soul upon things which contribute to his comfort and gratification of his physical instincts and passions, or whether he will make as his life's purpose and aim the acquisition of spiritual qualities." In my opinion, President McKay's preoccupation of ascending from the animal to the spiritual plane and striving to reach to something higher than self was his dominant teaching as president of the Church.

26. Spencer W. Kimball, Conference Report, October 1977, 123.

27. Adam S. Bennion, "'Men Are, That They Might Have Joy,'"

Improvement Era, June 1955, 433. Elder Neal A. Maxwell, "'Brim with Joy' (Alma 26:11)," *Speeches of the Year, 1995–96* (Provo, UT: Brigham Young University, 1996), 144, speaks on a similar wavelength. He notes that "joy is obviously of a higher order than mere pleasure. Pleasure is perishable. It has a short shelf life. Mere pleasure is not lasting because it is constantly feeding on itself. . . . The carnal pleasures cannot fully deliver. . . . Joy, on the other hand, is lasting. It involves the things that really matter. . . . One true test of ultimate value has to do with whether or not something is lasting."

28. John Taylor, *Millennial Star,* March 21, 1857, 182.

29. David O. McKay, "'Choose You This Day Whom Ye Will Serve,'" *Improvement Era,* June 1949, 351.

30. Smith, *Teachings,* 181. The Prophet's successor, President Young, in *Journal of Discourses,* 10:192, follows up on this crucial theme: "We cannot believe for a moment that God is destitute of body, parts, passions or attributes. Attributes can be made manifest only through an organized personage. All attributes are couched in and are the results of organized existence."

31. Here is one illustrative sentence in an exposition in Pratt, *Key to the Science of Theology,* 43: "Nonentity is the negative of existence."

32. Joseph Smith, *The Words of Joseph Smith,* ed. Andrew F. Ehat and Lyndon W. Cook (Provo, UT: Religious Studies Center, Brigham Young University, 1980), 207. In the book of Abraham, while planning the creation of the world, the members of the Godhead determine that they will prove the as yet unembodied spirits by sending them to the earth. "And they who keep their first estate shall be added upon; and . . . shall have glory added upon their heads for ever and ever" (3:26). This condition will depend on the human embodiment.

33. Smith, *History of the Church,* 5:339. Orson Pratt accepted and taught the Prophet's doctrine (see *Journal of Discourses,* 14:235–36).

34. Brigham Young, in *Journal of Discourses,* 9:287; *Millennial Star,* November 8, 1875, 706–7.

35. Smith, *Teachings,* 199–200. Elsewhere he said, "When our flesh is quickened by the Spirit, there will be no blood in this tabernacle" (*Teachings,* 367). Elder Parley P. Pratt, "A Sermon Delivered by Parley P. Pratt, at New Haven City, March, 1845," *Millennial Star,* June 15, 1845, 9, addressing Paul's distinction between natural and spiritual bodies in 1 Corinthians 15:44, spoke further on this to an audience in New England: "If I were to define a spiritual body, I should conceive my natural one abstracted from the element which sustains it. Let it be drained of all blood which circulates through it, and all other influences which minister to its sustenance, and then let it be

animated with what Moses terms the spirit of life, and I shall then stand before you an immortal being, with no loss or change in my composition, no change whatever, except that I am glorified. All the difference of my glorified from my natural body is the mode and power by which it is quickened." Elder Pratt also brought this out in *Writings of Parley Parker Pratt,* ed. Parker Pratt Robison (Salt Lake City, n.p., 1952), 77; see also Howard W. Hunter, "The Reality of the Resurrection," *Improvement Era,* June 1969, 107–8.

36. Spencer W. Kimball, "Absolute Truth," *1977 Devotional Speeches of the Year* (Provo, UT: Brigham Young University Press, 1977), 140.

37. Russell M. Nelson, "Doors of Death," *Ensign,* May 1992, 74. I suggest that the calling together of our primal bodily elements and their fusing with the elements of our spirit demonstrates the surpassing love of the Father and the Son, for in D&C 93:33–34 we are taught that "spirit and element, inseparably connected, receive a fulness of joy; and when separated, man cannot receive a fulness of joy."

38. Similarly, when John the Baptist appeared to bestow the Aaronic Priesthood upon Joseph and Oliver, his body was perfectly intact, in spite of having been decapitated many centuries earlier.

39. John Taylor, in *Journal of Discourses,* 21:15. Elder Taylor implies here that there will be a difference in resurrection between those who have honored God's laws and those who have not.

40. Melvin J. Ballard, in Conference Report, October 1917, 110.

41. Smith, *Teachings,* 368. Here the Prophet speaks of the "loveliness" of children in "the celestial glory. . . . No man can describe it to you—no man can write it."

42. Lorenzo Snow, in Conference Report, October 1900, 4, 63.

43. Snow, in Conference Report, October 1900, 63.

44. Although we acknowledge that our mortal world is fallen, President Brigham Young, *Millennial Star,* July 15, 1854, 438, points out that we do experience a similitude of the celestial kingdom, where people associate with family and friends. The loving relationships here can be a foretaste of the world to come. Projecting to our life ahead, the Prophet testified "that the same sociality which exists among us here will exist among us there, only it will be coupled with eternal glory, which glory we do not now enjoy" (Smith, *History of the Church,* 5:323).

45. Smith, *Teachings,* 295–96. The remarks in which this report is included came as a result of the death of missionary Lorenzo Barnes, who died in England.

46. See Brigham Young, in *Journal of Discourses,* 9:140.

47. Pratt, *Key to the Science of Theology,* 180.

CHAPTER NINETEEN

THE PROPHET'S "DAILY WALK AND CONVERSATION": THREE WOMEN WITNESSES

JENNIFER REEDER

Eliza R. Snow became acquainted with Joseph Smith during the winter of 1830–31, when he called at her father's home in Ohio. She later wrote, "As he sat warming himself, I scrutinized his face as closely as I could without attracting his attention, and decided that his was an honest face."[1] After her baptism four years later, Snow boarded at the Smith home in Kirtland, where she taught the family school. She later filled the same role in Nauvoo. There, she wrote, she had "ample opportunity to mark his 'daily walk and conversation,' as a prophet of God; and the more I became acquainted with him, the more I appreciated him as such."[2]

Many women were uniquely qualified to testify of Joseph Smith as a result of their proximity to him. Mary Alice Cannon Lambert met him when she was young in an impressionable moment: "I knew him the instant my eyes rested upon him, and at that moment I received my testimony that he was a Prophet of God." Emmeline B. Wells described Joseph's "majestic bearing." She wrote, "The one thought that filled my soul was, I have seen the Prophet of God, he has taken me by the hand, and this testimony has never left me." Jane Manning James wrote about working in the Smith home in Nauvoo: "He was the finest man I ever saw on earth." Others also described his physical presence or remembered hearing him speak, while many more recorded tender interchanges with him.[3] Nearly all

---

Jennifer Reeder is a graduate student at New York University.

witnessed of a personal spiritual testimony linking this man to God. As the recipient of such divine testimony, each woman participated in her own personal revelation, linking her as well with the divine.

Following a rich tradition of women actively involved in American religion through the eighteenth and early nineteenth centuries, many Latter-day Saint women raised their voices in a similar manner.[4] Speaking of their personal experiences with the Prophet and of their deep conviction of the Restoration, women have remembered and commemorated not only a mighty man but also a momentous movement, with each individual woman giving voice to a unique perspective. As Leonard Arrington, a past Church historian, observed, "Anyone who spends a substantial amount of time going through the materials in church archives must gain a new appreciation of the important and indispensable role of women in the history of the LDS church—not to mention new insights into church history resulting from viewing it through the eyes of women."[5] The wealth of their words adds a heretofore untapped depth to a modern understanding of Joseph Smith as Prophet of the Restoration, allowing for individual access and participation in the greater power of God's work on the earth.

A brief examination of three women whose intimate acquaintance with Joseph Smith and close connection to the Restoration through personal revelation reveals a living, dynamic, individual touch to an institutional memory. Lucy Mack Smith, Eliza R. Snow, and Helen Mar Whitney are three writing women whose intimate acquaintance with Joseph Smith and close connection to the Restoration through personal revelation reveals a woman's touch. The power of their words can be felt as the Spirit adds to their testimonies, for "in the mouth of two or three witnesses shall every word be established" (2 Corinthians 13:1).

The witness of these women, as a result of their personal experience, locates them in the Restoration, much as it can for every member. The personal construction of memory, according to historian David Thelen, as for these women, illuminates how individuals establish core identities and how they connect and even participate with large-scale historical events.[6] Elder M. Russell Ballard said: "A most significant evidence of our conversion and of how we feel about the gospel in our own lives is our willingness to share it with others. . . .

This is God's work. He wants us to participate with Him and His Beloved Son."[7] Our modern testimonies can then rise with theirs, as we too have ample opportunity to learn from them about Joseph Smith and to follow their pattern in full participation in the Restoration.

"MOTHER IN ISRAEL"—LUCY MACK SMITH

Lucy Mack Smith, mother of the Prophet Joseph Smith, is remembered with a term used by Brigham Young in October 1845, "a mother in Israel."[8] As a church matriarch, Sister Smith was honored and revered in her unique role as witness of the Restoration; she was the first woman to speak at a general conference of the Church in Nauvoo in October 1845, where she testified of the Book of Mormon and the Church's organization.[9] She is also recognized as the author of the first extensive biographical account of the Prophet following the martyrdom in June 1844. With the assistance of Nauvoo residents Howard and Martha Jane Coray, she penned the "History of Lucy Smith, Mother of the Prophet" in 1845 as a special effort to reaffirm the divine prophetic role during a crisis in leadership succession. The book was published in 1853 by Orson Pratt in England and later revised and published many times throughout the twentieth century as the *History of the Prophet Joseph Smith,* becoming, in the words of historian Jan Shipps, the "premier printed resource for information about young Joseph Smith and the beginnings of Mormonism."[10]

A close examination of Lucy Smith's words reveals her intimate connection to God and her subsequent intense desire to testify, an incumbent responsibility to witness of her participation within the Restoration. Of her own connection with the divine, in a time of great sickness, Lucy Smith wrote, "I made a solemn covenant with God, that, if he would let me live, I would endeavor to serve him according to the best of my abilities."[11] Her introduction stated: "I feel it a privilege as well as my duty to all candid inquirers after truth to give (as my last testimony to a world from whence I must soon take my departure) an account. . . . And inasmuch as no one on earth is so thoroughly acquainted as myself with the entire history of those of whom I speak I have been induced by these and other considerations to assume the task."[12] She followed the pattern of other nineteenth-century religious women, who, according to historian Catherine Brekus, "seem to have *wanted* to be remembered."[13] With many narrative accounts of spiritual experience and divine intervention throughout the history of her family, Sister Smith referenced her readers with her own divine role, which, she stated, may "tax the credulity of such as do not bear witness of the fact as I do who are not a few. . . . But what I say here I say with reference to Eternity and the judgment seat of the allmighty where I shall again meet my readers as a testater of the same."[14] Near the end of her account, she wrote, "As I hasten to the end of my story, the reader will be able to form an opinion with regard to the correctness of my conclusion."[15] Thus along with the role of recorder, she assumed the role of divine witness before God, following the counsel given by Joseph Smith as testimony "recorded in heaven" (D&C 62:3). The command to witness is an incumbent responsibility of testimony.

The crux of Lucy Smith's testimony is the prophetic role of her son in light of her own search for religious truth. "I began to feel the want of a living instructor in matters of salvation," she wrote following the death of her sister. "I was totally devoid of any satisfactory knowledge or understanding of the laws or requirements of that Being."[16] She then linked this sense of lacking with the fulfillment of the Restoration. "I had always believed confidently that God would raise up some one who would be able to effect a reconciliation among those who desired to do his will at the expense of all things else—But what was my joy and astonishment to hear my own son though a boy of fourteen years of age declare that he had been visited by an angel from Heaven."[17] Her writing, then, reflected her personal testimony and understanding of the Restoration.

Sister Smith had a unique position from which to report the unfolding of the Restoration. Because of her proximity to events such as the First Vision, the subsequent visits of the angel Moroni, the reception of the gold plates, the organization of the Church and its resulting persecution, and the martyrdom, she was able to mingle a chronicle of events of the Restoration with her own stirring testimony of its truth. She hefted the breastplates as a physical witness, and she boldly proclaimed her spiritual allegiance. For example, when Joseph Smith Sr. was imprisoned by a Quaker neighbor for debt, Lucy testified, "God has raised up my son to bring forth a book, which was written for the salvation of the souls of men, for the salvation of your soul as well as mine."[18] Sociologist Maurice Halbwachs noted the use of personal testimony as evidence to validate interpretation of personal experience.[19] As "a mother in Israel," Lucy Mack Smith embedded the chronicle of events she witnessed with her personal conviction. Her voice, as a result of proximity, is a valuable testimony of the Restoration.

"ZION'S POETESS"—ELIZA R. SNOW

Renowned women's leader and poet Eliza R. Snow was well acquainted with Joseph Smith. She boarded with his family in Kirtland and Nauvoo, taught his children, served in the Nauvoo Relief Society, and was sealed to him as a plural wife. She had great respect and love for him, calling him the "choice of my heart and the crown of my life."[20] As a practiced and published poet before joining the Church in 1835, it was natural for her to express her innermost convictions through verse. In the fall of 1838, Joseph Smith appointed her to write poems for and in behalf of Latter-day Saints in a role defined by historians Jill Mulvay Derr and Karen Lynn Davidson as Mormon "poet laureate," and she subsequently published more than seventy-five poems in Illinois.[21] She was later known as "Zion's Poetess," and her poems rallied the Saints in their celebration of a modern Prophet. Many of her pieces about Joseph Smith were published during his lifetime in the *Times and Seasons,* the *Nauvoo Neighbor,* the *Wasp,* and the *Millennial Star;* some were published again later in the *Frontier Guardian* of Iowa and the *Deseret News* in Utah, indicating her poetic popularity as well as a continuing commemoration of the Prophet long after his death. Unlike Lucy Smith's reminiscent biography of Joseph written after his death, Snow's contemporaneous efforts to laud his prophetic role had an immediate impact on readers.

Snow had not always held such a revered position. Her conversion as a Saint occurred after much time, observation, and study, following the universal process outlined in Moroni 10:3–5. Her unique proximity to the Prophet and her detailed study of the Bible provided her with the relevance and context of his work in the Restoration.[22] Her poetry reveals knowledge gained as she carefully examined the ancient prophetic pattern. In "Psalm," for example, she compared

Joseph Smith to ancient prophets with likewise humble beginnings, such as David and Elijah.[23] "In these last days the Lord hath call'd his servant Joseph . . . to be a prophet and a teacher: yea, to be a mighty instrument in rolling forward and establishing that kingdom which 'shall fill the whole earth.'"[24] Her grand epic poem, "Two Chapters in the Life of President Joseph Smith," was written in 1843 after she left Nauvoo for the nearby Morley settlement, where she had the time and solitude to pursue serious poetic endeavors. Like Lucy Smith's biography, this piece bears the metaphoric imprimatur of Snow's role as testator. The poem opens invoking the muse of the "Great Eternal of Eternity," asking him to "warm my minstrel with celestial fire." "The Seer and Prophet of the latter days / Is now my theme—his history help me trace; / For thy approval, Lord, shall prompt my pen, / Regardless of the praise or blame of men."[25] Snow's words clearly indicate her prominent sense of mission in writing, echoing Alma's heartfelt desire to "speak with the trump of God" (Alma 29:1).

Eliza Snow and Lucy Smith both wrote to chronicle the divine interventions in the life of the Prophet, indicating their own connections to divinity, their personal testimonies, and their consequent witnesses. Their words have provided sustenance for subsequent retellings of now famous Joseph Smith stories. Following a grand sweeping history of the Apostasy and ancient prophecy of a restoration in "Two Chapters," Snow highlighted the Prophet's divine role as one upon whom Jehovah's "eye was fix'd." The event of the First Vision is captured:

> *A pillar, brighter than the noon-day sun,*
> *Precisely o'er his head, descending, fell*
> *Around him; and he felt himself unbound. . . .*
> *He saw two glorious personages stand*
> *Above him in the air; surrounded with*
> *The light that had envelop'd him. . . .*
>
> *One of the*
> *Bright personages whom he saw, referr'd*
> *Him to the other, and address'd him thus,*
> *"Joseph, this is my well beloved Son,*
> *Hear him."*[26]

According to Derr and Davidson, this poem revealed Snow's "passionate conviction of the importance of Joseph's prophetic calling and the preeminent position of the First Vision in Mormonism's historical narrative."[27] Phrases in this poetic account may have influenced George Manwaring's well-known hymn, "Joseph Smith's First Prayer."[28] Snow's testimony of Joseph as Prophet as revealed through her poetry indicates her personal conviction of the hand of God throughout the events of the Restoration and her participation as a witness.

Snow's poetry dramatized the events of the Restoration as they happened, creating a communal form by which to understand, laud, and mourn Joseph Smith. "Jubilee Song," written January 18, 1843, was printed as a broadside and distributed throughout Nauvoo. The poem commemorated Joseph's triumphant return from a trial in Springfield, Illinois, and was recited at a celebratory dinner in his honor. "That deed—that time we celebrate," she chronicled, "the Lord who guides the Prophet's cause."[29] The ballad "The Kidnapping of Gen. Joseph Smith" reenacts an equally exciting event. After being illegally arrested by secret order of Missouri Governor Lilburn Boggs, this poem described how Smith "bared his breast" before the "rude ferocity" and "savage wildness," again coming out triumphantly according to the will of God.[30] The excitement of the events is clear, and the community celebration revering Joseph's prophetic role is apparent. Snow captured the immediate events in which she participated, recording the veracity from her valuable perspective.

Snow's poetic commemoration of Joseph's martyrdom was published just one week after the June 27, 1844, event. At a time most difficult for her personally, perhaps she found solace in penning words the community of Saints could share.[31] "Ye heav'ns, attend! Let all the earth give ear! / Let Gods and seraphs, men and angels hear— / The worlds on high—the universe shall know," she began.[32] The poem became a site of community mourning: "We mourn thy Prophet, from whose lips have flow'd / The words of life. . . . Now Zion mourns—she mourns an earthly head."[33] The poetic textual form allowed for immediate communal grieving, and as it was republished later, the poem reflected community memory re-creation. Following the sons of Mosiah, Snow "did impart much consolation to the church, confirming their faith, and exhorting them with longsuffering and much travail to keep the commandments of God" (Mosiah 27:33). As Snow consecrated her poetic talent to express her own testimony and to speak for the Saints, she was "fixed" as a stalwart witness of the Restoration.[34] She participated in the Restoration according to her own ability, and in so doing, she witnessed the universal access to study, understanding, and sharing.

POLITICAL COMMENTATOR—HELEN MAR WHITNEY

The third example of female rhetoric commemorating Joseph Smith comes from Helen Mar Whitney. The daughter of Heber C. Kimball, counselor and close associate of Joseph Smith, Helen Mar experienced the founding era of the Church from a child's point of view. As a young woman, she became one of Joseph's plural wives, and in her adult years, she was respected as a writer and Relief Society leader in Utah.[35] Whitney's editorial-style reminiscences were published in the *Woman's Exponent* from May 1880 through August 1886, certainly physically and temporally removed from Joseph Smith's lifetime. Although her mode of communication varied from that of Lucy Mack Smith and Eliza R. Snow, who both wrote from a much closer standpoint and for an intended audience of Latter-day Saints, Whitney filled a different political need dictated by her later context.

In a time marked particularly by antipolygamy legislation for the fledgling Utah territory, Whitney wrote with a specific purpose in defense of her institutional allegiance. Her audience was composed of a variety of readers, some of whom were not members of the Church and were deeply antagonistic towards its peculiar beliefs. In an attempt to connect with these readers, she wrote of her task, "I often find it a very difficult one to gather up the many broken threads of the almost forgotten past, and weave them into a shape for the perusal of others, and it is a pleasant relief, like a cooling draught to the thirsty traveler, to find here and there a scrap of our history interwoven with that of others, bringing before us objects and scenes which were once familiar, but had become dim and nearly effaced from our memory by the hand of time, which has been to me unsparing in its ravages."[36] She later wrote, "I am willing, nay, anxious, that they should know the true history."[37] Whitney's words echoed the efforts of Joseph Smith to write his own history: "Owing to the many reports which have been put in circulation"

(Joseph Smith—History 1:1). She felt a strong need to defend as well as find common ground with and connect with those not of her faith, a position often experienced for modern as well as historical participants in the Restoration.

Like Sister Smith and Sister Snow, Helen Mar Whitney boldly testified of revelation. To readers within the Church of a younger generation without the personal relationship to Joseph Smith to influence their own convictions, Whitney's testimony crossed generational lines, and she joined past testimony in declaring her own witness: "I truly rejoice that I have had the privilege of being numbered with those who have come up through much tribulation and gained a knowledge for myself that this is the work of God."[38] Historian Nathan Wachtel noted such a role as a living link between generations within a social group.[39] She defined the Church as "our glorious religion, the pure gospel of Christ, revealed through Joseph, the Prophet of God, by which, instead of bringing us into bondage, every soul is made free."[40] Whitney's joy in her membership of the restored Church declares her own personal testimony and reflects heartfelt conviction and active participation years after the defining moment of conversion.

As with Smith's and Snow's accounts, Whitney's personal experience with Joseph Smith indicated the hand of God in the events of the Restoration. Throughout her writing, Whitney listed personal recollections of the Prophet. "Those scenes," she wrote, "are fresh in my memory."[41] For example, she remembered an occasion in Kirtland praying as a young child when Joseph Smith was so touched by her earnest efforts that he wept.[42] She also remembered watching the Prophet bless and administer to the sick—a tender, Christ-like act of service that testified to Whitney of Joseph Smith's divine connection. Such accounts also made for her mixed audience a portrait of a concerned citizen rather than the manipulative sycophant often portrayed in anti-Mormon literature of the time. Whitney's record of personal proximity to the Prophet is one that may not be found in institutional records, yet it bears an important view of his compassionate and personable character. And an intimate connection with the Lord's prophet reveals an even deeper respect and closer understanding of the Lord Himself.

"AMPLE OPPORTUNITY"

The words of these three women invaluably commemorate Joseph Smith, for each speaks of him from a different perspective, for a different audience, and with a different purpose. Lucy Mack Smith's efforts to testify and remind members of the prophetic role of her son, Eliza R. Snow's work to rally the community, and Helen Mar Whitney's movement to defend Church beliefs all witness a close connection to the Prophet and a committed allegiance to the Restoration. Their varying ages, media, and purposes reveal the richness of historical experience and the need to witness.[43] Deeper analysis reveals modern application to gospel principles.

These intimate, individual relationships with Joseph Smith indicate the value of personal experience, personal participation in the Restoration, and personal voice. One common theme among these three women's accounts is an assertive notion of self-placement within institutional history. Women's history in general, according to historians Nancy F. Cott and Elizabeth H. Pleck, serves a "consciousness-raising" function with special attention to the individual.[44] Each woman had a strong personal experience producing personal testimony, and each accordingly became an active participant in the events of the Restoration—a pattern still asked of every member. It is a common religious experience, as noted by anthropologist Susan Friend Harding, to transform self and share with others.[45] Spiritual and personal implications follow.

Lucy Mack Smith, Eliza R. Snow, and Helen Mar Whitney bore record of Joseph Smith as the Lord's Prophet. Each of these women responded to her personal conversion, transforming self and sharing with others. The Lord promises all an individual conversion experience and relationship: "Draw near unto me and I will draw near unto you; seek me diligently and ye shall find me" (D&C 88:63). As these women testify of the Lord's hand in preserving Joseph Smith, they also testify of His hand in their own lives. He promises to stand by each individual in times of trouble: "When thou passest through the waters, I will be with thee; and through the rivers, they shall not overflow thee" (Isaiah 43:2). As Lucy Mack Smith, Eliza R. Snow, and Helen Mar Whitney note the Lord's hand in guiding and protecting His prophet, they in turn report how He has guided and protected them as Saints. He then charges His recipients, "Ye are my witnesses" (Isaiah 43:10).

Subsequently, these women, in the deepest sense, precipitate readers to witness of their own experiences and become active participants. "When thou are converted, strengthen thy brethren" is the apostolic counsel (Luke 22:32). Elder M. Russell Ballard taught: "We as members of the Church arise individually and collectively, with dedication and action, to help build the kingdom of God. Our duty lies in assisting others, through the power of the Spirit, to *know* and *understand* the doctrines and principles of the gospel. Everyone must come to *feel* that the doctrines of the Restoration are true and of great value. And everyone who accepts the message must strive to *live* the gospel by making and keeping sacred covenants and by participating in all of the ordinances of salvation and exaltation."[46]

As these three women worked in their own way to witness, they utilized their individual talents and voices. As a result, their reminiscences, poetry, and editorials reached different audiences and affected different purposes in their active roles in building the kingdom.

NOTES

1. "A Sketch of My Life," in *Personal Writings of Eliza R. Snow*, ed. Maureen Ursenbach Beecher (Logan, UT: Utah State University Press, 2000), 9.
2. Snow, "A Sketch of My Life," 11.
3. These accounts are taken from "Joseph Smith, the Prophet," *Young Woman's Journal*, December 1905, 548–58.
4. See Catherine A. Brekus, *Strangers and Pilgrims: Female Preaching in America, 1740–1845* (Chapel Hill: University of North Carolina Press, 1998), 3.
5. Leonard Arrington, "The Search for Truth and Meaning in Mormon History," in *The New Mormon History: Revisionist Essays on the Past*, ed. D. Michael Quinn (Salt Lake City: Signature Books, 1992), 7.
6. David Thelen, "Memory and American History," *Journal of American History*, March 1989, 1118.
7. M. Russell Ballard, "Now Is the Time," *Ensign*, November 2000, 75.
8. Joseph Smith, *History of the Church of Jesus Christ of Latter-day Saints*, ed. B. H. Roberts, 2nd ed. rev. (Salt Lake City: Deseret Book, 1970), 7:471.
9. Journal History of The Church of Jesus Christ of Latter-day Saints, Church Archives, Salt Lake City, October 8, 1845, 1. Lucy Smith

also spoke at a family meeting called by Brigham Young earlier that year.

10. Jan Shipps, *Mormonism: The Story of A New Religious Tradition* (Urbana: University of Illinois Press, 1987), 92.

11. Lucy Mack Smith, *Lucy's Book: A Critical Edition of Lucy Mack Smith's Family Memoir,* ed. Lavina Fielding Anderson (Salt Lake City: Signature Books, 2001), 277–78; spelling, punctuation, interlineations, and marginalia have been modernized here.

12. Smith, *Lucy's Book,* 220–21.

13. Brekus, *Strangers and Pilgrims,* 8.

14. Smith, *Lucy's Book,* 235.

15. Smith, *Lucy's Book,* 725.

16. Lucy Mack Smith, *The Revised and Enhanced History of Joseph Smith by His Mother,* ed. Scot Facer Proctor and Maurine Jensen Proctor (Salt Lake City: Bookcraft, 1996), 210.

17. Smith, *Lucy's Book,* 464–65.

18. Smith, *Revised and Enhanced History,* 239.

19. Maurice Halbwachs, *The Collective Memory* (1925); cited in Thelen, "Memory," 1122.

20. Eliza R. Snow, "Past and Present," *Woman's Exponent,* August 1, 1886, 37; cited in Jill Mulvay Derr, "The Significance of 'O My Father' in the Personal Journey of Eliza R. Snow," *BYU Studies* 36 (1996–97): 87.

21. [Emmeline B. Wells], "Pen Sketch of an Illustrious Woman: Eliza R. Snow Smith," *Woman's Exponent,* February 1, 1881, 131. See Jill Mulvay Derr and Karen Lynn Davidson, "The First Vision in Eliza R. Snow's Unfinished Epic on the Life of Joseph Smith," unpublished paper in the author's possession.

22. For an in-depth examination of Eliza R. Snow's religious background and conversion, see Jill Mulvay Derr and Karen Lynn Davidson, "A Wary Heart Becomes 'Fixed Unalterably': Eliza R. Snow's Conversion to Mormonism," *Journal of Mormon History* 30, no. 2 (Fall 2004): 98–128.

23. See Karen Lynn Davidson, "Eliza R. Snow, Psalmist of the Latter Days," *Covenants, Prophecies, and Hymns of the Old Testament: The 30th Annual Sperry Symposium* (Salt Lake City: Deseret Book, 2001), 307.

24. *Times and Seasons,* July 15, 1841; *Millennial Star,* October 1841.

25. "Two Chapters in the Life of President Joseph Smith," *Nauvoo Neighbor,* August 23, 1843; *Times and Seasons,* August 15, 1843; lines 1, 14.

26. "Two Chapters," in Eliza R. Snow, *Poems, Religious, Historical, and*

Personal (Liverpool: F. D. Richards; London: Latter-day Saints Book Depot, 1856), 15–27; lines 1, 14, 5–8, 118, 206–8, 223–27.

27. Jill Mulvay Derr and Karen Lynn Davidson, "The First Vision in Eliza R. Snow's Unfinished Epic on the Life of Joseph Smith," unpublished paper in the author's possession.

28. "Joseph Smith's First Prayer," *Hymns* (Salt Lake City: The Church of Jesus Christ of Latter-day Saints, 1985), 26. See also Karen Lynn Davidson, *Our Latter-day Hymns: The Stories and the Messages* (Salt Lake City: Deseret Book, 1988), 54–55.

29. Eliza R. Snow, Broadside, January 18, 1843, titled "Part Second" under general heading, "Jubilee Songs," LDS Church Archives, lines 1, 49. Also printed in *Times and Seasons*, February 1, 1843.

30. "The Kidnapping of Gen. Joseph Smith," *Nauvoo Neighbor*, July 26, 1843; *Times and Seasons*, August 1, 1843.

31. [Lula Greene Richards], "Eliza Roxey Snow," in *Latter-day Saint Biographical Encyclopedia*, comp. Andrew Jensen (Salt Lake City: Western Epics, 1971), 1:695.

32. "The Assassination of Gen's Joseph Smith and Hyrum Smith," *Times and Seasons*, July 1, 1844, lines 1–3.

33. "The Assassination of Gen's Joseph Smith and Hyrum Smith," lines 59, 67.

34. See Derr and Davidson, "A Wary Heart Becomes 'Fixed Unalterably,'" 127.

35. Todd Compton, "Introduction," in *A Widow's Tale: The 1884–1896 Diary of Helen Mar Kimball Whitney* (Logan, UT: Utah State University Press, 2003), 1–2.

36. *Woman's Exponent*, December 15, 1881, 106. Jeni Broberg Holzapfel and Richard Neitzel Holzapfel collected and published Helen Mar Whitney's editorials in *A Woman's View: Helen Mar Whitney's Reminiscences of Early Church History* (Provo, UT: Religious Studies Center, Brigham Young University, 1997), xxvi.

37. *Woman's Exponent*, July 1, 1880, 18; cited in Holzapfel and Holzapfel, *A Woman's View*, 14.

38. *Woman's Exponent*, May 15, 1880, 188; cited in Holzapfel and Holzapfel, *A Woman's View*, 1.

39. Nathan Wachtel, "Between Memory and History," *History and Anthropology* 2, no. 2 (October 1986): 213.

40. *Woman's Exponent*, March 15, 1881, 154; cited in Holzapfel and Holzapfel, *A Woman's View*, 81.

41. *Woman's Exponent*, May 15, 1881, 188–89; cited in Holzapfel and Holzapfel, *A Woman's View*, 3.

42. *Woman's Exponent,* 15 November 1880, 90; cited in Holzapfel and Holzapfel, *A Woman's View,* 52–53.

43. Nancy R. Cott and Elizabeth H. Pleck, "Introduction," in *A Heritage of Her Own: Toward a New Social History of American Women,* ed. Cott and Pleck (New York: Simon and Schuster, 1979), 17.

44. "Introduction," 9.

45. Susan Friend Harding, *The Book of Jerry Falwell: Fundamentalist Language and Politics* (Princeton: Princeton University Press, 2000), 34–35.

46. Ballard, "Now Is the Time," 75.

CHAPTER TWENTY

WHAT IF THERE WERE NO JOSEPH SMITH TRANSLATION OF THE BIBLE?

THOMAS E. SHERRY

When The Church of Jesus Christ of Latter-day Saints moved west to Utah in 1846, the unpublished manuscripts of Joseph Smith's translation of the Bible (JST) were left behind.[1] Thereafter, Church members largely lost access to and use of much of this "crowning achievement"[2] of the Prophet and the rich history related to the translation. For the next 135 years, the resulting deprivation had a rippling effect on the Church and its members who carried on largely as if there were no JST.[3]

Without access to the manuscripts, Latter-day Saints were hindered in understanding the intimate interplay between the production of the "new translation" and the making and tutoring of a prophet. In their absence it was more difficult to discern how, in Joseph Smith's words, "an obscure boy" became a mature spokesman for the Lord in the restoration of all things (see Joseph Smith—History 1:23). Additionally, much of what Latter-day Saints take for granted as essential doctrinal foundation to the Restoration was underappreciated.[4] Both the process and product of the new translation shaped the development of the Prophet Joseph Smith and the theological foundations of the Church in essential ways.

This paper explores these issues, looking specifically at three consequences of the manuscripts' loss to members of the Church. First, Latter-day Saints in general would not have been able to appreciate

---

Thomas E. Sherry is director of the Corvallis Oregon Institute of Religion.

the joy and wonder felt by the Prophet as a result of experiences related to the translation. Second, they were less able to recognize the strength, courage, and education received during the process. A third consequence was a diminished awareness of the enduring doctrinal impact on both the Prophet and the Church as Joseph Smith translated the Bible "by the power of God."[5]

JOY AND WONDER

The process of producing the JST was neither passive nor dispassionate. The Prophet Joseph worked hard at the new translation. He recorded that the endeavor was a "branch of [his] calling"[6] and that its demands caused "exceeding fatigue."[7] At times the Lord directed him to cease the translation because it was "expedient" that he tend to other matters (see D&C 37:1), but, the Prophet noted, "as soon as I could arrange my affairs, I recommenced the translation of the Scriptures, and thus I spent most of the summer."[8] Notwithstanding the demands, the Prophet was exuberant about the work and its results. He published bits and pieces of it in early periodicals and spoke enthusiastically about its value.[9] The work brought the Prophet a spiritual joy that filled him with wonder at the magnificence of communing with God and understanding the holy scriptures. Note those sentiments in the following:

December 1830. During the translation and while contemplating the "lost books" of the Bible, the Prophet Joseph received revelations concerning Enoch and recorded: "To the *joy* of the little flock . . . did the Lord reveal the following doings of olden times, from the prophecy of Enoch."[10]

January–February 1832. While Joseph Smith and scribe Sidney Rigdon were translating John 5:29, a great and glorious vision burst upon them, "not only one of the greatest revelations contained in the Doctrine and Covenants but one of the greatest ever given to mortal man."[11] "While we were doing the work of translation, which the Lord had appointed unto us, . . . [we saw a vision that] caused us to *marvel,* for it was given unto us of the Spirit" (D&C 76:15, 18; emphasis added). After recording the vision, the Prophet said, "Nothing could be more *pleasing* to the Saints upon the order of the kingdom of the Lord, than the *light* which burst upon the world through the foregoing vision . . . [which] is a transcript from the records of the eternal world."[12]

February 1843. Here in poetic verse, Joseph Smith reflects on the revelation recorded in Doctrine and Covenants 76 and again exults in the joy he felt at such magnificence:

"And while I did meditate what it all meant, / The Lord touch'd the eyes of my own intellect:—/ *Hosanna forever!* They open'd anon [immediately], / And the glory of God shone around where I was; / And there was the Son, at the Father's right hand, / In a fulness of glory, and *holy applause.*"[13]

We can sense in these statements the deep pleasure felt by the Prophet at the wonders of eternity revealed during the translation and at being an instrument in the hands of God to bring back that which had been lost (see Moses 1:41; 1 Nephi 13:23–29, 38–41).

STRENGTH, ENCOURAGEMENT, AND KNOWLEDGE

The joy and wonder the Prophet felt was tempered during the translation years (1830–33) by difficult trials. Historical records note that truths and information received during the translation strengthened and encouraged Joseph and early Church members in the demands of discipleship even in the face of these trials. The Prophet Joseph Smith appreciated these gifts of knowledge and noted their strengthening and refreshing value:

June 1830. "I will say . . . that amid all the trials and tribulations we had to wade through, the Lord, who well knew our infantile and delicate situation, vouchsafed for us *a supply of strength,* and granted us 'line upon line of knowledge' . . . of which the following was a *precious* morsel."[14]

December 1830. "It may be well to observe here, that the Lord greatly *encouraged* and *strengthened* the faith of His little flock, which had embraced the fulness of the everlasting Gospel, . . . by giving some more extended information upon the Scriptures, a translation of which had already commenced."[15]

Winter 1832–33. "The winter was spent in translating the Scriptures. . . . I had many glorious seasons of *refreshing.*"[16]

These statements inform us that the knowledge received and the process of translating strengthened, encouraged, and refreshed Joseph Smith and the Saints. The years spent on the new translation affirmed the truth of the scriptures and witnessed that God was guiding him in their restoration. Additionally, during the translation the Prophet repeatedly mentioned that he received explanations, visions, and revelation that expanded his knowledge of biblical passages, their meaning and application.[17] Perhaps this was all part of what the Lord intended in an 1831 revelation: "Wherefore I give unto you that ye may now translate it, that ye may be prepared for the things to come" (D&C 45:61). Both the translation experience and product helped prepare Joseph Smith to lay a sure foundation for the Church on the footings of restored and corrected doctrine.

ESSENTIAL DOCTRINE

The new translation was the revelatory means God chose as the "primary source of doctrine and to strengthen the Bible as a witness for the Lord Jesus Christ and His gospel. . . . Many of the doctrines that set our religion apart from the rest of modern Christianity derive from [the JST and] in many cases are revealed nowhere else and are unknown in the doctrines of Christian tradition."[18]

Excellent articles and books have previously been published on the doctrinal contributions, value, and importance of the JST.[19] A broad summary of those contributions might be approached by asking, "What doctrines define the mission, purpose, and foundation of the Church and set it apart from other religious organizations?" Essential items on the list would include the nature of God and our relationship to Him; the mission of Jesus Christ and the antiquity of His gospel; the plan of salvation, beginning with our premortal existence and extending through to immortality and eternal life; the reality, nature, and motives of Satan and the process of his apostasy; the Fall of Adam and Eve and their redemption; the establishment of Zion; and the role of priesthood ordinances, councils, and covenants. Each of these essential elements of the gospel was introduced or expanded through the new translation and were a significant source of Joseph Smith's doctrinal education. Not only does the new translation add and clarify truth, but it often restores relevant context that helps us better understand the meaning of sacred history and doctrine.[20]

Perhaps the easiest way to appreciate contributions of the JST is by contrasting the Bible text without the benefit of doctrines restored through the new translation. For example, let us look at messages conveyed in the first few chapters of Genesis as they might be viewed by a reader who does not have the blessing of restored knowledge found in the JST.[21]

Genesis 1–2. God creates heaven and earth as well as Adam and Eve and places them in the Garden of Eden, though we are not informed as to His purpose. He gives them apparently contradictory commandments that seem to leave them unable to make either choice without incurring the displeasure of God.

Genesis 3. A serpent appears and tempts Eve. She succumbs and persuades Adam to partake, thus breaking the commandment not to eat of a certain fruit. In apparent anger, God curses and summarily expels them from the garden.

Genesis 4. Adam and Eve's first child, Cain, is jealous of his younger brother Abel and assumes that God prefers Abel over him. Cain is incensed and kills Abel. God curses Cain and expels him from the family.

Genesis 5–8. Adam and Eve continue having children as does Cain. In time, much of their posterity forsake God and live riotously. God is sorrowful that He created man and feels to "repent" (Genesis 6:6). He calls Noah as a prophet to preach repentance and reclaim the people. Noah's apparent lack of success culminates in God's destruction of the earth's inhabitants save Noah and seven of his family, who are brought through the flood to repopulate the earth.

Even in a brief selection such as this, reading the sacred record without the purifying touch of revelation may not impress one as logical or inspiring. If this were the entire story, we would have difficulty loving and trusting God and seeing meaning in our earthly sojourn. Gratefully, the story remaining in current biblical text is not the whole story. The account told in the JST differs markedly and helps us draw nearer to God rather than being repulsed.[22] The events of this same period are covered in Moses 1–8 (the JST parallel of Genesis 1–6). The added light and understanding make an immeasurable difference to these first chapters in the Bible:

Moses 1. Moses, the author of Genesis, sought and found God, who appeared to him and declared His almighty sovereignty. God lovingly told Moses, "Thou art my son; . . . and I have a work for thee" to do (vv. 4, 6). Lucifer was allowed to tempt and dissuade

Moses from his mission, but Moses discerned between the divine and the imposter. God revealed the infinite majesty and purpose of His many creations, declaring, "This is my work and my glory—to bring to pass the immortality and eternal life of man" (v. 39). The Lord informed Moses that he should record the divine history of God's creations. In time, however, "the children of men shall esteem my words as naught and take many of them from the book which thou shalt write"; but not to fear, for God would "raise up another like unto thee [Joseph Smith]; and they shall be had again . . . among as many as shall believe" (v. 41).

Moses 2–3. Knowing why God created the earth, Moses understood that the Creation account was a brief narrative setting the stage for the coming of Adam and Eve and all who would issue from them. The earth was designed to assist them in their eternal progress. Since all mankind is of the family of God, He established the covenant of marriage and the commandment to multiply and replenish the earth that the spirit offspring of God might have a family in which to be raised in the ways of the Lord—the earthly pattern being a reflection of the heavenly.

Moses 4–5. To accomplish the purposes of God, the rebel Lucifer was allowed to act on earth to tempt us. We are told how Lucifer fell through pride and rebellion in hopes of aggrandizing himself at the cost of our moral agency. In response to the temptations of Lucifer (the serpent), Adam and Eve initiated the divine plan of God on behalf of each of us and cried out, "Blessed be the name of God, for because of my transgression my eyes are opened, and in this life I shall have joy, and again in the flesh I shall see God. . . . Were it not for our transgression we never should have had seed, and . . . known good and evil, and the joy of our redemption, and the eternal life which God giveth unto all the obedient" (Moses 5:10–11). They learned of Jesus Christ and His Atonement, of their redemption through the Only Begotten Son, and of baptism and the gift of the Holy Ghost. They, in turn, taught the same to their children, for this is the message of salvation in every age. Cain, one of their many children, eventually chose evil, making a pact with Lucifer to murder his brother Abel for gain.

Moses 6–8. Adam and Eve were forgiven their transgression in the Garden of Eden. Adam kept a record of the Lord's doings among them, and later the record was kept by his righteous posterity. Among those were Enoch and Noah, both of whom also declared the gospel of Jesus Christ to an increasingly wicked people. Enoch established a Zion, which was eventually translated, and from then until the Flood the righteous who hearkened to the prophets were likewise taken off the earth to join the holy city so that when the Flood came, the sheaves of Noah had been harvested with only the tares remaining to be washed away.

The JST contributions noted above are a sample of the rich historical context and doctrine found in the new translation. Beyond these early Genesis refinements that were preserved in the book of Moses, the JST goes on to enrich our knowledge of early patriarchs and prophets in the Old Testament. Hundreds of verses are added about Abraham, Melchizedek, Joseph, Moses, Isaiah, and others. Their knowledge of the eternal plan of salvation is greater than portrayed in the KJV, and their focus on Jesus, the priesthood, and covenants of salvation between God and mankind is consistent. The JST thus makes the Old Testament witness of the gospel consistent with the Book of Mormon witness and tells us that salvation through Jesus Christ has ever been the centerpiece of prophetic witness (see Jacob 4:4; 7:10–11).

Regarding the New Testament record, Robert J. Matthews writes: "The JST is more vivid and informative than all other translations of the Bible, the doctrine is stronger, situations are more focused, the disciples struggle more, Jewish rulers are worse, and Jesus is greater. The Prophet Joseph Smith understood Jesus and the New Testament better than anyone in this dispensation, and when we use the JST we honor both the Prophet and the Lord Jesus Christ who inspired him."[23] He joins coauthors Faulring and Jackson to further state: "The Bible is Judah's witness for God and for Jesus Christ. It was not sufficient for the Book of Mormon, the Doctrine and Covenants, and the Pearl of Great Price to restore missing doctrinal truth. Justice to Bible prophets required that the Bible itself be restored to its original power as a witness for Jesus and His gospel. The Bible must be made right, and the Joseph Smith Translation contributes powerfully to the restoration of its truths."[24]

It is this doctrinal restoration that led Elder Bruce R. McConkie to declare that the JST is "a thousand times over the best Bible now

existing on the earth."[25] Truly, the Prophet Joseph Smith was inspired
of the Lord as he translated and taught with power and authority
from biblical text. Near the end of his life, he frankly and boldly
stated, "I know the scriptures, I understand them."[26]

CONCLUSION

Regarding the position of the JST in The Church of Jesus Christ
of Latter-day Saints today, Elder Dallin H. Oaks has said: "There
should be no doubt about the current status of the Joseph Smith
Translation of the Bible. It is a member of the royal family of scripture . . . [and] should be noticed and honored on any occasion when
it is present."[27] But it is not just the richness of the text and its marvelous doctrine that should receive such attention.[28] We should also
note and honor the blessings which came to Joseph Smith while
engaged in the new translation. The Prophet progressively learned of
divine doctrine and history, text and context, of ancient prophets
and the spirit of prophecy and revelation. These elements made their
contribution to related modern revelation and guidance, all of which
helped establish and empower the fledgling Restoration.[29] The work
shaped both the Prophet and the doctrine of The Church of Jesus
Christ of Latter-day Saints as unique in the world of religion. Lastly,
we should remember that Joseph Smith found joy and pleasure in
this work that strengthened him and the early Saints in establishing
the restored Church of Jesus Christ in the latter days.

Could the Prophet have learned these same things if there were
no JST? While the Lord may have been able to impart necessary
learning and personal development through other avenues, *this* was
a primary avenue He chose. It was to the process of constructing the
new translation and experiences growing from it that God employed
to educate and nurture both the Prophet and the Church and to set
them firmly on the path to salvation.

By studying Joseph Smith's Translation of the Bible, we are better
able to appreciate the divine role it played in tutoring Joseph Smith
and contributing so richly to what made him the great prophet of
the Restoration.[30] In turn, we also gain access to unique truths and
messages of the Bible. "What would you give to know the Bible and
other scriptures as Joseph Smith knew them? Using the JST in our
study is like sitting at the same table with the Prophet Joseph Smith,

with the privilege of turning to him for counsel."[31] For such a privilege, I am deeply grateful.

NOTES

1. In response to divine directive, the Prophet Joseph Smith undertook an inspired translation of the King James Version of the Bible (which he and his contemporaries referred to as the *New Translation*). The endeavor occupied much of his time from 1830 to 1833. Periodically thereafter until his death in 1844, the Prophet sought unsuccessfully to prepare the work for publication (see Robert J. Matthews, "Joseph Smith's Efforts to Publish His Translation," *Ensign*, January 1983, 57–64). The translation manuscripts were retained by Emma Smith after the death of her husband and were subsequently transferred to her son Joseph Smith III and the newly emerged Reorganized Church of Jesus Christ of Latter Day Saints (now Community of Christ) in 1866. After it was published in 1867 with the title *Holy Scriptures,* in 1936 the subtitle *Inspired Version* was added and became the common title used by members of the RLDS Church. In 1979 the Church of Jesus Christ of Latter-day Saints published its first LDS edition of the King James Bible which by permission from RLDS leaders included footnote references to the new translation text. In that publication, the acronym JST was adopted for Joseph Smith's Translation of the Bible and is now the common term used by members of the LDS Church.

2. Elder Bruce R. McConkie of the Quorum of Twelve Apostles taught that "as a crowning achievement . . . [Joseph Smith] would begin the perfection of the Bible, a work destined to be greater and have more significance than any of us have yet realized. . . . The Joseph Smith Translation of the Bible is holy scripture. In one sense of the word, it is the crowning part of the doctrinal restoration" (see "The Doctrinal Restoration," in *The Joseph Smith Translation: The Restoration of Plain and Precious Things,* ed. Monte S. Nyman and Robert L. Millet [Provo, UT: Religious Studies Center, Brigham Young University, 1985], 10, 21–22). Note: The LDS Church did retain for use those portions of the new translation which were previously published by Joseph Smith in Church periodicals and which later became part of the Pearl of Great Price (the book of Moses and Matthew 24).

3. In a recent interview, Robert J. Matthews said, "I have frequently said that every person who has joined the Church since 1831 has been affected by the JST, even though he or she did not know it." For details on how they have been affected, see Ray L. Huntington

and Brian M. Hauglid, "Robert J. Matthews and His Work with the Joseph Smith Translation," *Religious Educator* 5, no. 2 (2004), 45.

The figure of 135 years is taken from the death of Joseph Smith in 1844 until the 1979 publication of the first LDS edition of the King James Version of the Bible which included JST text in footnotes and a sixteen-page appendix. For details on the odyssey of the JST from nonuse by the LDS Church to official inclusion in the 1979 LDS edition of the Bible, see Robert L. Millet, "Joseph Smith's Translation of the Bible: A Historical Overview," in *The Joseph Smith Translation: The Restoration of Plain and Precious Things*, 35–42. Also see the author's dissertation: "Attitudes, Practices, and Positions Toward Joseph Smith's Translation of the Bible: A Historical Analysis of Publications, 1847–1987" (Ph.D. diss., Brigham Young University, 1988), 162–63.

4. For a succinct review on this issue, see "The New Translation and Latter-day Saint Doctrine," in *Joseph Smith's New Translation of the Bible: Original Manuscripts,* ed. Scott H. Faulring, Kent P. Jackson, and Robert J. Matthews (Provo, UT: Religious Studies Center, Brigham Young University, 2004), 17–25.

5. Taken from a written note at the top of the first page of the new translation manuscript for the New Testament (NT1, March 8, 1831). The whole statement reads, "A Translation of the New Testament translated by the power of God" (*Joseph Smith's New Translation of the Bible,* 159).

6. Joseph Smith, *History of the Church of Jesus Christ of Latter-day Saints,* ed. B. H. Roberts, 2nd ed. rev. (Salt Lake City: Deseret Book, 1957), 1:238.

7. Smith, *History of the Church,* 1:368.

8. Smith, *History of the Church,* 1:273.

9. See Matthews, *Plainer Translation,* 52–53.

10. Smith, *History of the Church,* 1:132–33; emphasis added.

11. Robert J. Matthews, *A Plainer Translation: Joseph Smith's Translation of the Bible, A History and Commentary* (Provo, UT: Brigham Young University Press, 1975), 34; emphasis added.

12. Smith, *History of the Church,* 1:252; emphasis added.

13. Quoted in Larry E. Dahl, "The Vision of the Glories," in *Studies in Scripture: Volume One—The Doctrine and Covenants,* ed. Robert L. Millet and Kent P. Jackson (Sandy, UT: Randall Book, 1984), 297; emphasis added.

14. Smith, *History of the Church,* 1:98; emphasis added. This reference refers to the revelations regarding Enoch now contained in Moses 7.

15. Smith, *History of the Church,* 1:131–32; emphasis added.

16. Smith, *History of the Church,* 1:322; emphasis added.

17. See, for example, Smith, *History of the Church,* 1:242, 245, 253, 300, 331. These experiences helped Joseph Smith to know and restore the scriptures "even as they are in [the Lord's] bosom" (D&C 35:20).

18. See "The New Translation and Latter-day Saint Doctrine," in *Joseph Smith's New Translation of the Bible,* 18, 20.

19. A comprehensive summary is found in the previously cited article, "The New Translation and Latter-day Saint Doctrine," by Faulring, Jackson, and Matthews. Also see Robert J. Matthews, "The Role of the Joseph Smith Translation of the Bible in the Restoration of Doctrine" in *The Disciple As Witness,* ed. Stephen D. Ricks, Donald W. Parry, and Andrew H. Hedges (Provo, UT: FARMS, 2000), 327–53. Whole symposia were largely dedicated to the JST and its doctrinal contributions; see Nyman and Millet, *The Joseph Smith Translation,* and Robert L. Millet and Robert J. Matthews, eds., *Plain and Precious Truths Restored: The Doctrinal and Historical Significance of the Joseph Smith Translation* (Salt Lake City: Bookcraft, 1995).

20. "Since no originals of any part of the Bible are available today, only a prophet or seer could now correctly give the original author's intended meaning. . . . A seer can restore the proper meaning whether the passage is vague or incorrectly stated, or even if the text is entirely lost. I have noticed that often other Bibles tell *what* occurred anciently, but the JST adds *why*" (Robert J. Matthews, "The Role of the JST in the Restoration," in *Plain and Precious Truths Restored,* 47). For a pointed example of the significance of restored doctrine and context, see the author's article "The Savior's Rejection: Insights from the Joseph Smith Translation," in *Jesus Christ, Son of God, Savior,* ed. Paul H. Peterson, Gary L. Hatch, and Laura D. Card (Provo, UT: Religious Studies Center, Brigham Young University, 2002), 270–83.

21. For a book-length treatment, see Kent P. Jackson, *The Restored Gospel and the Book of Genesis* (Salt Lake City: Deseret Book, 2001).

22. In October of 1988, the television show *Donahue* hosted various ministers and a former minister turned atheist, to discuss God's plan for the salvation of his creations. At one point near the end of the broadcast, an audience member queried the former minister: "What made you change your mind? You were a minister, and now you're an atheist." To which the atheist replied: "What made me change my mind was I studied the Bible, and now I'm an atheist. The Bible is contradictory. It is nonhistorical. It is repugnant and it is harmful. I have no choice but to not believe in it" (transcription by the author from video recording).

23. "The Joseph Smith Translation: Restoring the Doctrinal Foundation

to the New Testament," handout for the CES Conference on the New Testament, Brigham Young University, 2000, 70.

24. "The New Translation and Latter-day Saint Doctrine," in *Joseph Smith's New Translation of the Bible,* 25.

25. Bruce R. McConkie, *Doctrines of the Restoration: Sermons and Writings of Bruce R. McConkie,* ed. Mark L. McConkie (Salt Lake City: Bookcraft, 1989), 289.

26. Thomas Bullock notes from the "King Follett Discourse" as published in Joseph Smith, *The Words of Joseph Smith,* comp. Andrew F. Ehat and Lyndon W. Cook (Provo, UT: Religious Studies Center, Brigham Young University, 1980), 353. Joseph Smith knew and understood the power of divine knowledge. He affirmed: "Knowledge does away with darkness, suspense and doubt; for these cannot exist where knowledge is. . . . In knowledge there is power. God has more power than all other beings, because he has greater knowledge" (*History of the Church,* 5:340).

27. "Scripture Reading, Revelation, and the JST," in *Plain and Precious Truths Restored,* 13.

28. This said, I do not wish to minimize the attention that should be paid to doctrinal text in the JST. In an interesting perusal of the last five years of general conference addresses (1999–2004) it is noted that JST texts are used nearly 150 times to establish and emphasize certain points of doctrine and constitute the major theme of about ten addresses. The most frequent users of the JST during that period were Elders Russell M. Nelson, Neal A. Maxwell, and Jeffrey R. Holland.

29. "Over 50 percent of the revelations in the Doctrine and Covenants were received during the time period associated with the inspired revision of the Bible" (Robert L. Millet, "Joseph Smith's Translation of the Bible and the Doctrine and Covenants," in *Studies in Scripture: Volume 1: The Doctrine and Covenants,* ed. Robert L. Millet and Keith P. Jackson [Salt Lake City: Randall Book, 1985], 139). "The Joseph Smith Translation of the Bible exerted a substantial influence on the content of the Doctrine and Covenants . . . [and] shows the [JST] for what it really is, a preliminary source for many of the theological statements in the Doctrine and Covenants. Such a view adds dignity, grace, and stature to the extensive labors of the Prophet Joseph Smith in making this translation" (Robert J. Matthews, "Doctrinal Connections with the Joseph Smith Translation," in *The Doctrine and Covenants: A Book of Answers,* ed. Leon R. Hartshorn, Dennis A. Wright, and Craig J. Ostler [Salt Lake City: Deseret Book, 1996], 27–28).

30. I concur with the view of Faulring, Jackson, and Matthews: "Joseph Smith's New Translation of the Bible has not received the attention

it deserves and has not been recognized for the important contributions it has made to Latter-day Saint scripture and doctrine. It has been neglected and even ignored by some LDS scripture scholars and historians. . . . Few Latter-day Saints appreciate what it has contributed to our faith" (in *Joseph Smith's New Translation of the Bible*, 17, 20).

31. Robert J. Matthews, "The Eternal Worth of the JST," in *Plain and Precious Truths Restored*, 175.

CHAPTER TWENTY-ONE

"Taught from on High": The Ministry of Angelic Messengers to the Prophet Joseph Smith

BRIAN L. SMITH

We often consider Joseph Smith's First Vision to mark the beginning of the current dispensation. But after the veil-piercing visitation of God the Father and His Son, Jesus Christ, to the Prophet Joseph Smith, many other heavenly messengers visited Joseph and helped usher in this final dispensation. Though we do not know how many angelic messengers appeared to the Prophet—or the purpose of some of their visits—we do know the circumstances and the nature of many of these visits. Heavenly beings came to Joseph Smith to unfold the majesty and glory of future events, to warn, to admonish, and to teach the maturing prophet. Former prophets and apostles returned priesthood keys to reestablish the Church with divinely recognized authority once again upon the earth.

A Reformation or Restoration?

The Church of Jesus Christ of Latter-day Saints is a *restoration*, not a reformation. This fundamental doctrine was forcibly impressed upon me when I served as the director of the Portland Institute of Religion in Oregon. There are a number of Bible colleges in the greater Portland area. Students from these institutions frequently sought interviews with members of the Latter-day Saint Church. In these interviews, I was often reminded of how unique our Church is among the other churches of today. They asked questions like "Why

Brian L. Smith is an instructor at the Orem Institute of Religion.

is your church different?" or "Where does your church fit in?" This was an opportunity to testify of the doctrinal restoration of the gospel and the return of the keys of the priesthood by the visitation of angels to the Prophet Joseph Smith. I would ask them to draw a simple diagram of where *their* church fit historically with other denominations. Then I would ask them to place The Church of Jesus Christ of Latter-day Saints on their charts. This often stymied them. I would draw a cloud to the side of their chart and label it "heaven," with angels coming down to a kneeling figure, and then explain the difference between a reformed church and the restored one. As you can imagine, this was visually startling to most of the students, particularly because it makes the claim of direct access to God and direct communication from Him and from angelic messengers. In these experiences I testified that Joseph Smith did communicate with God and angels and that the doctrines and ordinances found in the Church today are of divine origin.

WHY JOSEPH SMITH?

Joseph's call, like the calls of prophets and apostles of old, was to help us become heirs of salvation. Ancient prophets taught that Joseph Smith was foreordained to receive and reveal the hidden mysteries and wonders of God.[1] President Brigham Young said it well when he stated, "When I saw Joseph Smith, he took heaven, figuratively speaking, and brought it down to earth; and he took the earth, brought it up, and opened up, in plainness and simplicity, the things of God; and that is the beauty of his mission."[2] President Gordon B. Hinckley said this about the Prophet: "We acknowledge [Joseph Smith] . . . as an instrument in the hands of the Almighty in restoring to the earth the ancient truths of the divine gospel, together with the priesthood through which the authority of God is exercised in the affairs of His church and for the blessing of His people."[3]

Consider what Joseph Smith contributed and published to the world as an "unlearned" youth. Elder Bruce R. McConkie stated, "Here is a man who has given to our present world more holy scripture than any single prophet who ever lived; indeed, he has preserved for us more of the mind and will and voice of the Lord than the total of the dozen most prolific prophetic penmen of the past."[4] Elder Neal A. Maxwell shares the following insights:

> From Joseph Smith, one unlearned and untrained in the-
> ology, more printed pages of scripture have come down to us
> than from any mortal, including Moses, Paul, Luke, and
> Mormon combined.
>
> But it is not only a matter of impressive quantity; it is
> also a qualitative matter. Doctrines that came through the
> Prophet included key doctrines previously lost from the face
> of the earth, a loss which caused people to "stumble exceed-
> ingly." . . .
>
> What came *through* Joseph Smith was *beyond* Joseph
> Smith, and it *stretched* him! In fact, the doctrines that came
> through that "choice seer" (2 Nephi 3:6–7), by translation or
> revelation, are so light-intensive that, like radioactive mate-
> rials, they must be handled with great care![5]

How did Joseph Smith accomplish what he did, coming from
such an obscure, unlearned background? The explanation is simple:
God chose Joseph Smith and spoke to him. Heavenly messengers
taught him. This young prophet was entrusted with opening the
greatest dispensation. He experienced firsthand the restitution of all
things and was given the greatest volume of revelatory knowledge
known to man. Through inspiration he produced something far
superior to what the combined philosophy and wisdom of man
could produce. Joseph was given doctrine and authority from all the
previous dispensations. He saw in vision the writings of Enoch,
Abraham, Moses, John, and many others, and he understood the
writers' intent and original message. The ancient prophets likewise
knew of and prophesied of Joseph Smith and looked forward to his
day with great anticipation. And so we have ancient prophets tutoring a modern prophet, creating a cross-dispensational uniformity of
gospel principles.

President John Taylor shared this insight: "God chose this young
man. He was ignorant of letters as the world has it, but the most profoundly learned and intelligent man that I ever met in my life, and I
have traveled hundreds of thousands of miles, been on different continents and mingled among all classes and creeds of people, yet I
have never met a man so intelligent as he was. And where did he get
his intelligence from? Not from books; not from the logic or science
or philosophy of the day, but he obtained it through the revelation

of God made known to him through the medium of the everlasting gospel."[6]

DO ANGELS STILL APPEAR TO MEN?

In modern times many find it easy to scoff at the notion that angels minister to man. But those who believe in God should ask, "Is it likely that God would establish His Church today in a pattern different from what He has done in past dispensations?" Since the days of Adam, God has communicated with His children by the means of angels. Angels are messengers from God who deliver authority and information related to salvation. Mormon taught that "God knowing all things, being from everlasting to everlasting, behold, he *sent angels* to minister unto the children of men, to make manifest concerning the coming of Christ" (Moroni 7:22; emphasis added). We are led to Christ through faith, angels, prophets, and other diverse ways. Through the ministering of angels and by every word that comes from God, we can lay hold on every good thing, including miracles (see Moroni 7:21–27). Have angels ceased to appear to man? Only if man has lost faith in God! In fact, Mormon taught that as long as there is one man on earth to be saved, and he has faith, angels will appear (see Moroni 7:36–37).

In scripture we find heavenly messengers appearing to Adam (Moses 5:6), Abraham (Genesis 22:15), Hagar (Genesis 21:17), Moses (Exodus 3:2), the children of Israel (Exodus 14:19), Isaiah (Isaiah 37:36), Daniel (Daniel 6:22), Mary (Luke 1:30–33), Joseph (Matthew 1:20), Jesus (Luke 22:43), the women at the tomb (Matthew 28:5), and Peter (Acts 5:19), among others. Additionally, angels are referred to many times throughout the book of Revelation. Also, angels appeared to Nephi and his brothers (1 Nephi 3:29), Alma (Mosiah 27:11), a later Nephi (3 Nephi 7:15), and others during Christ's visit to the Nephites (3 Nephi 19:14).

FORMER PROPHETS AND APOSTLES
MINISTER IN THIS DISPENSATION

Many ancient prophets saw in vision the last days and looked forward to the dispensation of the fulness of times. Not only did they see many events of our day, but some of them were also privileged to return as messengers and be part of the restoration of all things. Here we have past prophets meeting face to face with a modern prophet. We learn from scripture that messengers who appear on this earth are individuals who belong to or have belonged to this earth (see D&C 130:5). Imagine having personally entertained angels anciently and now being sent as an angel to a later prophet. President John Taylor also stated, "The principles which [Joseph Smith] had, placed him in communication with the Lord, and not only with the Lord, but with the ancient apostles and prophets; such men, for instance, as Abraham, Isaac, Jacob, Noah, Adam, Seth, Enoch, and Jesus and the Father, and the apostles that lived on this continent as well as those who lived on the Asiatic continent. He seemed to be as familiar with these people as we are with one another."[7] Joseph B. Noble, an early Latter-day Saint convert, reported that Joseph Smith told him that he knew the angels so well that he could recognize them by the sound of their voices even before he saw their faces.[8]

Joseph Smith was preeminent among prophets in regard to the number of divine manifestations he experienced. Joseph received firsthand the restitution of all things (see Acts 3:21). It is remarkable that many of the visions and revelations given to Joseph were also experienced by others who were with him at the time the revelations were given. They were not just eyewitnesses to something happening; it happened to them too! This is not the mode of operation for an imposter who was trying to deceive people. Many testified that they saw and heard just what Joseph said he witnessed. He truly did bring heaven down to us, as Brigham Young said.

Hyrum Smith said of his brother, "There were prophets before, but Joseph has the spirit and power of all the prophets."[9] In 1882 George Q. Cannon, then a counselor in the First Presidency, said that Joseph "was constantly visited by angels" and given many visions. "In this respect he stands unique."[10] Wilford Woodruff taught that young Joseph Smith "was taught for years by visions and revelations, and by holy angels sent from God out of heaven to teach and instruct him and prepare him to lay the foundation of this Church."[11] Is it not reasonable to expect that when a prophet is called to open a gospel dispensation, he would be blessed with an abundance of God-given revelations, visions, and manifestations to guide him in the reestablishment of the gospel? Just as Enoch, Abraham, and Moses were tutored by divine messengers to preside over their dispensations, so was Joseph Smith. John Taylor taught:

> Why was it that all these people should . . . communicate with Joseph Smith? Because he stood at the head of the dispensation of the fulness of times, which comprehends all the various dispensations that have existed upon the earth, and that as the Gods in the eternal worlds and the Priesthood that officiated in time and eternity had declared that it was time for the issuing forth of all these things, they all combined together to impart to him the keys of their several missions, that he might be fully competent, through the intelligence and aid afforded him through these several parties, to introduce the Gospel in all its fulness, namely, the dispensation of the fulness of times.[12]

MORONI, JOSEPH'S TUTOR

It is difficult to determine how many heavenly messengers appeared to the Prophet Joseph Smith and who they all were. President Joseph F. Smith explained that Joseph Smith was taught by the angel Moroni and received his education from above, from God Almighty, and not from man-made institutions.[13] Moroni, who was the last prophet of the Book of Mormon, appeared more times than any other angel on record in this dispensation. Beginning with his first appearance in the Smith log home in Palmyra on September 21, 1823, he appeared to Joseph and others at least twenty-two times. Some fourteen hundred years after completing the scriptural record, Moroni revealed where the plates were hidden and began teaching the seventeen-year-old prophet. For the next six years (1823–29), Moroni prepared Joseph to receive and translate the plates and bring forth the Book of Mormon. President Cannon shared this insight of Moroni's influence in the Prophet's training: "[Joseph Smith] was visited constantly by angels. . . . Moroni, in the beginning, as you know, to prepare him for his mission, came and ministered and talked to him from time to time, and he had vision after vision in order that his mind might be fully saturated with a knowledge of the things of God, and that he might comprehend the great and holy calling that God has bestowed upon him."[14]

Joseph's mother related some details concerning the training

Joseph received from Moroni. She called these teaching moments "interviews." She observed that from the very first visit at Cumorah, Moroni attempted to impress upon Joseph the consequences of obedience and disobedience. Moroni repeatedly emphasized the concept of obedience, and "ever afterwards he [Joseph Smith] was willing to keep the commandments of God."[15] Joseph later learned that the very purpose of delaying reception of the plates was to wait until "he had learned to keep the commandments of God—not only till he was willing but able to do it."[16]

What did Moroni teach Joseph Smith? In a letter written by Oliver Cowdery to William W. Phelps, we find a partial list of Moroni's teachings at Cumorah:

1. The things of God must be done with the express view of glorifying God, not for gaining wealth.

2. Joseph could not obtain the plates unless he kept the commandments.

3. He must understand the difference between good and evil, holy and profane, in order never to be overcome by the wicked one.

4. If Joseph was ever to obtain the gold plates, it must be by prayer and faithfulness in obeying the Lord.

5. The Book of Mormon was sealed by Moroni with a prayer of faith.

6. The Book of Mormon contains the fulness of the gospel.

7. The Gentiles and the house of Israel would be brought into the fold if they believed in the Book of Mormon.

8. The former inhabitants of this land were promised that their descendants would receive the Book of Mormon record.

9. The plates contained sacred writings and could be obtained and understood only by the power of God. They could be translated only by the gift and power of God.

10. The Book of Mormon could not be translated through the learning of the world. The worldly would want the record only for the value of the plates of precious metal.

11. By the Book of Mormon, God would do a great and marvelous work, which would show the power of God, expose the unwise learning of the world, and comfort the faithful with great signs and wonders.

12. The record would go to every nation.

13. The workers of iniquity would seek Joseph's overthrow, to destroy his reputation, and even take his life.

14. Joseph would be preserved and would acquire the plates, after which the holy priesthood would be conferred and the Church would be established.

15. The Church would continue to grow, even though persecutions would increase.

16. In time, the ten tribes would return, and the Lord would come to Zion.

17. Joseph's name would be known among the nations, causing the righteous to rejoice and the wicked to rage.[17]

WHAT DID THE OTHER HEAVENLY MESSENGERS REVEAL TO JOSEPH SMITH?

From the numerous divine visits to Joseph, many foundational doctrines were established in the theology of the Church. For example, in the First Vision when God the Father and His Son Jesus Christ appeared to Joseph, we learn eternal truths, including: God lives, and He and His Son Jesus Christ are separate personages; God hears and answers prayers; the gospel in its fulness was not upon the earth; the Church, with divine authority, would soon be restored; the religions of the day had a "form of godliness, but [denied] the power thereof," and Joseph should join none of them. Finally, Joseph was told that he would be a disturber of Satan's kingdom (see Joseph Smith—History 1:17–20).[18]

The restoration of the Aaronic and Melchizedek Priesthoods occurred 15 May and late May or early June of 1829 (respectively), establishing divine authority once again upon the earth. When the Aaronic Priesthood was restored, John the Baptist informed Joseph Smith and Oliver Cowdery that Peter, James, and John would in due time confer the Priesthood of Melchizedek upon them (see Joseph Smith—History 1:70, 72). Of this event Joseph said, "The Priesthood is everlasting. The Savior, Moses, & Elias—gave the Keys to Peter, James & John on the Mount when they were transfigured before him. . . . How have we come at the priesthood in the last days? It came down, down in a regular succession. Peter James & John had it given to them & they gave it [to us]."[19]

WHICH OTHER PROPHETS APPEARED TO JOSEPH SMITH?

We do not know the precise nature of a number of other visits to the Prophet Joseph Smith. Some messengers may have given keys, while others taught him doctrine or gave him counsel. These personages include Seth, Isaac, Jacob, and the Jewish and Nephite Apostles.[20] In addition, Joseph saw other angels in vision, some of whom are identified in recorded revelations such as Doctrine and Covenants 107:53; 128:19–21.[21] These verses list Seth, Enos, Cainan, Mahalaleel, Jared, Enoch, Methuselah, Moroni, Jesus Christ, Michael, Peter, James, John, God the Father, Gabriel, Raphael, and "divers" others. George Q. Cannon added, "Moroni, who held the keys of the record of the stick of Ephraim, visited Joseph; he had doubtless, also, visits from *Nephi* and it may be from *Alma and others,* but though they came and had authority, holding the authority of the Priesthood, *we have no account of their ordaining him.*"[22] President John Taylor testified that "when Joseph Smith was raised up as a prophet of God, Mormon, Moroni, Nephi and others of the ancient Prophets who formerly lived on this Continent, and Peter and John and others who lived on the Asiatic Continent, came to him and communicated to him certain principles pertaining to the Gospel of the Son of God. Why? Because *they held the keys of the various dispensations, and conferred them upon him,* and he upon us."[23]

President Taylor also taught that Joseph "understood things that were past, and comprehended the various dispensations and the designs of those dispensations. He not only had the principles developed, but he was conversant with the parties who officiated as the leading men of those dispensations, and from a number of them he received authority and keys and priesthood and power for the carrying out of the great purposes of the Lord in the last days, who were sent and commissioned specially by the Almighty to confer upon him those keys and this authority."[24] (See the charts at the end of this article for a listing of messengers and other personalities who appeared to the Prophet Joseph Smith or whom he saw in vision.)

CONCLUSION

In 1839 Joseph Smith, Sidney Rigdon, and others traveled to Washington, D.C., to present their petitions for redress for the crimes committed against them by the Missourians. During the trip, they were invited to speak to about three thousand people in Philadelphia. President Rigdon addressed the group first. In an effort to avoid confrontation, he used Bible references in an attempt to prove that the Church was true, avoiding any reference to the visions and revelations of the Restoration. The Prophet was visibly disappointed at Sidney's defense. Parley P. Pratt observed that the Prophet could barely sit still:

> When he [Sidney Rigdon] was through, brother Joseph arose like a lion about to roar; and being full of the Holy Ghost, spoke in great power, bearing testimony of the visions he had seen, the ministering of angels which he had enjoyed; and how he had found the plates of the Book of Mormon, and translated them by the gift and power of God. He commenced by saying: "If nobody else had the courage to testify . . . of so glorious a record, he felt to do it in justice to the people, and leave the event to God."
>
> The entire congregation was astounded; electrified, as it were, and overwhelmed with the sense of truth and power by which he spoke, and the wonders which he related. A lasting impression was made; many souls were gathered into the fold. And I bear witness, that he, by his faithful and powerful testimony, cleared his garments of their blood.[25]

For each member of the Church, there must ultimately come a conviction that Joseph Smith was a prophet and revealer of truth. He did see the Father and the Son and received instruction and keys from heavenly messengers. Joseph Smith was foreordained and commissioned to establish the gospel of Jesus Christ on the face of the earth before the Second Coming of the Savior. Some have said they would consider belonging to the Church if we would take out the part about God and angels appearing to Joseph Smith. This cannot happen, because the appearance of divine messengers and other angels is a foundational doctrine of the Church.[26] John Taylor said it this way: "If God has not spoken, if the angel of God has not appeared to Joseph Smith, and if these things are not true of which we speak, then the whole thing is an impostor from beginning to end. There is no half-way house, no middle path about the matter; it is either one thing or the other."[27] Angels *did* help usher in this dispensation. Without them, it would not have happened. Millions can testify that Joseph did hear and see all that he claimed. As he said: "I had seen a vision; I knew it, and I knew God knew it, and I could not deny it, neither dared I do it; at least I knew that by so doing I would offend God, and come under condemnation" (Joseph Smith—History 1:25). Some may fear to make such claims, but not Joseph!

The following is a list of many of the personages who appeared to Joseph Smith and restored keys or delivered divine instructions.

Personage	Selected References	Keys given or nature of appearance
God the Father	JS—H 1:17; *HC* 1:5; D&C 76:2	Opened this dispensation; introduced the Son.
Jesus Christ	JS—H 1:17; *HC* 1:5–6; D&C 76:20–24; 110:2–10	Called Joseph as a prophet; accepted the temple.
Moroni	JS—H 1:30–49, 59; *JD* 17:374	Tutored Joseph; gave him keys of stick of Ephraim.
John the Baptist	D&C 13:1; *HC* 1:39–42	Restored Aaronic Priesthood and its keys.
Peter, James, John	D&C 27:12; 128:20; *JD* 18:326; *HC* 1:40–42	Restored Melchizedek Priesthood and apostleship and keys.
Moses	D&C 110:11; *JD* 21:65; 23:48	Restored keys of gathering and leading the ten tribes.
Elias	D&C 27:6; 110:12; *JD* 23:48	Committed the "gospel of Abraham."
Elijah	D&C 110:13–16; *JD* 23:48	Conferred the sealing power.
Adam (Michael)	*HC* 2:380; 3:388; D&C 128:21; *JD* 18:326; 21:94; 23:48	Restored keys (perhaps of the presidency over the earth).
Noah (Gabriel)	D&C 128:21; *JD* 21:94; 23:48	Restored keys (perhaps of the power to preach the gospel).
Raphael	D&C 128:21	Restored keys (perhaps of the dispensation of Enoch's day).
Various angels	D&C 128:21	Restored keys (all declaring their individual dispensation).

Personage	Selected References	Keys Given or Nature of Appearance
Lehi	JD 16:265–66	Ministered to him.
Nephi	JD 21:161; 16:266; 17:374	Tutored Joseph; gave him keys.
Mormon	JD 17:374	Tutored Joseph; gave him keys.
Unnamed angel	D&C 27; HC 1:106	Taught concerning use of wine in the sacrament.
Unnamed angel	*Life of Heber C. Kimball*[28]; *Temples of the Most High*[29]	Sent to accept dedication of the Kirtland temple.
Unnamed angel	*Biography and Family Records of Lorenzo Snow*[30]	Visited Joseph three times; commanded him to practice plural marriage, as previously revealed by the Lord.

Although keys, instructions, or information may have been given by some of the personages in the following list, they are generally noted as simply having been seen by Joseph.

Abel	JD 18:325; HC 3:388
Seth	JD 21:94; D&C 107:53–57; HC 3:388
Enos	HC 3:388; D&C 107:53–57; HC 3:388
Cainan	HC 3:388; D&C 107:53–57
Mahalaleel	JD 18:325; D&C 107:53–57; HC 3:388
Jared (Bible)	HC 3:388; D&C 107:53–57
Enoch	HC 3:388; D&C 107:53–57; JD 21:65
Methuselah	JD 18:325; D&C 107:53–57; HC 3:388
Lamech	JD 18:325
Eve	Oliver B. Huntington diary[31]
Abraham	D&C 27:10; JD 21:94; 23:48
Isaac	D&C 27:10; JD 21:94
Jacob	D&C 27:10; JD 21:94

Joseph, son of Jacob	D&C 27:10
Twelve Jewish Apostles (Peter, James, and John already counted above)	*JD* 21:94 (Names in Matthew 10:1–4, Luke 6:13–16)
Twelve Nephite Apostles (Includes the Three Nephites)	*JD* 21:94 (Names recorded in 3 Nephi 19:4)
Zelph the Lamanite	*Times & Seasons*, 6:788
Alvin Smith (Joseph's deceased brother)	*HC* 2:380
Paul	*TPJS* 180
Alma	*JD* 13:47
"I saw many angels"	Warren Cowdery's account of the First Vision[32]
Satan and his associates	JSH 1:15–16; D&C 128:20; *JD* 3:229–30

Notes

1. See W. Jeffrey Marsh, "A Mission Long Foreknown," *Ensign*, January 2001, 30–36.
2. Brigham Young, *Discourses of Brigham Young*, ed. John A. Widtsoe (Salt Lake City: Deseret Book, 1954), 458–59.
3. Gordon B. Hinckley, *Be Thou an Example* (Salt Lake City: Deseret Book, 1981), 119.
4. Bruce R. McConkie, "Joseph Smith—The Mighty Prophet of the Restoration," *Ensign*, May 1976, 95.
5. Neal A. Maxwell, "A Choice Seer," *Ensign*, August 1986, 6.
6. John Taylor, in *Journal of Discourses* (London: Latter-day Saints' Book Depot, 1854–86), 21:163.
7. Taylor, in *Journal of Discourses*, 21:94.
8. Mark L. McConkie, *Remembering Joseph* (Salt Lake City: Deseret Book, 2003), 24.
9. Hyrum Smith, in *History of the Church of Jesus Christ of Latter-day Saints*, ed. B. H. Roberts, 2nd ed. rev. (Salt Lake City: Deseret Book, 1957), 6:346.
10. George Q. Cannon, in *Journal of Discourses*, 23:362.
11. Wilford Woodruff, in *Journal of Discourses*, 16:265.
12. Taylor, in *Journal of Discourses*, 18:326.

13. Joseph F. Smith, *Gospel Doctrine* (Salt Lake City: Deseret Book, 1963), 484.

14. Cannon, in *Journal of Discourses,* 23:362.

15. Lucy Mack Smith, *History of Joseph Smith by His Mother* (Salt Lake City: Bookcraft, 1979), 81.

16. Smith, *History of Joseph Smith by His Mother,* 81.

17. Oliver Cowdery to William W. Phelps, *Messenger and Advocate,* October 1, 1835, 198–200.

18. See also James E. Faust, "The Magnificent Vision Near Palmyra," *Ensign,* May 1984, 67; Milton V. Backman Jr., *Joseph Smith's First Vision* (Salt Lake City: Bookcraft, 1971), 206–8.

19. Joseph Smith, *The Words of Joseph Smith,* comp. and ed. Andrew F. Ehat and Lyndon W. Cook (Provo, UT: Religious Studies Center, Brigham Young University, 1980), 9.

20. Taylor, in *Journal of Discourses,* 21:94.

21. See Smith, *History of the Church,* 3:388.

22. Cannon, in *Journal of Discourses,* 13:47; emphasis added.

23. Taylor, in *Journal of Discourses,* 17:374; emphasis added.

24. Taylor, in *Journal of Discourses,* 20:174–75.

25. Parley P. Pratt, *Autobiography of Parley P. Pratt* (Salt Lake City: Deseret Book, 1938), 298–99.

26. James E. Faust, "Lord, I Believe: Help Thou Mine Unbelief," *Ensign,* November 2003, 19–20.

27. Taylor, in *Journal of Discourses,* 21:165.

28. Orson F. Whitney, *Life of Heber C. Kimball, An Apostle: The Father and Founder of the British Mission* (Salt Lake City: Bookcraft, 1967), 91.

29. *Temples of the Most High,* comp. N. B. Lundwall (Salt Lake City: Bookcraft, 1968), 23.

30. Eliza R. Snow Smith, *Biography and Family Records of Lorenzo Snow* (Salt Lake City: Deseret News, 1884), 69–70.

31. Oliver B. Huntington diary, comp. H. Donl Peterson, vol. 2 (L. Tom Perry Special Collections, Harold B. Lee Library, Brigham Young University), 244; see also H. Donl Peterson, *Moroni: Ancient Prophet—Modern Messenger* (Bountiful, UT: Horizon, 1983).

32. Milton V. Backman Jr., *Joseph Smith's First Vision,* 2nd ed. (Salt Lake City: Bookcraft, 1980), 159.

CHAPTER TWENTY-TWO

"PRAISE TO THE MAN": A REVIEW OF THE ANNUAL JOSEPH SMITH MEMORIAL SERMONS

THOMAS E. THUNELL

One of the most significant ongoing tributes to the Prophet Joseph Smith is the annual Joseph Smith Memorial Firesides (also referred to as Memorial Sermons and Lectures) held in Logan, Utah. These firesides, sponsored by the Logan Institute of Religion, began in 1944 and have been held each year since, as close as possible to December 23, Joseph Smith's birthday. Speakers during the past six decades have included all the presidents of the Church (David O. McKay through Gordon B. Hinckley, prior to their calls as president), counselors in the First Presidency, members of the Quorum of the Twelve Apostles, other General Authorities, Church leaders, and scholars.[1] Their insights into the life, character, and doctrinal contributions of the Prophet Joseph, along with their testimonies of his divine calling, are invaluable resources in the reservoir of witnesses to the monumental contributions of the Prophet of the Restoration.

"Thumbnail History of the Logan Institute, 1928–1957" describes the inception of the Joseph Smith Memorial Sermons as follows: "One of the objectives of the LDS Educational System is to develop a testimony of the Divinity of the work of Joseph Smith. In harmony with this objective, the institute began the traditional Joseph Smith Memorial Sermons under the direction of Director Daryl Chase in 1944. Each year the institute invites an outstanding scholar and churchman to deliver a sermon dealing with some phase of the life

---

Thomas E. Thunell is an instructor at the Salt Lake University Institute.

and work of the Prophet Joseph Smith."[2] Brother Chase's intense interest in this topic was obvious, since in the same year, 1944, he published a small volume titled *Joseph the Prophet, As He Lives in the Hearts of His People*. This book was the product of his graduate work and years of studying the life of Joseph Smith. Some thoughts he expressed in the foreword cast light on his motivation for initiating the Joseph Smith Memorial Lecture Series. In it he expressed his opinion that "the definitive biography of the Prophet has not yet appeared." Nonetheless, he believed "that some day the great book on the life of Joseph Smith" would appear and that its author would have to be a first-rate scholar.[3]

This series began in the heat of World War II, when many students experienced a trial of their faith. These lectures were a wonderful source of inspiration, testimony, and direction in a chaotic world. The students and faculty of the Logan institute described the desired outcome of the series as follows: "It is hoped that these Memorial Sermons will help to keep the Prophet and his teachings in a vital and meaningful place before each succeeding generation."[4]

When the first sermon in the series was delivered by then Acting Patriarch of the Church, Joseph F. Smith,[5] on February 6, 1944, the Logan institute consisted of the director, two instructors,[6] and fewer than eight hundred institute students.[7] The early sermons were intended to be not only inspirational but also of a scholarly nature, reporting new research and blazing new territory. In recent years, most of the sermons have focused on personal testimony of Joseph's character and works. By the 2004 memorial fireside (also the seventy-fifth anniversary of the Logan institute), the institute faculty included thirty-four instructors and 7,500 students.

The array of distinguished speakers who have been invited to speak at the Memorial Firesides has included fifty-three brethren and three sisters: Barbara B. Smith, Elaine Cannon, and Janette Hales (Beckham). These three sisters were serving as general auxiliary presidents at the time of their presentations. The speakers have included two Brigham Young University presidents (Howard McDonald and Jeffrey R. Holland), eminent scholars (Sidney B. Sperry, Lowell L. Bennion, G. Homer Durham, T. Edgar Lyon, Daniel H. Ludlow, Richard L. Bushman, Truman G. Madsen, Robert K. Thomas, and Robert J. Matthews), and General Authorities (mostly from the

Twelve and First Presidency). Three of these speakers, Elders L. Tom Perry, Robert J. Matthews, and Truman G. Madsen, have presented twice at the memorial firesides, and Elder Henry B. Eyring has spoken three times.

In 1953 William E. Berrett observed: "It is an appropriate thing to remember the birthday of the Prophet Joseph. . . . This is the birthday of our greatest countryman. Joseph Smith is the only American whose birthday is heralded around the world. . . . People of every land and of every race are coming to honor the birthday of the Prophet Joseph Smith."[8] In this spirit, this article brings together insights shared by these presenters on the life and mission of Joseph Smith the Prophet. The wide variety of topics addressed by these speakers is fascinating, instructive, and awe-inspiring. Obviously, a comprehensive summary would be impractical. Therefore, the major topics discussed here are the testimony of Joseph's divine calling and mission, the doctrinal restoration through Joseph Smith, and Joseph's lasting legacy.

Testimony of Joseph's Divine Calling and Mission

The essential and most consistent theme of all the presentations was the powerful witness that testifies of Joseph Smith's divine calling, the centerpiece of the Restoration. Elder Russell M. Nelson identified the appearance of the Father and the Son to Joseph Smith in 1820 as the "center from which the very pulse of life for this Church has emanated." It "is at the very heart of our religion. . . . The prophetic mission of Joseph Smith and the doctrines he taught . . . [are] central to this work. God knows it. We know it. Satan knows it."[9]

Elder Richard G. Scott amplified the centrality of Joseph Smith's role by sharing the familiar story of President McKay's father, who, while serving a mission in the 1880s, had become downcast and gloomy. In despair he "retire[d] to a cave near the ocean . . . and pour[ed] out his soul to God and asked why he was oppressed. . . . He entered that place and said, 'Oh, Father, what can I do to have this feeling removed?' He heard a voice . . . say, 'Testify that Joseph Smith is a Prophet of God.' . . . Always, we need to be valiant in the testimony of Joseph Smith."[10]

The pivotal role that the testimony of Joseph Smith plays in missionary work and the conversion process was characterized by a survey conducted in the Canadian Mission under the direction of the mission president, Thomas S. Monson. Elder Monson reported that converts were asked: "Of all the things which came together to bring you into membership in the Church, what aided you most? Almost invariably the response to that question would be this: That which aided me most in my conversion was the humble, simple testimony of the Prophet Joseph Smith."[11] Speaking of his own conversion, Elder Gary J. Coleman recalled, "Coming to know the Prophet Joseph Smith was the key to my conversion, along with reading the Book of Mormon."[12]

Discussing 2 Nephi 3 and elaborating on the similarities between the lives of Joseph of Egypt and Joseph Smith, his latter-day descendant, Elder Sterling W. Sill, concluded:

> Joseph, the son of Jacob, was sent before the face of the Egyptian famine to preserve life. Joseph Smith was to go before the face of the spiritual famine. . . . Joseph, the son of Jacob, opened the Egyptian graineries that people might not perish in the famine for bread. . . . God touched the life of Joseph Smith and through him opened the graineries of spiritual truth to abate the famine of hearing the word of the Lord mentioned by Amos. . . . But the spiritual graineries are now open. All things that were lost have now been restored. . . . The greatest information of our lives might well be the personal testimony of Joseph Smith.[13]

The divine and heavenly preparation the boy Joseph received was what made him into a prophet, according to President Harold B. Lee. He stated: "We come to the sure conclusion that a prophet does not become a spiritual leader by studying books about religion, nor does he become one by attending a theological seminary. . . . One becomes a prophet or a religious leader by actual spiritual contacts. The true spiritual expert thus gets his diploma direct from God."[14] Howard W. Hunter further explained in his sermon: "History does not indicate that prophets have been chosen for their great learning, for their acquisition of worldly culture, or for their social position. They have been called from the more humble stations of life, they were chosen before they were born."[15]

In this light Elder Coleman cited John Taylor's observation that

"[Joseph] was ignorant of letters as the world has it, but the most profoundly learned and intelligent man that I ever met in my life."[16]

"The Lord had shepherded the unveiling of this work," stated Elder David B. Haight.[17] Elder Russell M. Nelson pointed out that Joseph was known to the ancient prophets, and they appeared to and tutored him.[18] He was not a self-made man; rather, God prepared, molded, fashioned, and endowed him.

After rehearsing the key elements of what constitutes a prophetic calling, Elder Hugh B. Brown testified, "I have the sacred honor to be a witness for Him, and now with the solemnity of an oath, standing before you as in a witness box, I declare that our Heavenly Father . . . commissioned the Prophet Joseph Smith to establish His Church and through him the priesthood was restored by which men today are authorized to speak and act in the name of God, as did the prophets of old."[19] Elder Boyd K. Packer reasoned that by all standards Joseph qualifies for and is "worthy of the designation of prophet, seer, and revelator."[20]

Many of the Joseph Smith memorial speakers emphasized the need for all those present to obtain this personal witness of Joseph Smith. Elder James E. Faust put into perspective the vital role of a personal testimony, pointing out that "the beginning point of the restoration is the story of Joseph Smith. . . . Joseph Smith lies at the heart of it all. . . . Every person who claims membership in the Church must have his own personal witness concerning the truthfulness of the story of Joseph Smith. . . . That which makes [the Church] live is the individual testimony of the members of the Church."[21] Regarding personal testimony, Patriarch Joseph F. Smith observed that some people do not yet believe Joseph was a prophet, to whom he said, "That is not a disgrace. Honest doubt was never shameful." It was this questioning state of mind that led Joseph to the grove. "Honest doubt is a salutary thing. Dynamic doubt is a good thing."[22] He then concluded, "I promise you young people that if you will make the Gospel of Christ the cornerstone of your education, and live according to the principles of the Gospel. . . . You will be given a greater insight and a wider wisdom. . . . You will know that Joseph Smith was a Prophet of the Lord, and no amount of sophistry, no amount of worldly learning, can move your faith."[23]

An eloquent summary to the testimonies of all the memorial

speakers came in the words of President David O. McKay, who asked, "Whence hath this man wisdom?" Then he answered as follows: "Praise to the man who communed with Jehovah! Jesus anointed that Prophet and Seer. . . . As absolute as the certainty that you have in your hearts that tonight will be followed by dawn tomorrow morning, so is my assurance that Jesus Christ is the Savior of mankind, the Light that will dispel the darkness of the world through the Gospel restored by direct revelation to the Prophet Joseph Smith."[24]

The Doctrinal Restoration through Joseph Smith

The most significant contribution of the Prophet Joseph Smith was the vast reservoir of revealed truth that flowed almost continually from heaven through him. Of all the topics discussed by the Joseph Smith memorial speakers, this theme, the doctrinal restoration, was by far the most prevalent. The nature and reality of the Godhead, additional scripture, the restoration of lost truths, and doctrines related to the plan of salvation were among the topics most frequently addressed. Elder Joe J. Christensen depicted the Prophet Joseph's revelatory capacity in the words of Truman G. Madsen, who wrote:

> [Joseph Smith's] Biblical teachings, letters and counsels are so extensive as to transcend the grasp of any one historian. . . . He spoke profoundly of eternal law, of the . . . cosmos, of the relationship of matter and spirit, of space and time, of the nature of freedom, of causation and process, of the meaning and unity of truth, of the foundations of ethics, and of history, education and languages. . . . He testified firsthand of the revealed personalities of God and Jesus Christ, the origins of man. . . . He manifested such grasp of the meaning of life as to exceed, even, the aspirations of men of faith in every age. . . . That it could have come from, or even through, a mind as taxed by a thousand other matters as was Joseph Smith's, staggers the imagination.[25]

The First Vision and the Godhead. The event of Joseph's life most frequently referred to by memorial sermon speakers was the First Vision. As a result of that consummate event, Joseph, and the world, would never be the same. Elders John A. Widtsoe and Spencer W.

Kimball dedicated the bulk of their remarks to the significance of the
First Vision. Of this experience Elder Kimball testified: "This young
boy was entrusted with the greatest block of knowledge known to
men." No one "in the world had absolute knowledge of God. . . . But,
here was a boy who knew . . . God lives. . . . He is a person with flesh
and bones and personality. . . . The Father and the Son were two distinct beings. . . . The gospel was not on the earth. . . . The true church
was absent from the earth. . . . He must join none of the many religious sects. . . . Joseph knew from firsthand experience the attributes
of the Father and the Son and the program that was to be restored
through him."[26]

"The First Vision," Elder Widtsoe stated, "was not only the
Prophet's first great religious experience and, therefore, of great consequence, but it seems to me to be an epitome of the approach to all
truth, whatever it may be."[27] Two great lessons may be gleaned from
this theophany: "First, divinity is personal. . . . We in this day can
hardly understand the greatness of that message, for in that day men
were taught that God could not or would not speak anymore. . . . The
second lesson . . . was a simple lesson: order must prevail among us.
. . . The law of order rules the universe."[28]

"At no time has God made himself common by appearing to
people in general," stated Elder Mark E. Petersen, "but always in the
past He has restored the true knowledge of himself by appearing to
divinely chosen instruments on the earth. . . . Their testimonies then
would become a basis for a proper and intelligent worship of the
Deity and through that worship, with proper obedience, mankind
could be saved. This is why . . . Joseph Smith was permitted to see
the Father and the Son."[29]

The primary role of the First Vision in the Restoration leads us to
what Sidney B. Sperry called "the first and in many respects, the most
important contribution of Joseph Smith in this realm . . . his concept
of God,"[30] or the nature of God. In light of this theme, Elder Jay E.
Jensen titled his sermon "'Joseph Smith—The First and the Last
Lesson.' . . . Based on a statement by President Joseph F. Smith, 'The
knowledge of God and of his Son Jesus Christ, . . . is the first and the
last lesson.' . . . The foundation of the restored gospel is the correct
knowledge of God."[31] Elder Petersen stated that "no one can be saved

in ignorance of a true knowledge of God." We become like him by learning of his attributes and applying them to our lives.[32]

Additional scripture. Discussing the doctrinal restoration, Elder Joe J. Christensen said that one can hardly overlook Joseph's "literary labors. . . . He produced more scripture, that is, the revealed word of God, than any other man of whom we have record. Indeed, his total scriptural productions would almost equal those of all others put together."[33] Standing first and foremost was the foundation work of translating and publishing the Book of Mormon. Many of the memorial fireside speakers addressed the keystone role of the Book of Mormon. William E. Berrett referred to the Book of Mormon as a living book: "We see not only the organization of the Church but we see some books, living books. I could count on the fingers of my two hands every book published in America a hundred years ago that is still being printed. Most books are dead in a half dozen years. And when a book survives a century we come to call it a living book." The Book of Mormon, the Doctrine and Covenants, and the Pearl of Great Price are, therefore, living books, having passed the test of time.[34]

"The Book of Mormon," Robert K. Thomas concluded, "claims to be essentially Hebraic history. . . . The Hebraic theory of history is devastatingly simple and exclusive: History is God's dealings with his chosen people—no more, no less."[35] The Book of Mormon stands as "Another Witness of Jesus Christ," and that witness "is the heart of the Book of Mormon," concluded Truman Madsen. "It is . . . the most revealing, relieving, releasing portrait of Jesus Christ in the world today. To say that it is crucially different from other prevailing portraits is an understatement. . . . This is a segment of the life of Christ, otherwise unknown, given with clarity. Here he is a resurrected, a composite self. . . . He is in all the highest senses of flesh and spirit a personality. He can be seen, felt, embraced . . . loved. He is the revelation of the Father not because 'two natures' are combined, but because He is now exactly like the Father in nature."[36]

Another major body of scripture, often overlooked, that played a pivotal role in the Restoration was Joseph's translation of the Bible. Both times Robert J. Matthews spoke, he addressed the Joseph Smith Translation. Of it he said, "The Joseph Smith Translation, or JST, is not just a better Bible; it was the channel or the means of doctrinal restoration in the infancy of this Church. Or in other words, several of the major doctrines and practices of the Church today were first revealed by means of the Bible translation by the Prophet Joseph Smith."[37] "If we select the great doctrinal revelations of the Doctrine and Covenants, we can immediately see that it was during the time of the Bible translation that such sections as D&C 29, 42, 45, 76, 77, 84, 86, 88, 93, 107, 132, and 133 were received."[38] Among the doctrines clarified by the Genesis account in the JST were "the spiritual and temporal creations, agency, the rebellion of Lucifer, the fall of Adam and the introduction of the gospel to Adam and his posterity."[39] The Lectures on Faith and even the temple ceremony were greatly influenced by what Joseph received while translating the Bible.[40] "There are at least 3,400 verses that contain alterations by him."[41] "The translation was not just a process of pouring information from one vessel to another, nor was it a matter of inserting doctrine already understood. The manuscripts suggest that the Prophet received inspiration line upon line, here a little and there a little. It was a learning experience for him."[42]

The house of Israel and Zion. Many other familiar doctrines became new at the hands of Joseph Smith. The revelations, teachings, and prophecies regarding Judah and the house of Israel led Daniel H. Ludlow to postulate: "I am convinced in my heart Joseph Smith knew more about Israel than any other person of his century."[43] Joseph taught that "there are three aspects of the gathering of Israel, just as there were three aspects of the scattering: The lost tribes, the dispersed of Israel, and Judah. Some peoples of the world understand one of these aspects, but I honestly do not know anyone except the Latter-day Saints who understand all three of those aspects."[44]

Another doctrine unique to our theology is that of building up the latter-day Zion. Speaking to this theme, Elder Alvin R. Dyer said, "It is the responsibility, the obligation, of every servant of God in this dispensation, according to the revelations, to bear record unto the children of men that the foundation of Zion has been laid, that the celestial principles upon which it will be redeemed have been revealed."[45] Elder Dyer quoted Joseph on the destiny of Zion: "You know there has been a great discussion in relation to Zion—where it is, and where the gathering of this dispensation is, and which I am now going to tell you. The prophets have spoken and written about it; but I will make a proclamation that will cover a broader ground. The whole of America is Zion itself, from north to south."[46]

The plan of salvation. Many of the doctrines revealed through Joseph Smith deal with the plan of salvation. These revelations stand supreme in teaching mortals the eternal truths of their origin, mortality, and destiny. It is not surprising that the plan would be addressed by many of the memorial speakers. Stressing the importance of man's knowing the plan, Elder L. Tom Perry stated: "The Plan of Salvation provides direction and purpose to the eternal scheme of things and is available to everyone in every condition. Unless people understand and act upon the principles found in the Plan of Salvation, the fullness of happiness will slip from their grasp."[47] In 1966 President N. Eldon Tanner said we learn from Joseph's teachings "about man's relationship to God, our pre-existence, the council in heaven. . . . Here also we learn about the resurrection. . . . We are taught also how we can do work for our dead, thereby making available the blessings of the Gospel to millions of our ancestors who died without a knowledge of it. Then we have the principle of Celestial Marriage and eternal progression."[48] "To me," concluded Brother Tanner, "this is the greatest story in all the world."[49]

Of the plan of salvation, President Jeffrey R. Holland said, "You go back I suppose from the very beginning and think of all of the things we know about the premortal existence, the council in heaven, the conflict, the role of Satan, the role of Christ, our role, whatever our testimony was even then clear back with Christ. If you took away what the Prophet Joseph has contributed to that we wouldn't know a lot."[50] No other Christian religion teaches anything about premortal existence or the general plan of salvation. "If you just begin there," continued Brother Holland, "[you can] make that leap forward to all this business about three degrees of glory and rather detailed doctrine about sons of perdition and all that it takes to get there, the fall and the atonement, . . . relationship of faith to works, . . . the nature of man, . . . baptisms for the dead, . . . the attributes of God. The list is as long as your arm."[51] "All of the significance of all these temples moving throughout the world, well, that alone . . . is a legacy from Joseph Smith."[52]

Elder Dallin H. Oaks addressed another aspect of the plan of salvation, the eternal nature of man in regard to his agency. He concluded: "What the Prophet Joseph Smith taught about the nature of man and his relationship to God and the role of free agency contrasted sharply with the accepted Christian doctrine of his day. These are among the most distinguishing doctrines of the restoration. . . . Our understanding of the principles of free agency is traceable almost entirely to revelations received and taught by the Prophet Joseph Smith."[53]

"Joseph Smith made clear the part played by this earth life in the eternal scheme of things," stated Sidney Sperry. "We came to this earth that we might have a body and present it pure before God in the celestial kingdom. The great principle of happiness consists in having a body."[54] The great and anticipated climax of the plan is to return to God and become one with Him. Dr. Henry Eyring, an eminent scientist, said: "One other idea that was revolutionary and is still revolutionary is to take away the idea of the limitation that one supposes exists for man. . . . He replaced it with the idea . . . that there is no limit to how high man might go, man the son of God, might go, if he lived the gospel . . . that through the eternities he could go beyond any limit. That great idea is something that can't help catching hold of our imaginations."[55]

These doctrines are but a sampling of those discussed by the Joseph Smith memorial speakers. President Henry D. Moyle expressed it well when he related, "President McKay frequently has impressed upon my mind the fact that if the Prophet Joseph had given us nothing but the 89th Section and the 121st Section of the Doctrine and Covenants, he would have given us enough to justify our recognizing him fully as a Prophet of God with a mission to perform here upon the earth."[56] Joseph Smith revolutionized the doctrinal world of his day and changed the world for the centuries to come.

JOSEPH'S LASTING LEGACY

As significant as the life, teachings, and works of Joseph Smith were to his day, the greatest measure of importance lies in their endurance. "Our concern with history, Joseph Smith's or any other," asserted G. Homer Durham, "is not merely for what happened in the past, but in what history suggests by way of principle for the present and the future."[57] Does the message and the work outlast the man, not only outlast but grow and increase with time? This last section will consider the spiritual heritage left by Joseph Smith and what impact and lasting difference his life, mission, and doctrines have made in our twenty-first-century world.

Regarding the test of time, Elder Bruce D. Porter quoted Joseph's own projection: "I intend to lay a foundation that will revolutionize the whole world."[58] Of this prophetic vision, Elder M. Russell Ballard quoted Joseph's prophecy that "this Church will fill North and South America—it will fill the world," and observed, "You will detect in this statement by Joseph Smith no element of cautious forecasting. He certainly did not predict future growth based on past trends. He gave a bold statement, a prophecy—given by the Spirit of the Lord to a prophet of the Lord."[59]

Many of the speakers of the memorial firesides sought to acquaint their audiences with the Prophet Joseph, sharing anecdotal insights from his life and citing personal appraisals by friends and prominent figures of his day. President Howard McDonald cited an 1843 *New York Times* article that stated, "This Joe Smith must be set down as an extraordinary character, a prophet hero. . . . He is one of the great men of his age, and in future history will rank with those who, in one way or another, have stamped their impress strongly upon society."[60] Leaders of his day esteemed Joseph Smith to be one of the greatest Americans of the nineteenth century who left his mark on future generations.[61]

Such admiration of the Prophet has often been misconstrued. Elder Neal A. Maxwell clarified: "We do not, as some occasionally charge, worship Joseph Smith, nor place him on a par with Jesus. But we do venerate him, remembering, hopefully, that the highest and best form of veneration is emulation."[62] Modestly, Joseph "made no attempt to hide his errors or the Lord's rebuke,"[63] Elder Joseph B. Wirthlin reminded his listeners. Elder Russell M. Nelson quoted Joseph's personal assessment of himself: "I never told you I was perfect; but there is no error in the revelations which I have taught."[64]

"Time judges all men," observed William E. Berrett, "most of us rather severely. Few of us are remembered long after the grave is closed except by our most intimate friends and family. . . . It is

interesting to note that at the end of a century there are more
devoted followers of [Joseph Smith], more who are paying obedience
to those things he taught."[65] In the same light, Elder Ezra Taft Benson
commented: "I have thumbed through more than a score of volumes
on the Prophet in my own library and recalled there are, it is
reported, more than 1,600 separate volumes and more than 20,000
books and pamphlets which refer to the prophet in the library of the
Church."[66]

It is not in the least surprising that the most frequently quoted
statement and scripture by all of the memorial speakers in esteeming
the Prophet Joseph was John Taylor's tribute found in the 135th section of the Doctrine and Covenants. "Joseph Smith, the Prophet and
Seer of the Lord, has done more, save Jesus only, for the salvation of
men in this world, than any other man that ever lived in it" (D&C
135:3). Dr. Eyring said, "I do believe and I don't see how others can
help but believe that there is no greater man in the last two centuries
and no other person who has more effectively caught hold of
people's minds and led them than has Joseph Smith, with the exception of the Savior Himself who lived about 2,000 years ago."[67]

Elder Widtsoe identified the qualities that contributed to Joseph's
greatness, "the cornerstones of his character": "First, he had an
unchanging faith and trust in God. Second, he loved the truth.
Third, he was humble, and fourth, he loved his fellow men."[68] "The
Prophet Joseph Smith was creative," asserted Lowell L. Bennion,
"Everything he touched became a new thing. In him was something
of the curiosity of a child, the imagination of an artist, the practical
zeal of a reformer, the idealism of a Utopian and the fire of a Prophet.
His theology is dynamic. He used religion to remake life."[69] Brother
Bennion then concluded, "Joseph Smith stood upon a wall with a
plumb line in his hand, and every important institution of life which
was not in line with the fundamental principles and purposes of religion and human welfare must needs be made straight."[70]

Wesley P. Lloyd assured that each of us "will recognize with gratitude the mission of the Prophet and his part in affecting where and
how we live; his part in the determination of our present associates,
his part in the actual makeup of our families."[71] As to the makeup of
families, Elder Hartman Rector Jr., a convert to the Church, quipped:
"My wife and I had two children at the time the elders knocked on

the door, and we were expecting our third, and that was all that we were going to have. That was one for me, one for my wife, and one unplanned; then we found out why we are here. Now we have seven, and expecting another. Joseph Smith is responsible for five of my children."[72]

On a tender note, Elder Richard G. Scott related how the restored truths of the eternal plan of salvation affected how he and his wife dealt with the passing of their two infant children. He related his assurance that "we knew that Joseph Smith had promised that any child born before the age of accountability inherited the Celestial Kingdom. Difficult as it was to lose Richard and Andrea, we knew that we would live with them again." Elder Scott then posed a probing question: "What does Joseph Smith mean to you? What will he mean to you as your life unfolds? Will the truths he gave his life to sustain guide your life? Will you share them with others on both sides of the veil?"[73]

Elder Benson noted, "The greatest activity in this world or in the world to come is directly related to the work and mission of Joseph Smith."[74] The effects of the ministry of Joseph Smith do not merely linger on; rather, they grow in crescendo. Joseph's works and teachings affect virtually all aspects of our lives. The Book of Mormon, the Doctrine and Covenants, priesthood, love, eternal marriage and family, knowledge of truth, agency, and even the Constitution and politics[75] were but a few of the doctrinal legacies discussed in these sermons. Even "the JST has affected every member of the Church, including those who have not even heard about the JST," concluded Robert Matthews. How? Doctrines concerning the age of baptism, the three degrees of glory, Zion, celestial marriage, and priesthood quorums all came as a result of Joseph's work on the Bible.[76]

Barbara B. Smith, as president of the Relief Society, spoke about Joseph Smith's contribution to all women. She stated, "I think it is significant that all of the saving ordinances of the gospel are for women as well as men. From the beginning the freedom of truth, as revealed by the Prophet Joseph, has been available to all women."[77] Sister Smith then identified what she felt was one of the most enduring blessings bestowed upon the women of the Church, the organization and commission of the Relief Society. Joseph charged them to render service, to teach one another, to strengthen the community, and to unite the sisters around the world.[78] This inspired organization continues to grow in strength and number as a result of Joseph's turning the key in their behalf.

Focusing on the personal nature of restored truths, Elder Eyring observed, "Yes, his work will touch the lives of all who have lived on the earth. That is a contribution of breadth. But how has it touched your life? That is another way to think about it: as a contribution of depth. And for you, that will matter more."[79] Elder Eyring emphasized how to receive and respond to revelation, using Joseph Smith as our model: "More than for any other prophet, we have a clear and lengthy record from Joseph Smith of how we can communicate with God. . . . Your problem and mine is not to get God to speak to us. . . . Our problem is to hear. The Prophet Joseph is our master example in that art."[80]

Elder Christensen concluded his sermon with this admonition and promise: "Now what does this mean for all of us here this evening? . . . We should study more about the prophet. . . . Of greater importance, we should strive to incorporate into our lives the principles that he taught. . . . If [anyone] will receive and apply the teachings of Joseph Smith he will be made happy. Doubt and uncertainty will leave him. Glorious purpose will come into life. Family ties will be sweeter. Friendships will be dearer. Service will be nobler, and the peace of Christ will be his portion."[81]

A fitting concluding testimony to all Joseph has done for us was given in 1980 by Elder Gordon B. Hinckley, who testified: "I stand before you as one who has both heard and spoken testimony of him across [the world]. . . . We are inclined to exclaim, What hath God wrought through the instrumentality of His servant Joseph! As we assess the present we find strength. The Church flourishes in a world of secularism. It is a refuge of spirituality. . . . Never has it taken a step backward."[82]

President Hinckley concluded: "'When a man gives his life for the cause he has advocated, he meets the highest test of his honesty and sincerity that his own or any future generation can in fairness ask. When he dies for the testimony he has borne, all malicious tongues should ever after be silent, and all voices hushed in reverence before a sacrifice so complete.' . . . He was the servant of God, this Joseph raised up to become the mighty prophet of this dispensation, the restorer of the ancient truth."[83]

The annual Joseph Smith Memorial Sermons are truly a treasure trove, filled with nuggets of testimony, insight, wisdom, and inspiration. Reading them is an enriching experience in deepening one's love and appreciation for and testimony of this noble prophet of God. They constitute one of the most enduring tributes to the legacy of the Prophet Joseph Smith and his divinely directed mission. These sermons confirm what Leo Tolstoy observed, that Joseph was the one great American, "the only man who has brought forth any new ideas that could in the long range of time change the history of men."[84] This being the case, appropriately we sing, "Praise to the man who communed with Jehovah! . . . Praise to his memory. . . . Honored and blest be his ever great name!" For the time is not far distant when "millions shall know Brother Joseph again."[85]

APPENDIX

Joseph Smith Memorial Firesides, 1944–2005

	Date	Speaker	Title of Presentation
1	6 February 1944	Patriarch Joseph F. Smith	Joseph Smith— a Prophet
2	10 December 1944	BYU President David O. McKay	The Prophet Joseph Smith— on Doctrine and Organization
3	9 December 1945	President Howard S. McDonald	The Prophet Joseph Smith
4	8 December 1946	Elder John A. Widtsoe	Joseph Smith—Significance of the First Vision
5	17 December 1947	Sidney B. Sperry	An Evaluation of Joseph Smith and His Work
6	5 December 1948	Lowell L. Bennion	Joseph Smith—His Creative Role in Religion
7	4 December 1949	President J. Reuben Clark Jr.	The Prophet Joseph Smith— Equally Burdened with Moses
8	3 December 1950	G. Homer Durham	Joseph Smith and the Political World

9	2 December 1951	President Joseph Fielding Smith	Joseph Smith—Prophet of the Restoration
10	7 December 1952	President Stephen L. Richards	Joseph Smith—Prophet, Martyr
11	6 December 1953	William E. Berrett	Joseph Smith and the Verdict of Time
12	5 December 1954	T. Edgar Lyon	The Wentworth Letter & Religious America in 1842
13	4 December 1955	Elder Harold B. Lee	Joseph Smith, His Mission Divine
14	2 December 1956	Elder Wesley P. Lloyd	A New Dimension in Religious Thought and Action
15	15 December 1957	Henry Eyring	Religion in a Changing World
16	7 December 1958	Elder Hugh B. Brown	Joseph Smith Among the Prophets
17	6 December 1959	Boyd K. Packer	Joseph, Prophet Teacher
18	15 December 1960	Elder Howard W. Hunter	Joseph Smith—The Seer
19	5 December 1961	Elder Sterling W. Sill	The Leadership of Joseph Smith
20	6 December 1962	President Henry D. Moyle	The Prophet Joseph's Work
21	11 December 1963	Elder Thomas S. Monson	The Prophet Joseph Smith—Teacher by Example
22	6 December 1964	Robert K. Thomas	Joseph Smith Memorial Sermon (Untitled)
23	5 December 1965	Truman G. Madsen	Joseph Smith and the Source of Love
24	4 December 1966	President N. Eldon Tanner	Joseph Smith the Prophet
25	3 December 1967	Elder Ezra Taft Benson	Joseph Smith—Man of Destiny
26	8 December 1968	President Alvin R. Dyer	The Foundation in the Center Place of Zion

27	14 December 1969	Elder Mark E. Petersen	The Prophet and the True Knowledge of God
28	13 December 1970	President Spencer W. Kimball	The Prophet JosephSmith and the First Vision
29	12 December 1971	Bishop Victor L. Brown	The Prophet Joseph Smith— A Beacon in Our Lives
30	10 December 1972	Elder Hartman Rector Jr.	The Prophet Joseph Smith
31	9 December 1973	Robert J. Matthews	A Walk through the Bible with the Prophet Joseph Smith
32	19 January 1975	Elder Neal A. Maxwell	The Prophet Joseph Smith: Spiritual Statesman
33	18 January 1976	Richard L. Bushman	The Teachings of Joseph Smith
34	16 January 1977	Daniel H. Ludlow	Joseph Smith's Contribution to Understanding of Israel
35	15 January 1978	President Marion G. Romney	Joseph Smith the Seer, and Truth
36	28 January 1979	Barbara B. Smith	Joseph Smith—A Life of Love
37	3 February 1980	Elder Gordon B. Hinckley	Joseph Smith from the Perspective of 150 Years
38	25 January 1981	Elder James E. Faust	Joseph Smith, the Beloved Leader
39	January 1982	Truman G. Madsen	(No transcript available)
40	30 January 1983	Elder David B. Haight	Joseph Smith, the Stalwart
41	January 1984	Elaine Cannon	(No transcript available)
42	3 February 1985	Elder Russell M. Nelson	At the Heart of the Church
43	25 January 1986	President Jeffrey R. Holland	Joseph Smith Memorial Lecture (Untitled)
44	25 January 1987	Robert J. Matthews	The Joseph Smith Translation—A Blessing to the Church

45	17 January 1988	Elder Dallin H. Oaks	Free Agency and Freedom
46	29 January 1989	Elder M. Russell Ballard	The Prophet Joseph Smith and Later Prophets
47	21 January 1990	Elder Joseph B. Wirthlin	The Prophet Joseph Smith
48	13 January 1991	Elder Richard G. Scott	The Prophet Joseph Smith
49	19 January 1992	Elder Henry B. Eyring	For the Salvation of Men in This World
50	17 January 1993	Janette C. Hales	The Prophet Joseph Smith
51	16 January 1994	Elder L. Tom Perry	A Visit with the Prophet Joseph Smith
52	22 January 1995	Elder Joe J. Christensen	In Memory of the Prophet Joseph Smith
53	21 January 1996	Elder Henry B. Eyring	(No transcript available)
54	26 January 1997	Elder Vaughn J. Featherstone	The Unspeakable Gift of the Prophet Joseph Smith
55	8 February 1998	Elder Jay E. Jensen	The Prophet Joseph Smith— The First and the Last Lesson
56	31 January 1999	Elder Gary J. Coleman	Joseph Smith Memorial Lecture (Untitled)
57	27 February 2000	Elder Bruce D. Porter	Joseph Smith Memorial Lecture (Untitled)
58	25 February 2001	Elder D. Todd Christofferson	Joseph Smith—The Revelator of Jesus Christ
59	10 February 2002	Elder Henry B. Eyring	He Could Not Do Otherwise
60	February 2003	Elder Cree-L Kofford	(No transcript available)
61	25 January 2004	Elder L. Tom Perry	(No transcript available)
62	3 February 2005	F. Melvin Hammond	The Prophet Joseph Smith

NOTES

1. A complete *list* of speakers is found in the appendix (above).

2. Thumbnail History of the Logan Institute, 1928–1957, unpublished manuscript, Special Collections Library of the Logan Institute of Religion.

3. Daryl Chase, *Joseph the Prophet, As He Lives in the Hearts of His People* (Salt Lake City: Deseret Book, 1944), 7–8.

4. The Annual Joseph Smith Memorial Sermons, Vol. 1 (Sermons 1–10), Logan, UT, 1966.

5. Oldest son of Hyrum Mack Smith, son of President Joseph F. Smith—President of the Church, 1901–1918.

6. Director Daryl Chase later became president of Utah State University. The two instructors were Milton R. Hunter, who was called to the First Council of the Seventy a year later, and Wilford W. Richards, who succeeded Chase as Logan Institute director.

7. No number was available for this year. The Logan institute enrollment for 1945–46 was 846.

8. William E. Berrett, "Joseph Smith and the Verdict of Time," transcript, Logan institute, 1953, 1.

9. Russell M. Nelson, "At the Heart of the Church," transcript, Logan institute, 1985, 1.

10. Richard G. Scott, "The Prophet Joseph Smith," transcript, Logan institute, 1991, 3–4.

11. Thomas S. Monson, "The Prophet Joseph Smith—Teacher by Example," transcript, Logan institute, 1963, 1.

12. Gary J. Coleman, transcript, Logan institute, 1999, 12.

13. Sterling W. Sill, "The Leadership of Joseph Smith," transcript, Logan institute, 1961, 8–9.

14. Harold B. Lee, "Joseph Smith, His Mission Divine," transcript, Logan institute, 1955, 5.

15. Howard W. Hunter, "Joseph Smith—The Seer," transcript, Logan institute, 1960, 3.

16. Coleman, transcript, 5–6; quoting *Journal of Discourses* (London: Latter-day Saints' Book Depot, 1854–86), 21:163.

17. David B. Haight, "Joseph Smith, the Stalwart," transcript, Logan institute, 1983, 3.

18. Nelson, "At the Heart of the Church," 4.

19. Hugh B. Brown, "Joseph Smith Among the Prophets," transcript, Logan institute, 1958, 10.

20. Boyd K. Packer, "Joseph, Prophet Teacher," transcript, Logan institute, 1959, 1.

21. James E. Faust, "Joseph Smith, the Beloved Leader," transcript, Logan institute, 1981, 1–2.
22. Joseph F. Smith, "Joseph Smith—A Prophet," transcript, Logan institute, 1944, 2.
23. Smith, "Joseph Smith—A Prophet," 6.
24. David O. McKay, "The Prophet Joseph Smith on Doctrine and Organization," transcript, Logan institute, 1944, 7–8.
25. Joe J. Christensen, "In Memory of the Prophet Joseph Smith," transcript, Logan institute, 1995, 4. quoting "Joseph Smith Among the Prophets" (The New England Mission of The Church of Jesus Christ of Latter-day Saints, 1963), 5–6.
26. Spencer W. Kimball, "The Prophet Joseph Smith and the First Vision," transcript, Logan institute, 1970, 7.
27. John A. Widtsoe, "Joseph Smith—Significance of the First Vision," transcript, Logan institute, 1946, 1.
28. Widtsoe, "Joseph Smith—Significance of the First Vision," 3–4.
29. Mark E. Petersen, "The Prophet and the True Knowledge of God," transcript, Logan institute, 1969, 6–7.
30. Sidney B. Sperry, "An Evaluation of Joseph Smith and His Work," transcript, Logan institute, 1947, 2.
31. Jay E. Jensen, "The Prophet Joseph Smith—The First and the Last Lesson," transcript, Logan institute, 1998, 1.
32. Petersen, "The Prophet and the True Knowledge of God," 1–3.
33. Christensen, "In Memory of the Prophet Joseph Smith," 3.
34. Berrett, "Joseph Smith and the Verdict of Time," 4.
35. Robert K. Thomas, transcript, Logan institute, 1964, 4–6.
36. Truman G. Madsen, "Joseph Smith and the Source of Love," transcript, Logan institute, 1965, 2–3.
37. Robert J. Matthews, "The Joseph Smith Translation—A Blessing to the Church," transcript, Logan institute, 1987, 1.
38. Matthews, "The Joseph Smith Translation—A Blessing to the Church," 6.
39. Matthews, "The Joseph Smith Translation—A Blessing to the Church," 4.
40. Matthews, "The Joseph Smith Translation—A Blessing to the Church," 5.
41. Robert J. Matthews, "A Walk through the Bible with the Prophet Joseph Smith," transcript, Logan institute, 1973, 14.
42. Matthews, "The Joseph Smith Translation—A Blessing to the Church," 2.

43. Daniel H. Ludlow, "Joseph Smith's Contribution to an Understanding of Israel," transcript, Logan institute, 1977, 2.
44. Ludlow, "Joseph Smith's Contribution to an Understanding of Israel," 10.
45. Alvin R. Dyer, "The Foundation in the Center Place of Zion," transcript, Logan institute, 1968, 8.
46. Dyer, "The Foundation in the Center Place of Zion," 5–6; quoting *History of the Church*, VI, 318–19.
47. L. Tom Perry, "A Visit with the Prophet Joseph Smith," transcript, Logan institute, 1994, 5.
48. N. Eldon Tanner, "Joseph Smith the Prophet," transcript, Logan institute, 1966, 8.
49. Tanner, "Joseph Smith the Prophet," 10.
50. Jeffrey R. Holland, transcript, Logan institute, 1986, 18.
51. Holland, transcript, Logan institute, 1986, 19–22.
52. Holland, transcript, Logan institute, 1986, 21.
53. Dallin H. Oaks, "Free Agency and Freedom," transcript, Logan institute, 1988, 2.
54. Sperry, "An Evaluation of Joseph Smith and His Work," 7–8.
55. Henry B. Eyring, "Religion in a Changing World," transcript, Logan institute, 1957, 3.
56. Henry D. Moyle, "The Prophet Joseph's Work," transcript, Logan institute, 1962, 1.
57. G. Homer Durham, "Joseph Smith and the Political World," transcript, Logan institute, 1950, 3.
58. Bruce D. Porter, transcript, Logan institute, 2000, 7.
59. M. Russell Ballard, "The Prophet Joseph Smith and Later Prophets," transcript, Logan institute, 1989, 2.
60. Howard S. McDonald, "The Prophet Joseph Smith," transcript, Logan institute, 1945, 2.
61. McDonald, "The Prophet Joseph Smith," 2.
62. Neal A. Maxwell, "The Prophet Joseph Smith: Spiritual Statesman," transcript, Logan institute, 1975, 12.
63. Joseph B. Wirthlin, "The Prophet Joseph Smith," transcript, Logan institute, 1990, 17.
64. Nelson, "At the Heart of the Church," 6; quoting Joseph Smith, *Teachings of the Prophet Joseph Smith,* comp. Joseph Fielding Smith (Salt Lake City: Deseret Book, 1938), 368.
65. Berrett, "Joseph Smith and the Verdict of Time," 1.
66. Ezra Taft Benson, "Joseph Smith—Man of Destiny," transcript, Logan institute, 1967, 1.

67. Eyring, "Religion in a Changing World," 2.

68. Widtsoe, "The Prophet Joseph Smith," 14.

69. Lowell L. Bennion, "Joseph Smith—His Creative Role in Religion," transcript, Logan institute, 1948, 2.

70. Bennion, "An Evaluation of Joseph Smith and His Work," 7.

71. Lloyd, "Joseph Smith—His Creative Role In Religion," 7.

72. Hartman Rector Jr., "The Prophet Joseph Smith," transcript, Logan institute, 1972, 3.

73. Scott, "The Prophet Joseph Smith," 18.

74. Benson, "Joseph Smith—Man of Destiny," 3.

75. Maxwell, "The Prophet Joseph Smith: Spiritual Statesman," 1.

76. Matthews, "The Joseph Smith Translation—A Blessing to the Church," 7–8.

77. Barbara B. Smith, "Joseph Smith—A Life of Love," transcript, Logan institute, 1979, 8.

78. Smith, "Joseph Smith—A Life of Love," 9–11.

79. Henry B. Eyring, "For the Salvation of Men in This World," transcript, Logan institute, 1992, 1.

80. Eyring, "For the Salvation of Men," 2.

81. Christensen, "In Memory of the Prophet Joseph Smith," 10.

82. Gordon B. Hinckley, "Joseph Smith from the Perspective of 150 Years," transcript, Logan institute, 1980, 10.

83. Hinckley, 12; quoting Ezra Dalby, Dec. 12, 1926.

84. Berrett, "Joseph Smith and the Verdict of Time," 5.

85. "Praise to the Man," *Hymns* (Salt Lake City: The Church of Jesus Christ of Latter-day Saints), no. 27.

CHAPTER TWENTY-THREE

THE CALLING OF THE TWELVE APOSTLES AND THE SEVENTY IN 1835

RICHARD E. TURLEY JR.

The Zion's Camp march of 1834 helped refine those who participated in it, providing them not only with experience that they could apply later in life but also proving to Church leaders which members were willing to "hearken . . . unto the counsel which . . . the Lord their God, shall give unto them" (D&C 103:5; see also Abraham 3:25).[1] Part of the revelation calling for the organization of Zion's Camp commanded, "Let no man be afraid to lay down his life for my sake; . . . and whoso is not willing to lay down his life for my sake is not my disciple" (D&C 103:27–28). Zion's Camp thus became an Abrahamic test of worthiness, and when that test was over, the Lord declared, "There has been a day of calling, but the time has come for a day of choosing; and let those be chosen that are worthy." The revelation designated Joseph Smith as the one through whom "the voice of the Spirit" would manifest those who "are chosen" (D&C 105:35–36).

On Sunday, February 8, 1835, the Prophet Joseph Smith invited Brigham Young and his brother Joseph Young to his home in Kirtland and "proceeded to relate a vision to these brethren, of the state and condition of those men who died in Zion's Camp, in Missouri." Some persons had worried about those who died on the march, and Joseph's vision responded to their concern, moving and

Richard E. Turley Jr. is managing director of the Family and Church History Department of The Church of Jesus Christ of Latter-day Saints.

comforting both him and those who accepted his testimony of it. "Brethren," he told his visitors tearfully, "I have seen those men who died of the cholera in our camp; and the Lord knows, if I get a mansion as bright as theirs, I ask no more."[2]

The Prophet wept for some time before turning to Brigham Young and directing, "I wish you to notify all the brethren living in the branches, within a reasonable distance from this place, to meet at a General Conference on Saturday next. I shall then and there appoint twelve special witnesses, to open the door of the gospel to foreign nations." Pointing to Brigham, he said, "And you . . . will be one of them." After further describing the responsibilities of the Twelve, the Prophet turned to Joseph Young and said, "Brother Joseph, the Lord has made you President of the Seventies."[3]

The Young brothers marveled at what they had been told. Joseph Young later recalled that "they had heard of Moses and seventy Elders of Israel, and of Jesus appointing other Seventies, but had never heard of Twelve Apostles and of Seventies being called in this Church before."[4]

Soon word went out to the branches of the Church in that area, announcing "a meeting of the brethren in General Conference" to be "held in Kirtland, in the new school house under the printing office" the next Saturday.[5] The meeting was open to Church members generally but was intended especially for "those who journeyed to Zion for the purpose of laying the foundation of its redemption."[6]

On Saturday, February 14, 1835, Joseph Smith opened the meeting by reading John 15 from the New Testament, a chapter that resounded with verses meaningful to the Zion's Camp members and pertinent to the meeting's purpose.[7] "After an appropriate and affecting prayer," Joseph spoke directly to the Zion's Camp veterans, telling them that the meeting was being held because "God had commanded it and it was made known to him by vision and by the Holy Spirit."[8]

After relating "some of the circumstances attending us while journeying to Zion, our trials, sufferings, &c.," Joseph "said God had not designed all this for nothing, but he had it in remembrance yet." Joseph revealed that it was God's will that "those who went to Zion, with a determination to lay down their lives, if necessary, . . . should be ordained to the ministry and go forth to prune the vineyard for the last time." Joseph said that "even the smallest and weakest among" them could accomplish "great things." He predicted, "From this hour . . . you shall begin to feel the whisperings of the Spirit of God, and the work of God shall begin to break forth from this time, you shall be endowed with power from on high." Joseph invited all Zion's Camp members who "agreed with him" to stand; they all rose to their feet. He asked the remaining members of the congregation "if they would sanction the movement. They all raised the right hand."[9]

After an intermission, Joseph declared the first order of business to be "for the three witnesses of the Book of Mormon, to pray each one and then proceed to choose twelve men from the Church as Apostles to go to all nations, kindred, to[ngue]s and people." The Three Witnesses prayed and "were then blessed by the laying on of the hands of the Presid[e]ncy." Having prepared their hearts and minds, "they then according to a former commandment, proceeded to make choice of the *twelve.*"[10]

The "former commandment" was a revelation given in June 1829 before the Church was organized. In it, the Lord spoke to Oliver Cowdery and David Whitmer "even as unto Paul mine apostle," telling them that they were called "with that same calling with which he was called" (D&C 18:9).[11] The revelation outlined qualifications for the Twelve and commanded Oliver and David to "search out the Twelve," who would "have the desires of which I have spoken," instructing the Witnesses that "by their desires and their works you shall know them" (D&C 18:37–38).[12]

One of the Zion's Camp veterans attending the meeting of February 14, 1835, Heber C. Kimball, would cite this revelation and recall, "This was the day appointed for choosing." The Three Witnesses "proceeded to call forth those whom the Lord had manifested by his spirit to them, that they might make known their desires."[13] The names had earlier been reviewed by Joseph Smith.[14] Those called to the first Quorum of the Twelve in this dispensation were Lyman Johnson, Brigham Young, Heber C. Kimball, Orson Hyde, David W. Patten, Luke Johnson, William E. McLellin, John F. Boynton, Orson Pratt, William Smith, Thomas B. Marsh, and Parley P. Pratt.[15]

During that first meeting, Lyman Johnson, Brigham Young, and

Heber C. Kimball were ordained by the Three Witnesses. The next day, a Sunday, Oliver "Cowdery called forwar[d] Orson Hyde, David W. Patten and Luke Johnson and proceeded to their ordination & blessing." William E. McLellin, John F. Boynton, and William Smith were ordained the same day. On Saturday, February 21, "Parley P. Pratt was called to the stand and ordained as one of the Twelve" by Joseph Smith, David Whitmer, and Oliver Cowdery.[16]

Although each blessing was unique to the Apostle who received it, Heber C. Kimball summed them all up when he wrote that they "predicted many things which should come to pass, that we should have power to heal the sick, cast out devils, raise the dead, give sight to the blind, have power to remove mountains, and all things should be subject to us through the name of Jesus Christ, and angels should minister unto us, and many more things too numerous to mention."[17]

While organizing the Twelve, the Prophet Joseph Smith prepared to organize the Seventy. On February 28, Joseph Smith, Sidney Rigdon, and Oliver Cowdery began to ordain "certain individuals to be Seventies, from the number of those who went up to Zion." The next day, March 1, the meeting reconvened, Joseph Smith spoke, and other Seventy were ordained.[18]

According to Elder Kimball, the ordained members of the Twelve "assembled from time to time as opportunity would permit, and received such instruction as the Lord would bestow upon us, and truly he blessed us with his spirit, and inspired his prophet to speak for our edification."[19] On March 28, 1835, the members of the Twelve who had been ordained to that point met in council. In a few weeks, they would leave together on a mission, and in preparation for that experience, they "unitedly asked God, our Heavenly Father to grant unto us through his Seer, a revelation of his mind and will concerning our duty this coming season."[20] Heber C. Kimball wrote that while they "were assembled to receive instructions, the revelation . . . on Priesthood was given to Brother Joseph as he was instructing us, and we praised the Lord."[21] The revelation declared, among other things, that "the twelve traveling councilors are called to be the Twelve Apostles, or special witnesses of the name of Christ in all the world—thus differing from other officers in the church in the duties of their calling. . . . The Seventy are also called to preach the gospel, and to be especial witnesses" (D&C 107:23, 25). The Twelve were "to officiate . . . under the direction of the Presidency," and the Seventy "under the direction of the Twelve" (D&C 107:33–34).

The remaining two members called to the original Twelve in the last dispensation, Thomas B. Marsh and Orson Pratt, were away on a mission at the time, and thus had not yet been ordained. Brother Marsh returned to Kirtland from his mission on April 25.[22] On April 26, the eleven new Apostles met together, awaiting the arrival of Orson Pratt to complete their quorum.[23]

Twenty-three-year-old Orson had apparently known for years that he would be an Apostle. Sometime after the 1829 revelation was received directing the Three Witnesses to select the Twelve, Joseph Smith had shown it to Orson, telling him he would "be one of this Twelve." Joseph's words startled him. "I looked upon the Twelve Apostles who lived in ancient days with a great deal of reverence— as being almost superhuman," Orson later said. "They were, indeed, great men—not by virtue of the flesh, nor their own natural capacities, but they were great because God called them." The idea that he might become an Apostle awed Orson.[24]

Later, he had gone to Missouri with the Prophet in Zion's Camp and remained there for months on a mission before returning to Ohio. Reaching Columbus, he asked directions "of a man who was standing in the street" and was surprised to discover that he was a Church member. Orson followed the man home, where he saw the Latter-day Saint paper published in Kirtland.[25] In the paper was a notice that Thomas B. Marsh and Orson Pratt were "desired to attend a meeting of the elders" in Kirtland on April 26. "We hope that circumstances may render it convenient for them to attend," the paper continued, "as their presence is very desirable."[26] With assistance, he hurried by stage and foot to Kirtland, arriving at the meeting "valise in hand."[27] Orson was "invited to take [his] seat as one of the 12."[28]

The eleven members of the Twelve meeting in Kirtland on April 26 had waited expectantly for him. Orson would learn that during that meeting and in previous ones "it had been prophesied . . . [that] I would be there on that day. They had predicted this, although they had not heard of me for some time, and did not know where I was." Yet "the Lord poured out the spirit of prophecy upon them, and they predicted I would be there at that meeting." When Orson walked in, "many of the Saints could scarcely believe their own eyes, the pre-diction was fulfilled before them so perfectly."[29] "At this time while we were praying, and wishing for his arrival," Elder Kimball recalled, "while opening the meeting he entered the house, [and] we rejoiced at his presence, and thanked the Lord for it."[30] Thomas B. Marsh and Orson Pratt were ordained later that day by Oliver Cowdery and David Whitmer.[31]

Under the direction of Joseph Smith, Oliver Cowdery spoke to the Twelve and gave them an apostolic charge. He prefaced it by cit-ing the revelation directing "that in process of time there should be Twelve chosen to preach his gospel to Jew & Gentile." During the intervening years, Cowdery reflected, "Our minds have been on a constant stretch to find who these Twelve were."[32] Those directed to select the Twelve did not know "when the time should come" but earnestly "sought the Lord by fasting and prayer to have our lives prolonged to see this day, to see you, and to take a retrospect of the difficulties through which we have passed." The day having come, he gave the Twelve a lengthy charge describing the importance of the calling, the sacrifices it would require, and the blessings that would flow through humble and obedient service to the Lord.[33]

Having delivered the charge, President Cowdery took each mem-ber of the Twelve "separately by the hand" and asked, "Do you with full purpose of heart take part in this ministry, to proclaim the gospel with all diligence with these your brethren, according to the tenor and intent of the charge you have received?" Each in turn committed to do so.[34] The Twelve was then fully organized, and its members pre-pared to set off on a mission together.[35]

On May 2, a "grand council" of the Church's General Authorities was held in Kirtland at which Joseph Smith presided. The conference opened with a prayer by Brigham Young, and Joseph instructed the Twelve on how to organize for conducting business. The eldest was to preside in the first meeting, the second oldest in the second meet-ing, and so on until each had presided, then start over again.[36] This approach made sense at first when the Twelve had all been called and ordained at roughly the same time. Later, however, the system was changed, gradually developing into the current practice by which "the date . . . a person becomes a member of the Quorum (usually the date he is sustained as an apostle) establishes his position of seniority in the Quorum relative to other quorum members."[37]

The May 2 meeting also dealt with the question of the Twelve's jurisdiction, another feature that would change over time. Joseph Smith instructed the Twelve that they had "no right to go into Zion or any of its stakes and there undertake to regulate the affairs thereof where there is a standing High Council." Instead, their jurisdiction extended only to the areas outside Zion, the Church's center place in Missouri, "or any of its stakes."[38] The separate jurisdictions between the Twelve and the high councils in Zion and its stakes would raise questions of overall seniority in Church administration, and after the members of the Twelve returned from their second mission to Great Britain in the early 1840s, Joseph Smith broadened the Twelve's jurisdiction to cover the entire Church worldwide. The Quorum of the Twelve then stood second only to the First Presidency in overseeing Church affairs across the globe.[39]

At the May 2 meeting, Joseph also provided for the new system of seventies to expand as necessary to meet the Church's growing needs. He explained that if the first Seventy were all employed in the Lord's work and more help was needed, the seven presidents had a duty "to call and ordain other Seventy and send them forth to labor in the vineyard." At the same time, although the Seventy as a quorum were considered in one sense "equal in authority" (D&C 107:26) as a body to the Twelve, they were clearly subordinate in terms of day-to-day administration.[40] Joseph made it clear in the meeting, for example, that "the Seventy are not to attend the conferences of the Twelve unless they are called upon or requested to by the Twelve." After Joseph spoke, additional seventies were called forward and ordained, as were yet others after the conference adjourned and reconvened.[41]

After calling the Twelve and the Seventy, Joseph responded to elders in Kirtland who were disappointed when the men of Zion's Camp did not fight in Missouri.[42] "Let me tell you," Joseph said, "God did not want you to fight. He could not organize his kingdom with twelve men to open the gospel door to the nations of the earth, and with seventy men under their direction to follow in their tracks, unless he took them from a body of men who had offered their lives, and who had made as great a sacrifice as did Abraham." With apparent satisfaction, he added, "Now, the Lord has got his Twelve and his Seventy, and there will be other quorums of Seventies called, who will make the sacrifice, and those who have not made their sacrifices and their offerings now, will make them hereafter."[43] Although further changes would occur over time, Joseph Smith's organization of the Twelve and the Seventy in Kirtland in 1835 would provide the foundation for leading the Church in the generations that followed.

NOTES

1. On the impact of Zion's Camp, see B. H. Roberts, *A Comprehensive History of the Church of Jesus Christ of Latter-day Saints* (Provo, UT: Brigham Young University Press, 1965), 1:370–71; Joseph Young Sr., *History of the Organization of the Seventies* (Salt Lake City: Deseret News, 1878), 14; *History of The Church of Jesus Christ of Latter-day Saints,* ed. B. H. Roberts, 2nd ed. rev. (Salt Lake City: Deseret Book, 1976), 2:182n; Brigham Young, October 23, 1853, in *Journal of Discourses* (Liverpool: F. D. Richards, 1855), 2:10; Church Educational System, *Church History in the Fulness of Times: The History of the Church of Jesus Christ of Latter-day Saints,* 2nd ed. (Salt Lake City: The Church of Jesus Christ of Latter-day Saints, 2000), 151; Ronald K. Esplin, "The Emergence of Brigham Young and the Twelve to Mormon Leadership, 1830–1841" (Ph.D. diss., Brigham Young University, 1981), 122–25, 128.

2. Young, *History of the Organization of the Seventies,* 1; Smith, *History of the Church,* 2:180–81.

3. Young, *History of the Organization of the Seventies,* 1–2.

4. Young, *History of the Organization of the Seventies,* 2. Apostles had been mentioned in earlier revelations. For example, in June 1829, the Lord spoke to Oliver Cowdery and David Whitmer "as unto Paul mine apostle" because they were "called . . . with that same calling with which he was called" (D&C 18:9). The Articles and Covenants of the Church described Joseph Smith and Oliver Cowdery each as "an apostle of Jesus Christ" (D&C 20:2–3). On Moses and seventy elders of Israel, see Exodus 24:1, 9–11; Numbers 11:16–17, 24–25. On Christ's appointment of "other seventy," see Luke 10:1–20.

5. Young, *History of the Organization of the Seventies,* 2.

6. Kirtland High Council Minutes, 147, in Richard E. Turley Jr., ed., *Selected Collections from the Archives of The Church of Jesus Christ of Latter-day Saints* (Provo, UT: Brigham Young University Press, 2002), vol. 1, DVD 19; Smith, *History of the Church,* 2:181. Heber C. Kimball recalled that the "meeting was called for the camp of Zion to be assembled, to receive what was called a Zion's blessing"

("Extracts from H. C. Kimball's Journal," *Times and Seasons*, April 15, 1845, 868).

7. Kirtland High Council Minutes, 147; *History of the Church*, 2:181. Roberts, *Comprehensive History of the Church*, 1:373, writes:

"The Prophet read at the opening of the conference the 15th chapter of *St. John;* the appropriateness of it is striking. In it is stressed the needed union with the Christ. So close that it must be as the branch to the vine, if it would have life; love so great that it will not withhold life as a sacrifice to friendship—and greater love hath no man than this, that a man lay down his life for his friends; the apostles are declared to be friends to the Christ. Ye have not chosen me but I have chosen you and ordained you that ye may bring forth much fruit. Love one another;" and "if the world hate you, ye know that it hated me before it hated you. . . . the servant is not greater than his Lord. If they have persecuted me they will persecute you. . . . They hated me without a cause. . . . But when the Comforter is come . . . even the Spirit of Truth . . . he will testify of me; and ye also shall bear witness. How fitting the scripture to the occasion!"

8. Kirtland High Council Minutes, 147; *History of the Church*, 2:181–82. Since others were in attendance besides the Zion's Camp members, "the Brethren who went to Zion, were requested to take their seats together in one part of the house by themselves" (Kirtland High Council Minutes, 147).

9. Kirtland High Council Minutes, 147–48; *History of the Church*, 2:182. Not all who were ordained participated in Zion's Camp, but most did, including nine of the Twelve and all of the original members of the First Quorum of Seventy (Milton V. Backman Jr., *The Heavens Resound: A History of the Latter-day Saints in Ohio, 1830–1838* [Salt Lake City: Deseret Book, 1983], 199; *Church History in the Fulness of Times*, 151). The three Apostles who did not were Thomas B. Marsh, John F. Boynton, and William E. McLellin (Esplin, "Emergence of Brigham Young and the Twelve," 129).

10. Kirtland High Council Minutes, 149; emphasis in original; *History of the Church*, 2:186–87.

11. According to Brigham Young, April 7, 1852, in *Journal of Discourses* (Liverpool: Asa Calkin, 1859), 6:320, "Joseph Smith, Oliver Cowdery, and David Whitmer were the first Apostles of this dispensation." Brigham Young, April 6, 1853, in *Journal of Discourses* (Liverpool: F. D. and S. W. Richards, 1854), 1:134, clarified, "Joseph was ordained an Apostle." Heber C. Kimball, November 8, 1857, in *Journal of Discourses*, 6:29, said that Joseph ordained all three Book of Mormon witnesses Apostles (see D&C 27:12). Martin Harris's

ordination as an Apostle seems confirmed by Doctrine and Covenants 19:8–9.

12. B. H. Roberts opined that "it was designed from the first that the Three Witnesses should choose the Twelve" but that "Martin Harris was out of favor with the Lord" when Doctrine and Covenants 18 was given, "for which reason doubtless his name is not there associated with those of his fellow Witnesses when they were designated to choose the Twelve." Roberts suggested that Joseph was later inspired of the Lord to include Martin "in choosing the Apostles" (*History of the Church*, 2:186–87n).

13. "Extracts from H. C. Kimball's Journal," 868.

14. At least one substitution was made in the original list of those chosen (see Esplin, "Emergence of Brigham Young and the Twelve," 147–48n108).

15. Kirtland High Council Minutes, 149; *History of the Church*, 2:187; "Extracts from H. C. Kimball's Journal," 868.

16. Kirtland High Council Minutes, 149, 151, 153–54; *History of the Church*, 2:187, 189–91. The record does not name who ordained each person. For B. H. Roberts's best guess on who ordained whom, see *Comprehensive History of the Church*, 1:374–75n13. After the ordination, Oliver Cowdery gave Parley P. Pratt a charge, not to be confused with the one Cowdery gave to the Twelve later.

17. "Extracts from H. C. Kimball's Journal," 868. For the text of the blessings, see Kirtland High Council Minutes, 149–55; *History of the Church*, 2:188–92.

18. *History of the Church*, 2:201–4; Kirtland High Council Minutes, 164, 169, 172. Smith, *History of the Church*, 2:203, also lists the presidents and members of the newly called Seventy. Individual blessings of members of the Seventy can be found in the Kirtland High Council Minutes, 164–86.

19. "Extracts from H. C. Kimball's Journal," 868–69.

20. Kirtland High Council Minutes, 198; Robert J. Woodford, "The Historical Development of the Doctrine and Covenants" (Ph.D. diss., Brigham Young University, 1974), 3:1398.

21. "Extracts from H. C. Kimball's Journal," 869; Woodford, "Historical Development of the Doctrine and Covenants," 3:1399.

22. *History of the Church*, 2:193.

23. "Extracts from H. C. Kimball's Journal," 869.

24. Orson Pratt, August 11, 1867, in *Journal of Discourses*, 12:86.

25. Orson Pratt Diary, vol. 2, April 20, 1835, Church Archives, The Church of Jesus Christ of Latter-day Saints, Salt Lake City; Pratt, August 11, 1867, in *Journal of Discourses*, 12:86.

26. *Latter Day Saints' Messenger and Advocate*, March 1835, 90; Pratt

Diary, vol. 2, April 20, 1835; Pratt, August 11, 1867, in *Journal of Discourses*, 12:86.

27. Pratt, August 11, 1867, in *Journal of Discourses*, 12:87.

28. Pratt Diary, vol. 2, April 26, 1835.

29. Pratt, August 11, 1867, in *Journal of Discourses*, 12:87.

30. "Extracts from H. C. Kimball's Journal," 869.

31. Pratt Diary, vol. 2, April 26, 1835.

32. Kirtland High Council Minutes, 158; *History of the Church*, 2:195. On October 26, 1831, Oliver Cowdery wrote that he and David Whitmer "had received this morning [directions] respecting the choice of the twelve . . . that they would be ordained & sent forth from the Land of Zion" (Donald Q. Cannon and Lyndon W. Cook, eds., *Far West Record: Minutes of The Church of Jesus Christ of Latter-day Saints, 1830–1844* [Salt Lake City: Deseret Book, 1983], 26). The Missouri persecutions, however, required changing the location from Zion to Kirtland.

33. Kirtland High Council Minutes, 159–64; *History of the Church*, 2:194–98.

34. Kirtland High Council Minutes, 164; *History of the Church*, 2:198. An apostolic charge would continue to be administered to new Apostles in subsequent generations. See, e.g., Francis M. Gibbons, *George Albert Smith: Kind and Caring Christian, Prophet of God* (Salt Lake City: Deseret Book, 1990), 45; Francis M. Gibbons, *Joseph Fielding Smith: Gospel Scholar, Prophet of God* (Salt Lake City: Deseret Book, 1992), 152; Francis M. Gibbons, *Harold B. Lee: Man of Vision, Prophet of God* (Salt Lake City: Deseret Book, 1993), 155; Francis M. Gibbons, *Spencer W. Kimball: Resolute Disciple, Prophet of God* (Salt Lake City: Deseret Book, 1995), 149; Neal A. Maxwell, in Conference Report, October 1981, 8, or *Ensign*, November 1981, 8; Jeffrey R. Holland, in Conference Report, October 1994, 40, or *Ensign*, November 1994, 32.

35. Pratt Diary, vol. 2, May 4, 1835; "Extracts from H. C. Kimball's Journal," 869; Esplin, "Emergence of Brigham Young and the Twelve," 157, 162, 163–66; Backman, *The Heavens Resound*, 251; Dean C. Jessee, ed., *The Papers of Joseph Smith* (Salt Lake City: Deseret Book, 1992), 2:143–49.

36. Kirtland High Council Minutes, 187; *History of the Church*, 2:219.

37. William O. Nelson, "Quorum of the Twelve Apostles," in *Encyclopedia of Mormonism*, ed. Daniel H. Ludlow (New York: Macmillan, 1992), 3:1188; see also Roberts, *Comprehensive History of the Church*, 5:519–24. This seniority, in turn, affects succession to the Presidency of the Church. "There is no mystery about the choosing of the successor to the President of the Church," Joseph

Fielding Smith wrote. "The Lord settled this a long time ago, and the *senior apostle automatically becomes the presiding officer of the Church*, and he is so sustained by the Council of the Twelve which becomes the presiding body of the Church when there is no First Presidency" (*Doctrines of Salvation*, comp. Bruce R. McConkie [Salt Lake City: Bookcraft, 1956], 3:156; emphasis in original). See also Gordon B. Hinckley, in Conference Report, April 1986, 61–62, or *Ensign*, May 1986, 46–47; James E. Faust, in Conference Report, October 1994, 94–95, or *Ensign*, November 1994, 72–73; Boyd K. Packer, in Conference Report, April 1995, 5–6, or *Ensign*, May 1995, 7; Hoyt W. Brewster Jr., *Prophets, Priesthood Keys, and Succession* (Salt Lake City: Deseret Book, 1991), 111–17; Backman, *The Heavens Resound*, 425n63.

38. Kirtland High Council Minutes, 187; *History of the Church*, 2:220; D&C 107:36–37.

39. "Conference Minutes," *Times and Seasons*, September 1, 1841, 521–22; *History of the Church*, 4:403; Backman, *The Heavens Resound*, 250, 426n64; Reed C. Durham Jr. and Steven H. Heath, *Succession in the Church* (Salt Lake City: Bookcraft, 1970), 47–54. See also Brewster, *Prophets, Priesthood Keys, and Succession*, 41–49; Roberts, *Comprehensive History of the Church*, 2:87–88, 368–71.

40. Kirtland High Council Minutes, 188; *History of the Church*, 2:221.

41. Kirtland High Council Minutes, 188; *History of the Church*, 2:221. For a list of Seventies called in Kirtland, see Young, *History of the Organization of the Seventies*, 2–4.

42. On the rumblings in Kirtland about Zion's Camp, see Joseph Smith to Lyman Wight and Others, August 16, 1834, in Dean C. Jessee, ed., *Personal Writings of Joseph Smith*, rev. ed. (Salt Lake City and Provo, UT: Deseret Book and Brigham Young University Press, 2002), 347–50; Backman, *The Heavens Resound*, 196; Marvin S. Hill, "Cultural Crisis in the Mormon Kingdom: A Reconsideration of the Causes of Kirtland Dissent," *Church History* 49, no. 3 (September 1980): 287–88.

43. Joseph Smith, address to the elders assembled in Kirtland, in Young, *History of the Organization of the Seventies*, 14. In the revelation releasing the members of Zion's Camp, the Lord declared, "I have heard their prayers, and will accept their offering; and it is expedient in me that they should be brought thus far for a trial of their faith" (D&C 105:19). Wilford Woodruff testified, "God accepted our works as He did the works of Abraham" (Woodruff, December 12, 1869, in *Journal of Discourses*, 13:158).

CHAPTER TWENTY-FOUR

JOSEPH SMITH'S RESTORATION OF THE ETERNAL ROLES OF HUSBAND AND FATHER

MARY JANE WOODGER

Brigham Young felt that Joseph Smith would "unite heaven with earth."[1] Part of that heaven as described by the Prophet Joseph was to put in place the family organization established by our Father in Heaven for His children. Joseph was a prophet, seer, and revelator. He was also a father, husband, and patriarch of a family unit. In all these roles he was exemplary. Professors Susan Easton Black and Larry C. Porter concur: "Those things done behind closed doors and unknown to the masses must be considered if one is to get a true picture of Joseph Smith, the man of God. . . . The Prophet Joseph understood well his exemplary role in a family unit. A busy life did not excuse him from a divine appointment, because he understood that the home is the basis of a righteous life and that it was the Lord's will for him to be an exemplary child, brother, husband, and father."[2]

By studying the life and teachings of the Prophet Joseph Smith, we can see that he exemplified principles declared one hundred fifty-one years after his death in "The Family: A Proclamation to the World."[3] Joseph told the Quorum of the Twelve Apostles, "A man filled with the love of God, is not content with blessing his family alone, but ranges through the whole world, anxious to bless the whole human race."[4] Joseph Smith's prophetic legacy blessed all

Mary Jane Woodger is an associate professor of Church history and doctrine at Brigham Young University.

humanity as he restored doctrine regarding the roles of husband and father that are also reflected in the proclamation.

As a husband, Joseph Smith treated his wife as an equal partner and fulfilled his solemn responsibility to love and care for her.

Joseph restored the correct pattern of marriage taught anciently by the Apostle Paul. This pattern of equal partnership and a husband's responsibility to love and care for a spouse are outlined in Colossians and Ephesians. These verses were repeated by Joseph in the November 1835 edition of the *Messenger and Advocate,* wherein he signed his epistle "In the bonds of the New and Everlasting Covenant"[5]:

> Wives, submit yourselves unto your own husbands, as unto the Lord, for the husband is the head of the wife, even as Christ is the head of the Church; and He is the Savior of the body. Therefore, as the Church is subject unto Christ, so let the wives be to their own husbands, in everything. Husbands, love your wives, even as Christ also loved the Church and gave Himself for it, that He might sanctify and cleanse it with the washing of water by the Word, that He might present it to Himself a glorious Church, not having spot or wrinkle, or any such thing, but that it should be holy and without blemish, so ought men to love their own wives as their own bodies. He that loveth his wife, loveth himself, for no man ever yet hated his own flesh, but nourisheth and cherisheth it, even as the Lord the Church, for we are members of His body, of His flesh, and His bones. For this cause shall a man leave his father and mother, and shall be joined unto his wife, and they two shall be one flesh. . . ." (Ephesians 5:22–31.)

> Husbands, love your wives, and be not bitter against them."(Colossians 3: 18–22.)

Joseph not only taught husbands to love their wives as Christ loves the Church, but he also exemplified it in his own marriage. He called Emma Hale his "choice in preference to any other woman [he had] ever seen,"[6] and his marriage to her on January 18, 1827, was the beginning of an affectionate relationship of equal partners.

Joseph learned early that the Lord valued Emma's "divine nature and destiny."[7] Emma was willing to marry Joseph at a time of persecution in his life—persecution and hardship that never ceased. Joseph learned early that the Lord valued not only Emma's role as a wife but also her role in the Restoration of the gospel of Jesus Christ. Early in their marriage, it was a blessing for Joseph to have the support, assistance, and strength of a wife while translating the Book of Mormon. The story is told of Joseph's trying to translate the Book of Mormon one morning after having a disagreement with Emma. "Going into the Whitmer orchard where he could be alone, Joseph spent an hour in supplication with the Lord. When he returned to the house, he asked Emma's forgiveness. He was then in the proper spiritual position to continue the translation."[8] Joseph learned through this experience and others that the Lord felt it was a solemn responsibility to be a husband. Things had to be right with him as a spouse before things were right with him as a prophet.

Entries in the Prophet's journal reveal that his and Emma's lives became completely entwined as they helped one another.[9] Joseph looked to her as a valued voice. In 1832, Joseph confided to Emma, "I should like [to] . . . converse with you on all the subjects which concern us, things . . . [that are] not prudent for me to write. I omit all the important things which, could I see you, I could make you acquainted with."[10] Joseph valued Emma's opinion, and conversing with her increased his joy and sustained him through his trials.

During 1838, Joseph faced severe trials as he was arrested and incarcerated in Missouri. Letters back and forth reveal the Smiths' equal partnership as Joseph expressed trust in Emma's ability to make good decisions as a mother in his absence.[11] In a letter on November 12, 1838, the Prophet wrote, "Act according to your own feelings and best judgment."[12] In another letter on April 4, 1839, he complimented Emma on her actions in his absence, saying, "I find no fault with you at all, I know nothing but what you have done the best you could." After spending five months in prison, he divulged, "The contemplations of the mind under these circumstances defies the pen, or tongue, or Angels to describe or paint to the human being, who never experienced what we experience."[13] In this communication he crossed out "I" and replaced it with "we," showing that Joseph was mindful of Emma's suffering in his persecutions.[14]

Joseph seems to have been consistently cognizant of Emma's contribution. For instance, Jesse S. Crosby observed Joseph doing what he called "women's work" and concluded that Joseph was "mismanag[ing] Emma." Crosby argued, "Brother Joseph, my wife does much more hard work than does your wife." The Prophet gave Crosby a "terrible reproof," saying that "if a man cannot learn in this life to appreciate a wife and do his duty by her, in properly taking care of her, he need not expect to be given one in the hereafter." Crosby said, "After that I tried to do better by the good wife I had and tried to lighten her labors."[15]

Such instances of Joseph's publicly honoring his wife were common. On one occasion, while having dinner at the Nauvoo Mansion House, Joseph remarked to W. W. Phelps that Emma was "a kind, provident wife," and if he just "wanted a little bread and milk, she would load the table with so many good things, it would destroy [his] appetite." Emma walked in on the conversation as Phelps replied, "You must do as Bonaparte did—have a little table, just large enough for the victuals you want yourself." Emma quipped, "Mr. Smith is a bigger man than Bonaparte: he can never eat without his friends." Joseph, complimenting his wife, responded, "That is the wisest thing I ever heard you say."[16] In similar fashion, on a Sunday morning while sitting with Benjamin Johnson in the mansion dining room, two of the Prophet's children came to Joseph just after Emma had changed their clothes. Joseph turned to his visitor and asked, "Benjamin, look at these children. How could I help loving their mother?"[17]

Joseph expressed such love for his wife constantly, addressing her as "My dear and beloved companion," "Dear and Affectionate Wife," and simply "My beloved Emma."[18] This sentiment written in 1839 would make any wife's heart tender: "If you want to know how much I want to see you . . . I would gladly walk from here to you barefoot, and bareheaded, and half naked, to see you and think it great pleasure, and never count it toil."[19] Joseph felt that his heart was entwined around Emma's.[20] Such tender feelings were also expressed through physical affection. In another letter dated November 12, 1838, he wrote of pressing his wife and children to his bosom and kissing their lovely cheeks.[21] Exemplifying his solemn responsibility of lovingly caring for his wife and children when denied this opportunity in prison, he expressed, "If God will spare my life once more to have the privilege of taking care of you, I will ease your care and endeavor to comfort your heart."[22] And in 1842, thinking back on his marital experiences, Joseph recalled, "Again she is here, even in the seventh trouble—undaunted, firm and unwavering—unchangeable, affectionate Emma."[23] Expressing admiration for Emma, Joseph emulated those principles espoused in the proclamation.

When Joseph was with Emma, his consideration for her was noticed by others. Mercy Rachel Thompson observed the Prophet "exhibiting all the solicitude and sympathy possible for the tenderest of hearts and the most affectionate of natures to feel" toward his wife.[24] During 1842, the Prophet's journal reports much concern over Emma's impending childbirth though the Prophet was not feeling well. As Emma became ill with a fever, the Prophet stayed by her bedside for several days. She worsened, and his extreme concern becomes evident in his journal:

> *Wednesday, 5.*—My dear Emma was worse. Many fears were entertained that she would not recover. . . . I was unwell, and much troubled on account of Emma's sickness.

> *Thursday, 6.*—Emma is better; . . . she appears considerably easier. May the Lord speedily raise her to the bosom of her family, that the heart of His servant may be comforted again. Amen. My health is comfortable.

> *Friday, 7.*— . . . Emma is somewhat better. I am cheerful and well.

> *Monday, 10.*— . . . Emma gaining slowly. My health and spirits are good.

> *Thursday, Nov. 1, 1842.*—I rode with Emma to the Temple for the benefit of her health. She is rapidly gaining.[25]

Later, one day after Christmas, Emma gave birth to a son who did not survive, and, as on many occasions, Joseph and Emma wept together. Though Emma recovered physically, Joseph continued to be concerned for her emotional well-being. Margarette Burgess tells of Joseph's coming to her mother and asking if he could borrow one of her twin girls to comfort Emma. Mrs. Burgess agreed, providing he would bring the child home each night. He punctually came for the twin every morning and returned the baby each night. After Emma became more emotionally stable, he stopped taking the baby, but he often visited the Burgesses to caress the baby and play with her.[26] Such actions reveal that Joseph fulfilled his solemn responsibility to love and care for his wife as outlined in the proclamation.

JOSEPH SMITH PRESIDED OVER HIS FAMILY IN LOVE AND RIGHTEOUSNESS AND TRIED TO PROVIDE THE NECESSITIES OF LIFE ALONG WITH PROTECTION.

Presiding. John Taylor remembered Joseph's teaching him the following doctrine about a father's responsibility to preside: "It is right for heads of families to get their families together every morning and evening, and pray with them."[27] Joseph practiced what he preached and was seen by others as the head of his household. Orson Pratt witnessed the Prophet leading his family in morning and evening devotionals, where "the words of eternal life flow[ed] from [the Prophet's] lips," words that were "nourishing and soothing and comforting [to] his family."[28] Another visitor to the Smith home, William H. Walker, arrived at the Prophet's house at nine o'clock in the evening to observe Joseph's family singing before evening prayer with Emma leading the music.[29] William F. Cahoon was assigned to be a ward (home) teacher to visit the Smiths when he was just seventeen years old. When Cahoon knocked, the Prophet came to the door and invited Cahoon in. Cahoon relates:

> They soon came in and took their seats. He [Joseph Smith] then said, "Brother William, I submit myself and family into your hands," and took his seat. "Now, Brother William," said he "ask all the questions you feel like."
> By this time all my fears and trembling had ceased, and I said, "Brother Joseph, are you trying to live your religion?"
> He answered "Yes."
> I then said "Do you pray in your family?"
> He said "Yes."
> "Do you teach your family the principles of the gospel?"
> He replied "Yes, I am trying to do it."
> "Do you ask a blessing on your food?"
> He answered "Yes."

"Are you trying to live in peace and harmony with all your family?"

He said that he was.

. . . I then turned to Joseph and said, "I am through with my questions as a teacher; and now if you have any instructions to give, I shall be happy to receive them."[30]

Joseph also encouraged wives to treat their husbands with respect, thus facilitating their husbands' ability to preside in the home. In remarks given to the first Relief Society on April 28, 1842, he taught wives to be more careful in their conversations. He urged, "You need not be teasing your husbands because of their deeds, but let the weight of your innocence, kindness, and affection be felt, which is more mighty than a millstone hung about the neck; not war, not jangle, not contradiction, or dispute, but meekness, love, purity—these are the things that should magnify you in the eyes of all good men. . . . When you go home, never give a cross or unkind word to your husbands, but let kindness, charity and love crown your works henceforward."[31]

As counseled above, Joseph Smith's mission to restore the gospel in its purity included restoring the principle of wives showing deference in their marital discussions. Such consideration encourages the placement of the husband as the head of the household. As the prophet of the Restoration, Joseph offered the glad tiding that husbands had the right and responsibility to preside in the homes they provided.

Providing. Susan Easton Black and Charles D. Tate Jr. tell us that the Smiths had little formal education because they all had to work just to stay alive. Joseph was known throughout his entire life as a hard worker.[32] Because Joseph was constantly moving and was also busy with preaching the gospel, it was difficult for him to do the work of the Lord and simultaneously provide for his family. Joseph was told in July 1830 that "in temporal labors thou shalt not have strength, for this is not thy calling" (D&C 24:9). Particularly after the organization of the Church in 1830, the Prophet's lifestyle necessarily shifted from that of an independent farmer to businessman and Church administrator. With this shift in responsibility, Emma was told in a revelation contained in the Book of Commandments, "Thy husband will support thee *from* the Church."[33] Later the word "from" was replaced with "in." Emma surely expected that their family would be supported by the Church. With Joseph's full-time Church calling, he was to receive full-time pay; however, when Joseph tried to obtain financial support from believers, more times than not it was withheld. He was constantly in need of aid, whether it was to publish the Book of Mormon or to supply his family's needs in Missouri. Records from Far West show Joseph not only being denied financial support but also being chastised for asking for it. During an 1840 high council meeting, Alma Babbitt accused Joseph of being extravagant for merely buying Emma a dress.[34]

During the years the Smiths spent in Nauvoo, between 1839 and 1844, Joseph had the opportunity to more fully provide for his family than he had previously done by becoming the trustee in trust of the Church and opening a store. "Of the thirty-five general stores in Nauvoo, the most important, if not the most profitable, was the Joseph Smith Red Brick Store."[35] Joseph opened the building in December 1841. A store daybook was kept from June 1842 to June 1844 showing that a wide variety of goods was sold. However, prophetically, Joseph proved to be unsuccessful in temporal concerns. Historian George W. Givens tells us, "A well-stocked store, a good location, a steady supply of customers, and a congenial proprietor would usually mean success in any store, but within months Joseph had turned his store over to others."[36] Church educator William E. Berrett explains: "The Prophet Joseph was in debt. . . . There were no funds to support the Presidency of the Church. The members of the Church were taking advantage of him. They were getting goods on credit and not paying their debts, knowing the Prophet would hardly sue them."[37] Joseph's tender heart may have always been at odds with his satisfactorily providing for his family.

Few would doubt that Joseph desired to provide for his family, but circumstances and situations precluded him from fulfilling that desire. Though he was often unable to personally provide for his own family because of his high calling, he offered solace to women, for through him the Lord decreed, "Women have claim on their husbands for their maintenance" (D&C 83:2). Reflecting this gospel principle, the Lord, through the Prophet Joseph Smith, gave this personal commandment to Brigham Young at Far West on April 17, 1838: "Let my servant Brigham Young go unto the place which he has bought, on Mill Creek, and there provide for his family until an effectual door is opened for the support of his family, until I shall command him to go hence, and not to leave his family until they are amply provided for."[38] As seen in the examples above, Joseph Smith reinstated a doctrine repeated in "The Proclamation": Husbands are to provide food, clothing, and shelter for their wives and children.

Protecting. Providing physical protection for his family was also difficult, though Joseph felt it was a God-given responsibility, a doctrine that is reiterated in the proclamation. Joseph expressed, "There is one principle which is eternal; it is the duty of all men to protect their lives and the lives of the household, whenever necessity requires, and no power has a right to forbid it."[39] In his journal in November 1839, Joseph describes his wish to protect his family in Far West:

> Who can realize my feelings which I experienced at that time; to be torn from my companion, and leaving her surrounded with monsters in the shape of men, and my children too, not knowing how their wants would be supplied; to be taken far from them in order that my enemies might destroy me when they thought proper to do so. My partner wept, my children clung to me and were only thrust from me by the swords of the guard who guarded me. I felt overwhelmed while I witnessed the scene, and could only recommend them to the care of that God, whose kindness had followed me to the present time; and who alone could protect them and deliver me from the hands of my enemies and restore me to my family.[40]

Joseph's desire to protect his family was constant, but drastic situations such as the one listed above denied him the privilege.

JOSEPH SMITH EXEMPLIFIED A FATHER'S SACRED DUTY BY TEACHING HIS CHILDREN IN LOVE AND RIGHTEOUSNESS.

The Prophet and his wife had eleven children, nine natural and two adopted; six of these children did not survive infancy.[41] Joseph can be viewed as a hands-on father. John M. Bernhisel observed Joseph participating in "the gentle charities of domestic life, as the tender and affectionate . . . parent," and he said that Joseph's heart was "felt to be keenly alive to the kindest and softest emotions of which human nature is susceptible."[42] As recorded in his journal, Joseph chose to spend time with his children.[43] In these entries Joseph displays himself as "devoted to his family and they to him."[44] He developed relationships in activities such as carriage rides, spending holidays together, singing together, teaching his children grammar, reading to his children, or sliding with them on the ice. Lucy Meserve Smith observed that little children, including his own, "were very much attached to the Prophet," since he played with them as if they were his equals.[45] Joseph clearly advocated recreational activities with his family, as does "The Proclamation," recognizing that physical activity "benefited the mind and spirit as well as the body."[46] John Hess and Enoch E. Dodge both recall the Prophet playing with his children in their games.[47] As he participated in domestic activities, Joseph often commented that his family brought him "great joy."[48]

Joseph also encouraged his growing family. In one letter he told his wife, "Tell the children that I am alive and trust I shall come and see them before long. Comfort their hearts all you can, and try to be comforted yourself."[49] The tenderness of a father's heart is expressed in this letter written November 9, 1839, from Springfield, Illinois: "I shall be filled with constant anxiety about you and the children until I hear from you and in a particular manner little Frederick. It was so painful to leave him sick. I hope you will watch over those tender offspring in a manner that is becoming a mother and a saint." Always teaching, the Prophet went on, "Cultivate their minds and learn them to read and be sober. Do not let them be exposed to the weather to take cold, and try to get all the rest you can."[50]

Right before he was martyred, Joseph was very concerned that his children continue to grow and progress. In 1842, the Smith's adopted daughter Julia told Lucy Meserve Smith that "her papa talked to her before he left, and told her to be a good girl; and he particularly enjoined it upon her to never mistreat any of her playmates, and then he should be happy to meet her again. 'Oh,' she said, 'how bad I should feel if I thought I should not be prepared to meet my dear papa!'"[51] Edwin Rushton remembers Joseph asking his wife the following when he was on his way to Carthage: "Emma, can you train my sons to walk in their father's footsteps?" She answered, "Oh, Joseph, you are coming back." Joseph repeated the question three times, reiterating its importance.[52]

Even in his last moments, Joseph was concerned about his sacred responsibility to teach his children.

Latter-day Saints owe a debt of gratitude to Joseph Smith, who reinstated the sacred responsibility of fathers to teach their children in love and righteousness. At the funeral of Judge Higbee, Joseph stressed the importance of this principle when he promised family members, "Do as the husband and the father would instruct and you shall be reunited."[53] As professed by the Prophet and in the proclamation, fathers who fulfill their sacred duty of loving and teaching children unite their families both in mortality and eternity.

JOSEPH SMITH RESTORED THE DOCTRINE THAT THE FAMILY IS ORDAINED OF GOD AND CENTRAL TO THE CREATOR'S PLAN.

Most Latter-day Saints are familiar with a statement Joseph made to a man who asked him, "How do you govern such a vast people as this?" "Oh," said Joseph, "it is very easy. . . . I teach them correct principles and they govern themselves." Brigham Young added, "And if correct principles will do this in one family they will in ten, in a hundred, and in ten hundred thousand."[54] Prophetically, the correct principles Joseph taught about marriage and families continue to govern thousands of Latter-day Saint families today.

One Latter-day Saint who was personally taught these restored doctrines about the family was Parley P. Pratt. In 1839, Joseph Smith defined for Pratt the eternal gender roles that are now repeated in "The Proclamation." Joseph revealed "a heavenly order of eternity" that consisted of an "eternal family organization, and the eternal union of the sexes." Before this, Pratt had esteemed "kindred affections and sympathies as appertaining solely to [mortality]." As Joseph revealed, "The true dignity and destiny of a son of God, [is to be] clothed with an eternal priesthood, as the patriarch and sovereign of his countless offspring. . . . The highest dignity of womanhood [is], to stand as a queen and priestess to her husband, and to reign for ever and ever as the queen mother of her numerous and still increasing offspring." In addition, these teachings revolutionized Pratt's feelings for his wife. He explained, "I had loved before, but I knew not why. But now I loved—with a pureness and intensity of elevated, exalted feeling, which would lift my soul from the transitory things of this groveling sphere and expand it as the ocean. I felt that . . . the wife of my bosom was an immortal, eternal companion; a kind of ministering angel, given to me as a comfort, and a crown of glory for ever and ever. In short, I could now love with the spirit and with the understanding also."⁵⁵ As Joseph revealed such principles, it elevated both men and women in marriage, defining the family as central to the Father's plan.

JOSEPH RECEIVED THE KEYS THAT RESTORED SACRED ORDINANCES UNITING FAMILIES ETERNALLY.

Sealing ordinances are of utmost significance in the plan of salvation as restored by the Prophet. These ordinances were also of great importance to him personally, as he often spoke of his family relationships existing beyond mortality. In 1838, he expressed to his wife, "If I do not meet you again in this life may God grant that we may meet in heaven. . . . I am yours forever."⁵⁶ In April 1836, Joseph received the keys of the sealing ordinances in the Kirtland Temple that made his desires possible. Placing the sealing of husbands and wives as the pinnacle of priesthood ordinances, Joseph revealed, "In the celestial glory there are three heavens or degrees; and in order to obtain the highest, a man must enter into this order of the priesthood [meaning the new and everlasting covenant of marriage]" (D&C 131:1–2).

Telestial words are inadequate to describe the celestial blessings Joseph Smith brought back to the earth. As he received priesthood keys from Elijah, generations were, as Joseph put it, rescued.⁵⁷ These restored covenants not only turn our hearts to one another, but, as Joseph explained, they also seal them eternally, creating a "chain that binds the hearts of the fathers to the children, and the children to the fathers." As Joseph defined it, this doctrine "is one of the greatest and most important subjects that God has revealed."⁵⁸ Joseph described a blessing of this knowledge as follows: "When we lie down we contemplate how we may rise in the morning; and it is pleasing for friends to lie down together, locked in the arms of love, to sleep and wake in each other's embrace."⁵⁹ One of the great blessings of restoring the sealing ordinances is the knowledge that "when we depart, we shall hail our mothers, fathers, friends, and all whom we love, who have fallen asleep in Jesus."⁶⁰

As brought to light by the Prophet, the blessings associated with keeping the covenants of this ordinance astound the human mind. Faithful Latter-day Saints are promised thrones, kingdoms, principalities, powers, dominions, all heights and depths, exaltation and glory in all things, and a continuation of seed forever (see D&C 132:19).

CONCLUSION

With such glorious promises looming, one understands why John Taylor wrote that Joseph Smith "left a fame and name that cannot be slain" (D&C 135:3). John Taylor saw the Prophet in various circumstances and testified that "he was a good, honorable, and virtuous man, that his private and public character was irreproachable, and that he lived and died a man of God."[61] Joseph Smith was an exemplary husband and father. Those ideas taught by him about families and exemplified during his life have now been declared in "The Proclamation" through his successor President Gordon B. Hinckley.

Joseph Smith's God-given principles about eternal families are filled with hope. The doctrines Joseph taught and the Church organization he perfected welds people of all nations into family units where love and happiness can bind those on the earth into eternity.

NOTES

1. Brigham Young, *Discourses of Brigham Young,* comp. and ed. John A. Widtsoe (Salt Lake City: Deseret Book, 1966), 459.
2. Larry C. Porter and Susan Easton Black, eds., *The Prophet Joseph: Essays on the Life and Mission of Joseph Smith* (Salt Lake City: Deseret Book, 1988), 46–47.
3. "The Family: A Proclamation to the World," *Ensign,* November 1995, 102.
4. Joseph Smith, *Teachings of the Prophet Joseph Smith,* comp. Joseph Fielding Smith (Salt Lake City: Deseret Book, 1976), 174.
5. Smith, *Teachings,* 88–89.
6. Mark L. McConkie, *Remembering Joseph: Personal Recollections of Those Who Knew the Prophet Joseph Smith* (Salt Lake City: Deseret Book, 2003), 304.
7. "The Family: A Proclamation to the World," 102.
8. Porter and Black, *The Prophet Joseph,* 43.
9. "The Family: A Proclamation to the World."

10. Joseph Smith to Emma Smith, June 6, 1832, in *The Personal Writings of Joseph Smith,* comp. and ed. Dean C. Jessee (Salt Lake City: Deseret Book, 1984), 239.

11. "The Family: A Proclamation to the World," 102.

12. Joseph Smith to Emma Smith, November 12, 1838, in *Personal Writings* (Salt Lake City: Deseret Book, 1984), 368–69.

13. Joseph Smith to Emma Smith, April 4, 1839, in *Personal Writings,* 427, 425.

14. Joseph Smith to Emma Smith, in *Personal Writings,* November 12, 1838, 368–69.

15. Jesse S. Crosby in Hyrum L. Andrus and Helen Mae Andrus, comps., *They Knew the Prophet* (Salt Lake City: Deseret Book, 1999), 145; and W. Jeffrey Marsh, "Dealing with Personal Injustices: Lessons from the Prophet Joseph Smith," *Religious Educator* 4, no. 3 (Fall 2003): 109–10.

16. Joseph Smith, *History of the Church of Jesus Christ of Latter-day Saints,* ed. B. H. Roberts, 2nd ed. rev. (Salt Lake City: Deseret Book, 1978), 6:165–66.

17. Andrus and Andrus, *They Knew the Prophet,* 88.

18. Porter and Black, *The Prophet Joseph,* 44.

19. Joseph Smith to Emma Smith, April 4, 1839, in *Personal Writings* (Salt Lake City: Deseret Book, 1984), 426.

20. Joseph Smith to Emma Smith, January 20, 1840, in *Personal Writings,* 454.

21. Joseph Smith to Emma Smith, in *Personal Writings,* 368.

22. *Church News,* April 27, 1968, 3.

23. Smith, *History of the Church,* 5:107.

24. McConkie, *Remembering Joseph,* 58; Andrus and Andrus, *They Knew the Prophet,* 120; Porter and Black, *The Prophet Joseph,* 43, and "Recollections of the Prophet Joseph Smith," *Juvenile Instructor,* July 1, 1892, 399.

25. Smith, *History of the Church,* 5:167–69; 182.

26. McConkie, *Remembering Joseph,* 71.

27. John Taylor, in *Journal of Discourses* (London: Latter-day Saints' Book Depot, 1854–86), 26:112.

28. Ezra C. Dalby, "Joseph Smith, Prophet of God," manuscript of talk delivered December 12, 1926, Salt Lake City, 14, as cited in Gordon B. Hinckley, "The Lengthened Shadow of the Hand of God," *Ensign,* May 1987, 52.

29. McConkie, *Remembering Joseph,* 98.

30. "William Cahoon Autobiography," in Stella Shurtleff and Brent Farrington Cahoon, eds., *Reynolds Cahoon and His Stalwart Sons* (Salt

Lake City: Paragon Press, 1960), 80; see also William Cahoon, "Recollections of the Prophet Joseph Smith," *Juvenile Instructor*, August 15, 1892, 492–93.

31. Smith, *Teachings*, 227.

32. Susan Easton Black and Charles D. Tate Jr., eds., *Joseph Smith: The Prophet, the Man* (Provo, UT: Religious Studies Center, Brigham Young University, 1993), 169.

33. Book of Commandments 26:8 or Doctrine and Covenants 25:9. The Doctrine and Covenants says "in," but the Book of Commandments says "from."

34. Smith, *History of the Church*, 4:187.

35. George W. Givens, in *Old Nauvoo: Everyday Life in the City of Joseph* (Salt Lake City: Deseret Book, 1990), 82.

36. Givens, *Old Nauvoo*, 84.

37. William E. Berrett, "The Life and Character of the Prophet Joseph Smith," *BYU Speeches of the Year, 1963–64* (Provo, UT: Brigham Young University Press, 1964).

38. Smith, *Teachings*, 118.

39. Smith, *Teachings*, 391.

40. Joseph Smith Journal Extract, November 1839, in *Personal Writings*, 439.

41. Joseph and Emma Hale Smith's children: Alvin Smith, born June 15, 1828, died same day; Thaddeus Smith, born April 30, 1831, died same day (twin); Louisa Smith, born April 30, 1831, died same day (twin); Julia Murdock Smith, adopted daughter, born April 30, 1831 (twin), died 1880; Joseph Murdock Smith, adopted son, born April 30, 1831 (twin), died March 30, 1832, from exposure caused by the mob at Hiram, Ohio; Joseph Smith III, born November 6, 1832, died December 10, 1914; Frederick G. W. Smith, born June 20, 1836, died April 13, 1862; Alexander H. Smith, born June 2, 1838, died August 2, 1909; Don Carlos Smith, born June 13, 1840, died August 15, 1841; stillborn son, born 1842; David Hyrum Smith, born November 17, 1844, died August 29, 1904.

42. Letter of John M. Bernhisel to Governor Thomas Ford, June 14, 1844, Church Historian's Library, Salt Lake City; Washington Franklin Anderson, "Reminiscences of John M. Bernhisel," typewritten manuscript, Church Historian's Library, Salt Lake City, 1–4, as cited in Andrus and Andrus, *They Knew the Prophet*, 177.

43. Joseph Smith Diary, October 1835–March 1836, *Personal Writings*, 64, 66, 73, 161–62, 169–71.

44. Porter and Black, *The Prophet Joseph*, 36.

45. McConkie, *Remembering Joseph*, 23, 98, 73; and Porter and Black, *The Prophet Joseph*, 45–47.

46. "Recollections of the Prophet Joseph Smith," *Juvenile Instructor,* August 1, 1892, 302, as cited in Black and Tate, *Joseph Smith: The Prophet, the Man,* 143.

47. "Joseph Smith, The Prophet," *Young Woman's Journal,* December 1906, 544, as cited in Black and Tate, *Joseph Smith: The Prophet, the Man,* 144.

48. *History of the Church,* 2:45, and Joseph Smith Diary, March 28–29, 1834, in *Personal Writings of Joseph Smith,* 31.

49. Joseph Smith to Emma Smith, November 12, 1838, Community of Christ Library Archives, as cited in Linda King Newell and Valeen Tippetts Avery, *Mormon Enigma: Emma Hale Smith* (Urbana and Chicago: University of Illinois Press, 1994), 76.

50. Joseph Smith to Emma Smith, November 9, 1839, in *Personal Writings,* 448.

51. McConkie, *Remembering Joseph,* 73.

52. McConkie, *Remembering Joseph,* 410–11; "Edwin Rushton (Related by his Son)," in Andrus and Andrus, *They Knew the Prophet,* 171.

53. Smith, *Teachings,* 321.

54. Brigham Young, in *Journal of Discourses,* 10:57–58; see also Erastus Snow, in *Journal of Discourses,* 24:159.

55. Pratt, *Autobiography,* 260.

56. Joseph Smith to Emma Smith, November 4, 1838, in *Personal Writings,* 362–63.

57. See Smith, *Teachings,* 323.

58. Smith, *Teachings,* 337.

59. Smith, *Teachings,* 295.

60. Smith, *Teachings,* 359–60.

61. Dalby, "Joseph Smith, Prophet of God," as cited in Hinckley, "The Lengthened Shadow of the Hand of God," 52.

INDEX

through, 20; eternal marriage
and, 82–84; Joseph Smith learns
of infinite, 152–53; covers
children, 192; at core of Book of
Mormon, 224–25; priesthood
and, 241–43; bodies and, 291–92;
bodies and spirits and, 294–96
Attempts, on life of Joseph Smith,
254–61, 267–71
Australia, railroad in, 275–76
Authority, 51–52; of Joseph Smith,
179
Autobiography, of Joseph Smith,
35–36

Baby, 385–86
Ballard, M. Russell: on sharing
gospel, 306–7; on living gospel,
315; on growth of Church, 357
Ballard, Melvin J.: on spirit
children, 78–79; on bodies and
resurrection, 298
Baptism: Parley P. Pratt's anguish
over, 50–51; infant, 61, 190–94;
Catholic views on infant, 201;
Book of Mormon and infant,
202
Baptisms for the dead, 114–20,
168–69
Battle, Joseph Smith won't fight in
mock, 258–59
Behavior, 76
Bennett, John C., 258–59
Bennion, Adam S., on joy, 295–96,
302–3
Bennion, Lowell L., 347; on Joseph
Smith, 358
Benson, Ezra Taft: on First Vision,
12; on priesthood, 126; on
priesthood and marriage, 237;
on knowing God, 275; on
legacy of Joseph Smith, 358; on
mission of Joseph Smith, 359
Bernhisel, John M., on Joseph
Smith as father, 389–90

Berrett, William E.: on observing
birthday of Joseph Smith, 348;
on Book of Mormon, 353; on
legacy of Joseph Smith, 357–58;
on Joseph Smith's store, 388
Bible: as word of God, 54–55; age
of accountability in, 194; Joseph
Smith and, 221–22; Book of
Mormon establishes truth of,
226; Joseph Smith translation
of, 226–29; Joseph Smith
translates, 320–22; ex-minister
on, 329. *See also* JST
Bible sermons, 232–33
Black, Susan Easton, on Joseph
Smith's role as husband and
father, 381
Blessings, 279
Body: as purpose of life, 81; Satan
and, 81; views on, 288–89; of
Jesus Christ as model, 289–92; in
mortality, 292; premortal
anticipation of, 293; spirit and
Atonement and, 294–96; of God,
296–97; in resurrection, 297–98;
marital union of, 298–300;
connection to temple of, 302;
Mark E. Peterson on spirit and,
302; Parley P. Pratt on spiritual,
303–4; as sign of God's love, 304.
See also Mortality
Body guards, 258–59
Book of Abraham, 230–32
Book of Mormon: article of faith
on, 54–55; translation and
publication of, 95; translation
of, 148–49, 224; Joseph Smith
repents after losing, 149–51;
salvation of children and,
191–94; infant baptism and,
202; Joseph Smith as translator
of, 210–12; as keystone of
Restoration, 224–26; restoration
of doctrine and, 353

pamphlet, 35–36; on Satan's damnation, 86; on Kirtland Temple, 111; on translation of books, 212; on priesthood, 277; on heavenly and earthly riches, 280; on heaven, 282; called as Apostle, 371, 373–74

Pratt, Parley P.: on repentance, 50; on gifts of Spirit, 53–54; on eternal families, 118; understands purpose of love, 249, 391–92; on body of Jesus Christ, 290; on spirit and body, 293; on being without body, 296; on offspring in resurrection, 299–300; on spiritual body, 303–4; called as Apostle, 371; ordination of Apostles and, 378

Prayer: dedicatory, 112–13; family, 386

Predestination, 48–49, 49–50, 59

Premortal existence, 69–70; agency in, 70–72; foreordination and, 72–73; marriage and, 77–80; Joseph Smith on, 80–81; Book of Abraham teaches of, 231; decrees and decisions in, 278–79; anticipation of body in, 293

Presbyterianism, 146

President of High Priesthood, 204

Presiding, 386–87

Priesthood: keys and, 26–27; sealing power and, 28–29; article of faith on, 51–52; as vocation, 61; restoration of, 61–62, 244, 339; temples and, 118–19; taught to Relief Society sisters, 125–26; Elijah to restore keys of, 159–61; President of High, 204; in Book of Abraham, 231; as power of God, 238–39; order and, 239–40; marriage and, 240–41, 248–49;

Atonement and, 241–43; responsibilities in, 243–45; Relief Society and, 245–48; as fixed principle, 276–78; decreed in premortal existence, 278; chain, 279

Principles, 391

Printing press, 259–60, 262–63

"Proclamation to the World," 281–82

Procreative powers, 81

Progression, 79–80

Prophecies: on Elijah, 158–61, 161–62; on Joseph Smith, 173–77

Prophet(s), 274; Joseph Smith as, 3, 212–15; Joseph Smith taught by, 9–11; essential job of, 14; hold keys to kingdom, 27–28; prophesy of Joseph Smith, 173–77; dispensation concept and, 181; restoration of, 203–4; symbols of, 204–6; as revelators, 210, 233–34; Book of Mormon and, 225; ancient, 335–37, 340, 342–44; requirements for, 349–50

Protecting, 389

Protestantism, 46–47

Providing, 387–89

Punishment, 48–49, 149–51

Quincy, Josiah, on Joseph Smith, 172–73

Quorum of Twelve Apostles, seniority in, 374–75, 379–80

Railroad, 275–76

Record keeping, Church of Jesus Christ of Latter-day Saints and, 163–68

Rector, Hartman Jr., on Joseph Smith's effect on family, 358–59

Redemption, 273

Reformation, 332–33